Shakespeare and the Victorian Stage

Shakespeare and the Victorian Stage

Edited by
RICHARD FOULKES

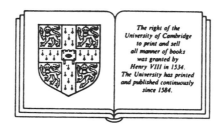

The right of the
University of Cambridge
to print and sell
all manner of books
was granted by
Henry VIII in 1534.
The University has printed
and published continuously
since 1584.

CAMBRIDGE UNIVERSITY PRESS

Cambridge
New York   New Rochelle   Melbourne   Sydney

Published by the Press Syndicate of the University of Cambridge
The Pitt Building, Trumpington Street, Cambridge CB2 1RP
32 East 57th Street, New York, NY 10022, USA
10 Stamford Road, Oakleigh, Melbourne 3166, Australia

First published 1986
Reprinted 1987, 1988

Printed in Great Britain by
the Athenaeum Press Ltd, Newcastle upon Tyne

British Library cataloguing in publication data

Shakespeare and the Victorian Stage.
1. Shakespeare, William — Stage
history — England — 1800–1950.
I. Foulkes, Richard
792.8'5   PR3106

Library of Congress cataloguing in publication data

Main entry under title:
Shakespeare and the Victorian stage.
Bibliography: p. 295
Includes index.
1. Shakespeare, William, 1564–1616 — Stage history —
1800–1950 — Addresses, essays, lectures.   2. Theater —
Great Britain — History — 19th century — Addresses, essays,
lectures.   I. Foulkes, Richard.
PR3099.S5   1986   822.3'3   85–31326

ISBN 0 521 30110 6

wv

Contents

Contents

Contents

Illustrations

Contributors

DR KATHLEEN BARKER is long-standing Honorary Secretary of the Society for Theatre Research. Her numerous publications include *Theatre Royal Bristol* (1974) and *Bristol at Play* (1976).

RALPH BERRY is Professor of English at the University of Ottawa. His books include *On Directing Shakespeare* (1971) and *Shakespeare and the Awareness of Audience* (1985).

PROFESSOR MICHAEL R. BOOTH returned to Canada – University of Victoria – in 1984 after a decade at the University of Warwick. His extensive publications on nineteenth-century theatre range from *English Melodrama* (1965) to *Victorian Spectacular Theatre* (1981).

DR J. S. BRATTON is Reader in English, Royal Holloway and Bedford New College, University of London. Her book *The Victorian Popular Ballad* was published in 1975. She is editing a theatre-history edition of *King Lear*.

CAROL CARLISLE is Professor of English, University of South Carolina. She is the author of *Shakespeare from the Green Room* (1969) and of numerous articles, including studies of Helen Faucit.

JEREMY CRUMP has recently completed a doctoral thesis on recreational provision in Leicester 1850–1914 at the Centre for the Study of Social History, University of Warwick. He has contributed to *Theatre Note-book* and taught for the Department of Adult Education, University of Leicester. He now teaches at Lutterworth Grammar School.

RICHARD FOULKES is Assistant Director (responsible for Northamptonshire), Department of Adult Education, University of Leicester. He is the author of a range of articles on theatre history and of *The Shakespeare Tercentenary of 1864* (1984).

DR JAMES FOWLER is Assistant Keeper of the Theatre Museum, Victoria and Albert Museum. He edited *Images of Show Business from the Theatre Museum* (1982) and contributes to the *Year's Work in English Studies*.

DR ARNOLD HARE concluded his career in the Department of Extra-mural Studies, University of Bristol, as Reader in Theatre History. His publications include *Theatre Royal Bath – The Orchard Street Calendar* (1977) and *George Frederick Cooke: The Actor and the Man* (1980).

ARTHUR JACOBS retired as Professor of Music, Huddersfield Polytechnic in 1984. He has edited successive editions of *The Penguin Dictionary of Music.* His *Arthur Sullivan: A Victorian Musician* was published in 1984.

MARION JONES has taught at several universities in Britain and overseas. She was a major contributor to *The Revels History of Drama in English, Volume I: Medieval Drama* and *Volume V: 1660–1750.*

CARY MAZER, Assistant Professor of English, University of Pennsylvania, is the author of *Shakespeare Refashioned: Elizabethan Plays on Edwardian Stages* (1981). He is Secretary of the American Society for Theater Research.

THE REVEREND EMERITUS PROFESSOR W. MOELWYN MERCHANT is the author of *Shakespeare and the Artist* (1959). In 1964 he prepared an Arts Council Exhibition, Shakespeare in Art. Since retiring from the University of Exeter he has devoted much time to his work as a sculptor.

DR CHRISTOPHER MURRAY is a statutory lecturer in the Department of English, University College, Dublin. His publications include *Robert William Elliston, Manager* (1975) and *Selected Plays of Lennox Robinson* (1982).

KENNETH RICHARDS, Professor of Drama, University of Manchester, is co-editor with Peter Thomson of *Nineteenth Century British Theatre* (1971) and *The Eighteenth Century English Stage* (1972).

GEORGE ROWELL, Reader in Theatre History, Department of Drama, University of Bristol, is the author of many books on the Victorian Theatre. His publications include *Theatre in the Age of Irving* (1981), *The Repertory Movement* with Anthony Jackson (1984) and *Plays by A. W. Pinero* (1986).

DR CHRISTOPHER SMITH is Senior Lecturer in the School of Modern Languages and European History, University of East Anglia. He has edited plays by Jean de la Taille and Antoine de Montchrestien. He is editor of the journal *Seventeenth-Century French Studies.*

JANE STEDMAN, Professor of English, Roosevelt University, Chicago, edited *Gilbert Before Sullivan: Six Comic Plays* (1967) and has added *The Blue-Legged Lady* to the Gilbert canon. She has been a reviewer for *Opera News* for over twenty years.

Contributors

PETER THOMSON, Professor of Drama, University of Exeter has written *Brecht*, with Jan Needle (1981), and *Shakespeare's Theatre* (1983), and has recently edited *Plays by Dion Boucicault* (1984).

SIMON WILLIAMS is Associate Professor of Dramatic Art, University of California, Santa Barbara. He is the author of *German Actors of the 18th and 19th Centuries: Idealism, Romanticism and Realism* and of translations of Schnitzler and Kaiser.

Acknowledgements

All the contributors to this volume have their own debts of gratitude: to friends and colleagues, librarians and curators, secretaries and spouses. As editor I have an additional obligation to all my fellow-contributors, who have made their essays available for this book and responded to my urgings and askings with promptness and tolerance.

R. G. F.

Introduction: Shakespeare and the Victorian Stage

RICHARD FOULKES

> There is a certain isle beyond the sea
> Where dwell a cultured race . . .
> 'Tis known as Engle-land. Oh, send him there!
> If but the half of them be true
> They will enshrine him on their great good hearts,
> And men will rise or sink in good esteem
> According as they worship, or slight him!

These lines, spoken by Ophelia in W. S. Gilbert's *Rosencrantz and Guildenstern* (1891), refer to the exiled Hamlet's likely reception in England, but they can be applied with remarkable aptness to the esteem in which Shakespeare himself was held by the Victorians. For during the reign of Queen Victoria Shakespeare was indeed enshrined not only in individual hearts, but also in the institutions of national life; and men worshipped him not only as an act of veneration, but also as a means of imbuing themselves and their enterprises with the status that was increasingly ascribed to the realm's immortal laureate.

It might be assumed that the Victorians venerated Shakespeare pre-eminently as a dramatist, but such was the uncertain status of the theatre at the beginning of the reign that actors sought respectability for their profession by invoking the respect in which Shakespeare was held outside the theatre, as author and poet. The point was well made, as late as 1892, by Henry Irving in *The Henry Irving Shakespeare*:

SHAKESPEARE AS A PLAYWRIGHT

I daresay that it will appear to some readers a profanation of the name of Shakespeare to couple with it the title of playwright. But I have chosen this title for my introduction because I am anxious to show that with the mighty genius of the poet was united, in a remarkable degree, the capacity for writing plays intended to be acted as well as read. One often finds that the very persons who claim most to reverence Shakespeare, not only as a poet but also as a dramatist, carry that reverence to such an extent that they would almost forbid the representation of his plays upon the stage, except under conditions which are, if not impossible, certainly impracticable. (1892, vol. 1, p. lxxxi)

1

Irving's insistence upon Shakespeare's genius as a practical dramatist is coupled with a certain defensiveness about the current style of staging his plays. It was the theatre's determination to claim Shakespeare as its own, and to accord his plays productions whose lavishness persistently exceeded their appropriateness, that characterised Shakespeare's fortunes upon the Victorian stage.

During this period the theatre was led by a series of remarkable actors and actresses. The career of William Charles Macready (1793–1873) began as early as 1810 with Romeo in Birmingham, and his final appearance, after a prolonged sequence of farewell performances, was as Macbeth in 1851. Known as the 'Eminent Tragedian' (taken by Alan Downer as the title for his 1966 biography of the actor), his most influential achievements in terms of Shakespearean production were his managements of the two patent theatres, Covent Garden (1837–9) and Drury Lane (1841–3), during which he established high standards of rehearsal and preparation. The actress with whom Macready is most closely associated is Helen Faucit (1817–98), who married Theodore Martin, the biographer of Prince Albert.

The actor who was widely regarded as Macready's heir, Samuel Phelps (1804–78), benefited from the abolition of the Patent Theatres Monopoly in 1843, whereby the restrictions on performing legitimate drama in the capital were removed. Phelps, initially with Mrs Warner, set up in management at the outlying Sadler's Wells Theatre in 1844 and by 1862 had staged all of Shakespeare's plays except *Henry VI*, *Troilus and Cressida*, *Richard II* and *Titus Andronicus* (Allen, 1971, pp. 314–15).

Coinciding with the middle years of Phelps's management was that of Charles Kean (1811–68), the Eton-educated son of Edmund, at the Princess's Theatre in Oxford Street between 1851 and 1859. Kean had previously taken charge of the royal theatricals at Windsor for eleven seasons from 1848 (Rowell, 1978, pp. 47–65), establishing important contacts between the theatre and the court. Formidable support in all Kean's endeavours came from his wife, Ellen Tree (1806–80). Phelps and Kean both continued to act after retiring from management, and Phelps was still performing Shakespeare in 1878, the year in which Henry Irving took over the management of the Lyceum Theatre. In the last decades of the century Irving's extraordinary personality dominated the profession as a whole and achieved for it unprecedented social and artistic status. He became the first actor–knight in 1895. For much of his reign at the Lyceum Irving was partnered by Ellen Terry (1847–1928), offspring of an old theatrical family.

Irving's tenure of the Lyceum ended in 1902, but already lavish

Introduction

Shakespearean productions by Herbert Beerbohm Tree (1853–1917) at Her Majesty's Theatre, which he built and occupied from 1897, were a powerful counter-attraction. The Lyceum itself proved to be a training ground for actor–managers, notably Johnston Forbes-Robertson (1853–1937), whose Hamlet was so highly regarded by Shaw, Frank Benson (1858–1939), the tireless purveyor of Shakespeare to the provinces, and John Martin-Harvey (1863-1944), all of whom were knighted.

Although Macready, Phelps, Kean, Irving and Tree were the pre-eminent Shakespearean actor–managers of the period, there were, of course, many others: Madame Vestris (1797?–1856) with a notable *Midsummer Night's Dream* at Covent Garden in 1840; Ben Webster (1797–1882) with an Elizabethan-style *Taming of the Shrew* at the Haymarket in 1844 and 1847; the French actor Charles Fechter's (1824–79) revolutionary *Hamlet* in the 1860s; the Bancrofts' (Sir Squire, 1841–1926; Marie, 1839–1921) *Merchant of Venice* with sets by E. W. Godwin (1833–86) at the Prince of Wales's Theatre in 1875, to mention but a few, all of them in London. But of course London has no monopoly of Shakespeare, whose plays were performed all over his own country and overseas in languages not his own.

By the turn of the nineteenth–twentieth century new and original talents were directing their attention to Shakespeare, as J. L. Styan (1977) has shown. Foremost amongst these were William Poel (1852–1934), exponent of the Elizabethan style; Edward Gordon Craig (1872–1966), combining the inherited gifts of his parents, Ellen Terry and E. W. Godwin, with his own piercing vision of stagecraft; and Harley Granville-Barker (1877–1946), actor, dramatist and scholar, whose productions of *The Winter's Tale* and *Twelfth Night* in 1912 and *A Midsummer Night's Dream* in 1914 remain amongst the most significant in the history of the Shakespearean stage.

The recurring debate about Shakespearean production during the Victorian period centred on the conflicting demands for spectacular scenery and for the restoration of Shakespeare's texts. The plays had been written for a non-scenic theatre which allowed rapid changes from location to location. The taste for localised and elaborate sets necessitated extensive rearrangement and cutting. For instance, in *The Merchant of Venice* the casket scenes (or those that survived) were often run together to reduce the number of scene-changes. Scene-changes were nevertheless numerous (ten to twelve on average) and very time-consuming, requiring extensive cuts to the plays to keep performances within a reasonable timespan. The Victorians also inherited other accommodations of the text, prompted by public distaste for certain aspects of Shakespeare

unadulterated. Nahum Tate's *Lear* (1681) was the most notorious example, and his exclusion of the Fool was perpetuated until Macready's
restoration in 1838, when he cast an actress, Priscilla Horton, in the role.

The theatre's awareness of the importance of textual probity was
heightened by the increasing scholarly attention devoted to Shakespeare's
plays. Victorian Shakespearean scholarship was not without its own
controversies, notably that surrounding John Payne Collier and the so-
called 'Perkins First Folio' (Ganzel, 1982); but Collier, J. O. Halliwell-
Phillipps, Alexander Dyce, Edward Dowden, F. J. Furnivall (Benzie,
1983) and H. H. Furness, with the Variorum editions from 1871,
constituted a corpus of editorial industry and expertise which, even
allowing for the individual distinction of earlier editors, was unprecen-
ted. A school of literary criticism was also developing, with A. C. Bradley
making the most enduring contribution (Stavisky, 1969). In its pursuit of
respectability the theatre recognised the kudos that could be derived from
association with this scholarly endeavour. Edward Dowden, Furnivall and
Furness all contributed to Irving's Shakespeare edition.

Hitherto only the classics of ancient literature had been thought worthy
of such treatment, but now English literature was deemed to be a fit subject
for university study. Henry Morley, an enthusiastic chronicler of the stage,
was Professor of English Literature at University College, London, the
prolific editor of popular classics and a supporter of a School of Dramatic
Art. At Oxford University, Arthur Bourchier took a lead in establishing
OUDS (the Oxford University Dramatic Society) in 1885, together with
the future Archbishop of Canterbury, Cosmo Gordon Lang, cousin of
actor Matheson Lang. Frank Benson and Irving's son Harry (H.B.) were
amongst the first university-educated actors, and Benson always cultivated
schools' patronage for his touring companies. Shakespeare's potential as
an educator was widely recognised amongst the Mechanics' Institutes
across the land and in the university extension work emanating from
Cambridge, Oxford and London.

Actors, at least nominally, produced editions of the plays. E. L.
Blanchard prepared a complete works, which bore Samuel Phelps's name.
The Henry Irving Shakespeare, in eight volumes (L. Irving, 1951, pp. 522–
4), was undertaken for him by Frank A. Marshall 'with notes and
introductions to each play by F. A. Marshall and other Shakespearean
scholars and a life of Shakespeare by Edward Dowden, LL.D.'. Irving also
produced acting editions of his productions, printed by the Chiswick
Press, as did Charles Calvert for his Manchester revivals. H. B. Irving's
edition of *Hamlet*, as arranged for performance at the Shaftesbury Theatre
in February 1909, is prefaced by a note concerning 'the adoption in the

Second Act of the sequence of scenes as given in the earlier Quarto of 1603'. On the other hand editions of the plays (including examples by Halliwell-Phillipps and Charles Knight) contained illustrations of stage performances.

However, whilst actors might lend their names to complete works in print, in the theatre (with the creditable exception of Phelps and later of Benson) the canon was very much smaller, with the same plays – the major tragedies, the romantic comedies and the popular histories – recurring to the almost complete exclusion of the remainder. Furthermore, the individual acting editions revealed the extent to which the theatre still cut and rearranged the plays. Cuts of up to and over a thousand lines were not unusual, particularly for Charles Kean. But a complete *Hamlet* is rarely feasible, and the acting text is best prepared with a knowledge of the possiblities available, as demonstrated by H. B. Irving.

The editions of Shakespeare's plays as 'arranged for representation at the Princess's Theatre with historical and explanatory notes by Charles Kean' (printed by John Chapman) emphasise the conflict between textual purity and spectacular scenery. Kean's editions abound in scholarly paraphernalia, but it is directed not at the plays themselves, but at the historical period in which they are set. The depth and range of this scholarship is undeniably impressive, and it demonstrates again the theatre's zeal for accruing respectability by association with other non-theatrical pursuits. Kean became a FSA in 1857, the most important public accolade thereto accorded to an actor.

Macready, Phelps to a lesser extent, Irving more selectively, and Tree more extravagantly, all subscribed to the fashion for lavish historical scenery and costumes. This was reinforced by the Victorians' appetite for exhibitions of all kinds. The British Museum accumulated antiquities from all over the world – from the Elgin Marbles to A. H. Layard's discoveries at Nineveh, which were a direct source for Kean's revival of Byron's *Sardanapalus* and, more improbably, for Phelps's *Pericles*.[1] Richard Altick, in *The Shows of London* (1978), reveals the public enthusiasm for historical and geographical panoramas and dioramas, the latter being a favourite scenic device in the theatre.

The Great Exhibition of 1851 crowned all. Kean's biographer, J.W. Cole, acclaimed it: 'The six months which followed were pregnant with instruction' (1859, vol. 2, p. 6). Its historical displays were every bit as popular as those of contemporary industry and were permanently installed in the Crystal Palace on its new site at Sydenham in 1854. The profits from the Great Exhibition were used to establish the South Kensington museums.

5

The predilection for spectacular scenery inevitably influenced the style of acting to be found in Victorian productions of Shakespeare. G. H. Lewes recognised genius in Edmund Kean, but only talent, albeit 'so marked and individual that it approaches very near to genius' (1875; repr. 1952, p. 39), in Macready. The quality of Macready's that Lewes singled out was his voice, 'capable of delicate modulation in quiet passages . . . and having tones that thrilled and tones that stirred tears'. His declamation may have been 'mannered and unmusical', but it was accompanied by an intelligence which followed 'the winding meanings through the involutions of the verse'. This vocal power, attuned to the meaning and measure of the verse, characterised Macready's Shakespearean performances and those of Samuel Phelps. Both actors perpetuated traditional stage conventions in their classical roles.

By the 1860s this style was becoming outmoded, and, as Shirley Allen (1971, p. 192) observes, Charles Fechter's Hamlet 'was the greatest single event in this evolution from the traditional to the modern school of acting'. Fechter eschewed the declamatory style and ignored established conventions; he was more conversational in speech, plucking from the lines fresh meanings which cast a new light upon character.

Undoubtedly Charles Kean had been moving in the same direction the previous decade, but without the benefits of grace and charisma possessed by Fechter. Furthermore, so preoccupied was Kean with scenic detail that the actors were often regarded as little more than accessories to the stage picture. Such a subsidiary role could not be ascribed to Ellen Terry, whose remarkable beauty and warmth of character presented such a glowing physical presence on the stage, with so strong an appeal to the eye, that the ears and mind were stilled in their expectations.

If Macready's and Phelps's acting was characterised by vocal power and Ellen Terry's by pictorial effect, Henry Irving was not naturally well endowed either vocally or physically. Edward Gordon Craig (1930, pp. 70–1) undertook to defend Irving against William Archer's criticisms that he 'murdered our mother tongue . . . could not speak English . . . And . . . that his locomotion is the result of an involuntary spasm.' It is a measure of Henry Irving's extraordinary quality as an actor that he offset his lack of natural gifts of voice and form with compelling performances which transfixed his audiences with his distinctive insights into the inner reaches of his characters, often extending to the darker sides which had rarely been explored before.

Acting styles – declamatory, pictorial, psychological – developed through the long years of Victoria's reign, and interpretation of character varied also. But by and large the prevailing taste inclined towards the domestic and sentimental, and this is reflected in realisations of Shakespeare's characters in other art forms, notably the graphic arts of portraiture and book illustration. The established status of the fine arts – the Royal Academy, with its president and academicians and summer exhibitions – lent a further respectability to the theatre by its association with them.

As Victoria's reign progressed Shakespeare's name and reputation were upheld in an increasing variety of ways. John Payne Collier established, in 1840, the first Shakespeare Society, which spearheaded the advance of Shakespeare scholarship with an extensive range of publications. It survived only until 1853, but in 1874 the New Shakespeare Society was founded by F. J. Furnivall at a meeting at University College, London. Shakespeare's birthplace was purchased by public subscription in 1847 with the help of actors, writers and politicians. In the succeeding years J. O. Halliwell-Phillipps, under the aegis of his National Shakespeare Fund, set about the acquisition of the other Shakespeare properties in Stratford-upon-Avon.

The Shakespeare tercentenary of 1864 (Foulkes, 1984) provided the occasion for national – indeed international – celebrations of the Bard, with Stratford and London vying with each other for the prior claim. Edward Fordham Flower masterminded the celebrations in Stratford, which involved, with not a little controversy, leading actors, public figures and all levels of society. The London celebrants, invoking the status of the capital, dubbed themselves the National Shakespeare Committee and were led by W. Hepworth Dixon, editor of the *Athenaeum*. They were dogged by misfortune and mismanagement and never achieved their goal of a statue of Shakespeare in the nation's capital.

Nevertheless, as London, like the other capitals of Europe, vested itself with the institutions of national government – Parliament, ministries, museums and galleries – the literary heritage was pressed into the service of national pride. Characteristically for Britain, the initiative was left largely to private enterprise, with the Lyceum Theatre becoming a national theatre in all but name. Similarly, it fell to a private individual (albeit a MP), Albert Grant, to acquire the dilapidated Leicester Fields in 1873 and to commission Signor Fontana to reproduce Peter Scheemakers' statue of Shakespeare as the centre-piece of Leicester Square, as it remains today. In an age in which religious belief came less easily, the Victorians created their own immortals, in whose hall of fame Shakespeare's place was assured.

In Birmingham George Dawson founded the Birmingham Shakespeare Library, and when Charles Flower realised his ambition of a Shakespeare

Memorial Theatre in Stratford in 1879 it contained, as well as a stage, a library and art gallery. In 1887 a commemoration monument in the form of an ingenious architectural marriage of a clock and fountain in the Gothic style was erected in Rother Market, and in the following year Lord Ronald Gower presented to Stratford his group of bronze statues representing Shakespeare surrounded by Hamlet, Hal, Falstaff and Lady Macbeth. The poet's home town was progressively translated from an unexceptional market town to a mecca, which attracted visitors from all over the world.

The distinctive quality of the theatre was that it could give living expression to Shakespeare's plays and, being the most popular form of entertainment of its day, could reach the mass of the population. This it succeeded triumphantly in doing. Shakespeare's plays figured in the Windsor theatricals, encouraging a widespread transference of Queen Victoria's enthusiasm for the theatre to Shakespeare's own sovereign Queen Elizabeth, who, it was happily supposed, was on close and friendly terms with the author. The audiences at Windsor included the British royal family, courtiers, clergy and visiting royalty from overseas. The Queen, until Prince Albert's death, also patronised London theatres, a tradition maintained by her son, the future Edward VII. Whereas in the early nineteenth century the theatre was largely ignored by the upper classes, Irving's Lyceum first nights were a high point of the London season, as were Tree's at Her Majesty's.

The theatre was certainly not the exclusive preserve of the upper classes. The Lyceum and Her Majesty's incorporated extensive gallery seating. The pit at Sadler's Wells in Phelps's day was exceptionally large, and he prided himself on attracting the local Islington populace to attend Shakespeare's plays, which they did with an enthusiasm and intelligence which impressed Charles Dickens and Bishop Tait of London alike.

For the provinces, with admitted exceptions and fluctuations, a similar tale is told. Douglas Reid asserts, of the Birmingham Theatre Royal, 'that Shakespearian productions drew consistently good popular audiences' (Bratby, 1980, p. 82), and for the week of so-called 'Popular Entertainments', following the main tercentenary celebrations, in Stratford audiences flocked in from all over the West Midlands, facilitated by the new network of railways.

Shakespeare was indeed the poet of all the people, from the court at Windsor to the Leicester Shakespearean Chartist Association, and it was to his interpreters in the theatre that the population turned on an unprecedented scale. If the theatre is the most collaborative of the arts, it is also the most ephemeral. Whereas the Victorian buildings, books, statues and paintings inspired by Shakespeare still, for the most part, survive, the stage productions have like insubstantial pageants faded, leaving behind the occasional costume, set-design, photograph, prompt-book, memoir and review. These are the materials from which theatre historians assay their task of reconstruction and reassessment. Those Victorian Shakespeareans were well served by their contemporary chroniclers[2] – Morley, G. H. Lewes, Clement Scott, William Archer, Shaw and Max Beerbohm; we, the contributors to this volume, must hope that we have served them in like measure.

NOTES

1 Richard Foulkes, 'Samuel Phelps's *Pericles* and Layard's Discoveries at Nineveh', *Nineteenth Century Theatre Research*, 5.2 (1977), 85–92.
2 Rowell, 1971. For a summary of scholarly work on Victorian productions of Shakespeare's plays, see Russell Jackson, 'Before the Shakespeare Revolution: Development in the Study of Nineteenth-Century Shakespearian Production', *Shakespeare Survey*, 35 (1982), 1–12.

PART I

Shakespeare in the Picture Frame

PREFACE

ALTHOUGH it was not until 1880 that Squire Bancroft encased all four sides of the Haymarket Theatre's proscenium arch in a picture frame,[1] the tendency to regard Shakespeare's plays as pictorial subjects, both on canvas and on stage, was long-standing. The enterprise of John Boydell's Shakespeare Gallery of 1789, which exhibited paintings on Shakespearean subjects by virtually all the leading artists of the day, was unmatched in the theatre. It was not just the scale of eighteenth-century Shakespearean paintings and their freedom from current theatre practice that placed them in advance of contemporary stage interpretations, but also the nature of their insight into the plays. Whilst Sir Joshua Reynolds adhered to the classical precepts of composition, William Blake – not represented in the Boydell Collection – revealed the romantic potential of his subjects in a manner which the theatre was not to witness until the advent of Edmund Kean.

The degree of convergence between the artist's studio and the stage designer's paint-frame fluctuated throughout the nineteenth century, with Clarkson Stanfield, W. R. Beverley, Ford Madox Brown and Sir Lawrence Alma-Tadema producing important work in both spheres of activity.[2] A key figure is James Robinson Planché, whose long life (1796–1880) and career spanned much of the period under consideration here. The author of burlesques, his more substantial contribution was in the field of historically accurate costume. His designs for Charles Kemble's *King John* in 1824 are generally regarded as a turning-point in stage practice, and, as Dr Fowler asserts (below, p. 31), his *History of British Costume* – first published in 1834 and extended into *A Cyclopaedia of Costume or Dictionary of Dress* (1876–9) – was the source book for many a Victorian costume designer. Planché's importance as a link between the theatre and the art world is indicated by his responsibility for the armour display at the Art Treasures of the United Kingdom Exhibition at Manchester in 1857, referred to by Richard Foulkes.

David Scott's preoccupation with the intricacies of Elizabethan dress emerges clearly from Dr Fowler's account of his painting *Queen Elizabeth Viewing the Performance of the 'Merry Wives of Windsor' in the Globe Theatre*. Here the focus was upon Shakespeare's theatre, which was reconstructed with the same diligence as was lavished upon historical settings for his plays. With the exception of Ben Webster's *The Taming of the Shrew* in 1844 and 1847 (Richards and Thomson, 1971, pp. 157–70) it was not until William Poel's revivals (Speaight, 1954) that the historical reconstruction of Shakespeare's own theatre was applied to the staging of his plays in Britain. Even then the effect tended towards a picture-frame restoration of the Elizabethan stage rather than a thoroughgoing application of Elizabethan principles of staging.

In the mean time the scenic theatre dominated, pre-eminently with Charles Kean's management at the Princess's Theatre in the 1850s, which Moelwyn Merchant (below, p. 20) describes as 'a massive if blinkered achievement'. Kean's management coincided with the heyday of the Pre-Raphaelite Brotherhood, and Richard Foulkes argues that his scene designs shared important characteristics with works by Walter Deverell and Holman Hunt in particular. Certainly, as Geoffrey Ashton has shown (1980, p. iv), 'the 1850's were the bumper years for Shakespearean subjects (at the Royal Academy Exhibition) and the average increased to about twenty works a year'. It was not simply a matter of quantity: the choice of Shakespearean subjects (the history plays, *The Tempest*, *A Midsummer Night's Dream*, *Romeo and Juliet* and *King Lear*) and the interpretation (pathetic, domestic) given to them was very much in line with theatrical taste.

However, the essential difference between a Shakespearean painting and stage designs was, as Professor Merchant, Miss Jones and Mr Foulkes all aver, that the artist was limited to the momentary, silent, two-dimensional image, whereas stage designers had to encompass the flow of the – albeit heavily cut – play. As Miss Jones points out, this placed a basic requirement – that of kinetic movement – upon the costume designer, a requirement which Lewis Wingfield, for one, found irksome.

As the nineteenth century closed, Shakespearean picture-making took on a new meaning with the invention of film. There the two-dimensional, silent image was at last endowed with kinetic movement. Robert Hamilton Ball (1968) has made a detailed study of this phenomenon, which as Roger Manvell (1971, p. 17) records, accounted for 'some four hundred [silent] films adapted from Shakespeare's plays'. The first of these was made in 1899 on the London Embankment, with Sir Herbert Beerbohm Tree as King John signing Magna Carta – a scene which does not occur in Shakespeare's play. Dr Manvell refers to this as 'a harbinger of many other "inspired" additions', but it was also a legacy from those Victorian artists and stage designers who had so frequently strayed beyond the confines of Shakespeare's text for the historically interesting and pictorially effective.

NOTES

1 Richard Southern, 'The Picture-Frame Proscenium of 1880', *Theatre Notebook*, 5.3 (1951), 59–61.
2 Hilary Norris, 'A Directory of Victorian Scene Painters', *Theatrephile*, 1.2 (1984), 38–52; van der Merwe, 1979.

Artists and Stage Designers

W. MOELWYN MERCHANT

IT is not surprising that, since the critic's customary medium is the word, he should show a certain reluctance to admit such a concept as 'visual criticism'. Yet the history of European art and literature shows that the great majority of our major themes in literature, music and the pictorial arts have common sources (substantially classical literature and the Bible) and that artists in every medium comment on the work of their predecessors and in so doing pass latent or overt judgement on the earlier work. It is my contention that this is a peculiarly active principle in drama and that Shakespeare has for three centuries been uniquely subjected to this kind of criticism. The Victorian age experienced with especial intensity the symbiotic relationship between dramatist, artist and actor, and this process merits exploration.

The innocent-seeming phrase 'visual criticism' is not, however, a simple concept. Painting and engraving, book-illustration and stage design and setting have each their peculiar problems – some distinct, some, as we shall see, closely interrelated. Each may be a sensitive extension of the dramatic text (and lend a 'critical gesture' towards it); the painters, from Runciman and Blake to Gordon Craig, will focus upon one significant moment; the stage designer from Planché to Godwin or Gordon Craig will demand of himself at once a greater subservience to the text and a more mobile, flexible art.

And what of the actor and director? Many academic critics today appear to endow the actor with unique insights which lead the critic to declare that a dramatic work is 'incomplete', 'unrealised', until it is produced on the stage. It would seem, if this be true, that the actor (and *a fortiori* the director) has a like status to the artist, who produces a new and unique work springing from the dramatist's words. This should be scanned.

A good starting-point is a very moving and penetrating account by Dame Janet Baker of her experience first in rehearsing with Benjamin

14

Britten and then in performing his operas (Herbert, 1979, p. 3). Of herself as performer and Britten as creator she says:

I have always believed that the creative person inhabits a world unknown to others. The gulf which exists between his world and that of the re-creative artist is wide indeed. Even at their most sublime, performers are still only able to go as far as the entrance and look from afar towards the land where the composer is perfectly at home.

She goes on, with the humility of the superlative performer, to deny the claim made by some performers that they are as important as the creative artist 'because they bring the work to life':

I cannot agree; even if a composition is never heard, the process of seizing an inspired idea, and shaping it into concrete form, makes the composer what he is.

This is, of course, not to say that 'the re-creative artist' brings little creative criticism to bear upon a creator's material; Redgrave's Hamlet, Jacqueline Du Pré's performance of Elgar's Cello Concerto, Peter O'Toole's Shylock, Dame Janet herself in *Phaedra*, created for her by Britten – these not only vibrate in the memory beyond the evanescence of the stage or concert platform; they reveal depths perhaps only suspected before.

We seem therefore to be granted multiple possibilities in this matter of critical gesture. The painter or engraver meditating on the text creates a wholly new work, valid and independent in its own terms, yet pointing to and enhancing the significance of the earlier work – as Picasso, from a perspective of more than three centuries, by his studies and final large canvas, changed our critical perspective in relation to Velasquez's *Las Meninas* – and we shall note this regularly in relation to eighteenth- and nineteenth-century painters of Shakespearean themes.

Then there is the theatre designer, perhaps himself a painter (W. R. Beverley) or an architect (E. W. Godwin) who will submit himself to the complex demands of text and stage and thereby prepare the way for the third critical extension of the dramatist's text, the 're-creative' performer. It is a subtle pattern, to the complex relationships of which more attention should have been given by academic commentators.

Shakespeare in the Victorian theatre cannot, visually, be studied in isolation; at least a century and a half of creativity must be taken into account before the true significance of Victorian experiment can be seen in perspective.[1] We must begin with Tonson's complete *Shakespeare* of 1709, the first edition of the playwright's works to be illustrated with a frontispiece to each play. Most of these are rather undistinguished reflections of contemporary stage practice, but one of them the frontis-

15

piece to *Coriolanus*, has a remarkable history. It is based on an engraving after Poussin's painting of Coriolanus confronting his wife and his mother. With great skill the engraver of the frontispiece has converted Poussin's horizontal composition to the vertical one demanded by the book illustration. It is additionally piquant that Poussin's painting is, of course, derived from Plutarch and not from Shakespeare, involving subtle modification of Shakespeare's dramatic tensions. The story does not end there: we may trace this derivation by way of the frontispiece to the play in Hanmer's *Shakespeare* of 1744, the artist in this instance being Francis Hayman, of significantly greater stature than Tonson's engraver, Kirkall; we are fortunate in the survival in the Folger Library, Washington, of Hayman's original drawing for Hanmer's edition. The final stage in the story (omitting some interesting detours) is reached in a drawing by Rowlandson and Pugin (a fascinating conjunction of talents) now to be seen in the Deering Collection, the Art Institute of Chicago. It was intended for the plate 'Drury Lane Theatre' in Ackermann's *Microcosm of London*, and a startling transformation has again taken place; for Rowlandson has here almost certainly depicted Kemble in his greatest role, and the scene, Volumnia pleading with her son before the Volscian camp, returns wholly to the horizontal composition of Poussin, with remarkable fidelity to detail, even to the great classical drape which backs the throne of state. One can only speculate: did the classical Kemble know of Poussin's painting or one of the engravings based on it? or did his designer, Capon? or did either of them follow the Tonson or Hanmer version, and constrained by the proportions of the proscenium arch, return by happy accident to the form of Poussin's original work? Whatever the speculation, this is a remarkable union of the three elements which establish 'visual Shakespeare' – painter, engraver and scene-designer.

Before we finally enter the world of Macready, Kean and the later Victorians, two major artists must have their say, in the establishment of the visual tradition. The first, John Runciman, could scarcely be bettered in his clinical isolation from the theatre. Brought up in Edinburgh and dying at the age of twenty-seven, his major work, *King Lear in the Storm* (pl. 1), is wholly without debt to *King Lear* in the eighteenth-century theatre (which in any event he had scarcely the opportunity to see). For this splendid picture, in the National Gallery of Scotland in Edinburgh, defies all the canons of 'illustration'. It has the full complement of the characters in the heath scenes, though the Fool had not been seen in the theatre since the seventeenth century; half the composition explores a stormy sea, with on the horizon a foundering ship and in the foreground a rock surrounded by water on which the King, Gloucester, Kent, the Fool and 'Poor Tom' are isolated. In short it 'illustrates' no scene in Shakespeare's *King Lear* and is certainly worlds apart from Colman's or Garrick's rewriting of the text for the theatre; rather, it renders with epic power the imagery of deluge, inundation and chaos within the play, and, ignoring the contemporary or any other theatre performance of the work, goes to the core of Lear's mind and the desolation which brought him to his purgation and reconciliation with Cordelia.

Later, at the turn of the century, our second artist, Blake,[2] shows us a similar independence of the conventions of the theatre. He was the only considerable artist omitted from the stately if over-comprehensive gathering of the talents for the Boydell Gallery. Here was the climax, at the turn of the century, of attempts in the classical tradition to render Shakespeare exclusively for the eye, and there were some splendid works; thirty-five artists (among them Reynolds, Romney, Hamilton, Fuseli, Opie) covered the whole range of Shakespeare's work, for Boydell's aim was no less than

1. *King Lear in the Storm*; a painting by John Runciman, 1767

17

to establish an 'English School of History Painting'. But the disclaimer in his Preface to the 1789 catalogue shows the dilemma of visualisation divorced from theatrical presentation:

It must not, then, be expected that the art of the Painter can ever equal the sublimity of our Poet. The strength of Michael Angelo, united to the grace of Raphael, would here have laboured in vain – for what pencil can give to his airy being, 'a local habitation and a name'?

No such considerations inhibited Blake. His works based on Shakespeare had none of the comprehensive majesty of his Dante, Milton or studies of Biblical subjects; but among the two dozen or so of Shakespearean themes, two stand out massively in themselves and in their relevance to our present argument; they are the two 'colour-prints', *Pity* and *The Triple Hecate*. The former gathers into one pattern the images of 'the naked babe', the 'Cherubim, hors'd' and the tempestuous flight, distancing and objectifying Macbeth's speech in 1.7. *The Triple Hecate* is a far more complex work and appears to me to put a period to the attempt up to Blake's day to render Shakepeare visible outside the theatre. For this work, regarded by Rossetti as 'altogether not to be surpassed in Blake's special range of power', is not only an elaborate rendering of the triple goddess surrounded by her familiars, but, in removing itself from overt illustration of one single play, draws together the dark references to Hecate in the tragedies (*Hamlet*, *Macbeth* and *King Lear*), but most potently attaches sinister depth to Puck's final speech in A *Midsummer Night's Dream*:

> . . . we Fairies, that do runne,
> By the triple *Hecates* teame,
> From the presence of the Sunne,
> Following darknesse like a dreame.

This dire expansion of Puck's significance – the dark undertone of this play not only enhancing its grace, charity and vision, but establishing also comedy's relationship to tragedy – is something that the artist of stature can achieve but that is rarely attainable in the theatre. Blake is a significant end-term, his stature as an interpreter of literature unmatched until our own day – and then rarely.

For with the Victorian theatre and its immediate predecessors we enter a new and different world. The key signature is provided by Planché in his settings in 1824 for *King John* (though substantially hinted at by de Loutherbourg in the previous century and by William Capon's work for Kemble at Drury Lane). Planché's unambiguous aim may be seen in the playbill for *King John* at Covent Garden on 19 January 1824:

Shakespeare's Tragedy of King John with an attention to Costume never equalled on the English Stage. Every Character will appear in the precise HABIT OF THE PERIOD, the whole of the Dresses and Decorations being executed from indisputable Authorities. (Odell, 1920, vol. 2, p. 171)

The age of Charles Kean was upon us.

It has been fashionable to decry the 'pedantry' and 'meretricious elaboration' of Kean's productions, such overloading of precise detail as frustrated the delicate ambiguities of Shakespeare's text. There is truth in this, but not the whole truth. For this is not a matter of an energetic actor–manager's employing a large team of antiquarian researchers and scene-designers. It is true that Kean worked with families of theatre artists – Grieve, Telbin, Gordon – whose expertise and practicality dominated the visual in the theatre throughout the century. But in the preceding period of Macready and Phelps scenery had been substantially in the hands of artists, notably Clarkson Stanfield and W. R. Beverley, who were as much at home in the Royal Academy as in the theatre; and Gordon, who with Grieve and Telbin was largely responsible for the atmospheric landscapes in Charles Kean's productions, took background setting sufficiently seriously to produce a setting for A Midsummer Night's Dream which was virtually a copy of Turner's Golden Bough. It is important to stress this painterly approach, for a clear line may be traced from de Loutherbourg's Eidophusikon in the previous century to the dioramas which the professional painters provided for the Victorian theatre and in each case landscape and townscape settings were enriched by the increasing experimentation with light.

Yet for all its roots in eighteenth-century art, in Charles Kean's team painting was wholly in the service of the theatre and a theatre which was dominated by certain clearly formulated ideals. Kean's tenure of the Princess's Theatre (1851–9) is summarised by his friend and biographer, J. W. Cole:

[Kean] had long felt that, even by his most eminent predecessors, Shakespeare in many respects had been imperfectly illustrated . . . The time had at length arrived when a total personification of Shakespeare, with every accompaniment that refined knowledge, diligent research, and chronological accuracy could supply, was suited to the taste and temper of the age, which had become eminently pictorial and exacting beyond all earlier precedent. (1859, vol. 2, p. 26)

Beginning with King John and following with four more Shakespeare histories, Kean regarded even such productions as those of The Winter's Tale, A Midsummer Night's Dream and The Merchant of Venice as demanding vast labours in historical reconstruction. The first page of the

Macbeth playbill (Feb. 1853) runs to some eleven hundred words of archaeological argument to establish 'the dress worn by the inhabitants of Scotland in the eleventh century', and with similarly scrupulous argument it was decided that 'the architecture previous to the Norman Conquest [should be] used throughout the play'. To these ends, the artists Gordon, Lloyds and Dayes produced sheet upon sheet of designs; the architectural settings are usually in two states, the first a plain set and the second with actors and properties prepared for a scene.

Though in all this industry there is no understanding of the creative ambiguity whereby Shakespeare, in both *Macbeth* and *King Lear*, achieves the dual perspective of a primitive society and the equivocal values of contemporary statecraft, Kean at least, with single-minded devotion, paid Shakespeare the compliment of thorough scholarship and highly professional team-work; this gave his productions at the Princess's Theatre a stature which we can still recreate for ourselves as we examine the designs preserved in the Victoria and Albert Museum and the Kean prompt-books in the Folger Library. His was a massive if blinkered achievement.

It might indeed be argued that without the productions of Charles Kean the subtler, more sensitive work of E. W. Godwin would have been impossible. His training as an architect imbued Godwin with both the historical expertise and the practical discrimination which gave to his explorations of Shakespeare a quality hitherto not found in the theatre. And he was free of the whole-hearted dogmatism which is on the whole too oppressive in Kean's work. We are fortunate that the articles he wrote for *The Architect* in 1875 were reprinted by his son, Gordon Craig, in *The Mask* (1909–11) with important editorial notes. In one of these Craig quotes his father's comment on the Royal Academy pictures of 1865 – 'The accessories in pictures, whether on canvas or on the stage, should be altogether wrong or wholly right' – and he goes on to comment on the justice of the insight that 'they may be altogether "wrong"':

Either the producer was to represent that purely imaginative realm of the poetic drama removed from all realities, furnished and peopled with purely imaginative forms or to give a reflection of reality as clear as the reflection of Narcissus in a pool.

(Merchant, 1959, p. 127)

It is fascinating that Gordon Craig should have held to this conviction derived from his father throughout his life: in a correspondence of 1948 he wrote to me with particular reference to Shakespeare setting and production:

Shakespeare is at times so realistic – calls for reality so sharply – and at other times exactly the reverse – so that designers should (and don't) take care to serve him in the two ways.

In this temper Godwin's researches almost wholly dominated Squire Bancroft's production of 1875, and Godwin's article in *The Architect* mobilises an historical expertise which greatly exceeds that of Charles Kean's researchers. He details not only the buildings which might provide models for the stage setting, but also the intermixture of styles ('the Byzantine, the Gothic and the Renaissance') which Venice's peculiar power as a trading city had brought about. But his sensitive discrimination goes beyond this historical detail to an insight into the cultural decay of the city which we feel Shakespeare to have sensed in his ambiguous treatment of the Venetian Christians. Godwin writes:

Venice was then in the full swing of the pride of life, and the very notion of decay or dilapidation must have been hateful to her, all the more hateful from an occasional gleam of consciousness that her power was already rapidly decaying.

This was a vastly different insight from the more pedestrian historical realism of Kean, and it is pleasing that *The Times* provides a coda to this work of Godwin (though in fact reviewing Bancroft's production, which gave only grudging acknowledgement of Godwin's work): 'No attempt is made to emulate the gorgeous revival of Mr Charles Kean, but the most thorough feeling for propriety and finish prevails throughout' (19 Apr. 1875).

This rigour and sensitivity were not to be found consistently through the remainder of the century, and the productions of Irving, Tree and lesser theatrical personalities might arouse a proper critical irony; but the tradition had been well founded, so that Godwin's sensitive scholarship was extended in two valuable and related directions. William Poel applied the same historical perspective to an imaginative recreation of the atmosphere and physical conditions of the Elizabethan and Jacobean theatre; and though among some of his pedestrian successors there has been more than a little ludicrous antiquarianism, no director can today be unaware of the pace, the flexibility and the early-Baroque ambiguities of Shakespeare's stage – at least let us say that no director *should* be so unaware.

Whatever the power of Poel's work, however, and whatever correctives he so salutarily applied to the visual excesses of the Victorian actor–managers, the true heir to the more delicate insights of the Victorians was the still greatly undervalued Gordon Craig. With the architectural heritage from his father, E. W. Godwin, and the powerful instinct for 'theatre' inherited from his mother, Ellen Terry, he established – more in his drawings, paintings and wood-engravings than in his actual work in the theatre – a visual chastity and discrimination which could traverse the range of stage setting from the monumental and epic to the most intimately domestic. *Macbeth*, *Electra* or *The Crown Pretenders* could evoke majestic and yet essentially simple monumentality; the engravings in the Cranach Press *Hamlet* had equal insight in such claustrophobic designs as *Now Might I Do it Pat*. We are fortunate that his work in the theatre has been focussed and preserved for us in these works, published by Count Kessler.

We have come, then, full circle. In the pre-Victorian period the artist at his easel was dominant, even at those moments, with Hogarth, Zoffany or Fuseli, when a theatre scene was the source of their inspiration and where the very gesture of Garrick or Mrs Siddons is made to live. And yet the most powerful insights come from those artists – John Runciman, Romney or Blake – who by-passed the theatre and went directly to Shakespeare's words. Throughout the Victorian period the journeyman scene designer was joined on equal terms by the painter, the ultimate spring of whose inspiration was outside the theatre. And at the end of that age, and thrusting design into our own time, Gordon Craig is the forerunner of those whose work lay in both centres of creativity: their own personal imaginings and the demands of Shakespeare's text in the theatre. Each is a fertile tradition, and both painter and designer have contributed to that discipline which we may hopefully call 'visual criticism'.

NOTES

1 Many of the paintings and designs referred to in this chapter are reproduced and discussed in W. Moelwyn Merchant, 1959.

2 All Blake's works based on Shakespeare were reproduced, with a commentary by W. Moelwyn Merchant, in *Apollo*, Apr. 1964, celebrating the Shakespeare quatercentenary.

David Scott's *Queen Elizabeth Viewing the Performance of the 'Merry Wives of Windsor' in the Globe Theatre* (1840)

JAMES FOWLER

D AVID Scott, RSA (1806–49), began his oil painting of *Queen Elizabeth Viewing the Performance of the 'Merry Wives of Windsor' in the Globe Theatre* (pl. 2) in 1839, completing it in time for the summer exhibition at the Royal Academy of 1840. It was bought by the Theatre Museum, Victoria and Albert Museum, in 1983 for display in the Museum's new premises in Covent Garden. The picture deserves to be better known for what it reveals of Shakespeare, his age and his theatre as seen through early Victorian eyes, and because it appears to be the first serious attempt to depict the inside of the first Globe.

In this history-painting, Scott seeks to epitomise the spirit of Queen Elizabeth's reign through a famous dramatic event. The focus of interest is both on Shakespeare, who stands in the foreground, and on the Queen as they watch Falstaff frolicking on stage in the final scene of the play. The design, as one Victorian critic observed, is 'well composed, with the interest admirably concentrated in spite of the multiplicity of component parts' (Gray, 1884, p. 26). Instead of restricting himself to the years 1601–2, the then supposed date of *The Merry Wives of Windsor*, Scott adopts a broader time scheme that allows him to include leading courtiers, statesmen and literary celebrities of the era. The figures and costumes fall mainly between *c.* 1580 and *c.* 1610; the former range from Sir Philip Sidney (d. 1586) who wears dress of 1577, to Beaumont and Fletcher, who only established themselves as successful dramatists towards the end of the first decade of the seventeenth century. Even the Queen appears, though it has been well known at least since the late eighteenth century that she never attended public playhouses (Malone, 1790; repr. 1821, vol. 3, p. 166). By featuring her, Scott exploits the tradition first recorded by Dennis and Rowe early in the eighteenth century that Shakespeare wrote *The*

2. *Queen Elizabeth Viewing the Performance of the 'Merry Wives of Windsor' in the Globe Theatre*; an oil painting by David Scott, 1840 Photograph by Graham Brandon.

Merry Wives of Windsor to satisfy Elizabeth's desire to see Falstaff 'in Love'. This singular acknowledgement of Shakespeare's art fuelled the avid interest taken in his life by the nineteenth century, which would surely have invented the legend had it not already existed. As one biographer, Charles Symmons, wrote in a Shakespeare edition of 1837, the Queen's acute literary and theatrical tastes made it 'impossible that she should overlook; and that, not overlooking, she should not appreciate the man, whose genius formed the prime glory of her reign' (p. x). Such an idea proved irresistible to novelists, playwrights and artists, who took it upon themselves to elevate Shakespeare further in the Queen's favour. In *Kenilworth* (1821), Walter Scott has Shakespeare's compliment to the 'fair vestal, throned by the West' relayed anachronistically to the Queen by Raleigh (Schoenbaum, 1970, p. 369). Shakespeare then actually appears before her at court in Charles Somerset's popular play *Shakespeare's Early Days* (1829), outwitting the Master of the Revels in a poetry competition. In 1835, John Wood's painting of *Shakespeare Reading one of his Plays to Queen Elizabeth* was exhibited at the Royal Academy (no. 342; see Strong, 1978, pp. 161–2). The subject re-emerged in various guises in the work of later artists, such as Eduard Ender's *Shakespeare before the Court of Queen Elizabeth Reciting 'Macbeth'* (reproduced in Schoenbaum, 1981, p. 198), or in Charles Cattermole's watercolour of *Shakespeare Reading the 'Merry Wives of Windsor' to Queen Elizabeth*, where the Queen sits Cleopatra-like upon a barge (*Catalogue of . . . Royal Shakespeare Theatre Picture Gallery*, 1964, no. 37). In 1838, Shakespeare made his début as hero in Robert Folkstone Williams's three-volume novel *Shakespeare and his Friends*, which tells how the Queen attends *The Merry Wives of Windsor* at the Globe, having first had Shakespeare read it to her at court. This occasions a colourful description of the Globe interior that David Scott may have read (vol. 1, pp. 69, 198–9). Bringing the Queen to Shakespeare's theatre was, as C. Walter Hodges writes, 'a conjunction of ideas natural enough in a world of Popular Historicals. Impossible to imagine that Good Queen Bess never even met the Swan of Avon. After all, they were both famous, and lived in London, and his theatre was only a little way down the river from her home' (letter of 27 May 1984 in the Theatre Museum). One might add that at a time when the young Queen Victoria regularly attended public theatres (Rowell, 1978, p. 128) such a practice could naturally have been projected on to the past.

David Scott was the eldest son of Robert Scott, the engraver, and brother of the Pre-Raphaelite artist William Bell Scott, whose *Memoir of David Scott R.S.A.* (1850) is the most important source for his life and work. Spending most of his short life in his native Edinburgh, David Scott began as an engraver in his father's business and then dedicated himself to painting from 1828. In his art he generally avoided contemporary subjects, often preferring scenes of a spiritual nature taken from literature or history which could be invested with a powerful symbolism.[1] Shakespeare, a favourite author, inspired several works including the violent and sinister *Lady Macbeth Leaving the Daggers by the Sleeping Grooms* (1836); essays in the supernatural such as *Puck Fleeing from the Dawn* and *Ariel and Caliban* (both 1837), and historical subjects, for example *Richard III Receiving the Children of Edward IV from their Mother* (c. 1842). After a visit to Italy in 1832–4, Scott started to produce major historical paintings such as the *Alchemystical Adept (Paracelsus) Lecturing on the Elixir Vitae* (1838), which was much admired by his contemporaries (W. B. Scott, 1850, pp. 209–10). This was followed by *Philoctetes Left in the Isle of Lemnos by the Greeks in their Passage towards Troy* (1840), which shows the intense anguish of the hero abandoned by his comrades to a certain death. The threat of personal annihilation found further powerful expression in *The Traitor's Gate* (1842) featuring the arrival of the Duke of Gloucester at Calais where he was murdered on Richard II's orders.[2] Though exhibited in the same year as *Philoctetes*, *Queen Elizabeth . . . in the Globe Theatre* is in very different vein as it celebrates Shakespeare in his finest hour, achieving the ultimate recognition by his contemporaries for his art. To convey the sense of gala occasion Scott uses colour exuberantly, picking out major figures in reds, yellows and blues in accordance with his theory of colour (see W. B. Scott, 1850, p. 282). He also adds lively details such as the Queen's jester, who leans against the royal box, the fiddler in the foreground whom a maidservant plies with drink, and the pack of playing cards tucked behind the horn and flute players in the bottom right-hand corner. But at the same time he undercuts the festive tone with slightly disturbing elements such as the dangerous-looking knife which the Fool holds at the side of the stage; or close by, Ben Jonson 'clenching his hand, and enjoying the practical jibes of the Merry Wives' (W. B. Scott, 1850, p. 218).

Queen Elizabeth . . . in the Globe Theatre is history-painting on the grand scale. Measuring approximately six feet high by nine feet wide, it is 'the most laborious and extended exhibition of character ever accomplished' by David Scott, according to his brother (W. B. Scott, 1850, p. 218). First exhibited at the Royal Academy in 1840 (no. 410), the picture was hung there 'in an obscure place out of reach of particular examination' (*ibid.*, p. 216) and was coolly received in consequence, much to Scott's resentment. After a further showing at the Royal Scottish Academy in 1841 (no. 249), it stayed in Scott's studio until his death in 1849 and was then included in a posthumous exhibition of his work held at 29 Castle Street, Edinburgh (no. 24). It was probably at about this time that the painting came into the possession of the eminent Scottish lawyer George Young (1819–1907), who became Lord Young in 1874. Certainly he was the owner of it in 1866–7, when an etching by William Bell Scott (see pl. 3) was published by the Art Union of Glasgow, giving the painting wider currency than it would otherwise have had in private hands. As a record taken in the 1860s, the etching almost certainly preserves features of the original apparently lost through later restoration, such as the dots between the stripes of Shakespeare's sleeve. It is possible that in rendering the work of another artist – even one he knew so well – William Bell Scott unconsciously modified faces in accordance with his own taste, although recent restoration makes it difficult to be certain of this. Certainly the etching omits significant details which warn against accepting the evidence it offers too uncritically: it loses, for instance, the rings for working the curtain on the beam crossing the stage, the feather in Raleigh's hat and a woman who sits in the middle tier, her face partly obscured in the painting by the slack rope hanging from the same beam.

In 1880 Lord Young lent the painting for exhibition at the Royal Scottish Academy (no. 505), and in the following year to the inaugural exhibition of the Picture Gallery of the Shakespeare Memorial Theatre, Stratford-upon-Avon (no. 8). There it happily complemented the drop-scene W. R. Beverley had painted for the opening of the theatre in 1879, which according to the *Stratford-on-Avon Herald* showed 'Queen Elizabeth in her carriage, going to the Globe Theatre, to witness a new play of Shakespeare's' (see also the *Stratford-on-Avon Chronicle*, 22 Apr. 1881).

As early as 1884 the physical condition of *Queen Elizabeth . . . in the Globe Theatre* began to arouse concern. John Gray, in his study of Scott's work, noted how 'the colour, though still rich and fine, seems to have changed and darkened with time and over-varnishing, so that we can scarcely feel that we see the canvas as it left the artist's hand' (1884, p. 26). Its condition had seriously deteriorated by the beginning of the 1970s, when it was put up for auction by Dowells Ltd of Edinburgh,[3] apparently by Lord Young's descendants. The canvas was then relined and the paint surface cleaned, rather too zealously in places, and partly repainted. Examination with ultra-violet light reveals overpainted areas, which include Shakespeare's jerkin and stockings, though not his face; the heads and hands of Lord Burleigh and son, behind Shakespeare; the lady's and gentleman's faces in the grand side box to the right of the royal box; part of the Fool's hood in the foreground; the bodice of the merry wife to the right

3. An etching of David Scott's painting (pl. 2), by William Bell Scott, 1866–7

of Falstaff; Raleigh's stockings; and part of the stage surface. Faces of other individuals have also been partly retouched in order to highlight them. Not always executed with the greatest sensitivity, this restoration must remain a permanent addition, since it is largely irreversible. But it can at least claim the merit of rescuing the painting from oblivion, enabling us now to appreciate fully the content of Scott's work and the sources he drew upon.

According to his brother, David Scott researched *Queen Elizabeth . . . in the Globe Theatre* intensively, amassing 'notes relating to the men of the era, their ages, costumes, and portraits, and on the form and fittings of the theatres of the time' (1850, p. 218) – notes which have since disappeared.[4] Many characters, however, can be identified from the description that accompanied the painting at the Royal Academy in 1840:

In the royal box, in attendance on the Queen, are the Earl of Leicester, in armour, the Earl of Essex, and Walsingham. Towards the foreground is Sir Walter Raleigh, in a light red dress, between whom and Shakespeare, who stands upon the landing-place at the end of the seats, are Spenser, his hands on his breast, the Earl of Southampton, Fletcher, and Beaumont. To the other side of Shakespeare are Ben Jonson, in a black doublet, Thomas Sackville, Earl of Dorset, and Dr. Dee, who addresses a youth. The group behind the figure of Shakespeare represents Cecil, Lord Burleigh, Mildred, his wife, and a son and daughter. In the line of seats before these, but farther from the spectator, stands Sir Philip Sidney, and higher, towards the left, Francis Bacon and Drake, Massinger, Harrington, etc. are meant to be represented by other figures.　　　　　(Graves, 1970, vol. 4, p. 56)

Essex stands at the front of the royal box, with Walsingham to the rear behind Leicester. Who the maid of honour is between Walsingham and the Queen is not clear: possible candidates include Elizabeth Throckmorton and Mary Fitton. Neither the lady nor the gentleman, attended by a dwarf in the side box to the right of the Queen, is named. In view of the preponderance of literary celebrities present, the lady might be Sidney's sister, Mary, Countess of Pembroke,[5] accompanied by her husband, the Second Earl. The identity of the man who sits between Shakespeare and Raleigh with his back to us remains obscure. Massinger's and Harington's locations are uncertain – unless it is Massinger who stands immediately in front of Drake, and Harington who raises his hat behind the helmeted Earl of Southampton. A revised version of the above description which appeared in the posthumous exhibition catalogue of 1849 names Dr Dee's interlocutor in the foreground as 'Fairfax the poet' (*Catalogue of . . . the Works of . . . David Scott*, 1849, p. 8).

Although engravings on which many portraits are based can be determined, it is almost impossible now that Scott's working notes are missing, to be certain precisely which source he consulted for these. In his

Autobiographical Notes, W. B. Scott recalls how in his youth he and David enjoyed thumbing through 'volumes of illustrations in Bell's and Cook's little editions of English poets and dramatists' in their father's print collection (Minto, 1892, p. 14). More specifically, in his account of the present painting the same writer suggests Aubrey's *Brief Lives* as a source for Jonson's costume: 'in plain black, a humble dress in those gay days – (Old Aubrey describes his doublet as somewhat split under the arm)' (1850, p. 218). Doubtless, David Scott knew major sources of engraved portraits such as Edmund Lodge's *Portraits of Illustrious Personages of Great Britain* (1821–34), *Granger's Biographical History of England* (1769–74) in one of its many editions or amplified versions, or Vertue and Houbraken's portrait work endlessly reproduced from the 1730s onwards (see Strong, 1978, p. 61). Even when he uses a single engraving as his model, Scott frequently introduces variations of his own. Shakespeare, whose head derives from the 'Chandos' portrait, loses his earring; Southampton acquires a helmet; Sidney gains a cloak, and Burleigh a black staff in place of his white wand of office.[6] Alternatively, Scott may combine two separate engraved sources. For instance, Raleigh's dress, ruff and hat with feather and pearl come from one source while his scarf comes from another which was believed in the nineteenth century to be of Walter Raleigh but has since been identified as of his brother, Carew (Strong, 1969a, vol. 1, pp. 258–9). In the case of Mildred, Lady Burleigh, he supplies a double ruff fashionable from the 1580s onwards (Cunningtons, 1970, p. 167) in place of the small single ruffs worn in the two known original portraits of her dating from *c.* 1565 (Strong, 1969b, p. 116). How Scott obtained her likeness is not clear. No reproductions of her appear in the British Museum *Catalogue* earlier than 1904 (O'Donoghue, 1908, vol. 1, p. 292), so maybe he had access to an actual painting of her. The Queen seems to be a composite figure with details drawn from several sources. W. B. Scott relates how a distinguished London critic wrote to Scott calling into question the Queen's expression, which seemed too staid in view of the fact she had commanded the performance. Scott's reply justified his portrait of her in terms that reveal a key motive of his painting – to express the essence of the historical character:

Doubtless among equals, or indeed in any society, politeness and indulgence would mark the reception of any effort to please, but in the case of a queenly command, this would not necessarily be seen – in a proud-tempered queen certainly not; and, after all, the right thing to be done was to give the general and true character of Queen Elizabeth, in which I hope I have in some measure succeeded.   (W. B. Scott, 1850, p. 219)

Studies of Elizabethan costume were scarce at the time Scott worked on this painting (see Strong, 1978, pp. 49–60). Joseph Strutt's monumental

4.   *The Fool and Double-Bass Player*; a sketched detail by David Scott for his painting (pl. 2)

works went no further than the early Tudors; James Robinson Planché's *History of British Costume* (1834) contains a few pages on the subject, but this was a very slim work compared to his massive two-volume *Cyclopædia of Costume* of 1876–9. Planché records how ruffs were starched in many different colours, and how women wore masks in Elizabeth's reign (1834, pp. 258, 261). Scott includes ruffs in different shades – Sidney's for instance, is lilac-coloured – as well as masked women in the audience. (He may also have seen the female masks described and engraved in Francis Douce's *Illustrations of Shakspeare* (1807, vol. 1, pp. 76–8).) Apart from such works, Scott probably relied mainly on portrait sources for details of costume. Douce's 'Dissertations on the Clowns and Fools of Shakespeare' probably inspired details of the dress of the Fool who sits beside the stage, such as a red and green colour-scheme for the hood and the bells at the base of it, together with the serrated knife in his hand (1808, vol. 2, p. 325, and pls. III, IV). A preliminary study[7] of the Fool and the bass player (pl. 4), 'made apparently to be painted as a small picture' (W. B. Scott, 1850, p. 218), shows how the bells have been added and the knife substituted for what seems to be a mask or bauble. Judging from the lofty headgear of one of the ladies and the style of the bass player's hat, the sketch is set in the second half of the fifteenth century (Cunningtons, 1969 pp. 149, 159). Curiously, Scott retains the same hat for the bass player in *Queen Elizabeth . . . in the Globe Theatre*, despite the fact that it appears an anachronism in the late sixteenth century. The sketch suggests a further borrowing: the lady with the tall head-dress has a tilt to her head and a smile rather like that of the merry wife who grips Falstaff's antlers.

Scott clearly makes no attempt to portray the merry wives as though played by boys. It is possible that the grouping of the wives with Falstaff reflects staging in Scott's own day: *The Merry Wives of Windsor* was successfully revived at the Edinburgh Theatre Royal in 1837 with William Murray playing Falstaff (Dibdin, 1888, p. 372). Alternatively, he may have been influenced by an earlier painting, such as Robert Smirke's *Falstaff at Herne's Oak*, painted for the Boydell Shakespeare Gallery (see Friedman, 1976, figs. 225–7). Smirke's female figures seem similarly animated, although his Falstaff, a genial old buffer, has nothing of the rather bestial expression Scott gives the character.

Scott's attempt to portray the Globe Playhouse reflects a revival of interest in Elizabethan architecture during the 1830s, when 'Elizabethan' and 'Gothic' were chosen as the two possible styles for the design of the new Houses of Parliament (Girouard, in Summerson, 1968, pp. 21–2; Pevsner, 1972, p. 84). So far as the structures of Shakespearean playhouses were concerned, he had little visual evidence to work on. The foremost authority on the subject, Malone's *Historical Account of the Rise and Progress of the English Stage* (1790; repr. 1821), reproduces a view of the Globe exterior after Visscher's 1616 Panorama of London, which shows it as a hexagonal building with a triple-gabled superstructure supporting a flag. An alternative view of the Globe after Hollar's Long View of 1647 shows it as round with a stairtower, but with no superstructure to support its flag of St George whose pole emerges from the centre of the arena (see *Dramatic Table Talk*, 1825, vol. 1, title-page). (Owing to Hollar's mislabelling, this so-called view of the Globe is actually of the Hope, but the error was not realised until 1948 (I. A. Shapiro, *Shakespeare Survey*, 1, 25–37).) For the interior of the Globe, Scott could, in theory, have gained clues from the vignette of a stage in the frontispiece to Alabaster's play *Roxana* (1632) before Charles Knight popularised this in his *Old England* of 1845–6 (vol. 2, p. 113). Or he might have consulted methodical reconstructions of other Elizabethan playhouses such as the Tieck/Semper version of the Fortune, or von Baudissin's 'Old English Indoor Theatre' both published in Germany in 1836 (Hodges, 1968, pp. 112–14). Yet he shows little sign of so doing, or of having read the Fortune contract closely in Malone, otherwise he would have made the structural posts of his Globe round not square (see Collier, 1831, vol. 3, p. 291), and made his galleries overhang one another. Instead, he simply drew freely on the accounts of Malone and possibly also on John Payne Collier's *History of English Dramatic Poetry* (1831). These two authorities sometimes disagree: Malone for instance, dates the building of the Globe 'not long before 1596' (1821, vol. 3, p. 63) while Collier puts it in the spring of 1594 (1831, vol. 3, pp. 296–7). Yet they provided a consensus on many points for Scott to follow – or to modify – where it suited him.

Scott accordingly gives the Globe a circular auditorium made of wood, partly thatched and partly open to the sky, with audience on three levels standing and sitting, some being accommodated in 'rooms' or boxes (Malone, 1821, vol. 3, pp. 64–7, 72–4; Collier, 1831, vol. 3, pp. 297, 303). The stage is railed at the front and lined with curtains at about head height which draw apart along a rod. Malone allows musicians to play between the acts and locates them aloft in a balcony (1821, vol. 3, pp. 111–12; cf. Collier 1831, vol. 3, pp. 447–8); Scott, showing nothing of the tiring-house behind the stage, locates them by the side of the stage. Malone has the stage covered with rushes or matting; a clown who appeared between acts or scenes; masked women in the audience; alcohol consumed in the playhouse; and table-books used during performance (1821, vol. 3, pp. 78, 116, 131, 142–3; Collier, 1831, vol. 3, pp. 414–16). These features all appear in various forms in the painting: a table-book, for instance, is being used by a man in the first section of the top gallery, to the right of the royal box, to scribble down passages from *The Merry Wives of Windsor* – tempting one to speculate whether this might not be another 'bad' quarto in the making.

Collier holds that the Globe had only two entrances, one leading into the tiring-house, the other into the auditorium; and mentions the office of doorkeeper (1831, vol. 3, pp. 297, 341–2). Scott shows a main entrance beneath the royal box which gives access both to the yard and to the top gallery via a single staircase on which a man stands. Another entrance, through the turnstile in the bottom left-hand corner, serves the middle tier, and seems to be guarded by a man with a truncheon and a bunch of keys – but not a box for takings as would be expected of a doorkeeper. (It is uncertain whether or not this turnstile reflects a method of controlling admission possibly used in some Victorian theatres instead of the usual crush-barrier system (see Leech and Craik, 1975, ill. 1b).)

Both the construction and the decoration of Scott's auditorium reinforce the different social levels of the audience. The elaborate fretwork of the middle tier and royal box contrasts with the plain red canvas curtains – reminiscent of a Victorian penny gaff (Sheridan, 1981, p. 66) – which hang above before each section of the gallery. The royal box occupies a central position as it did in the Restoration when Charles II visited the public theatres – the first reigning English monarch to do so (Lawrence, 1935, pp. 143–51). Although the source of structure of the royal box has remained elusive, Scott probably consulted Thomas Wille-ment's *Regal Heraldry* (1821) for the Queen's personal motto SEMPER EADEM and the design of the Tudor dragon which he includes in the coat of arms on the front (pl. XX). Willement warns that his illustration of Elizabeth's arms is not entirely typical (p. 81), yet Scott follows it to the extent of including in his quartering the Irish harp, a feature that did not become standard in the royal arms until the accession of James I in 1603 (Pinches, 1974, p. 154). Scott flies a flag (Malone, 1821, vol. 3, pp. 64–5; Collier, 1831, vol. 3, p. 365), seemingly of St George, on top of the royal box – an idea possibly inspired by the illustration after Hollar already described. The flagpole is set in a golden globe bearing the theatre's motto: TOTUS MUNDUS AGIT HISTRIONEM. This offers an ingenious solution to the problem of where the motto was actually displayed in the theatre; Malone and Collier disagree on the matter (1821, vol. 3, p. 67; 1831, vol. 3, p. 298).

The royal box has a fringe of gold and green, a colour-scheme re-used in the striped curtains that contain the upstage area. These are suspended by means of rings from a rod that runs down to the stage pillar and then turns away at right angles from the stage. The pillar supports a permanent cut-out border-piece that spans the acting area in the manner of a frontispiece (if such a term may be used of a frame stationed half-way down a thrust stage). Beneath the border-piece runs a cross-beam supporting with rings a dark curtain spangled with stars which seems to cover the upper half of the stage. The 1849 catalogue entry explains this as 'the means then adopted to indicate night' (p. 8), which is appropriate for this nocturnal scene, but cites no authority. If the curtain is meant to represent a stage canopy of 'heavens', it hardly tallies with Malone's suggestion of 'pieces of drapery tinged with blue . . . suspended across the stage' (1821, vol. 3, p. 108). The curtain may possibly be intended to have a dual function. If pulled forward over the cross-beam it might serve as house tabs, which Collier believed to be a feature of the Globe: 'besides the curtain in front of the stage, which concealed it from the spectators until it was drawn on each side upon a rod, there were other curtains at the back of the stage, called traverses' (1831, vol. 3, p. 372). At the very top of the painting, towards the right of the open sky, appears a very strange feature, a kind of tarpaulin with rope attached. Its function is obscure – unless it is a cover or 'heavens' designed to protect both stage and yard from the elements.

The curtains immediately above the stage seem to be worked with lines by the man who is perched on the end of the curtain rod behind the bass player. He could be a machinist or, more likely, the prompter or 'book-holder', judging by the bell above his head at the top of the pillar. A bell was a traditional feature of the prompt corner from the second half of the seventeenth century onwards (Langhans, 1981, pp. xx, xxvii), though Elizabethan references to it are lacking. Instead of being within the tiring-house (see Collier, 1831, vol. 3, p. 445), Scott's prompter sits stage left beside a pseudo-scenic frontispiece – an arrangement conditioned by proscenium theatre. The auditorium also betrays the influence of the first half of the nineteenth century in having a middle tier extending over the yard like the dress circle over the pit, instead of a yard contained by boxed galleries which slightly overhang one another (see Leech and Craik, 1975, p. 82). Another such detail is the child who sits upon the shoulders of a groundling, reflecting an era in which it was still possible to take even babes-in-arms to the theatre (Reid, in Bradby, 1980, p. 75). Paradoxically, Scott's inclusion of a toddler turns out to be an authentic touch, for as we now know the Globe audience did not entirely consist of adults.[8] Although he does not accommodate members of the audience on stage, Scott does link the stage with the middle tier by means of terraces, thereby suggesting the close interaction of players and audience characteristic of Elizabethan theatre. This is consistent with other features, such as the dark curtains that represent the night in a daytime performance, which Scott uses to convey the idea of a non-illusionist stage.

That Scott should reflect the theatre of his own day in the Globe was inevitable, especially as he was working almost fifty years before the publication in 1888 of the vital sketch of the Swan interior (c. 1596) by van Buchell after de Witt (Schoenbaum, 1975, p. 109). A measure of

Scott's achievement can be gained by comparing his version of the Globe with that of George Pycroft MRCS (1819–94), which C. Walter Hodges dated c. 1860 in *The Globe Restored* (1968, pp. 114–15), but which he now, on stylistic grounds, dates earlier, as 'perhaps contemporary with Scott, or not much after' (letter of 27 May 1984 in the Theatre Museum). Pycroft's work resembles Scott's in certain respects in showing the Queen in attendance watching Falstaff, on this occasion in *I Henry IV*, and in having a similar curtain-and-rail system running round the upper half of the stage down to the stage pillars. On the other hand, Pycroft depicts the interior of the Globe as a crude octagon having only two tiers, not three; this represents an unfortunate step backwards. But it is easy to criticise such efforts with hindsight. As Hodges says of Pycroft's work, not the least of its many merits is 'that it demonstrates the discomfiture that waits upon even the best-intended of historical reconstructions in the end' (1968, p. 115).

Queen Elizabeth . . . in the Globe Theatre dates from that era when efforts to restore Shakespeare's own text to the stage were coming to a head, notably in William Charles Macready's productions of *King Lear* and *The Tempest* at Covent Garden in 1838 (Odell, 1920, vol. 2, pp. 195–7, 200–1). Madame Vestris followed suit with a relatively pure version of *A Midsummer Night's Dream* (1840) at the same theatre, having revived there in 1839 the most 'Elizabethan' of the early comedies, *Love's Labour's Lost*, unstaged since the seventeenth century.[9] Apparently the earliest study of the Globe interior, Scott's painting belongs to the first wave of reconstructions of Elizabethan theatres that began with Ludwig Tieck and Gottfried Semper's version of the Fortune of 1836. Tieck's designs bore fruit in the theatre when he produced *A Midsummer Night's Dream* in 'Elizabethan' style at the royal palace of Potsdam in 1843 (Speaight, 1973, pp. 106–7). It was probably Tieck rather than Scott who inspired Planché to revive Shakespeare's text of *The Taming of the Shrew* in an 'authentic' manner at the Haymarket in 1844 and 1847 (McDonald, in Richards and Thomson, 1971, pp. 151–70). Yet it is Scott's painting that remains – despite 'Time's injurious hand' – as a feat of historical imagination, reflecting the preoccupation of his day with Shakespeare's life and times and the incipient interest in his theatre.

NOTES

1 For recent critical appreciation of David Scott's works, see Irwin, 1975, pp. 263–77; P. Smith, 'David Scott's *Vasco de Gama encountering the Spirit of the Cape*', unpublished MA dissertation, University of Edinburgh, 1980, pp. 1–18; Maas, 1969, p. 24.

2   The paintings mentioned here are all located in the National Gallery of Scotland, apart from *Lady Macbeth* (auctioned by Januarys of Newmarket, 27 Mar. 1985) and *Richard III* (unlocated).

3   Information concerning provenance has been supplied by Mr Tom Fidelo of Edinburgh, who says he bought the picture from the purchaser at the Dowells auction before eventually selling it himself to the Theatre Museum. The extreme scarcity of Dowells painting-sales catalogues has prevented verification of the sale date and lot number. (Phillips of Scotland, who took over Dowells in the mid-1970s, have the best run of catalogues, but even they lacked those for 1969–70 when their holdings were kindly checked for me by Caroline Stephen in February 1985.)

4   No working notes relating to this painting have been located, despite enquiries at Penkill Castle, Girvan, the Manuscript Departments of the British Library and National Library of Scotland, and the University of British Columbia Library. An appeal for information as to possible whereabouts published by *The Times Literary Supplement*, 26 June 1984, yielded no further leads. (Many thanks to all who assisted in the quest.)

5   My gratitude to Sir Roy Strong for suggesting Mary, Countess of Pembroke and others, and to other Victoria and Albert Museum colleagues for their generous help: Avril Hart (Department of Textiles & Dress), Michael Holmes (National Art Library), Lionel Lambourne (Department of Prints, Drawings, Photographs and Paintings), and Peter Young (Department of Conservation).

6   For portrait engravings that Scott could have used as sources for the present painting, reference is made where possible to O'Donoghue, 1908–25, as follows:

> Beaumont, I (1908), 148: nos. 1–9
> Burghley, Lord, I, 291: nos. 1–7
> Dee, II (1910), 26: nos. 1–2
> Dorset, II, 73–4: nos. 2–5
> Drake, II, 85–6: nos. 20–6
> Essex, II, 172: nos. 4–9
> Fletcher: see engraving by J. H. Robinson, after drawing by J. Thurston from a portrait in the Earl of Clarendon's collection, published by W. Walker, 8 Gray's Inn Square, 1 May 1821. Cf. Strong, 1969a, vol. 2, p. 244
> Harington, II, 446: no. 4
> Jonson, II, 661: nos. 7–10
> Leicester, III (1912), 38: nos. 1–3 (cf. Strong, 1969b, p. 165)
> Pembroke, Earl of, III, 439: no. 1
> Pembroke, Mary, III, 437: nos. 1–2; and cf. engraving by Bocquet, published by J. Scott, Strand, 20 May 1806
> Raleigh, III, 538–9: nos. 5–18 combined with nos. 2–3
> St Albans, IV (1914), 4: no. 2
> Shakespeare, IV, 65: nos. 64ff.
> Sidney, IV, 106: nos. 1 ff.
> Southampton, IV, 151: nos. 1–2, and cf. 4
> Spenser, IV, 166: no. 1 ff.
> Walsingham, IV, 395: nos. 7–10

7   The sketch, in pencil on wove paper (309×252 mm), is in the Department of Prints and Drawings, National Gallery of Scotland (D3545). On the verso is 'another drawing of the same subject, but showing the fool harassing the bass player . . . and includ[ing] many more figures' (information kindly supplied by Duncan Bell of the National Gallery of Scotland).

8 Maija Jansson Cole, 'A New Account of the Burning of the Globe', *Shakespeare Quarterly*, 32 (1981), 352.
9 Edith Holding, 'Revels, Dances, Masques, and Merry Hours: Madame Vestris's Revival of *Love's Labour's Lost*, 1839', *Nineteenth Century Theatre Research*, 9.1 (1981), 1–22; also Odell, 1920, vol. 2, pp. 223–6).

Charles Kean's *King Richard II*: A Pre-Raphaelite Drama

RICHARD FOULKES

AMONGST Charles Kean's services in reviving Shakespeare's *Richard II* at the Princess's Theatre on 12 March 1857 was providing the public with an opportunity to see a little-known and generally lowly regarded play. As J. C. Trewin recounts (1955, p. 233), W. C. Macready presented the play, at John Forster's suggestion, at the Haymarket Theatre on 2 December 1850, but it ran for only two performances. Not even Phelps staged *Richard II* during his Sadler's Wells management and Odell speculates: 'Did Kean's magnificent production anticipate one by Phelps and render it therefore useless, not to say hazardous?' (1920, vol. 2, p.346). This may be so, but by 1857 Phelps had been in management for thirteen years and inevitably he and Kean produced many of the same plays, so a more likely explanation is that he was not attracted to that particular Shakespearean drama. However, if in terms of stage history *Richard II* was an unexpected choice on Kean's part, in other respects it was a most timely selection during a decade in which antiquarian, artistic and public interest in the medieval past reached a new intensity.

The Great Exhibition of 1851 was a showplace for industrial progress and as such it promoted a process of manufacture and way of life which were abhorrent to many, not least John Ruskin, leader of what Kenneth Clark (1928) has called the 'Ethical Gothic' movement. Ruskin made his own contributions to the debate, but even he must have derived some consolation from the inclusion of historical exhibits within the Great Exhibition, in particular the Medieval Court prepared by A. W. Pugin: 'Among all the numerous attractions of the Great Exhibition, perhaps, on the whole, the Medieval Court, as a department, excited the most general interest.'[1] That commentator considered the Medieval Court to be 'a little too theatric in taste', this no doubt being attributable to Pugin's early experience as a stage designer, which included the scenery for a new opera based on Scott's *Kenilworth* in 1831 – the year in which he married a great-niece of George Dayes, who became one of Kean's leading scenic artists.

Pugin's Medieval Court remained in the public eye when it was installed in the Crystal Palace on its new site at Sydenham (from 10 June 1854), where it was joined by other Courts of Antiquity. During the 1850s interest in all forms of medieval art and architecture continued with such notable examples as Woodward's Natural Science Museum and Union Library, both in Oxford. These buildings were of course modern attempts to apply medieval principles and aesthetics in a functional way. Foremost amongst the exponents of this creative medievalism was the group of painters known as the Pre-Raphaelite Brotherhood, members of which, together with William Morris, executed the ill-fated murals in the Union Library during the summer of 1857.

The position of Shakespeare in this medieval revival was, to say the least, ambivalent. He was, of course, nearer in time to the artistic and architectural glories of the Middle Ages and presumably knew many buildings, artefacts and works of art which had subsequently been destroyed, altered or lost. Several of his plays were set in that age, notably *Richard II*, whose protagonist's court was upheld by Kean as a high point of artistic and cultural achievement, the milieu of Geoffrey Chaucer, 'whose elegant taste refined and smoothed our native tongue'.[2] But in Ruskin's view Shakespeare was irredeemably a product of the Renaissance: 'in the midst also of the fever of the Renaissance he [Shakespeare] writes, as everyone else did, in praise of precisely the most vicious master of that school – Giulio Romano'; in 'matters of art' he admired 'two things, – mockery of life (as in this instance of Hermione as a statue), or absolute splendour –, as in the close of Romeo and Juliet'. Culturally therefore Shakespeare belonged to an age in which medievalism had been supplanted; 'he was wholly incapable of entering into the spirit of the Middle Ages', wrote Ruskin, comparing him unfavourably with Browning who, in *The Bishop Orders his Tomb in St Praxed's Church*, 'is unerring in every sentence he writes of the Middle Ages'. Furthermore even critics less committed to upholding and recapturing the medieval past would have to agree with Ruskin that: 'They will find, if they look into his [Shakespeare's] work closely, as much antiquarianism as they do geography and no more' (1900, vol. 4, pp. 387–90).

A product of the Renaissance, certainly no antiquarian and 'wholly incapable of entering into the spirit of the Middle Ages' – Shakespeare, in Ruskin's estimation at least, was hardly promising material for the Pre-Raphaelite Brotherhood. Similarly, a theatre manager with the antiquarian zeal of Charles Kean was bound to find a degree of contradiction and conflict between Shakespeare's treatment of his historical subject in a play such as *Richard II* and the opportunity which it irresistibly presented for a painstaking reconstruction of medieval life. This aesthetic problem confronted Pre-Raphaelite painters and scene-designers alike; the resolution achieved behind the proscenium arch had much in common with that within the picture frame.

From the formation of the Pre-Raphaelite Brotherhood in 1848, its members and their followers were repeatedly drawn to Shakespeare's plays for subject-matter. The first Pre-Raphaelite exhibits at the Royal Academy in 1849 were Millais's *Ferdinand Lured by Ariel* (*The Tempest*, 1.2), together with his *Isabella*. In 1850 Walter Deverell, 'who took important parts on suburban stages',[3] completed *Twelfth Night*, (2.4), portraying himself as Orsino, Elizabeth Siddal as Viola and D. G. Rossetti as the Fool (pl. 5). Elizabeth Siddal appeared as Sylvia in Holman Hunt's *Valentine Rescuing Sylvia from Proteus* (*The Two Gentlemen of Verona*,

5. *Twelfth Night*; an oil painting by Walter Howell Deverell, 1850

41

5.4), which was exhibited, to a hostile response, at the Royal Academy in 1851. In 1852 Millais and Arthur Hughes coincidentally exhibited paintings of Ophelia, the former using Elizabeth Siddal as his model, Perhaps the finest Pre-Raphaelite Shakespearean painting, Hunt's *Claudio and Isabella* (*Measure for Measure*, 3.1), although completed in 1850, was not exhibited at the Royal Academy until 1853. Ruskin considered that 'such works as Mr. Hunt's "Claudio and Isabella" have never been rivalled, in some respects never approached, at any other period of art' (1904, vol. 4, p. 160). This extensive – but by no means comprehensive – list of Pre-Raphaelite Shakespearean paintings testifies to the dramatist's appeal to the Brotherhood and shows that their favoured model Elizabeth Siddal assumed a combination of Shakespearean roles unmatched by contemporary actresses.

These paintings appeared singly, but in 1857, within weeks of the opening of Charles Kean's *Richard II*, the public had an opportunity to see a collection of Pre-Raphaelite art in close juxtaposition to examples of medieval art such as inspired the Brotherhood.

If imitation is the sincerest form of flattery the Great Exhibition of 1851 was indeed highly regarded, for during the 1850s it spawned many imitations – Dublin in 1853, Paris in 1855 and, in 1857, Manchester. As exhibition succeeded exhibition it became apparent that some new emphasis was necessary, and when the city fathers of Manchester, under the chairmanship of Lord Ellesmere, made the obligatory approach to the Prince Consort he replied:

The mere gratification of the curiosity and the giving of intellectual entertainment to the dense population of a particular locality would be praiseworthy in itself, but hardly sufficient to convince owners of works of Art . . . to send them to Manchester for exhibition . . . national usefulness might, however, be found in the educational function that may be given to such a scheme.[4]

Accordingly the Manchester Exhibition became the Art Treasures of the United Kingdom Exhibition. A huge purpose-built, but temporary, gallery of 18,000 square yards was constructed at Old Trafford, two miles from the city centre; some 16,000 art objects were loaned, mainly by private owners, and ultimately seen by 1,336,715 visitors. The Pre-Raphaelites were assured a sympathetic response for, as Holman Hunt recorded, his 'good friend Mr. Thomas Fairbairn was one of the Council . . . and a guarantor. The collection was partly hung by my true defender, Augustus L. Egg, who had placed all my pictures well' (1913, vol. 2, p. 124). Theatrical expertise was present in the form of J. R. Planché (in charge of the armour display) and George Scharf jun., FSA (in charge of Works of Ancient Masters). Scharf, who had earlier recorded Macready's productions at Covent Garden, was acknowledged by Charles Kean in the Preface to *Richard II*: 'I am also indebted to G. Scharf, esq., jun., F.S.A., for many valuable suggestions.' In due course Scharf became the first director of the National Portrait Gallery for which the Manchester Exhibition was an effective preparation.

That the single most imposing portrait in the whole exhibition should be of King Richard II exceeds the bounds of mere coincidence. Of this portrait Scharf wrote:

From the year 1775, when the Westminster portrait of Richard II was removed into the Jerusalem Chamber, to the time of the Manchester Exhibition in 1857, the public no longer had access to it. Under the auspices of Dean Buckland, the chapter consented to lend their treasure to the great exhibition about to be opened in Manchester in May 1857, when this picture, partly it may be from its size, partly the subject, and, most of all, from its Gothic quaintness, attracted universal attention. (1867, p. xxxiv)

Kean's text of *Richard II* acknowledged: 'The costume of the king in this scene [1.1] is taken from the curious and authentic portrait of Richard preserved in the Jerusalem Chamber at Westminster Abbey' (p. 11).

Enthusiastic restoration in 1866 has robbed us of the Jerusalem Chamber portrait in the form in which Kean knew it, but comparison between production photographs and the portrait as it exists today reveals his debt to it (see pls. 6 and 7). The portrait's Shakespearean associations accounted for much of the interest in Manchester: 'The face claims pity, rather than scorn and anger. Shakespeare himself saw a deep and tragical bearing fraught with importance to all of us, in the king's career' (*The Art Treasures Examiner*, 1857, p. 52). The implication is that Shakespeare knew the painting and that it influenced his characterisation of Richard, a view which Oscar Wilde endorsed thirty years later: 'And that Shakespeare examined Richard II's tomb in Westminster Abbey seems to me certain'.[5] If Richard's tomb, then surely his portrait?

The dual attraction of the Jerusalem Chamber portrait in Manchester and of Kean's dramatic portrayal at the Princess's betokened the extraordinary appeal that that particular medieval monarch held for the Victorians – 'fraught with importance to all of us'. This was more than an antiquarian curiosity, it was an emotional sympathy bordering on identification which spanned the intervening centuries.

Pre-Raphaelite paintings were exhibited in the gallery of Modern Masters adjacent to the Jersusalem Chamber portrait at Manchester. Nineteenth-century pictures of Shakespearean subjects were a significant element in this section, as the catalogue reveals: Frith's *Anne Page* (no. 313); J. R. Herbert's *Lear Disinheriting Cordelia* (no. 329); C. R. Leslie's

43

6.   The 'Jerusalem Chamber' portrait of King Richard II, Westminster Abbey

7. Charles Kean as King Richard II, at the Princess's Theatre, 1857

Henry VIII (no. 378) and *Juliet* (no. 390); W. Gale's *Guiderius and Arvigarus Repeating the Dirge over Imogen* (no. 396); C. W. Cope's *Lear and Cordelia* (no. 567); Egg's *Scene from 'The Taming of the Shrew'* (no. 596); D. Maclise's *Macbeth* (no. 522) and *Scene from 'As You Like It'* (no. 612); and R. Dadd's *Puck on a Mushroom* (no. 335) and *A Midsummer Night's Dream* (no. 477). Not all were in the Pre-Raphaelite style. Indeed Daniel Maclise's work was criticised for the absence of the qualities which characterised the Pre-Raphaelites: 'where we want intensity, his personages are vehement; where we require concentration and self-repression, they are expansive and gesticulatory, full of parade and attitudinising display'.[6]

Gesticulation, attitudinising, vehemence on the one hand; intensity, concentration and self-repression on the other. It was indeed the latter qualities that the Pre-Raphaelites upheld and that were to be found in Holman Hunt's *Claudio and Isabella* (no. 565) and *Valentine Rescuing Sylvia from Proteus* (no. 570), both of which were on exhibition. The same observer found *Claudio and Isabella* 'far and away the most impressive work . . . in the whole English Gallery. The artist has chosen the moment when the first doubt of Claudio's courage grows up in his sister's brain. You can see the slow flush of scorn still striving with doubt in her eyes, and in every lineament of her noble face.' This was the essence of Pre-Raphaelitism, the truthful depiction of a character's appearance, conveying his/her inner thoughts and feelings at that moment. *Valentine Rescuing Sylvia from Proteus* 'though . . . a much more difficult achievement in all technical respects than "Claudio and Isabella", contains no such perfect expression as that face of Isabella's' (p. 97).

This view was very much in accordance with Ruskin's: 'But all this thoughtful conception, and absolutely inimitable execution, fail in making immediate appeal to the feelings, owing to the unfortunate type chosen for the face of Sylvia' (1904, vol. 12, p. 325). In theatrical parlance Elizabeth Siddal was miscast. Ruskin did visit Manchester during the Art Treasures Exhibition and there delivered 'A Joy for Ever: Two Lectures on the Political Economy of Art Delivered at Manchester July 10th and 13th 1857'. He had expressed his views on the Pre-Raphaelites many times, including in *Modern Painters* and in a lecture in Edinburgh in November 1853 in which he defended them against recurring critical calumnies:

Pre-Raphaelitism has but one principle, that of absolute, uncompromising truth in all that it does, obtained by working everything, down to the most minute detail, from nature, and from nature only. Every Pre-Raphaelite landscape background is painted to the last touch, in the open air, from the thing itself. Every Pre-Raphaelite figure, however studied in expression, is a true portrait of some living person . . . Again you must observe that as landscape painters, their principles must, in great part, confine them to mere foreground work.   (1904, vol. 22, pp. 157–60)

These characteristics – 'uncompromising truth', 'minute detail', painted 'from nature', 'living persons', 'landscape background', 'foreground work' – also informed Charles Kean's stage productions in which he created 'an historical picture, in which the creations of the painter's art [are] endowed with associated reality' (*King Richard II*, p. viii). Like the Pre-Raphaelite figures Kean's casts were made up of 'true portraits of some living persons', but there were more of them, they moved, had lines to speak and were called actors. But their style of performance, as we shall see, aspired to those qualities of inner and outer truth which distinguished Hunt's *Claudio and Isabella*.

For both the Pre-Raphaelites and Charles Kean the surroundings in which their figures appeared had to be as detailed, authentic and truthful as possible. Even 'landscape background' should be painted 'from the thing itself', but, as Ruskin recognised, this presented problems of perspective as a result of which the Pre-Raphaelites 'must, in great part' confine themselves 'to mere foreground work'. This was one of Kean's most acute problems, for as he developed his box-sets[7] with increasing sophistication, the contrast with painted two-dimensional backcloths was stubbornly inescapable.

The sense of a three-dimensional foreground and a two-dimensional background/backcloth is apparent in most Pre-Raphaelite Shakespearean paintings. In Deverell's *Twelfth Night* the foreground figures of Viola, Orsino and the Fool are of a substance totally lacking in the background figures of the Arab band and the landscape of the steps and trees. Similarly in Hunt's *Valentine Rescuing Sylvia from Proteus* the russet glade and horsemen appear shallow in comparison with the four foreground figures. In both cases there is a distinct line where, in theatrical terms, the backcloth meets the ground. True to Ruskin's precepts Hunt used the woods at Knole in Kent for *Valentine Rescuing Sylvia from Proteus*, as Millais used the River Ewell in Surrey for *Ophelia*, in which, for all his intense observation, the natural surroundings are little more than a 'border' for the stark figure of Elizabeth Siddal. Hunt's *Claudio and Isabella* is particularly interesting, showing an interior which the artist took from the Lollards' prison at Lambeth Place. This method was used by Kean's designers, and Hunt's painting has all the appearance of a theatrical box-set, with a backcloth of sky and trees visible through the window, itself carefully exploited as a source of 'natural' light. Indeed the whole composition recalls the Tallis print of Miss Glyn and Mr Hoskins in the same scene, from Samuel Phelps's Sadler's Wells production of *Measure for Measure* in 1846 (Laver, 1964, p. 132).

The restraints of perspective and the relationship between foreground and background were common problems for the Pre-Raphaelites and contemporary scene-designers, in the solution of which they showed remarkable uniformity. The correspondence between the two art forms is enforced by the surviving scene designs in the Print Room of the Victoria and Albert Museum. Of these Martin Hardie wrote:

Though it is hardly fair, owing to the necessary limitation and conventions imposed by stage requirements, to consider these drawings as original water-colours, yet a large number, regarded purely from a pictorial point of view, are of considerable merit. A striking point in all is the excellence of the composition, and one cannot help thinking that the artist has been helped by always seeing his picture, as it were, in the framework of the stage. (*St James's Gazette*, 17 Apr. 1902)

This is borne out by the recurrence of painterly terms in reviews of *Richard II*: 'a true living picture' (*The Times*, 13 Mar. 1857); 'a faithful picture . . . a vivid portraiture of contemporaneous customs . . . like an elaborately painted picture, every scene and personage stands boldly out of the canvas with a reality and delusion of effect at times perfectly startling' (*Era*, 15 Mar. 1857).

Kean's team of scenic designers was extremely talented with distinct specialisms, as W. Moelwyn Merchant (1959, p. 101) has observed: 'These artists fall into two broad groups: Grieve, Gordon, and Telbin were at their best in landscape and atmospheric settings . . . The second group is mainly represented by Cuthbert and Lloyds, with detailed architectural draughtsmanship and painstaking archaeology in properties and set pieces . . . Dayes lies between these two.' In all cases – whether concerned with landscape, architectural exterior or interior – the principle, as with the Pre-Raphaelites, was 'absolute uncompromising truth'. For the stage designers it was rarely a simple matter of visiting the River Ewell, Knole or the Lollards' prison, since most of the locations they were charged to represent had been destroyed or drastically altered. The nearest Kean got to complete authenticity was the command performance of *Richard II* on 5 March 1857 in St George's Hall, Windsor, in which part of the castle he specifically located his 4.4 (Shakespeare's 4.6). The reconstruction for the Princess's stage was by Frederick Lloyds, who was advised by Anthony Salvin, FSA, the foremost authority on medieval military architecture, whose restorations included the Tower of London and Caernarvon Castle as well as Windsor Castle. Salvin also advised for the sets of the Welsh castles and the Tower of London.

In his quest for historical truth Kean enlisted other antiquarian experts. Henry Shaw, FSA, advised on the Lists at Coventry and John of Gaunt's room at Ely House and on many of the accesssories introduced into other scenes; this, as the author of *A Series of Details of Gothic Architecture* and *Specimens of Ancient Furniture*, he was well qualified to do. George Godwin, FSA, advised on the Streets of Old London (the historical episode of Richard's return), Westminster Hall, the Dungeon at Pomfret and the Garden at King's Langley, which was based on the MS of the *Roman d'Alexandre* in the Bodleian Library. Another important source was the magnificently illuminated French Metrical History in the Harleian Collection at the British Museum, which provided the original designs for many of the costumes (in particular 3.1 – Shakespeare's 3.2). Other costumes were based on the Cotton MS (Gaunt in 1.2) and the effigy of Henry IV in Canterbury Cathedral (Bolingbroke in 5.4 – Shakespeare's 5.6). As Julian Treherz has shown, the Pre-Raphaelites consulted many of the same authorities and manuscript sources.[8]

Audiences lauded each succeeding portrait of people and places past without a qualm of concern for the 1300 discarded Shakespearean lines. The yardstick of authenticity was unequivocally historical not textual. In three key scenes the actors achieved their effect pictorially, relying more on silent by-play than on Shakespeare's lines. In 2.1 Kean cut 169 lines and presented Gaunt's death on stage (pl. 8). The scene afforded Lloyds – advised by Shaw – the opportunity of recreating a medieval interior in great detail. Gaunt's bed was resplendent with armorial bearings, all irreproachably authentic; the walls were decorated with paintings, selected from an illuminated manuscript in the British Museum; a chandelier and a fireplace provided sources of 'natural' light as did a window. The detail was, of course, far greater than the audience could see or appreciate, but that was not the point: the whole scene was based, *pace* Ruskin, on 'but one principle, that of absolute, uncompromising truth . . . down to the most minute detail'. Kean avowed with pride that 'in no single instance have I permitted truth to be sacrificed to theatrical effect' (Nagler, 1952, p. 490). This 'truth' served the purpose of establishing a context and atmosphere which validated the human experience set in it. Thus of this scene *The Times* of 16 March 1857 wrote:

The second act opens with a 'room in Ely-house' – the room where John of Gaunt dies, not to be surpassed as a representation of a baronial interior, not only in archaeological accuracy shown in all its decorative details, but a picture is produced in accordance with the sentiment of the situation.

Kean's main liberty with the text was the presentation of the historical

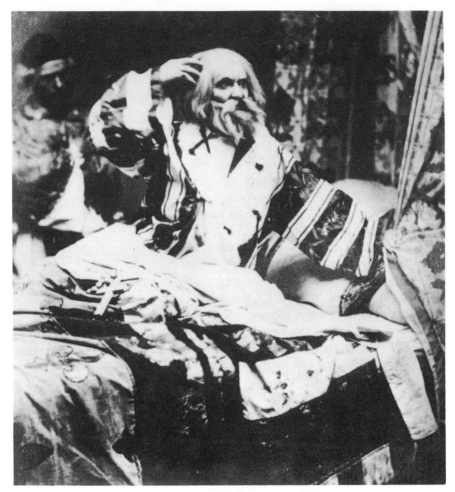

8. Walter Lacy as John of Gaunt, at the Princess's Theatre, 1857

episode of Richard and Bolingbroke's return to London, as described by the Duke of York (5.2). This incident had already formed the subject-matter of one of the most imposing pictures in the Boydell collection – James Northcote's *The Entry of Bolingbroke* (pl. 9). The painting is in just the Academy style against which Ruskin and the Pre-Raphaelites rebelled, and the illustrations of Kean's staging of this scene reveal that he too eschewed any imitation of Northcote. Northcote's figures are, as Maclise's were accused of being, 'expansive and gesticulatory, full of parade and attitudinising display'. The background is vestigial and the onlookers – in particular the two conventionalised eighteenth-century women in the

50

9. *The Entry of King Richard and Bolingbroke into London;* an engraving by R. Thew of the painting by J. Northcote, RA

bottom right-hand corner – as self-consciously theatrical as the principals and their horses.

Instead of this formalised artifice Kean sought at least the illusion of truth (pl. 10) with a carefully researched architectural set populated by a stage crowd of hundreds, each member of which, as Ellen Terry and Edward Righton recalled, was drilled to make an individual contribution by Oscar Byrn, Kean's dancing-master and director of crowds.[9] The *Era* reviewer revealed:

he [Kean] has given us a street of the olden times, with a veritable London crowd, eager and curious, filling every window, balcony, and crevice with innumerable heads, and harmonising the whole by those accessories that give vitality and intelligence to the picture. Here we have chiming bells, flags, music, mountebanks, beggars, grotesque dancers, love making, and all the motley ingredients, pastimes and enjoyments of a tumultuous mob, at once servile and brutal, while, to crown all, we have the triumphant progress of the 'haught insulting Bolingbroke', bowing to the applauding citizens with that mock humility that Richard, in an omitted scene, so admirably described upon his going into banishment; while, last of all, to add insult to indignity, the deposed monarch follows, to give eclat to his rival's triumph, and expose the unhappy Richard to the detestation and revilings of an infuriate mob. The moral of the picture is perfect, and the effect on the spectator astounding. (15 Mar. 1857)

Since Shakespeare provided no dialogue for this scene (Kean inserted a few interjections for the mob) the effect was achieved visually: 'The moral of the picture is perfect.'

In this scene, as indeed in all scenes, observers were struck by the apparent absence of theatricality: 'of theatrical convention there is not a trace . . . It seems a real mob – nay, a real people' (*The Times*, 16 Mar. 1857); 'we no longer look on actors' (*Era*, 15 Mar. 1857). Every leading actor in the company was commended for the truthfulness of his playing – even stalwarts of the older more declamatory school, such as Walter Lacy as Gaunt, Cooper as York and the forceful Ryder as Bolingbroke.

Charles Kean and his wife, Ellen Kean, had developed a more naturalistic acting style during the 1840s and 1850s, for which Kean, in

10. Charles Kean as King Richard II entering London, at the Princess's Theatre, 1857

particular, had been widely ridiculed. But public taste was moving with him, and Westland Marston (1890, pp. 123–4) recounted that even G. H. Lewes conceded 'Charles Kean is changing his style into a natural one. He will convert me yet.' In the 1860s the Bancrofts perfected the 'cup and saucer' style in their productions of Tom Robertson's social comedies at the Prince of Wales, where naturalistic sets and naturalistic acting were seen to be inextricably linked.

This association was perceived by one critic of *Richard II*: 'he has studied the psychological attributes of the character itself as thoroughly as he has the nature of the appointments that serve as the gorgeous framework of the picture' (*Era*, 15 Mar. 1857). Nowhere was this psychological truth more apparent than in the departure scene between Richard and his queen (pl. 11):

In the parting scene however Mrs Kean shows how a consummate artist can make a great deal out of a scanty material. This shadowy, unsubstantial Queen can be supposed a remarkable instance of feminine devotion, and the words she utters, though not many, bear out the supposition. On this hypothesis Mrs Kean, when Richard is torn from her arms, displays such an agony of tearful grief, is so completely broken up with heartrending sorrow, that, although the pageantry of the play is over, this scene is one of the most effective of the whole performance. When the hapless king has departed she carries out still further her illustration of feeling by rushing towards the parapet, and leaning over it to catch a last glimpse of the beloved object. (*The Times*, 16 Mar. 1857)

'The illustration of feeling' was the essence of paintings such as Hunt's, and here, with few words at her disposal, Ellen Kean achieved her effect through the inner truth which she created and expressed for her character – if indeed the distinction between actress and character applied, for, as one admirer wrote: 'And how beautifully did you cry and sob in parting from your husband, no it was not acting, I have never heard such sobs, or seen such true natural sorrow!'[10] For Ellen Kean the fact that the living person portraying Richard was her own husband produced a merging of personalities between actor and part. William Archer in *Masks or Faces?* (1888, p. 171) recounts a similar incident in *The Gamester*: 'After the death of Beverley [Kean] . . . Mrs Kean had become so absorbed in her part that she could not shake off the illusion even when the play was over . . . crying piteously "Oh, my Charles! – my poor darling – you are not dead; say you are not dead!"' For her performance as Queen Anne, Mrs Kean drew 'plaudits . . . [which] spring from a genuine sympathy with a distress so forcefully portrayed' (*Spectator*, 14 Mar. 1857).

This representation of 'distress so forcefully portrayed' by both Ellen Kean and Charles Kean on the Princess's stage had its counterpart in the clearly depicted moral dilemmas of the protagonists in Pre-Raphaelite Shakespearean paintings and, indeed, in the Jerusalem Chamber portrait

11.   Charles Kean as King Richard II and Ellen Kean as the Queen, at the Princess's
Theatre, 1857

of Richard II, with 'its deep and tragical bearing fraught with importance to all of us'. In each case past and present merged in the creation of 'a true portrait of some living person' generating a sense of emotional immediacy which spanned the centuries. Integral to this effect was the realisation of the character's historical environment in 'the most minute detail' with outdoor scenes painted from life, historical architecture faithfully restored, and costumes, armour and furnishings based on thorough scholarly research.

As interpreters of Shakespeare, Kean and the Pre-Raphaelites presented the plays in a manner which caught the spirit of the time in which they were living, when historical events, social forces and cultural tastes combined to create conditions uniquely suited to their talents and aspirations. This convergence of taste and talent was short-lived. Charles Kean continued to act until his death in 1868, but he concluded his management at the Princess's Theatre in 1859; Holman Hunt lived on until 1910, but the Pre-Raphaelite Brotherhood did not survive the 1850s. How authentically Shakespeare was seen and heard during that decade may be questionable, but for Kean and the Pre-Raphaelites it was their inalienable moment in time.

NOTES

1 *Tallis's History*, 1851, vol. 1, p. 227.

2 Kean, 1857; repr. 1970, p. vi. Kean's prompt-book is in the Folger Shakespeare Library.

3 Hunt, 1905; 2nd edn (1913), vol. 1, p. 137. Deverell acted for Mr N. Angel, the actor–manager of the Richmond Theatre: see Mary Lutyens, 'Walter Howell Deverell', in Parris, 1984, p. 88.

4 *Circular, No. 1 and Other Official Documents and Forms, Issued by the Executive Committee of the Manchester Art Treasures Exhibition*, Manchester, 1857.

5 Oscar Wilde, 'Shakespearean Stage Costume', *The Nineteenth Century*, May 1885, p. 814.

6 *A Handbook to the Gallery of British Paintings in the Art Treasures Exhibition Being a reprint of critical notices originally published in 'The Manchester Guardian'*, London, 1857, pp. 89, 97. Although no author is acknowledged, most of the articles in the *Manchester Guardian* were by Tom Taylor. An extract is reprinted in Hunt, 1905; 2nd edn (1913), vol. 2, pp. 409–10.

7 M. Glen Wilson, 'Charles Kean's Production of *Richard II*', *Educational Theatre Journal*, 19 (1967), 41–51.

8 Julian Treuherz, 'The Pre-Raphaelites and Medieval Illuminated Manuscripts', in Parris, 1984, pp. 153–69.

9 Terry, 1933, p. 19; Godfrey Archer, 'First Nights of My Young Days', *The Theatre*, 1 July 1887, pp. 13–18. See also Muriel St Clare Byrne, 'Charles Kean and the Meiningen Myth', *Theatre Research*, 6.5 (1964), 137–53.

10 Manuscript letter from T. Greenwood in the Folger Shakespeare Library (y.c. 1130).

Stage Costume: Historical Verisimilitude and Stage Convention

MARION JONES

J UST over half a century into Victoria's reign, that glossy periodical *The Magazine of Art* ran a series on 'Art in the Theatre': each paper was by a different hand, each took a different standpoint; but each was wedded to the concept of historical verisimilitude in the mounting of period plays, and each revealed exact personal knowledge of specific ventures in this field. Taken together, these papers provide a useful framework for discussion of the costumes which were used in Victorian productions of Shakespeare, with special reference to the question 'What degree of historical verisimilitude was in fact achieved on stage by managements that attempted it?'

The erudite Henry Herman, now best remembered for his collaboration with Henry Arthur Jones on *The Silver King*, called his paper 'The Stage as a Servant of Art and Archaeology'. After strongly deprecating the ignorance of most theatre critics about the clothes that were worn by earlier generations, he took a lofty stance on his own ideal of theatre costume for plays set in the past:

I think I may lay it down as an axiom in regard to art and archaeology on the stage that *that* is the most artistic which, being as nearly as possible archaeologically correct, is the most pleasing to the educated eye. (*The Magazine of Art*, Aug. 1888, p. 334)

The 'archaeologically correct' and the 'picturesque' are two values which are continually canvassed by writers on this subject in the period.

Descending sharply to personalities, Herman went on to point out how few eyes were in fact educated. In London, as he saw it, the costume designers were almost as ignorant as the critics. Only one of them could really design a period dress, as distinct from copying it slavishly from an illustration in some standard collection of historical plates. Too few research workers were available:

We had one great worker in the field of archaeology and art among us, the late E. W. Godwin, and we still have the Hon. Lewis Wingfield; but outside cultured student minds like these, the realm of art and archaeology on the stage is simply fertile ground ready to produce a great harvest, but barely ploughed, much less properly cultivated.   (p. 334)

E. W. Godwin, Ellen Terry's mentor, was a pundit who also concerned himself with details of practical stagecraft. Terry records the pains he took with a Titania costume in 1863:

He showed me how to damp it and 'wring' it while it was wet, tying up the material as the Orientals do in their 'tie-and-dye' process, so that when it was dry and untied, it was all crinkled and clingy.   (Terry, 1933, p. 38)

Godwin had given the Bancrofts 'valuable archaeological help' with their heavily documented and pictorial *Merchant of Venice* at the Prince of Wales's Theatre in 1875; but more recent in the minds of Herman's readers would have been the complaints about the 'early Danish' costumes Godwin had designed for Wilson Barrett's *Hamlet* in 1884. The *Illustrated London News* critic was bold to say 'with the exception of Hamlet and Polonius, I have seldom looked upon such a set of guys as those whom historical accuracy has placed upon the stage of the Princess's' (25 Oct. 1884), while the October number of *Dramatic Notes* was unsparing: 'We have no doubt that Mr Godwin's archaeology of the costumes and furniture is strictly correct, but picturesque effect has been sacrificed.'

Perhaps Herman was relying on *nil nisi bonum* here; Lewis Wingfield, however, was very much alive,[1] and had received a mixed press on both his *Romeo and Juliet* for Mary Anderson at the Lyceum (during Irving's American tour of 1884), and his *As You Like It* for the Kendals at the St James's Theatre in 1885. Yet, since Wingfield's share of Mary Anderson's credit for well-managed draperies in *The Winter's Tale* (Lyceum, 1887) was more freshly in the public's mind, Herman was able to proceed without a rearguard action to attack Irving's *Romeo and Juliet* of 1882 for its ambitious inaccuracy. Much money had certainly been spent, many sources consulted, but, alas, the actors had worn 'a mixture of dresses ranging over a period of a hundred years or so' (p. 335). Those who had praised this production for authenticity were (like Irving himself) only less grossly ignorant than the run of managers and critics, and for the same reason:

In costume-books designs are often huddled together in classes of centuries or so, and it is considered sufficiently near the mark if the average stage-manager or costumier comes within fifty years of the period which he desires to represent.   (p. 335)

The remedy, as Herman had already pointed out, would lie in deeper research, but most managements would not know where to start:

A visit to the Tapestries in the South Kensington Museum, for instance, would no more suggest itself as a proper and useful expedient than a journey to the mountains of the moon.
(p. 334)

Charles Kean was, of course, well known for resorting to such expedients in support of his English-history-play series at the Princess's: and even while Herman wrote – had the rumour not reached him? – Charles Cattermole and Alice Comyns Carr were busy seeking authorities at the British and South Kensington Museums for every detail of the eleventh-century setting of Irving's forthcoming *Macbeth*.

Herman, who believed in art for art's sake, went on to remind his readers that others did not:

A manager, after all, let him preach as much as he likes about high art (of the very definition of which he often has not the faintest idea), has but one object in view – one *ultima thule* – to make money; and if, by any chance, he works for a second purpose, it is to make more money.
(p. 335)

Sadly but resolutely, Herman drew his grim conclusion:

the prize to be gained by the highest endeavours of art is not sufficiently dazzling to compensate a manager for the additional great outlay he would have to incur. He is perfectly aware that his work will be just as much appreciated by the vast army of play goers, that it will be just as much praised by the marshalled army of the critics, if he simply uses such ordinary care as will avoid very glaring defects, as it would if he had employed Alma-Tadema to make his designs.
(p. 335)

Perhaps Herman knew that Irving had indeed approached Sir Lawrence Alma-Tadema in 1879 to design the projected but long-deferred *Coriolanus*.

The truth of the view that lavish productions rarely justify themselves in terms of box-office receipts did not need Herman to point it out. Kean wrote at the end of his decade at the Princess's:

Wonderful as have been the yearly receipts, yet the vast sums expended – sums, I have every reason to believe, not to be paralleled in any theatre of the same capability throughout the world – make it advisable that I should now retire from the self-imposed responsibility of management, involving such a perilous outlay; and the more especially, as a building so restricted in size as the Princess's, renders any adequate returns utterly hopeless.
(Fly-leaf to *Henry V* bill, 1859; quoted Cole, 1859, vol. 2, p. 341)

That a modicum of historical knowledge was enough to satisfy the public in the second half of Victoria's reign can be readily shown from two reviews by Dutton Cook. In April 1872, surveying an oddly assorted *Cymbeline* at the Queen's Theatre, in which Miss Hodson, wife of the joint manager Henry Labouchère, was playing Imogen, he took the ground that there are plays to which pedantry about historical period is unsuited:

The anachronistic nature of the story is, no doubt, a source of much bewilderment to the stage decorator who sets value upon archaic accuracy. Shakespeare did not concern himself on this head, took a fabulist's licence, and was content to send historic truth adrift upon a glorious sea of poetry. Nor does the question of correct appointments much move a general audience. As Hazlitt observed, 'Managers are not the Society of Antiquaries', and the same may be said of ordinary playgoers.   (Cook, 1883, vol. 2, p. 203)

The second review, expressing Dutton Cook's hearty admiration for George Rignold as Henry V in Drury Lane's production under Augustus Harris in 1879, speaks of the mounting as a good example of 'stock':

Drury Lane is rich in scenery suitable to the legitimate drama, and in costumes, armour and weapons of a mediaeval pattern; the play is presented, therefore, quite in the manner of a 'grand revival', if not absolutely with fresh appliances.   (Cook, 1883, vol. 2, p. 230)

This production had originated in Manchester with Charles Calvert, travelled to New York and returned, with Rignold its constant star, to London. It was at least seven years old when Cook saw it and is likely to have been refurbished during its tour from the stock of more than one theatre. No Royal Academician, no zealous antiquary, boasted of its accuracy. Yet when, 'falchion in hand, clothed in complete steel, with a richly emblazoned tabard', Rignold stood centre-stage in the limelight, he seemed as striking a stage figure as Dutton Cook had ever seen.

Chastened as he was by his reflections, Herman still thought it worthwhile to tack on a passionate plea for self-sacrifice and dedication on the part of the managers, harder and better-directed work from those whose duty it was to educate the public in history and art, more research by the critics, more discrimination all round. With hindsight on the development of taste since Herman wrote, we can afford to leave 'the stage as a servant of art and archaeology', and turn to the lone eminence he had praised, the artist and scholar Lewis Wingfield. Writing in the next issue of *The Magazine of Art*, under the title 'Costume-Designing', Wingfield improved Herman's initial metaphor into a full-blown allegory:

History and Archaeology are sisters, and the Historic Drama is their handmaid. By her faithful services both are made familiar to the public as instruments of instruction as well as of recreation. Moving hand-in-hand under her guidance, they perfect each the other, conjuring before the mental retina a picturesque vision of the past.

(*The Magazine of Art*, Oct. 1888, p. 403)

Not even the most pedagogic of Victorian directors – not Charles Kean himself when he followed the long list of his costume authorities for *Richard II* with the remark 'By the preceding statement I guarantee the truthfulness and fidelity of the entire picture' – had believed that the function of the elaborate presentation of Shakespeare's plays in costume styles from the past was solely – or even principally – to promote public familiarity with the history of art and with applied art and the fruits of antiquarian research. The true perspective was given by Kean in the same *Richard II* playbill of 1857:

An increasing taste for recreation wherein instruction is blended with amusement, has for some time been conspicuous in the English public; and surely, an attempt to render dramatic representations conducive to the diffusion of knowledge – to surround the flowing imagery of the great Poet with accompaniments *true* to the time of which he writes – *realizing* the scenes and actions which he describes – exhibiting men as they once lived – can scarcely detract from the enduring influence of his genius,

(Quoted Scott, 1899, vol. 1, p. 292)

As it happens, we also know what Irving thought on this point. In *The Drama: Addresses* (1893) he included a lecture which enshrined an earlier view he apparently did not wish to revise, strange as those who had seen his production of *Henry VIII* in 1892 were bound to find it:

For the abuse of scenic decoration, the overloading of the stage with ornament, the subordination of the play to a pageant, I have nothing to say. That is all foreign to the artistic purpose which should dominate dramatic work. Nor do I think that servility to archaeology on the stage is an unmixed good. Correctness of costume is admirable and necessary up to a certain point, but when it ceases to be 'as wholesome as sweet', it should, I think, be sacrificed. (p. 68)

'Up to a certain point': Wingfield explained carefully where, for his part, he would place that point:

the education of the masses is not far enough advanced as yet for an historic presentment to be made upon the stage in its bald truth. Concessions have to be allowed in a spirit of indulgence for weak vessels. There are certain details of costume, furniture or accessories of almost every past period which, too literally followed, would by unfamiliar quaintness or unexpected *bizarrerie* distract the attention of the spectator and give rise to inopportune laughter. Artistic effort being the pursuit of the beautiful, that which is ugly must be eschewed. (p. 403)

Only three years before, Wingfield had been slated by Austin Brereton for neglecting this precept in the costumes for the first act of the Kendals' *As You Like It*, set in the time of Charles VII of France.

His guards were doubtless attired with perfect accuracy; and I do not dispute the statement that Celia 'might have walked out of one of Froissart's illuminated pages'. But the appearance of the guards was certainly grotesque, and Celia's head-dress was exceedingly trying to the actress. (*Dramatic Notes*, Jan. 1885)

Though Brereton praised the rest of the costumes as 'rich in material and exquisite in design', he deplored one breach with stage tradition. The banished Duke and his followers were normally clad in Lincoln green like Robin Hood and his merry men: by making them 'courtly and gaily caparisoned foresters', Wingfield left Orlando open to the charge of churlishness in menacing them so roughly. The criterion here – that the spirit of the comedy should have priority – is one to which Wingfield in his paper paid lip-service: 'The intentions of the actor must not be hampered'; but the complaint about Celia's head-dress had fallen on stony ground. Wingfield thought that actors should practise costume management for stage purposes, since the people they represented had learned to manage such garments in real life.

To nineteenth-century actors there was nothing novel in being told to cope. We need only recall Macready, solemnly walking and sitting for two afternoons in his heavy armour for *Henry V* before he ventured to rehearse in it, or the child Ellen Terry with a flannel blanket 'pinned on in front and trailing six inches on the floor', decorously parading under the eye of old Oscar Byrn at the Princess's. We may also, however, recall Bram Stoker's horror story of the dazzlingly equipped army fitted out by Charles Calvert in the early sixties to support him as Richmond in a Manchester production of *Richard III*. Though Richard, played by Edwin Booth, was followed at Bosworth by mere scarecrows, his cause most unrighteously prevailed, for Richmond's men fell like skittles and lay helpless in their armour until the fall of the curtain veiled their shame (Stoker, 1906, vol. 1, pp. 91–2).

Wingfield quickly returned to what interested him most – the look of a garment on stage. Here he had a sound point to make, on why distinguished painters did not always succeed as costume designers:

from lack of technical knowledge; for oftentimes a dress which would look lovely on canvas or at a fancy ball will go for nothing on the boards. The long distance between the costumes and the eye has to be considered, and this will affect material pattern and trimming.

(p. 404)

Very true – and into this trap Charles Kean had marched as Hotspur, in his damask surcoat impeccably charged with armorial bearings. One look at this garment – which survives in the London Museum – and we know that only the three front rows had the benefit of that erudition which in 1857 earned Kean his Fellowship of the Society of Antiquaries. In stage parlance, the costume does not 'read': a few large painted devices would have had a better effect than the exquisitely worked replica of young Percy's correct heraldic entitlement. J. P. Kemble had played Hotspur in short jerkin and long smooth hose: with his Byronic collar and curls, his broad sash, high-crowned hat and plume of feathers, he had looked every inch the romantic hero. His one gesture towards local colour was to affect the insignia of the Garter, an order to which he knew well enough Hotspur had never been elected. William Creswick, who was playing Hotspur for Phelps in 1846, dressed rather like Hamlet in black tunic and tights, with a

12. *Ellen Terry as Lady Macbeth*; an oil painting by John Singer Sargent, 1888–9

little bright braid and dagging to suggest a military character. His portrait shows him posed with one hand on the dagger in his jewelled belt; beside him on a table lie his cloak and hat – high-crowned, but with merely a vestigial plume of feathers. His costume is quite unhistorical and – like Kemble's – vastly becoming. The eye does not pine for heraldry.[2]

The choice of fabric in suitably bold patterns was certainly limited in Victorian warehouses. Even at the end of the century Alice Comyns Carr was using the wrong side of a black satin with metallic weave to get the effect of large silver panels for Queen Catherine's trial-scene costume in *Henry VIII*. For the famous Lady Macbeth costume in which Ellen Terry posed to John Singer Sargent (pl. 12), Mrs Carr was obliged to crochet the fabric herself: she used a soft green silk thread twisted with blue tinsel to get the right suggestion of chain-mail. Wingfield's expedient was at once difficult and expensive: he had the curio-shops of London and Paris ransacked for genuine relics of Renaissance brocade and damask, some of them requiring continual repair. His description of how he disposed these rags of time in their 'half-faded gloomy magnificence' to clothe Mary Anderson's company in *Romeo and Juliet* makes strange reading. He worked surrounded by enlarged photographs of Carpaccio's series of pictures on the St Ursula legend, chosen as a basis for this production in a curiously arbitrary way: 'In the first place, we had to choose a period as remote from that selected by Mr Irving as the exigencies of the play would permit' (p. 406).

What fascinated and enraged Lewis Wingfield was the kinetic element in his commission. That, in the course of a play, actors move into different groupings and against different backgrounds was a trial to him. Not only had he to reckon with Miss Anderson's preferences in point of her Juliet costumes, but he knew that they 'must harmonize with Mr Terriss's (also difficult to please), and never jar with casual crowds and scenic changes'. He had positively to negotiate with the painters of the backcloths: 'Juliet's attire being a pale silvery blue, Mr O'Connor obligingly consented to avoid that colour in his picture' (p. 407).

Many of Wingfield's readers would have remembered the less than gracious reviews with which his efforts had been received. Clement Scott was severe on principle:

We are gradually overdoing spectacle so much that poetry must suffer in the long run. The question is no longer how this or that character in Shakespeare ought to be played, but how much money can be spent on this or that scene. (*Dramatic Notes*, Nov. 1884)

Even the *London Graphic*'s more kindly reviewer considered that the attempt to reconstruct thirteenth-century costumes from fifteenth-century pictures had been foredoomed to failure. On a high point of principle, however, he exempted Wingfield from censure:

The search for correct costume in relation to a Shakespearean legendary play is very much like the search for the absolute, or the true and infallible mode of squaring the circle.

(8 Nov. 1884)

Having caused the candid reader to set him down as a precious prig, Wingfield suddenly justified his reputation in a paragraph of key importance which places the duty of a costume designer in true perspective. After a searching look at the records of an earlier epoch of fashion, the designer of a period costume must try to lay bare its kernel, which resides in whatever gives it its distinctive character ('Is it in the glove or the garter, in the boot or in the neck-tie?'), and then redesign, 'so as to display the essence of a fashion while skilfully eschewing the absurd' (p. 408).

Thus by a seeming paradox in the matter of stage costume, the original and historical are one. There is no so-called 'original' dress but must have some period for a basis. The general scheme of colour that pervades a revival of importance is always original, evolved from the brain of the designer. Garments, of whatever epoch, are so modified and altered – the same, but *translated*, as it were, into another tongue – that, while seeming to be correct, they yet are in their way original.

(p. 407)

Wingfield's paper was published in October 1888; Irving's *Macbeth* opened at the Lyceum on 29 December, and in January 1889 *The Magazine of Art* gave space to M. H. Spielmann's account, written several weeks earlier, of the research and prodigious endeavours behind the mounting of this production. Spielmann, the distinguished art critic of the *Pall Mall Gazette* since 1883, had his feet well on the ground. After a long list of sources and documents for all aspects of the eleventh-century setting, he put his cards on the table:

But, after all is said and all is searched, history is somewhat reticent on the manners and costumes of the period, and much has had to be imagined, care being taken to keep all interpolations and creations thoroughly in the spirit of the time.

(*The Magazine of Art.* Jan. 1889, p. 98)

'Much has had to be imagined': three cheers for honest Spielmann! The other point which emerges from his long, factual account is the sheer scale of the undertaking:

Having collected his designs about him, Mr Cattermole forthwith gave out the work, and the large work-shops attached to the theatre, peopled with forty skilled 'hands', have been busily occupied for months ever since; no outside professional 'costumier' being employed as middleman. Altogether no fewer than 408 dresses have been made and 'passed', including 165 for soldiers (115 Scotch and 50 English), 80 for the 'Flight of Witches', 40 for lords and ladies, 16 for waiting-women, 8 for kings, 5 for cooks, and so forth. Besides these are the dresses for the principals, with their 'changes', all wrought in the house, in the midst of a scene every bit as busy and pictorial – for those who can appreciate it – as that afforded by bead stringers of Venice or coral workers of Naples.   (p. 99)

Alice Comyns Carr and her friend Mrs Nettleship had Ellen Terry's costumes in hand. We know from many sources that they applied real green beetles' wings to the crocheted 'chain-mail' costume to get that odd malachite sheen which Oscar Wilde had in mind when he joked that Lady Macbeth took care to do all her own shopping in Byzantium.[3] They also provided a great semicircular cloak of rich red corded silk – it survives in the London Museum – for her to wear in the gloomy scene after Duncan's murder. Irving took one look at it from a stage box at the first dress-rehearsal, congratulated the designer, and – for the sake of the stage picture – arranged to wear it himself. Tactfully working through his adviser Walter Lacy, he had shown the same sense of priority some years earlier, when Ellen Terry proposed to wear black for Ophelia's mad scene. Lacy, who had been with Charles Kean, took a firm line: 'My God, Madam! There must be only one black figure in this play, and that's Hamlet!' Though the costume had already been made, Ellen Terry gave way gracefully:

So instead of the crepe de Chine and miniver, which had been used for the black dress, I had for the white dress Bolton sheeting and rabbit, and I believe it looked better.
(Terry, 1933, p. 124)

Irving's workshops used quantities of Bolton sheeting. Bram Stoker reports that when Seymour Lucas had five specimens of gold cloth displayed under stage-lighting so that the choice could be made for *Henry VIII*, the 'real cloth of gold at ten guineas a foot' was rejected, while a Bolton sheeting at eighteen pence a yard, stencilled in the workshop, was acclaimed by all hands. Though Wingfield would never have made such a decision, his point about appearances at a distance held good here. An actor in *Henry VIII* who got a Duke to lend him a real and very valuable Collar of the Garter was piqued to find himself illustrating the same principle: because stage jewels are large and backed with foil to throw back the light, his fellow-actors in paste ornaments far outshone him.

It is ironic that Irving enjoyed the reputation of outdoing even Charles Kean in point of accuracy and lack of 'faked' materials. Writing of the Lyceum *Much Ado About Nothing* in 1882, George Augustus Sala had rhapsodised:

The costumiers have new models to work from, new materials to confect, new ornamentation to apply; and from such a theatre as the Lyceum, the old barbarous style of bedizening the subordinate characters – the plastering of girdles with zinc 'logies', the coarse tinselling of breast-plates and shields, the smearing with yellow ochre of the gauntlets and russet boots of the 'supers', and the substitution of glazed calico for real satin in 'back grooves' court dresses have been wholly banished. All is handsome, appropriate and honest.

(*Illustrated London News*, 28 Oct. 1882)

Of course Irving's productions did use very expensive materials as well as Bolton sheeting. Spielmann dwelt on Macbeth's second costume, of 'heavy bullion-gold damask, hand-embroidered with maroon-coloured silk, with sleeves of light blue silk' (p. 99). Irving liked to have his arms clearly visible across the body of his dress, so preferred pale sleeves. In the last act, as Spielmann tells us, Macbeth was made conspicuous by golden armour, 'low tones and sober harmonies' being prevalent in the mounting as a whole.

Such splendour for Macbeth was not traditional. It was Phelps who in 1847 had abandoned as anachronistic the tartan trappings which Macklin had brought in as a reform in 1773. We know that Tate Wilkinson's company at York in the early 1790s had several 'Plad Shaps' in its wardrobe – Mr Kennedy as Banquo was kitted out with a 'Plad gacket gould Las', 'Plad Breches' and a 'gould las Wascoat'. Charles Kean in 1853 had devoted much scholarship to underwriting his own compromise between the tunic and leg-straps affected by Phelps and the 'striped and chequered garb' peculiar to the Scots and favoured by recent stage tradition.[4] Attacked for this, Kean had bared his teeth upon retirement in 1859:

I have been blamed for depriving Macbeth of a dress never worn at any period, or in any place, and for providing him instead with one resembling those used by the surrounding nations with whom the country of that chieftain was in constant intercourse.

Irving's first appearance as Macbeth under the Bateman aegis in 1876 had eschewed plaid: his wrap-over tunic was bordered with dark, shaggy fur, and his leg-straps were of leather with metal studs and buckles. Though few critics cared for his reading of the role, then or in 1888, his costume for the cheaply mounted production of 1876 had suited his conception of the Thane rather better than did the well-documented and glorious semi-Viking lendings of Cattermole's design.

Turning from the Lyceum *Macbeth*, the expensive watershed of Irving's career, we come to the pronouncements on 'Spectacle' by Augustus Harris, the impresario of Drury Lane, in the February 1889 issue of *The Magazine of Art*. Harris spoke with authority: he was the son of A. G. Harris the opera manager, had made his own name famous for elaborate presentations, and worked with his sister Patience, the distinguished costumier who had dressed Ellen Terry until Alice Comyns Carr secured the preference. Something very like 'pearls before swine' was what Harris deplored as he reviewed the scholarly knowledge and artistic skill that lay behind the designs for spectacular productions and the immense effort and anxiety expended on worthily executing the designs. So few people understood how much work went into this; so many could not even distinguish the subtle gradations of colour in a calculated effect.

It is indeed a question whether all the exquisite colourings and delightful combinations are fully appreciated, except by a small and highly cultivated minority. Why then, many ask, take the trouble to do the thing properly? Why not follow the old Boucicaultian managerial axiom, 'never try to educate your audience'? Because the minority is fast becoming the majority, thanks to the march of education. (p. 111)

So Harris was more hopeful than Herman. Looking back at them both after nearly a century, we know that education has marched on to the extent that the history of costume and the history of theatre design are recognised subjects in colleges of art and at some universities, backed by excellent publications at a wide range of prices. Special museums and galleries are relatively numerous and easy of access. It would seem that adequate instruction is available at most levels to those who seek it. Yet the lobby for art and archaeology on the stage is no stronger. Academic productions favour the picturesque; but the most frequent ambition is to give the impression of a period by the use of stylised line – as Wingfield's advice had foreshadowed.

We are, however, free of the kind of costume convention with which Victorian actors had to reckon. There was comment when Charles Kean as Hamlet in his 'mad' phase would not wear one stocking down-gyved to the ankle, and when the First Gravedigger in Irving's *Hamlet* of 1874 'had not time to remove his ten waistcoats'; but Irving in 1874 retained the J. P. Kemble plumed hat (vestige of a hero's helmet and plume), and even left it with his long mourning cloak on the battlements for Horatio to gather up, as custom dictated and Dutton Cook deplored.[5] Irving rejected a whole range of precedents for Hamlet's neckwear: he wore neither a miniature of his father, nor the Star of the Garter, nor a medallion representing the order of the Danish Elephant, but a heavy gold chain to relieve his solemn black. Fechter in 1861 had introduced a flaxen 'Danish' wig, which Irving did not retain; but he followed the mode established by Charles Kean in 1838 in wearing a tunic rather than trunk-hose. For his own Lyceum production of *Hamlet* in 1878 Irving reverted to Elizabethan dress, but challenged convention by giving the Ghost 'a kind of dressing-robe' for the closet scene instead of armour. We know that when Garrick played Hamlet in black velvet breeches, the Ghost appeared in blue satin armour. In the majority of Victorian productions the Ghost's armour was both solid and self-consciously Gothic, much like the suit honoured by stage tradition in which the hunted hero of *The Castle Spectre* had taken refuge. But with all the ingenuities available from a generation of craftsmen familiar with the Corsican glide and Pepper's Ghost, innovative productions in which the Ghost's outline was softened by gauzy drapery and etherialised by illusions are also on pictorial record.

The concept of public decency also presses less heavily upon our own efforts towards historical verisimilitude on stage. Portraits of Henry VIII show a prominent cod-piece; the photograph of William Terriss as Henry VIII at the Lyceum in 1892 – despite the critical chorus that he had stepped straight out of a Holbein – does not. Even as hoops had sustained the great skirts of actresses in Shakespearean tragedy during the eighteenth century, to be discarded by Sarah Siddons in some roles when fashions in real life had changed to clinging draperies, so the crinoline petticoat of horsehair which, with many additional starched petticoats, bore out the classical robes or Scottish weeds of Isabella Glyn and Mrs Charles Kean gave way to a series of other underpinnings as the century advanced. The crinoline-cage in various forms, the bustle and the nip-waist corset are all apparent beneath the stage costumes of the Victorian era according to the date of the productions, not the periods in which they were supposed to be set. A single concession towards probability when fairies and spirits were costumed was a shorter skirt, often with gauze overskirt, which revealed ballet-fashion a pair of legs either permissibly juvenile or maturely proper to an accredited dancer – witness the costume of Madame Vestris as Oberon. Priscilla Horton hovered in plenty of gauze with narrow transparent dragonfly wings when she played Ariel for Macready, but the Ariel at Sadler's Wells in 1848, Julia St George, showed plump feminine contours beneath her plain *tutu*-style frock, and sported a pair of stiff, feathered wings like a Gothic angel.[6] At the end of the century, Ellen Terry preserved decorum as Cesario and Fidele in fully concealing and utterly improbable get-ups (her luckless brother Fred her parody as Sebastian); as Portia in lawyer's garb she wore a ground-length, closed robe. Though her basic costumes both as Ophelia and as Cordelia were skimpy to a degree unlikely in comparison with the solid wear of the men around her on stage, the high neck and long sleeves of her choice are severely decent (Hiatt, 1898, illustrations).

Another modifying factor, and one which has affected modern productions no less than Victorian, is the determination of players as a class to keep their period's 'line' beneath their stage-clothes and in their hairstyles. Even when a costumier provided correct and sufficiently modest undergarments they were set aside in favour of the current mode in corsetry and the undergarments appropriate to that. Hero's costume for the 'Elizabethan' *Much Ado About Nothing* at the Lyceum looks very different over its own farthingale from the way it was worn by Jessie Millward over a bustle on stage.[7] Ellen Terry's dress for Queen Catherine in the trial scene of *Henry VIII* was obviously worn over nip-waist corset and bustle – its line is that of a Paris-made model worn by Princess Alexandra at the same date and preserved in the Museum of Costume at the Bath Assembly Rooms. Hair too is a 'give-away' in most illustrations of professedly period productions. Mrs Kean always wore the central parting and smooth side sweeps of her own hairstyle, whether her part were Grecian, Scottish or Norman. Male actors, indeed, sometimes wore wigs (both Henry Irving's dressers had been wigmakers), but many principal women and nearly all 'supers' wore whatever style was in vogue. One of the funniest pictures of the period 'look' shows Isabella Glyn as Cleopatra in 1849 (*Illustrated London News*, 27 Oct.): her pose is that of Queen Victoria receiving the news of her accession, and both gown and hairstyle would have been suitable for an evening at Windsor Castle.

Very important are the deviations from authenticity made to exhibit an actor's good points. Irving was particularly adept at this – we know from his surviving costumes (see pls. 13, 14 and 15) that he wore his sleeves rather short to show off his hands, had his sleeves lighter in colour than the body of his dress to show off his arm-gestures, caught back the chain-mail on his *Macbeth* helmet's down-stage cheek to show off his profile, shortened the thrusting brims of fifteenth-century hats with the same object, widened his shoulders with heavy drapery for the first scene of *King Lear* to increase his majesty, and used a small shoulder-pad and shoes of unequal height to suggest only the most probable and becoming deformity in Richard Crookback.[8]

Another cause of modification of 'correctness' was the refusal of players to wear anything uncomfortable or unattractive. Ellen Terry had a special aversion to weight in costume: when Alice Comyns Carr had a metal crown expensively fabricated in Paris to a period design for Lady Macbeth, Terry called it a saucepan, ten pounds if an ounce. In despair, the designer faked a crown from buckram and tinsel, with stage gems: it was correct in shape and proved effective as well as acceptable. Terry also deprecated the stiff stomacher provided for her as Queen Catherine in *Henry VIII*: she called it a tea-tray. The report of Sarah Bernhardt's visit to her at this juncture is truly comic: Bernhardt thought that correct clothes were of necessity becoming; Terry would suffer nothing for art's sake, and chose to look well by modern standards (Terry, 1933, p. 215). We can see in photographs that Terry nearly always wore her hair to suit herself and let

13. The dress worn by Henry Irving on his first entrance as King Lear

15. Irving's last dress as Lear

14. The hunting-dress worn by Irving as Lear, together with a broken-down version worn after the storm scenes

the prescribed head-dress fit on as best it could. The 'Albanian' cap she affected as Viola, and Queen Catherine's French hoods and dying coif, are all worn at wrong angles. As Juliet, she shocked her daughter Edith ('a born archaeologist') by sporting a modish fringe – in view of the fact that many paintings of women in the Italian Renaissance period show shaven eyebrows and high, bare foreheads, this was particularly fatuous. As Lady Macbeth, she wore two long, auburn plaits, which were exchanged for duller, thinner tresses as she aged in the course of the play. Possibly to provoke comparison with the famous early nineteenth-century portrait of Siddons sleepwalking, Terry arranged that the long, white, knitted dress she wore in this scene should have a draped hood. Whether knitting (or indeed crochet) had really reached that perfection in the eleventh century did not worry her, and though Alice Comyns Carr professed to endure fearful pangs whenever her friend insisted on something incorrect, she would seem to have bitten on the bullet pretty often.

Correctness in colour is an area in which definitive statement is difficult at this distance – even surviving costumes have often faded, and descriptions vary with the observer. The cardinal's robe which Irving wore as Wolsey was what Ellen Terry called 'flame-coloured'. It was made of silk specially dyed for him in Coventry (not in Rome, as she was later to aver), and was the exact replica of a period garment lent him by the painter Rudolph Lehmann. Clement Scott wrote:

He is swathed from head to foot in what is miscalled the cardinal's scarlet. It is not scarlet at all, but an indescribable geranium-pink, with a dash of vermilion in it. The biretta on the head is of the same blush-rose colour.   (1896, p. 338)

Everyone agreed that Irving looked even more magnificent in this single robe than the King in his many gorgeous suits. We know that Henry VIII and his court did dress brightly; but it is dubious whether Prince Mamillius of Sicily in 350 BC would really have worn 'very pink' baggy tights (and rows of sausage-curls), as we know that the child Ellen Terry did in Charles Kean's production of The Winter's Tale. The natural dyes chosen for most of the cast in the Lyceum Macbeth were more probable than the peacock, malachite and flaring red ascribed in that production to 1056's top people.

Sometimes sheer whimsy prevailed. That the traditional dress of Time with hourglass and scythe should have given place to something classical in Kean's Winter's Tale is not unreasonable; but to dress Mrs Kean as Clio, Muse of History, was a bold stroke matched only by Irving when he presented the Chorus of his Florentine Romeo and Juliet as the poet Dante. Dutton Cook accused Irving of eccentricity when Iago in 1881 appeared as 'something between a Spanish bull-fighter and an Italian bandit': since in this case we have both Irving's own sketch for the costume and pictorial evidence that it was made up as he wished, there is no shifting the responsibility. Ellen Terry's costume as Desdemona was a travesty of Elizabethan style, similar except for the nipped-in waist-line to *Punch's* bugbear, Aesthetic Dress, as caricatured during the year before, 1880. A unique horror of 1871 was George Rignold's Caliban, with tusks and pasteboard jaws that hindered his articulation; but there are no rules for Calibans. To the chagrin of designers there were no cut-and-dried rules for togas: each successive actor chose his own compromise and sneered at the rest. Perhaps Alma-Tadema got it right at last for Irving's long-postponed *Coriolanus* in the year of the old Queen's death.

'Much has had to be imagined': Spielmann's confession is validated by surviving evidence. Some of the 'historical' costumes worn on the Victorian stage are still in existence, and provide incomparable evidence about basic design, type and quality of fabric, details of construction and ornament, modifications to suit the players' taste or convenience, and – to an extent varying with age and condition – the colours and combinations of colour that were chosen to look well under stage-lighting. Paintings of characters and scenes from productions are useful as evidence about colour-schemes, but, like the clever black-and-white sketches which illustrated newspaper and magazine reviews of plays in performance, they often suggest 'lines' and hairstyles which are entirely in keeping with current Victorian fashion, and possibly reflect in this respect the manner rather than the observation of their artists. That, so far as women's costumes were concerned, a fashionable 'line' was indeed effected by the retention of Victorian corsetry and body linen beneath reconstructions of historical garments is attested by the substantial number of photographs which survive of players posed in stage costume. Accessories and hair-styles are also put on record by photographs, though there is a 'studio only' air about some of the poses. Many of the elaborate designs and records painted by scenic artists such as the Grieves, Telbin and Hawes Craven contain groups of figures in action; but though they give vivid impressions of key moments in performance, they are hardly more satisfactory as evidence about costume than the chorus of newspaper critics who – when the craze for archaeological exactness was at its height – attributed this quality with lavish hand to many get-ups of which we know enough from other sources to be sure that they did not exhibit it. Yet 'the best in this kind are but shadows, and the worst are no worse if imagination mend them . . . If we imagine no worse of them than they of themselves, they may pass for excellent men.'

NOTES

1 Russell Jackson, 'The Shakespearean Productions of Lewis Wingfield, 1883–90', *Theatre Notebook*, 31.1 (1977), 28–41.

2 Kean's surcoat is one of the costumes catalogued in Holmes, 1968. John Boaden's painting of Kemble as Hotspur was engraved in 1820. Creswick as Hotspur is one of the 'Shakespere Gallery of Engravings' issued with *Tallis's Dramatic Magazine*, 1850–1.

3 Carr, 1923, pp. 211–12; Terry, 1933, p. 234, p. 248, n. 3 to ch. xii.

4 *Lloyd's Weekly Journal*, 27 Sept. 1847; Julia Curtis, 'Tate Wilkinson's Costume Notebook', *Theatre Notebook*, 32.1 (1978), 11–24; Cole, 1859, vol. 2, pp. 48–9.

5 Cole, 1859, vol. 1, p. 282; C. Scott, 1896, p. 66; Cook, 1883, vol. 1, pp. 43–4.

6 Priscilla Horton as Ariel on wires is compared to 'the fairies in *Cinderella*' by the *John Bull* reviewer of 21 October 1838: there is a print of her in flight, reproduced by Odell from the Harvard Theatre Collection (Odell, 1920, vol. 2, p. 220). *Tallis's Dramatic Magazine* paid frequent tribute to Julia St. George for her singing voice in its reviews 1850–1, and put her Ariel in its 'Shakespere Gallery'. She left Phelps for the Vestris management and starred in several of Planché's extravaganzas at the Lyceum, taking over Pandora in *The Olympic Devils* from Madame herself.

7 Hero's wedding-dress from the Lyceum *Much Ado About Nothing* is in the London Museum, and M. R. Holmes catalogues it as no. 103, with photographs of it displayed over a farthingale and over a bustle as pls. XII and XIII. Jessie Millward played Hero in 1882, Winifred Emery in the revival of 1891.

8 These modifications to Irving's costumes as they survive in the London Museum are noted, discussed and illustrated by M. R. Holmes in his catalogue. For the effectiveness of the Crookback costume, see C. Scott, 1896, p. 106.

PART 2
Shakespeare and the Lyceum Dynasty

PREFACE

LAURENCE IRVING, grandson and biographer of Sir Henry, takes as the title of his first book on Henry's sons, H. B. (Harry) and Laurence, *The Successors*, quoting Laurence's play *Peter the Great*: 'Emperors don't have sons, they have successors.' But Henry Irving did more than establish a family dynasty. Through the Lyceum, which he managed from 1878 to 1902, he created a theatrical commonwealth which survived in different forms for years to come. Actors and actor–managers such as William Terriss, George Alexander, Johnston Forbes-Robertson, John Martin-Harvey and Frank Benson served their apprenticeship with Irving, and the latter two continued their careers into the 1930s.

Irving's leading lady, Ellen Terry, also embodied and extended a family tradition (a *Pride of Terrys* as Marguerite Steen expressed it): the daughter of actors, a child actress for the Keans in the 1850s, Portia in E. W. Godwin's seminal *The Merchant of Venice* for the Bancrofts in 1875 and, of course, the mother of Godwin's son Edward Gordon Craig, whose personal testimony on Irving (*Henry Irving*) was published in 1930. The importance of Craig's own theories on Shakespearean production has been referred to by Moelwyn Merchant.

Irving's dozen productions of Shakespeare plays have been considered in detail by Alan Hughes in *Henry Irving, Shakespearean* (1981), but the emphasis here falls on acting style. Michael Booth's 'Pictorial Acting and Ellen Terry' resumes the discussion on pictorial acting begun in Richard Foulkes's account of Charles Kean's *Richard II*, again invoking Pre-Raphaelite painting. Ellen Terry's personal interest in stage costume (established by Marion Jones) is further illustrated both on stage and in portraits by her first husband, G. F. Watts, and by Sargent and others. Undoubtedly Ellen Terry's appeal as an actress lay more in the visual than in the verbal or psychological realisation of her characters.

The same was certainly true of William Terriss, as George Rowell recounts. He was the embodiment of Victorian manliness, the distinctive features of which he rarely completely disguised in his period roles, retaining, for example, his 'weepers' moustache as Mercutio (see Marion Jones on the resistance of hairstyles to historical authenticity). Terriss showed little aptitude for the beauty and meaning of his lines or the psychological state of the character, relying instead on by-play such as a snore to reinforce Mercutio's reference to sleep. Ironically for such a robust and uncomplicated actor, Terriss met a sinister end. He was stabbed as he entered the Adelphi Theatre by a small-part actor named Prince whom he had tried to help but who apparently resented Terriss's success. Prince's claim to fame as an actor-turned-murderer hardly rivals that of John Wilkes Booth, Abraham Lincoln's assassin, but it draws our attention to the more disturbing undercurrents inherent in the portrayal of the less salubrious aspects of human nature on stage and the relationship of this to the actor's own personality.

The essence of pictorial acting was that characters were what they appeared to be, but, as Peter Thomson and Cary Mazer demonstrate, both Henry Irving and his son Harry plumbed below surface appearance to explore the inner workings of human psychology and motivation. It is a measure of the Lyceum regime's catholicity that it could accommodate Ellen Terry's and William Terriss's pictorial acting alongside Irving's own disturbing studies of psychological neuroses. Irving's exploration of the two selves was, as Peter Thomson suggests, fully in tune with the theories of Dr Mesmer and Sigmund Freud, but it was probably primarily instinctive. By contrast, Harry added to undeniable inherited traits a more intellectual appraisal of human nature, arising from his Oxford studies (he was one of the first university-educated actors), and an interest in criminology.

The relationship between outward appearance and inner personality was the basis not only of diptych roles such as Lesurques and Dubosc in The Lyons Mail, but also of Macbeth, Iago and Hamlet, whose outer appearance concealed rather than revealed their true natures. This is of course the antithesis of pictorial acting and of the practice of painters, who express character through appearance. Indeed one of the most popular pseudo-sciences of Victorian times was phrenology and Stephanie Grilli has shown how the Pre-Raphaelites sought models with the right physical characteristics, notably Holman Hunt in Valentine Rescuing Sylvia, The Hireling Shepherd and The Awakening Conscience.[1] Henry Irving was himself the subject of an article on his phrenology (The Phrenological Magazine, Nov. 1882), but not surprisingly his son rejected allied theories on 'criminal anthropology'.

H. B. Irving's determination to penetrate a character's essential being, and the way in which this relates to the actor's own personality, raise the abiding question (re-examined by William Archer in *Masks or Faces?* (1888)) about the nature of acting – the extent of the actor's identification and emotional involvement with his role, one example of which has already been cited a propos of Charles and Ellen Kean. In his resolve to relate dramatic characters to real-life criminals, and for both to analyse the underlying causes of their behaviour, Harry Irving accords with his contemporary, the celebrated Shakespearean critic A. C. Bradley in *Shakespearean Tragedy* (1904; repr. 1961, p. 181): 'This question Why? is *the* question about Iago . . . But Shakespeare knew the answer, and if these characters are great creations and not blunders we ought to be able to find it too.'

NOTE

1 Stephanie Grilli, 'Pre-Raphaelitism and Phrenology', in Parris, 1984, pp. 44–60.

Pictorial Acting and Ellen Terry

MICHAEL R. BOOTH

IN THE 1980s, and indeed for many years past, the old and traditional bond between art and the stage has been virtually severed. An occasional artist like David Hockney will be asked to design *The Magic Flute*, but the now infrequent incursions of the artist into the theatre are confined to opera rather than the dramatic stage. The last flowering of the relationship between artist and theatre occurred in the first quarter of this century, when painters such as Picasso, Miró, Braque, Gris and Bakst experimented with stage and costume design for plays, operas and ballets alike. Here, though – and even in the 1890s in England, when a completely different kind of pictorial artist worked for the commercial stage – the emphasis was on design, on the scenic environment of the actor, on the clothes he wore, on the properties he used. The pictorial relationship between actor and design was important, but a much older relationship linked the actor directly with the arts of painting and sculpture irrespective of the scene and the stage world in which he moved.

The pictorialisation of the actor is still a common performance technique in, for instance, Kabuki and Indian classical dancing; in Western acting it was traditionally associated with tragic rather than comic acting, which reflected in a lifelike technique, exaggerated for stage and satiric effect, the real manners of the day. Tragic acting was an ideal art much larger than life, an art that aimed consciously at the physical communication, insofar as the imperfect human form would allow, of ideal beauty. The eighteenth century believed on the whole that the uniformity and harmony inherent in nature must be imitated in art, and this was also true of the art of acting, which, like painting, was concerned with both grace and dignity.

The use of stylised and sometimes stereotypical gesture, attitude and facial expression – at least in tragedy, poetic drama and melodrama – pictorialised both character and emotional response in a manner deliberately larger than life and in ways that had to be harmonious, pleasing, and beautiful. Essentially, the actor's elaborately codified visual sign language existed to accompany his utterance of the text with expressive and appropriate physical and pictorial images. To this end, a symbolic language of the face, arms, hands and legs was developed to pictorialise the passions of the character being played. The hands and fingers, for instance, assumed different positions for grief, anger, jealousy, remorse, etc. At its most complicated this sign language must have resembled the *mudras* of the Indian or Balinese dancer; on the Western stage, however, it accompanied the spoken text rather than music. The language of gesture, attitude and facial expression was universally accessible to the visual understanding of audiences. It was never a matter of the frozen pictorialism seen in numerous prints and drawings, but rather a continuous and kinetic flow of ordered and graceful attitudes that were themselves complete visual and emotional statements as well as being physical counterpoints to the vocal delivery of the text. Thus did the classical and melodramatic actor speak in pictures as well as words.

A consideration of the pictorialisation of the passions takes us into the direct association between art and pictorial acting. Not only did a knowledge of art make an actor a more moral and educated being, and therefore a better actor and a fitter person to tread the stage, but it could also greatly enhance the proper, graceful and aesthetically pleasing depiction of the passions as well as the force of their expression.

Such knowledge was not merely of intellectual and cultural value, but also of immediate physical use. Quintilian advised Roman orators to learn from the attitudes of statues; advice of this kind was given to actors in the eighteenth and nineteenth centuries. Theophilus Cibber (1753, p. 51) noted of an early eighteenth-century actor–manager of Drury Lane, Barton Booth, that 'Mr. *Booth*'s Attitudes were all picturesque. He had a good Taste for Statuary and Painting and where he could not come at original Pictures, he spared no Pains of Expense to get the best Drawings and Prints. These he frequently studied, and sometimes borrowed Attitudes from.' In 1827 Goethe (Oxenford, 1850, vol. 1, p. 380) told J. P. Eckermann: 'An actor should properly go to school to a sculptor and a painter; for in order to represent a Greek hero, it is necessary for him to study carefully the antique sculptures which have come down to us, and to impress on his mind the natural grace of their sitting, standing, and going.' Roger Pickering (1755, p. 38), the eighteenth-century author of a book upon the acting of tragedy, recommends 'to those who attempt to succeed *Capitally* upon the stage, the Study of the best Paintings, Statues, and Prints . . . Among these the Attitudes of the *four Limbs* are express'd, through the several *Passions*, in a very grand and masterly Manner, and, if happily hit off by an Actor, would place him to high Advantage upon the *Stage*.' This point is amplified by William Cooke (1775, pp. 199–201), twenty years after Pickering. Cooke confines his remarks to statuary and actually names the statues from whose study he believes that actors would benefit. For men, these include the Hercules Farnese, the Apollo Belvedere and the Dying Gladiator; for women the Venus De Medicis, Diana, Flora and the Graces. The performer must study these 'so as to adopt their attitudes with ease', as well as to understand the truth and justice of their artistic principles. 'In short', Cooke concludes, 'that inflexion of body, and composition of limbs, so as not to encumber each other, or appear divided by sharp, and sudden angles, form the whole of *grace*, and give that *Je ne sais quoi*, so much admired in the whole deportment of action.' Some of this advice to the actor to study statuary and paintings stemmed, as I have said, from the popular notion that the actor should be a thoroughly educated man conversant with the arts, but the greater part of it is concerned with the practical benefits an actor would attain through such study.

The notion that actors should study pose and attitude in the work of classical painters and sculptors bore curious fruit in the 1820s, when the great English equestrian and mime Alexander Ducrow appeared at Astley's Circus and elsewhere in an act called 'Grecian Statues'. This consisted of Ducrow posing in a picture frame, revealed by the drawing of a theatre curtain, as a famous classical statue. He then gradually changed his attitude to that of another statue, and then another, and so forth. The whole thing was done with a scenic background and costume appropriate to each statue. The two elements of painting and statuary were carried over into that popular upper-class drawing-room entertainment, the *tableau vivant*, a pictorial representation in authentic costume of subject-matter from art, history or classical myth. These *tableaux vivants* were playing to the general public by the 1830s, eventually passing into the music hall, where they became known as *poses plastiques*, and right until the demise of the music hall in the 1960s remaining a mildly salacious but undoubtedly statuesque form of entertainment.

Ducrow's combination of the impersonation of classical statues behind the actual frame of a picture with a theatre curtain in front brought all three arts together in a single visual image, and it is striking how common it was from the eighteenth century on to look at the stage and the actor in terms of pictures and to use the analogy of the painter in order to discuss the actor. Or the analogy of the sculptor: a former director of the National Gallery in London, Frederic Burton, said of the appearance of Helen Faucit in *Antigone* in 1845 that seen in profile the remarkable form and beauty of her face 'called vividly to mind the Greek ideal known to us in sculpture and in designs on the finer Athenian vases' (Martin, 1900, p. 151). The famous French tragedienne Rachel, an immediate contemporary of Helen Faucit, was noted for the force and power of her poses, and words like 'marble', 'statuesque', and 'sculptural' were frequently used by critics to describe her acting: her attitudes in certain roles were also compared to those of particular statues from antiquity. As for the painter, John Hill (1750, p. 6) pointed out that the player also required skill in colouring objects; 'he, like the painter, must be a master of the ingenious theory of shadows, the skilful application of which is by an insensible gradation to conduct the eye from the first and most striking part of the picture to whatever lies obscured in shades behind'. Later (1755, p. 231), Hill remarked of the actor that 'his looks and gestures are so many paintings made to be seen at a distance'.

By the nineteenth century, not only was the actor, with an essentially pictorial style, naturally being considered from a pictorial and painterly viewpoint, but theatre production itself was becoming increasingly pictorial, and the actor, according to the best principles of harmony and relationship in art, was more and more related to pictorial intentions.

Important developments in society and culture in the first half of the nineteenth century strongly influenced the stage and were all related to the multiplicity of visual stimuli that bombarded nineteenth-century man. Gaslight, plate glass, elaborate urban architecture, the kaleidoscope, the improved peepshow and magic lantern, the panorama, the diorama, the cosmorama, the stereoscope, the camera, the steel engraving, the illustrated newspaper and magazine – this was a world saturated in pictures, and the dissemination of the pictorial image to a mass audience became and remained the most popular form of public entertainment. Since it was a part of the pictorial movement in entertainment and also a social and cultural activity, the theatre disseminated the same kind of image.

Improvements in stage-lighting, notably in gaslight and limelight, meant that for the first time, despite the absence until early in the twentieth century of lighting from the auditorium, the area behind the proscenium arch could be adequately lit. The actor could retreat, as he did, behind the proscenium, and be illuminated properly; the scene could have a suffcent amount of light thrown on it to show details clearly. No longer did the actor perform on a forestage in front of a scenic background of wings and shutters; instead he was integrated with a scenic unit, a part of a pictorial composition in three dimensions, as well as a dramatic event.

The approach of the stage towards the status of painting is one of the most remarkable phenomena of dramatic art in the nineteenth century. The 'realising' of well-known paintings in tableau form on stage, the moving panorama, the careers of scene-painters like Cox, Roberts and Stanfield as easel painters and academicians, the installation of a real picture frame around the proscenium of the Haymarket in 1880, and the use of painters of great reputation like Alma-Tadema, Ford Madox Brown and Burne-Jones to design scenery and properties for Irving and Tree, are all characteristic of this cultural phenomenon. To look at the stage as if it were a painting was an automatic response in Victorian audiences, and to make the stage look as much like a painting as possible was equally a habit among managers and technical staff. This development was part of the principle of aesthetic beauty so significant in the nineteenth century, and also a consequence of the doctrine of illustration. Since Victorian art was anything but abstract, poetic beauty could only be actualised in lifelike pictorial images, and here the techniques of scene-painting and the use of romantic lighting effects were essential. Treating plays like books to be illustrated became a well-established method of producing Shakespeare or any work with a historical setting.

As the nineteenth century wore on, the tendency to more and more elaborate productions posed serious problems for the actor. Certainly he was now an integral part of the picture, but the very size, scale and colouring of that picture could obscure and even obliterate his own performance. Washed out by a blaze of gaslight, rendered indistinguishable by a mass of other actors in bright costume, dwarfed by spectacle – the difficulties he faced were many. Not only, therefore, could his identity be dissolved by effects of light, mass and colour, but there was also no easy way of separating him from the scenic environment in which he might merely have been a dab of paint on the canvas. The problems posed for the individual actor by the large-scale pictorial method of production were never really solved in his time; indeed, the only solution possible was the one eventually adopted – to eliminate this method altogether and concentrate upon the actor's relationship to light and space rather than the pictorial and environmental replication of the ancient or modern world.

Nevertheless, it was clear that this style of production demanded a particular style of acting. If the stage was a picture, the actor also had to be a picture, in other words to act pictorially, for this was the only acting style appropriate to the circumstances of production. We have seen how the classical actor pictorialised character and emotion through a set of stylised and symbolic physical responses. Tradition and experience thus enabled him to adapt this style to the necessities of the pictorial theatre. The beautiful pictures on the stage had to be matched by the actor composing his body in a continuous series of beautiful pictures, since in the nineteenth century poetic beauty remained one of the principal aims of acting.

Thus we find eminent performers assuming a pictorial style of acting and making of themselves living pictures. On the late nineteenth-century stage this style was very marked. Both Irving and Tree adopted it, especially in elaborate productions like the Lyceum *Faust* in 1885, where every pose of Irving's was, according to contemporaries, a subject for the painter. Specialist art journals reviewed *Faust* with some care; Irving and his public believed that Lyceum productions were simultaneously art and theatre. Tree was even more of a pictorial actor, and even more given to pantomimic glosses on his role, especially in Shakespeare; for he thought it was the actor's job as well as the scene-painter's to 'illustrate' Shakespeare.

The acting of Irving and Tree in the great spectacle productions of the late Victorian stage is an admirable demonstration of the way in which a pictorial acting style was an integral part of a pictorial production style closely related to easel painting. A final and even more perfect example of this union between art and acting style is Ellen Terry, Irving's co-star in *Faust* and his partner at the Lyceum from 1878 to 1902. The painter Graham Robertson (1931, pp. 54–5) described her as '*par excellence* the Painter's Actress' who 'appealed to the eye before the ear; her gesture and pose were eloquence itself'. Her charm, said Robertson, held everyone, but 'pre-eminently those who loved pictures'; she had learned how to create Beauty, 'not the stage beauty of whitewash and lip salve, but the painter's beauty of line, harmony, and rhythm'.

It is clear that Ellen Terry's great reputation and the idolatrous admiration which she received from certain artistic quarters were not entirely due to the merits of her *acting*: she possessed an appeal which, although arising from her work on stage, extended far beyond it into the realm of image-making. In this she resembled her contemporary, Sarah Bernhardt. When Ellen Terry returned to the stage in the 1870s, she expressed through a combination of physical appearance, movement, voice and indefinable *presence* a poetic and aesthetic ideal of Victorian womanhood, representing not so much the domestic or chastely maid-enish side of that ideal common in fiction and drama as a more physical temptress, whose sexuality was made acceptable and to an extent distanced by the conventions of poetic imagery and pictorial art. The lines in Oscar Wilde's sonnet upon her performance as Henrietta Maria in a

Lyceum revival of Wills's *Charles I* in 1879 express this sexual aspect as explicitly as it *could* be expressed:

> O Hair of Gold! O Crimson Lips! O Face
> Made for the living and the love of man!

In another sonnet, Wilde longed for Ellen Terry to play Cleopatra – with himself as Antony.

The hair of gold and the crimson lips recur in many descriptions of and rhapsodies on Ellen Terry in performance, a twinning of the sexual power of an enchantress with the aesthetic and virginal beauty of a medieval queen or madonna – the latter word occurring many times in these same descriptions. She was simultaneously seductress and innocent – a paradox at the heart of Wilde's sonnets to her, and at the heart of a painting like Waterhouse's *The Lady of Shalott*. Such twinning is familiar in Pre-Raphaelite art. Ellen Terry was never painted by a Pre-Raphaelite, except in a late work by Millais, but in her brief marriage to George Frederic Watts she had been the model for five of his paintings (including one of Ophelia before she played the role) and was widely admired by painters such as Robertson. When she first appeared in London at the Haymarket for a short season in 1863, at the age of sixteen, she suggested to an ardent Clement Scott (1900, pp. 17–18) and his circle 'the girl heroines that we most adored in poetry and the fine arts generally', reminding him of Tennyson's Elaine, a crowned queen in the *Morte d'Arthur*, Morris's Rapunzel, Browning's Porphyria, Undine and the paintings of Rossetti.

Such was Ellen Terry's image, of which she was no doubt quite aware. She transmuted that image into stage art by dressing for the part and through the techniques of pictorial acting already described. Through these means she created a resemblance, often noted by contemporaries, to a living picture or statue. Davenport Adams said of her Beatrice, which she played on tour in 1880, that she was 'a perfect vision of the picturesque . . . no lady on the modern stage is so much of a picture in herself, or falls so readily into the composition of the larger picture formed by the combinations of a drama' (Pemberton, 1902, p. 181).

Such views were specifically applied in criticisms of Ellen Terry's acting and her assumption of particular roles. Henry James, an especially severe critic, nevertheless observed that as Lilian Vavasour in a revival of Tom Taylor's *New Men and Old Acres* in 1876 she looked like a Pre-Raphaelite drawing or an illustration to a novel.[1] Her Lyceum Ophelia resembled, in James's opinion, 'a somewhat angular maiden of the Gothic ages'.[2] Charles Hiatt (1898, p. 115) believed that her Ophelia looked like a Pre-Raphaelite saint or a madonna by Giovanni Bellini. George Bernard Shaw wrote in the *Saturday Review* (17 July 1897): 'When I first saw her in Hamlet it was exactly as if the powers of a beautiful picture of Ophelia had been extended to speaking and singing.' To Joseph Knight (1893, p. 51), who saw her Pauline in *The Lady of Lyons* at the Princess's in 1875, her presentation 'comprised a series of pictures each more graceful than the preceding' – suitable illustrations, he thought, to a Border ballad or a legend of the Round Table. Ellen Terry's Camma in Tennyson's classically set *The Cup* (1881) reminded George Wedmore of both the Elgin Marbles and the paintings of Albert Moore (Hiatt, 1898, p. 155); her Hermione reminded Christopher St. John (1907, p. 83) of the statue of Niobe in the Louvre. For Clement Scott (1896, p. 201) Camma recalled the classical figures of Frederick Leighton and Alma-Tadema.

A list of parallels drawn by contemporaries between Ellen Terry on the stage and the women of art and literature could be extended to some length; the parallels, of course, are strongly pictorial, or, in the case of Greek art, statuesque. In the role of Portia, she was regarded by some critics as more a work of art than an actress. She first played Portia at the Prince of Wales's in 1875 under the Bancrofts, in a production that was a box-office failure but highly praised for its archaeological pictures of seventeenth-century Venice (following the precedent set by Charles Kean) and her own acting; she played the part again at the Lyceum in 1879. Irving's production was also highly pictorial, and replete with references to and recreations of the Venetian old masters: Moroni and Titian were the sources for the dove-coloured cloaks and jerkins, the hats and the frills, and Antonio's violet gown; Paolo Veronese provided the content and arrangement of several pictures. These large canvasses contained a smaller, Ellen Terry herself. In a letter thanking her for sending him photographs of her Portia, Tom Taylor said that he liked the profile best because 'it is most Paolo Veronesish and gives the right notion of your Portia, although the colour hardly suggests the golden gorgeousness of your dress and the blonde glory of the hair and complexion' (Terry, 1908, p. 115). In his review, Joseph Knight (1893, p. 305) noted that she was 'got up in exact imitation of those stately Venetian dames who still gaze down from the pictures of Paolo Veronese'; Dutton Cook (1883, p. 393), however, likened her Portia to a painting by Giorgione; and Clement Scott (1899, vol. 1, p. 587) declared that she looked 'as if she had stepped out of a canvas by Leighton'. All the critics were struck, like Oscar Wilde, with her hair of gold; the first Belmont costume was also gold.

All through the Ellen Terry literature runs this sub-text of gold; poets and Pre-Raphaelite painters alike were obsessed with the colour, and had the actress lived in Vienna she would undoubtedly have been painted by

Klimt. Graham Robertson (1931, p. 154) was later to praise her first appearance as Rosamund in Tennyson's *Becket* (1893) as 'a wonderful Rossettian effect of dim gold and glowing colour veiled in black, her masses of bright hair in a net of gold and golden hearts embroidered on her robe'. His memory of Portia is even more strongly pictorial, more intensely golden, and captures that trance-like effect she often created in audiences: 'A dream of beautiful pictures in a scheme of gold melting into one another; the golden gown, the golden hair, the golden words, all form a golden vision of romance and loveliness'(p. 55).

Criticism of this kind was unique to Ellen Terry; no performer in the history of the English stage had ever before been considered in quite these pictorial terms. However, such a point of view was the logical culmination of a century of theatrical development in which the production and the actor moved ever closer to the status of works of art, and the pictorial style in acting and production came to dominate the stage.

No longer is this style artistically fashionable or financially feasible. No longer is the depiction of poetic beauty one of the principal aims of actor and manager alike. No longer must the actor develop a graceful and aesthetically pleasing style to suit the prevailing style of scene-painting, set construction, costuming and lighting. While pictorialism and the earlier belief in the instructive and aesthetic powers of classical statuary were in vogue, however, the actor transformed himself into a painting, a statue, a work of art in his own right – a remarkable, unique, and now extinct historical phenomenon of the stage.

NOTES

1 'The London Theatres', *Galaxy*, May 1877, p. 110.
2 'The London Theatres', *Scribner's Monthly*, Jan. 1881, p. 143.

Mercutio as Romeo: William Terriss in *Romeo and Juliet*

GEORGE ROWELL

To those who recognise his name, William Terriss is first and foremost the hero of Adelphi melodrama: *Harbour Lights*, *The Union Jack*, *One of the Best*, and finally and tragically *Secret Service*. If we see him on the Lyceum stage, it is probably as an exuberant foil to Irving – cheeking him in *The Corsican Brothers*, stealing his daughter in *Olivia*, opposing secular might to clerical right as Henry II to his Becket.

Yet Terriss's cast of Shakespearean characters at the Lyceum was substantial: Bassanio, Laertes, Cassio, Don Pedro in *Much Ado About Nothing* and ten years later Claudio in the same play (surely a unique succession), Orsino, Edgar, Henry VIII. He also played Othello on an American tour with his own company, and on one occasion at the Haymarket to the Iago of Beerbohm Tree.

Nevertheless *Romeo and Juliet* was the Shakespeare play to which he returned most often. In all he played Romeo to four Juliets: Ellen Wallis, leading lady at Drury Lane in the 1870s; Bella Pateman at the Crystal Palace; Adelaide Neilson at the Haymarket; and Mary Anderson at the Lyceum during Irving's absence on his second American tour. His only appearance as Mercutio was also at the Lyceum with Irving and Ellen Terry; this was his longest run in this play – 161 performances broken by a brief recess in the summer of 1882.

The recurrence of *Romeo and Juliet* in his early career was no coincidence. Terriss was first and last a pictorial actor – handsome in a particularly Victorian way; athletic (his prowess as horseman and swimmer was only equalled by his courage); admirably proportioned and preserved. In the Victorian period *Romeo and Juliet* was widely regarded as the most pictorial of the tragedies. Irving spoke for his fellow actor–managers when he told Ellen Terry:

Hamlet could be played anywhere on its acting merits. It marches from situation to situation. But *Romeo and Juliet* proceeds from picture to picture. Every line suggests a

picture. It is a dramatic poem rather than a drama, and I mean to treat it from that point of view.
                                                                    (Terry, 1933, p. 162)

This approach explains the frequency with which Terriss was cast in a role for which he evidently lacked the vocal, intellectual and spiritual qualities needed. He looked like Romeo to a Victorian eye, and in the Victorian scale looks weighed most.

His first attempt came cruelly early in his career, the inception of which may effectively be dated to his joining the Drury Lane company in the autumn of 1871. Drury Lane in the 1860s and 1870s struggled to retain something of its role as a 'classical house', though the classics were more successfully represented by Walter Scott than by William Shakespeare. Terriss's Romeo in December 1874 formed part of a benefit week before pantomime took over, and was evidently a hasty, ill-prepared affair. The *Era* critic did not mince words:

When we heard him exclaim that he was 'the youngest of that name for fault of a worse' we could hardly help reflecting that it was the want of a better that had led to his being Romeo at all. Certainly he looked the character admirably, but this faint praise is all that can be bestowed. The role is a difficult one.   (20 Dec. 1874)

Between abject failure in 1874 and acceptability in 1878 Terriss had taken the measure of melodrama, if not of the metre of Shakespeare, by playing, amongst other parts, Captain Molineux in Boucicault's *The Shaughraun* at Drury Lane and Squire Thornhill opposite Ellen Terry in *Olivia*, W. G. Wills's dramatisation of *The Vicar of Wakefield*, at the Court. It was during the run of *Olivia* that he tackled his second Romeo at a Crystal Palace matinée – as always the sheer stamina of Victorian actors leaves us gasping – and his evening engagement may have necessitated substantial cuts. We are told 'the entire play was acted in very little more than two hours'. This time the *Era* critic found 'his acting in the balcony scene full of natural feeling as well as of finished art', adding significantly: 'As some ladies near us said "How nice" when he appeared, we may take it that the personal gifts of the Romeo were not without their attraction' (18 Aug. 1878).

If this comment strikes us as double-edged, the same source made amends when, almost a year later, Terriss played opposite one of the most famous of Victorian Juliets, Adelaide Neilson, in a brief season at the Haymarket during which he also played Orlando to her Rosalind:

Youth and good looks are no mean aids to the realisation of the love-sick and desperate hero, and these Mr. Terriss is fortunate enough to possess. But we have seen youthful and good-looking actors who, for lack of skill, have made but sorry Romeos. In Mr Terriss we are pleased to recognise one of the very best representatives of the character the English stage now boasts.   (27 July 1879)

Not everyone would agree, either then or later. But if Terriss lacked some of the essential qualities of a Romeo, he had most of the characteristics of Mercutio. He was endowed not only with Victorian good looks but also with a Victorian spirit of adventure. As a child he squeezed pocket money from his mother by insisting: ' "Give me £5 or I'll jump out of the window". And she at once believed that he meant it, and cried out: "Come back! Come back! and I'll give you anything" ' (Terry, 1933, p. 113). No school could hold him for long, and when in desperation his parents signed him on as a midshipman in the merchant navy, his service lasted only from Gravesend, where he embarked, to Plymouth, where he jumped ship. In the years before he settled to the stage he was in turn tea-planter in Assam, sheep-farmer in the Falklands, and horse-breeder in Kentucky. Sailing to the Falklands with his wife, who was then expecting the future Ellaline Terriss, he survived near-shipwreck off Cape Horn. Sailing back, the Swedish crew mutinied and elected him captain. Not only did he seek adventure; it constantly sought him, in life and unhappily in death.

Certainly his Mercutio, with Mrs Stirling's Nurse, were the popular successes of Irving's *Romeo and Juliet* at the Lyceum in 1882. Even so experienced a journalist and theatre man as Henry Labouchère told Ellen Terry that he should have played Romeo, adding:

I don't doubt Irving's intellectuality, you know. But as Romeo he reminds me of a pig who has been taught to play the fiddle. He does it cleverly, but he would be better employed in squealing. He cannot shine in the part like the fiddler. Terriss in this case is the fiddler.

(Terry, 1933, p. 165)

As for the public, they took his Mercutio to their hearts, from the galleryite who shouted 'Why don't you let him sit down?' as Benvolio tried to support the dying duellist,[1] to the heir to the throne who was present on the first night: 'The chivalrous and fresh Mercutio of Mr. W. Terriss well deserved the special recognition of the Prince and Princess of Wales', according to the *Illustrated Sporting and Dramatic News* (18 Mar. 1882), which suggests that their Royal Highnesses found the last two acts somewhat hard going.

In fact Irving's version of the play turned Mercutio into the loyal henchman Victorian audiences recognised from melodrama. Victorian taste found much of his dialogue indecent or incomprehensible: the comparisons of Rosaline to 'an open-arse medlar' and Romeo to 'a poperin pear' were wholly inadmissible, and his bawdy song to the Nurse was cut

16. *Romeo and Juliet*, 2.4, at the Lyceum Theatre, 1882. Left to right: Irving as Romeo, Mrs Stirling as the Nurse, Andrews as Peter, Terriss as Mercutio, Child as Benvolio. Set design by Hawes Craven

completely. True the Queen Mab speech presented Terriss with some problems, and it may have been this scene that moved one critic to comment:

Mercutio is neither a dancing master nor a Harlequin. A man may be gay and volatile without being either of these. Moreover there ought to be a limit in suiting the action to the word, and we may fairly assume that Mercutio would have spoken of sleep without accentuating the observation with a loud snore.[2]

But there was general approval of the performance, Queen Mab included. *The Times* spoke for most:

Mr. Terriss is a really excellent Mercutio, handsome, gay, vivacious, equally ready to run off into fantastic poetry for the amusement of his friends or to pick a mortal quarrel with his chance-met enemy.   (18 Mar. 1882)

Although *Romeo and Juliet* established new standards of spectacle and expense – Ellen Terry calls it the most *elaborate* of all the Lyceum productions – its scenic splendours are poorly recorded compared with those of *Faust* or *Henry VIII*. It predated the series of illustrated souvenirs, and magazine coverage focussed on Irving and Terry. The only full-stage illustration I know which includes Mercutio is Hawes Craven's design for his encounter with the Nurse and Peter, described as 'Verona: Outside the City' (pl. 16). It is evidently a design, not a record. The costumes do not match those in studio photographs, and Bram Stoker confirms that Irving discarded Alfred Thompson's suggestions in favour of sources of his own. But a glance at such impressions of Terriss as Mercutio as survive adds weight to the argument that his success was measured against Irving's and Ellen Terry's comparative failure. Both lovers were found to lack youthful spirit – they were respectively forty-four and thirty-five years old – and poetic passion. The *Theatre* spelt out the contrast:

The vociferous applause awarded to Mr. Terriss for certain passages in the life of Mercutio and in particular for his delivery of the Queen Mab speech, was due no doubt to the sense of relief that energy gives after so much depressed action and uneventful luxury.

(1 Apr. 1882)

The studio photographs of this Mercutio may suggest to our eyes Captain Molineux from *The Shaughraun* at a fancy dress ball, particularly as Terriss chose to retain his 'weepers' moustache in the part. But perhaps it was this feature of his performance that the Lyceum audience recognised and relished. In his Mercutio they looked for and found a 'walking gentleman' from melodrama, the hero's friend who fights and dies for him. In the Romeo and Juliet they looked for juvenile leads and found mature artists. It should be emphasised that, whatever view was taken of the two lovers' performances, the production pleased the public, running for 161 nights.

Romeo and Juliet did not figure in Irving's first American tour, and Terriss was therefore introduced to American audiences in a series of decidedly 'table-leg' parts (to use Gordon Craig's term): Christian in *The Bells* by Leopold Lewis; Moray in W. G. Wills's *Charles I*; Nemours in *Louis XI* (adapted by Boucicault from Casimir Delavigne) – with Bassanio and, towards the end of the tour, Laertes as his only Shakespearean roles. It may have been these limitations that tempted him to look elsewhere. Writing to his sister Harriet from New York in April 1884, he reflected: 'I could as you say remain with Irving for years, but I think now is my chance. If I do not take it, my chance is gone.'[3] It must have been about this time that he was approached by Mary Anderson, no doubt through Henry Abbey, who was managing Irving's tour as well as her season at the Lyceum. Her success, particularly in *Pygmalion and Galatea*, had encouraged her to plan a production of *Romeo and Juliet* at the Lyceum in the autumn, when Irving was due to return to America, and she sought a younger, more glamorous Romeo than her current leading man, J. H. Barnes. At any rate Terriss got the engagement, Mary Anderson's second season opened with *Pygmalion and Galatea*, and *Romeo and Juliet* followed on 1 November 1884.

The production was billed as 'under the direction of the Hon. Lewis Wingfield', and I am indebted to Russell Jackson's article on Wingfield's Shakespearean productions (*Theatre Notebook*, 33. 1 (1977), 28–41) for most of my information. How extensive Wingfield's control was must remain uncertain. He was undoubtedly responsible for the costumes, and in press interviews he stressed his part in training the dancers and supers, of whom there were 180. If the *Stage*'s estimate (7 Nov. 1884) of the cost ($6000) is accurate, the production was less expensive than Irving's by some $4000, but the name of Hawes Craven amongst the four scenic artists suggests access to the Lyceum's own resources. Certainly the production followed Irving's lead in elaborating and localising the settings. The opening brawl took place in the 'Piazza dell'Erbe' and the deaths of Mercutio and Tybalt in the 'Piazza Dante'. The treatment of Friar Laurence's cell was even more specific. It had been upgraded to 'The Monastery' and 'The Cloisters' by Irving. Mary Anderson's production offered 'A Chapel connected with the Monastery', in which the marriage of Romeo and Juliet took place before the audience's gaze, though not, as had been forecast, before a large congregation, which would have defeated the playwright's purpose.

Probably the most remarked feature was Bruce Smith's revolve for

Juliet's chamber and balcony, which showed to advantage Terriss's athleticism when quitting his bride's bedroom. From such evidence as survives it may be deduced that the strength of this *Romeo and Juliet* was visual rather than vocal. Mary Anderson's success, particularly as Galatea in W. S. Gilbert's *Pygmalion and Galatea*, was largely due to her beauty, and her childlike Juliet made a strong contrast to Ellen Terry's mature

17.   William Terriss as Romeo, at the Lyceum, 1884

woman. (Interestingly, they shared the same Nurse, the veteran Mrs Stirling.) Terriss's Romeo appeared correspondingly boyish (pl. 17) although he was in fact aged thirty-seven.

The speaking of verse, however, was never his strongest suit. In this context the best-known story relates to *Much Ado About Nothing*, when, after rehearsing interminably Don Pedro's line 'What needs the bridge much broader than the flood?', Irving asked 'Terriss, what's the meaning of that?', to be answered 'Oh, get along, Guv'nor, *you* know' (Terry, 1933, p. 174), or, in Graham Robertson's version, 'Oh, go along, Guv'nor, it's poetry, isn't it?' (Robertson, 1931, pp. 176–7) – an attitude confirmed when he played Edgar in *King Lear* and told Robertson: 'It doesn't do to take all this stuff so slow, you know, If you've *got* to say it, get it over. People pretend they like it, but they yawn their heads off.'

Not surprisingly, his delivery as Romeo met with much criticism. The *Pall Mall Gazette* voiced this powerfully:

Remembering the last revival of *Romeo and Juliet* upon these boards, one could but wish that some method of thought transference might be invented by which Mr. Irving's brains could be spirited for the nonce into Mr. Terriss's handsome head. The audience, however, admired the body and did not seem to miss the brains. He wore his clothes so well that they forgot to notice how ill he spoke his lines. (3 Nov. 1884)

In fact the first-night audience pursued its prejudice to the point of booing Mercutio, Herbert Standing – presumably for not being Terriss.

Probably the most telling comment on Terriss as Romeo, since it comes from a comrade and friend, was Ellen Terry's:

He was young truly, and stamped his foot a great deal, was vehement and passionate. But it was so obvious that there was no intelligence behind his reading. He did not know what the part was about, and all the finer shades of meaning in it he missed. Yet the majority would always prefer a Terriss as Romeo to a Henry Irving. (Terry, 1933, p. 165)

In fact her evidence is inadmissible, since Ellen Terry cannot have seen him as Romeo to Mary Anderson's Juliet. She left for North America with the Lyceum company in September 1884, six weeks before *Romeo and Juliet* opened, and did not return until six weeks after it had closed. The most likely explanation of her comment is that, writing more than twenty years after the event, she conflated one of Terriss's earlier performances (probably opposite Adelaide Neilson) which she had seen with adverse criticism and word of mouth about his Lyceum Romeo (pl. 18).

Despite the adverse comment, it should be stressed that this *Romeo and Juliet* was a considerable commercial success, running for 101 perform-ances between 1 November 1884 and 21 February 1885, and Miss Anderson took the production to New York later in the year with Forbes-

18. Terriss in the same production

Robertson as her leading man. Terriss remained at the Lyceum to play Squire Thornhill in *Olivia*, again with Ellen Terry in the title role and Irving now playing the Vicar of Wakefield. That autumn he moved along the Strand to the Adelphi, where he began his long and triumphant career as the hero of Adelphi melodrama. His appearances in *Romeo and Juliet* were over, though not his association with Shakespeare. During his second spell at the Lyceum under Irving between 1890 and 1894 he returned to the role of Bassanio, moved from Don Pedro to Claudio, and played Edgar and Henry VIII.

Gordon Craig, who looked up to Terriss very much as an elder brother, writes vividly of his hero as 'erect, head splendidly carried, with brows rather like Buonaparte'. He also notes Terriss's fondness for the Latin tag *Carpe diem* (make the most of today), sometimes varied to *Tempus fugit* – a fondness which he even extended to signing his letters 'Carpe Diem'. Craig quotes one such letter which concluded: 'And in the dim future give a few thoughts to old "Carpe Diem"', and adds: 'I have given many a thought to him since he died in 1897, but always the thoughts resolved themselves into remembrances of a *young* "Carpe Diem"' (Craig, 1930, p. 107). Ellen Terry's valediction is in the same vein: 'He died as a beautiful youth, a kind of Adonis, although he was fifty years old' (Terry, 1933, p. 113).

I began by touching on the similarities between Terriss's adventurous youth and Shakespeare's portrait of Mercutio: boyish, boisterous, brave – characteristics which make Mercutio perhaps the most rewarding of all the supporting parts in Shakespearean tragedy. Certainly more reputations have been sustained by playing Mercutio than established by undertaking Romeo, not least because his early departure from the play spares the actor the heavy demands made on the young lovers in the scenes which follow.

Without pressing too hard the parallel between Mercutio's sudden death and Terriss's violent end by the knife of Richard Archer Prince, there is surely a dramatic relevance in the stroke of fate which brought his career to a climax before his powers had begun to fail, and spared him the gradual eclipse suffered by his Lyceum colleagues, Frank Benson and Martin-Harvey, even by his 'Guv'nor' Henry Irving himself. Both on and off the stage William Terriss could be called the Mercutio of the late Victorian theatre.

NOTES

1 Unidentified cutting in Percy Fitzgerald Collection, Garrick Club Library, London, 7, p. 305.
2 Percy Fitzgerald Collection, 5, p. 238.
3 Letter kindly shown me by Robert Stuart (Terriss's great-grandson).

'Weirdness that lifts and colours all': The Secret Self of Henry Irving

PETER THOMSON

PERHAPS the most offensive feature of the successful late Victorian Englishman was his confidence. English and American people, living under the government of Mrs Thatcher and Ronald Reagan, have an opportunity to perceive and criticise a spectacular revival of the rhetoric of public confidence, used to divert attention from disturbing truths. The Victorians, we could probably agree, were better at it. Successive governments promoted to high office men whose particular skill lay in their ability to act out in public or to dramatise in parliamentary soliloquies the connection between prosperity and goodness. The early Victorian age of production had, in the words of G. M. Young (1936, pp. 7, 32), given way to the late Victorian age of finance: 'Knowledge of the facts and an apt handling of figures was now the surest proof of capacity, and among the most memorable feats of Victorian oratory are speeches on finance.' A representative voice is that of Samuel Smiles, whose heartlessness about an individual loser is papered over by an unctuous celebration of honest trade: 'The unhappy youth who committed suicide a few years since because he had been "born to be a man and condemned to be a grocer" proved by the very act that his soul was not equal even to the dignity of grocery' (Briggs, 1955, p. 134). Margaret Thatcher, rising from the dignity of Grantham grocery to the greater dignity of Downing Street, would have furnished Samuel Smiles with a splendid alternative to this wretched youth. But if you stop to wonder what Smiles is actually saying, rather than what he thinks he is saying or wants you to think he is saying, some disagreeable assumptions may emerge, and some dangerously contradictory ones too. For example:

1 The submerged (and anonymous) majority should accept its lot, but
2 if you are so unlucky as to be a grocer, you should at least aim at being a successful (i.e. prosperous) grocer. Why? Because
3 the best way to escape from grocery is to get rich at it, and

97

4 God will help you to do that, because He approves of a man whose soul is in his trade. Substitute a vapid patriotism, albeit with religious overtones, for God, and you have the outline notes for many a government statement during the 1984–5 miners' strike. My first assertion, then, is that Thatcherite England provides a context for a re-appraisal of the moral climate in which Irving's Lyceum throve.

It has never been easy for the theatre to behave well during a period of misplaced national confidence. I do not know whether Samuel Smiles went to the Lyceum, though I have no doubt that a large proportion of the Lyceum audience would have endorsed his values – at least in public. They are, after all, the values of contemporary melodrama and comedy. The stubbornly virtuous are rewarded with money; the incurably vicious lose it; the weak-willed, corrupted by drink or drawn to the gambling table, may, if they are lucky, get a ticket-of-leave, but they must earn it by a Leontes-like remorse. Such theatrical fictions are, in the *Proverbial Philosophy* of Martin Tupper and in the exemplary tales of Smiles's *Self-Help*, presented as social facts, the logical outcome of decency in a country that has the right priorities. Late Victorian stability was based, not simply on decency nor simply on finance, but subtly on the relationship between the two. A first step into the Lyceum foyer and a second into the auditorium were both likely to remind an observant spectator of this relationship. Michael Booth (1981, p. 95) has shrewdly pointed out that 'Irving conceived of entrance-hall, staircase, vestibule, and auditorium as entertainment'; but a theatre can entertain ideas as well as audiences. The presiding idea of Irving's Lyceum was that prosperity is a good servant to art. It was an idea that connected conspicuous expenditure with public virtue, and the reward of a knighthood seems entirely appropriate. And yet . . .

I need the pause of a new paragraph at that point, because I am moving resolutely into speculation. And yet . . . there is something in Irving's respectability that does not add up, something that has obsessed me for years and that I shall never satisfactorily express. I can offer images. There is, for example, this one from the biography by his grandson: 'Of all the entertainments Paris had to offer, Irving preferred the Morgue. He liked, in the early morning, to linger there and watch the procession of men and women who filed past the gruesome exhibits' (Irving, 1951, p. 498); or this, from Henry Arthur Jones's recollection of his Dubosc in *The Lyons Mail*: 'A wonderful touch was his blithe camaraderie in patting the horse as he murdered the postboy' (Jones, 1931, p. 44); or, less specifically, W. G. Wills's perception in Irving's playing of Mephistopheles of 'the weirdness which lifts and colours all' (Booth, 1981, p. 125). You cannot read much about Irving's acting without encountering adjectives like 'sly', 'sardonic', 'eerie', 'intense' or 'demonic'. These are not adjectives that we associate with Victorian stability. If there was uprightness on the Lyceum stage, it belonged to William Terriss or to honest Tom Mead, and it was there so that Irving could lean at a rakish angle away from it. The particular splendour of Irving's regime – and this is my second assertion – the reason for its unique hold on the theatrical public was that it simultaneously endorsed and threatened decency. We should not be surprised by that. Shaw would soon be revealing that 'decency is indecency's conspiracy of silence', and it is no secret that the godly text of Victorian manners concealed, but could not *always* conceal, a lurid sub-text. When I was an undergraduate, reading, I think, about Matthew Arnold, I encountered the curious information that Anna Kavan had detected in Victorian attitudes 'a manifestation of the anal complex operating upon the group psyche'. I did not understand what it meant, but I remember determining to slip it into an essay if the opportunity arose. It never did (I am not really sure that it has now), but the sentence awoke in me an obscure suspicion that my maternal grandmother was not necessarily as 'good' as I had been led to believe. Orderly, parsimonious and obstinate, she was simultaneously a representative Victorian and an exemplary anal erotic. If the nineteenth century had not existed, Freud would have had to invent it. So disciplined and constrained was the conscious mind that the upsurge of the subconscious, its precipitation into shameful deeds, was spectacular. The point I wish to make here has been made by Steven Marcus (1966, pp. 30–1): 'the development of social attitudes, of attitudes toward society and social problems, had outstripped the development of personal attitudes, of attitudes towards personal problems and conflicts, and of inwardness in general'. And I wish to make that point because I believe that Irving, against the tide of Victorian generality, offered to the Lyceum audiences a unique and dangerous access to the secreted self. Alan Hughes (1981, p. 92), by routes much cooler than my own, has arrived at the conclusion that Irving was naturally drawn to 'characters which were complex, introspective and individual to the point of eccentricity'. His preparedness to subject the characters he was to play to so searching a moral scrutiny implied, even if it did not require, a preparedness to do the same to himself, adding to Lyceum evenings a frisson of the forbidden, an attractiveness made more powerful by the counter-pressure of repulsion.

It was particularly in the profound study and detailed portrayal of guilt that Irving excelled. Hamlet and Iachimo, perhaps Shylock too, were his Shakespearean opportunities, and he took them finely. Macbeth he overloaded, mistakenly elaborating the role as he had done so triumphantly with Mathias in *The Bells*, Leopold Lewis's opportunistic adaptation of *Le Juif polonais* (Erckmann and Chatrian). There is an important truth in the observation of his old adversary, Shaw:

> He was utterly unlike anyone else; he could give importance and a noble melancholy to any sort of drivel that was put into his mouth; and it was this melancholy, bound up with an impish humour, which forced the spectator to single him out as a leading figure.
>
> (St. John, 1931, p. xx)

Shaw overlooks the technical and pictorial manipulation of audience attention, but his recognition of Irving's singularity is eloquent testimony from a hostile witness. And it is, of course, true that Irving could act better than most of the playwrights he commissioned could write. The literature of guilt had remained plentiful after the death of Byron and the dotage of Wordsworth and Coleridge, but it had lost its philosophical bite. Irving as Heathcliff in a dramatisation of *Wuthering Heights* is an appealing thought, or in a solo performance of *The Tell-Tale Heart*. Richard Mansfield beat him to T. R. Sullivan's dramatisation of *Dr Jekyll and Mr Hyde*, and Irving even had the courtesy to invite him to play it at the Lyceum. Mansfield's self-transformation, without artificial aids, from Jekyll to Hyde was deservedly famous in its time, but it was somatic. Irving was the unrivalled master of psychosomatic transformation through guilt. When he performed in it, *The Bells* was as profound a study of the human conscience as *Lord Jim*. The cultural significance of great actors has been insufficiently understood. Unlike Macready, Irving never tried to spearhead a literary revival, though it is, I suppose, possible that he thought W. G. Wills a great poetic dramatist; but he did, as Craig and Shaw in their different ways recognised, disturb the steady Victorian locomotion towards platitude. Occupationally an exhibitionist, the actor is always liable to do that, but few are as conscious as Irving was of cultural distinction. There was, as he confessed in his Harvard lecture of 1885, no way in which the off-stage actor could disguise his unorthodox beardlessness (1893, p. 74). It was a kind of nakedness, contributory perhaps to William Archer's claim that there was an intensely feminine streak in all that Irving did. Written at the height of the cult of the manly man, that compliment was intended as an insult. How could a sensitive actor avoid offending the devotees of such a cult? Not to pretend was the ultimate pretence of Victorian manliness. It was a hypocrisy that provoked Oscar Wilde into making of himself a social spectacle. Not so Irving, whose off-stage performance of respectability was usually faultless. It was on stage that he made a spectacle of himself, and it is the nature of that spectacle that intrigues me.

The Secret Self of Henry Irving

In a period that shunned, even denied, the neurosis of individuality, Irving emphasised it. The provocation of Victorian manliness would have been more obvious had his staging not so carefully assimilated it within pictorial conventions. But it was, I contend, the combination of pictorialism and provocation that gave Lyceum performances their fascination. Irving's acting disturbed and unnerved people. It was not simply what he did, but the whole-heartedness of his approach to what he had to do, the manner of his taking on a role, that challenged contemporary attitudes. When Richard Mansfield bemoaned the exhaustion of prolonged performance as Richard III, Irving asked him: 'Ah, then – a – why do you play him if you find him so unwholesome?' (Forbes-Robertson, 1925, p. 241). In 1905, when his son Harry took the terrifying risk of playing Hamlet at the Adelphi, Irving wrote in his notebook: 'Poor little H. . . . he'll never make anything of Hamlet', following this up with a first-night telegram of chilling comfort: 'I am thy father's spirit brooding o'er ye' (Irving, 1951, p. 661). Having gone with Ellen Terry to see the youthful Frank Benson as Hamlet, and having expressed some approval of the performance to her, he nevertheless confronted Benson with the question, 'Why do you play him?'. It was this quest for the source of his art, this self-punishing preparedness to ask the question 'why?', that gave his performances their peculiar intensity. Ellen Terry ascribed to his acting 'a kind of fine temper, like the purest steel, produced by the perpetual fight against difficulties' (Terry, 1908, p. 74). He was possessed by the possibilities of the characters he embodied, and it was the spectacle of a man possessed that he offered to his audiences. Anything less like a manly man (anything less like William Terriss) it would be hard to envisage.

My third assertion, then, is that Irving, despite the knighthood and despite his social success, belongs to the rogue tradition of acting, a tradition in which the actor dares to present himself as a critic of contemporary culture rather than as its mirror. It was Edmund Kean, not Macready and certainly not Charles Kean, whom he particularly admired. His choice of Ellen Terry as leading lady should properly be seen as an emblem of his intuitive radicalism. Their rightful successors are not Gielgud and Peggy Ashcroft but Jonathan Price and Glenda Jackson. It was Charles Reade who described Irving as an 'eccentric serious actor', in contrast with the more readily acceptable 'eccentric comic actor', Joseph Jefferson. That is to say that Reade did not think of Irving as a tragic actor. His Hamlet, by some way his most successful tragic role, was 'eccentric serious'. My impression is that John Barrymore's was of the same kind, and there were echoes of Irving's performance in Olivier's film version, but my own guess is that David Warner's student prince in the Stratford production of 1965 came closer to the spirit of Irving than either. It is Alan

Hughes's view that 'the peculiarities which would have hampered Irving if he had aspired to a generalizing style were developed until they became assets . . . He was never ordinary' (1981, p. 10). What I have been stressing, and will stress again, is that public behaviour in Victorian England aspired (or plodded) to a generalising style. Irving's particularity was inherently critical of that aspiration.

Consider his Hamlet: a fundamentally sane man, driven into solitude by bereavement and maternal betrayal, and then to outbursts of hysteria by the imposition of uncongenial duty. E. R. Russell (Hughes, 1981, p. 51) concluded, after seeing Irving:

Hamlet is evidently one of those who . . . find in solitude a licence and a cue for excitement, and who, when alone and under the influence of strong feelings, will abandon themselves to their fancies. Such men . . . will pace rooms like wild animals, will gaze into looking-glasses until they are frightened at the expression of their own eyes, will talk aloud . . . will do almost anything to find vent for emotions which their imagination is powerful enough to kindle, but not fertile or methodical enough to satisfy.

And here is a slightly earlier account:

Engaged in no social diversion, the patients of this group live alone in the midst of many. In their exercise they choose the quietest and most unfrequented parts of the airing-grounds. They join in no social conversation, nor enter with others into any amusement. They walk alone, or they sit alone. If engaged in reading, they talk not to others of what they may have read; their desire apparently is, in the midst of numbers, to be in solitude. They seek no social joys, nor is the wish for fellowship evinced.

The pale complexion, the emaciated form, the slouching gait, the clammy palm, the glassy or leaden eye, and the averted gaze, indicate the lunatic victim to this vice.

Apathy, loss of memory, abeyance of concentrative power and manifestation of mind generally, combined with loss of self-reliance, and indisposition for or impulsiveness of action, irritability of temper, and incoherence of language, are the most characteristic mental phenomena of chronic dementia resulting from masturbation in young men.

(Marcus, 1966, pp. 20–1)

Yes, I'm cheating. The second passage is from Acton's *The Functions and Disorders of the Reproductive Organs* (1857). But does it not sound like Irving ('The pale complexion, the emaciated form, the slouching gait')? I am not suggesting that Irving's Hamlet was to be seen as a martyr to Portnoy's complaint – though the idea opens the way to a nice reinterpretation of the Victorian insistence that the manly man should keep a grip on himself. What I am suggesting is that Irving's Hamlet, like so many of his melodramatic creations, referred his audiences, through the brilliance of its morbidity, not only to the friends and relations whose suffering they preferred to hush up (Mrs Rochester in the attic), but also to the insecurity of the self. It was a performance that embodied a criticism of Victorian confidence.

I move, then, to a fourth assertion. Irving's acting drew attention to the risk that, should the grip on the self slacken, another and very different self might emerge from the secreted depths. The emotional memories which he called, or seemed to call, upon in order to create his haunted heroes and villains were as dark as the Ancient Mariner's and their self-tormenting recollection almost as peremptory. It was, I suggest, a characteristic of the late Victorian temper to see things in pairs, often in polarities, black or white, innocent or guilty, greatly good or vastly evil, Jekyll or Hyde, Lesurques or Dubosc, one or the other. The assumption, widely expressed in painting as well as in literature, seems to have been that we are not one but two people, that lurking inside every Lesurques is a Dubosc who must be strenuously suppressed, even if the effort of suppression curbs all spontaneity. Keep a grip on the upright self or the buried self will take over. But often, says Matthew Arnold in *The Buried Life*:

> But often, in the world's most crowded streets,
> But often, in the din of strife,
> There rises an unspeakable desire
> After the knowledge of our buried life.

It is the territory of melodrama. At his most disturbing, Irving acted like a man who had satisfied the 'unspeakable desire', had been there, like Conrad's Kurtz, and could report back 'The horror! the horror!' Many of the stalwart Victorians in the Lyceum audience would have been familiar with duplicity; it is the price that rectitude exacts from sexual drive, and that fact must have endowed Irving's vivid portrayals of guilt with a curiously licentious, even erotic, power. For, make no mistake about it, Irving based his finest creations on the idea of the divided self. Macbeth, he explained in his Manchester lecture on 'The Character of Macbeth', 'was a poet with his brain and a villain with his heart'. As King Lear, he 'tried to combine the weakness of senility with the tempest of passion'. Almost equally suggestive is the point made by Alan Hughes (1981, p. 146):

Irving's Othello of 1881 was such a contrast to his Iago that they might almost have been designed to be played together, like one of those recordings of a popular singer in a duet with himself.

His Shylock, consumed by hatred, was built on a contrasting basis of dignity and nobility. I am almost persuaded that *all* of Irving's successful performances were of characters in whom he could combine opposite qualities, most memorably when text and pictorial staging permitted him to paint what George Rowell (1981, p. 24) has splendidly called 'the diptych of demon and saint'. It is self-evident, I think, that the literary

fashion for secret life and dual personality stories and plays gratified a wish
to escape from the light of Victorian virtue into the darker truths. Irving
exploited it because it suited him. I cannot prove, but I do suggest, that
Irving the actor appealed to the respectable addicts of the Lyceum because,
like theirs in this era of the double life, his respectability concealed its own
opposite. His theatre was dedicated to beauty. He (1893, pp. 162–3) made
that plain in his address to the Philosophical Institution in Edinburgh:

in the consideration of the Art of Acting, it must never be forgotten that its ultimate aim is
beauty. Truth itself is only an element of beauty, and to merely reproduce things vile and
squalid and mean is a debasement of Art.

A few years later, in *Principia Ethica* (1903, p. 201), G. E. Moore would
assert: 'The beautiful should be defined as that of which the admiring
contemplation is good in itself.' Irving would have applauded, because he
liked, in public, to turn his back on the dark angel who makes 'all the
things of beauty burn/With flames of evil ecstasy',[1] but the stage picture at
the Lyceum was rarely complete until that dark angel had stepped into it.

One of the most revealing of Victorian pairings – and one to which
Irving was often drawn – was that of hypnotist and victim. By the end of
the century, hypnotism was being widely discussed in serious medical
journals. Charcot demonstrated its efficacy in the treatment of hysterical
patients to, among many others, the twenty-nine-year-old Freud, who
began to practise it in 1887. But it was not scientifically controlled
hypnotism that preyed on the Victorian mind. The *pater familias*, watching Irving in *The Bells* and conscious of his family beside him, would have
been fearing the bogey-man whose sinister gift might expose his sexual
scuffles in the servants' quarters. It is easy to understand why, in this era of
private vice and public virtue, the image of the hypnotist exercised so
strong a fascination. There are hundreds of references to be found in
nineteenth-century plays, more I suspect even than in novels. Perhaps
that is because the actor's art has sometimes verged on the hypnotic.
Certainly Irving's did. He prepared his theatre, from foyer to final tableau,
as carefully as the notorious Dr Mesmer prepared his clinic:

gorgeously curtained and carpeted . . . where Dr Mesmer, armed with a wand, officiated in
'anti-magnetic' clothes to the strains of music [beside] the celebrated 'baquet', a large vat
filled with water and magnetic material such as iron filings. From this projected metal bars,
which the patients, who also held one another's hands as at table-turning seances, grasped
during treatments.[2]

It was the mumbo-jumbo of Mesmer – as Mesmer had been decanted –
rather than the clinical interest of Charcot that held sway in the Victorian
imagination; and Irving, with his gift for the sinister, exploited the

nervousness of his audience. There is, perhaps, something mesmeric in all great actors, but reviewers of Irving refer more frequently to his animal magnetism, his cobra-like ability to hold audiences, than can be shuffled off as journalistic hyperbole. It is the actor's business to deceive, but it is also the actor's business to expose what is conventionally concealed – himself. Richard Ellman has cleverly explored the focal motif of exposure in Oscar Wilde's plays, suggesting that Wilde's own compulsion to confess was so powerful that it drew him to invite the scandal that destroyed him. My fifth and final assertion is that the confessional impulse was powerful in Irving, too, and that he sublimated it through his acting. The Lyceum, during the last three decades of the nineteenth century, was a place to which you could take your family, and yet its atmosphere was almost licentious, certainly neurotic, possibly subversive. At its centre was a gaunt, expressive man, acting out his personal failures, exhibiting them to people who felt but resisted the same impulse. In part the hypnotist, and in part the hypnotist's victim, Irving presented his century's image in the gloom and glory of his secret self. Shaw (1932, vol. 3, p. 203) apprehended that when he wrote of 'that strange Lyceum intensity which comes from the perpetual struggle between Sir Henry Irving and Shakespeare'.

NOTES

1 The quotation is from the scholar–critic Lionel Johnson's poem *The Dark Angel*.
2 Quoted from Gilbert Frankau's introduction to the translation of Mesmer's *Mesmerism*, 1948, p. 15.

The Criminal as Actor: H. B. Irving as Criminologist and Shakespearean

CARY M. MAZER

As soon as [he] had completed his education he went to [the capital] to study for the bar; but his father, who was becoming gradually involved in pecuniary embarrassments, due to his unfortunate speculations, found himself unable to afford the money necessary to the completion of his son's legal studies. By this circumstance . . . he was deprived of the one career for which his gifts and his inclinations eminently fitted him.

SUCH might describe the early career of H. B. ('Harry') Irving, the elder son of Henry Irving, the great Victorian actor–manager. While Harry and his younger brother Laurence were being educated at Marlborough School, their father decided that neither of his sons was to go on to the stage professionally, and so Harry chose the bar as a career. But due to his father's changed financial circumstances at the Lyceum, he was obliged to become a professional actor after all. He ultimately donned the purple of management, played many of his father's famous roles, and assayed several important Shakespearean parts, most notably Hamlet.

The biographical passage at the beginning of this essay is taken, though, from a biography not of but *by* H. B. Irving. The source is a chapter in *Studies of French Criminals* (1901, p. 9), one of three volumes of criminal biography written by H. B. Irving, MA Oxon. The young man in the passage is not H. B. Irving but one Lacenaire; the capital in question is not London but Paris; and the professional activity which the young man pursued, when his father's change in financial fortune did not enable him to complete his legal studies, was not acting but murder.

The similarities between the lives of H. B. Irving, actor, and Lacenaire, criminal, simply cannot be coincidental. Writes Irving: 'It is not too much to say that in every man there dwell the seeds of crime; whether they grow or are stifled in their growth by the good that is in us is a chance mysteriously determined' (1918, p. 14). For many years Irving belonged to a 'Crime Club', and Edward Marshall Hall, KC, reports that he would privately develop elaborate theories about the identity of criminals in

106

notorious unsolved cases, and would not hide his admiration for note-worthy murderers (Irving, 1920, pp. xiv–xv).

I do not wish to infer from this that H. B. Irving was, secretly, Jack the Ripper. Rather, I wish to suggest that Irving's affinities with criminals, and his writings on their lives and crimes, are important documents for the theatre historian; that Irving is drawing an important analogy between the criminal and the dramatic character, and between the criminal and the professional actor; and that his writings on crime and criminality provide an important gloss on his approach as an actor to several significant dramatic roles, including his major appearances in Shakespeare.

Hall felt that Irving's interest in crime was based on his recognition of the intrinsic drama of the criminal trial; but it was not the drama of the courtroom that interested Irving so much as the drama of the criminal's life:

> The annals of criminal jurisprudence exhibit human nature in a variety of positions, are at once the most striking, interesting and affecting. They present tragedies of real life, often heightened in their effect by the grossness of the injustice, and the malignity of the prejudices which accompanied them. At the same time, real culprits, as original charac-ters, stand forward on the canvas of humanity as prominent objects of our special study.
>
> (Irving, 1901, p. vii)

As Irving states elsewhere, 'In studying the criminal case we . . . get a post-mortem on the diseases from which they suffered' (interview in the *Era*, 7 Nov. 1908).

The theatrical metaphor is prominent in Irving's biographies of crimi-nals. Here is a sample of the language he uses to describe the life of Lacenaire: 'Every human society has what is called in the theatres a third substage' (1901, p. 3, quoting Hugo). Elsewhere in the same work Irving refers to the 'theatre of life', (p. 13), to accomplices 'distributing roles' and acting as supernumeraries, and to criminals making their 'last public appearance' at their executions. (pp. 21, 45). The criminal himself is a consummate actor, living a double life, assuming one disguise after another in public, and creating a persona at his trial while concealing his true self. Some criminals are pathological liars and role-players (Henri Charles); others use elaborate disguises to commit their crimes or to effect their getaways (Charles Peace, Derues, the Abbé Auriol); some stage-manage their own trials (Holmes, Eyraud and several political terrorists); others feign madness during their trial or incarceration (Lebiez, Dr Castaing, the Abbé Boudes); and several live seemingly respectable lives under assumed identities (Peace, Holmes, Boudes). One of Irving's criminal subjects had actually been an amateur actor: Henry Wainwright, an East End brushmaker acquainted with the management of the Pavilion

Theatre, occasionally appeared on the stage reciting Hood's poem, 'The Dream of Eugene Aram', an account of the guilt-pangs of a schoolmaster and scholar living a double life and awaiting his inevitable apprehension for murder.[1] 'Externally, to the world', writes Irving, 'Wainwright was a kind, genial, generous sort of fellow, vain, caring much for the regard of his fellow-men, no doubt amiable and pleasant at his home . . . But under his pleasing exterior Wainwright concealed dangerous qualities' (1920, pp. xl–xli). Irving's description of Wainwright's 'double motive', 'his desire to stand well in the eyes of his fellow-men, and, unknown to them, to indulge to the full the gratification of his passions' (1920, p. xli), might, with only minor alterations, serve as a description of the late Victorian and Edwardian actor: an artist courting public respectability, playing the role of the gentleman among the best society, and yet able to indulge, or at least to feign, the passionate emotions of the darker, as well as the fairer, side of the human soul. That the actor parades the illusion of 'the baser side' of human character before the public, while the criminal lets these instincts and passions find expression through secretive, violent, anti-social acts, does not alter the fact that both the actor and the criminal are role-players, manipulating the public perception of their personae, and living double, and even multiple, lives.

Irving's actor–criminals are, in effect, the authors of their own roles, the creators of their own personae. Irving is particularly fond of quoting criminals who considered themselves to be poets or philosophers (Lacen-aire, Charles, Lebiez, Aram), and he deftly analyses their writings for any hints of self-dramatisation or romantic posturing. He condemns such people, but he is undeniably fascinated by them.

This aspect of Irving's writings on the lives of criminals is significant at a time when actors were asserting the right to be considered creative, and not merely interpretative artists. As the elder Irving argued in 1895,[2] actors are as much creators of their roles as the dramatists whose words they are speaking. Actors are artists of the self; their souls are their inspiration, and their bodies their medium.

H. B. Irving concurred with his father on this point, but he draws an important distinction between criminals and actors: the former use their roles to conceal and to deceive, their romantic posturing being a form of self-deception; actors use their role-playing as a salutary form of self-expression. The best example which Irving provides of a passionate individual who is denied a healthy artistic outlet for his passions is that of Judge Jeffreys, the infamous Lord Chancellor who presided over the 'Bloody Assizes' under James II. Popular histories before Irving's *Life of*

Judge Jeffreys portrayed him as a blood-thirsty criminal. Irving, surprisingly, sees Jeffreys as merely a weak, selfish and venal character:

He possessed one of those extreme dispositions that charm us in the artist but depress us in the Judge, – a temperament passing in one moment from the height of self-satisfaction to the utmost depths of gloom and depression, over-confident in success, unduly prostrate in failure, intemperate, emotional. In the artist, emotion of this kind is translated into his work and lends it passion and intensity. But Jeffreys was a lawyer, not an artist, and, had he confined himself strictly to the exercise of his profession, might have learnt to subdue his dangerous tendencies towards an emotional expression of life.   (1898, p. 111)

According to Irving, the corrupt British legal system forced Jeffreys to give vent to his passionate temperament through political opportunism. Criminals give vent to their creative genius through role-playing and self-presentation, which enable them to commit ghastly crimes; actors give vent to their creative genius through the more socially acceptable act of creative self-presentation on the stage.

As we have seen, Irving's criminals are almost all in some sense actors. But what is the true identity of the criminal? Beneath all the roles, is there a real 'self'? When are criminals, like actors, offstage, or out of character? These are precisely the questions that Irving himself raises in his *Book of Remarkable Criminals*:

There is always and must be in every crime a *terra incognita* which, unless we could ever enter into the very soul of a man, we cannot hope to reach. Thus far we may go, no further. It is rarely indeed that a man lays bear his whole soul, and even when he does we can never be quite sure that he is telling us all the truth, that he is not keeping back some vital secret.
(1918, p. 35)

In his biographies, Irving stands at the edge of the *terra incognita* of the human soul and peers into the void. Many of Irving's criminal subjects (Prado, Albert Pel) conceal their origins, identities and motivations, others (Holmes, Charles, Mme Weiss, Mme Fenayrou, Bompard) have victims or partners who claim to be the subject of hypnotic influence or possession. In these cases, Irving calls into question the very integrity of the human soul.

Irving's *Last Studies in Criminology* centres almost entirely on cases where criminal justice miscarried, and in most of which the question of identity was crucial. Perhaps the most interesting case is one with direct dramatic and theatrical ties to the careers of Irving and his father: that of Joseph Lesurques, accused of murdering a courier en route to Lyons with Napoleon's payroll – a crime actually committed by a professional criminal, Dubosc. This historical incident, so illustrative of the unreliability of physiognomy, served as the source material for *The Lyons Mail*, Charles

Reade's English version of the French melodrama, *Le Courier de Lyons*, one of the most enduringly popular plays in the repertoire of Sir Henry Irving. H. B. Irving seems to be fascinated by the inability of the judicial system to read into the heart and soul of the individual. The soul of the criminal is, for him, often completely unknowable; it is often malleable, subject to the influence of, or hypnotic possession by, another; and physiognomy is an inaccurate barometer of the soul.

One more feature of the soul of the actor is analysed in Irving's writings, and this too has important implications with regard to dramatic literature and the art of the actor. Are criminals, Irving asks, capable of remorse? In the elder Irving's dramatic repertoire, they indeed are: Mathias in *The Bells* is haunted by the crime buried in his past, the murder of the Polish Jew, and, after a lifetime of ill-gotten prosperity, relives his crime in his imagination, and has a vivid fantasy of his trial and hypnosis, before dying in a fit of apoplectic remorse; and Eugene Aram, both in Hood's poem and in W. G. Wills's adaptation, lives in terror of apprehension and has nightmares of remorse.

But are the younger Irving's criminals remorseful?[3] Wainwright, imitating Hood's Aram, appeared to be so.

But [Irving adds] such are not the emotions usually felt by murderers. It is difficult to believe that anyone as imaginative as Hood's Aram would ever have committed a murder; he is certainly unlike the Aram of real life, who would seem to have been very little troubled by feelings of acute horror and remorse. Apprehension would better describe, as a rule, the feelings of a murderer who has an awkward secret buried in, as he hopes, some unsuspected and inaccessible place.   (1920, p. xxvii)

Irving writes about the real historical Eugene Aram, in an essay in *The Nineteenth Century*, as 'a cold and deliberate murderer, justifying his act to himself by a kind of sentimental vanity which does not hesitate before slander and falsehood to accomplish its pitiful end' (repr. 1907, p. 153). For Irving, the fact that Aram was a scholar only confirms his heartless criminal genius. That he was an artist, and wrote poetry before his execution, is consistent with Irving's depiction of morally insensible criminals as hypocrites and poseurs. 'Are these lines', Irving asks of one of Aram's poems, 'the dignified farewell of a martyred philosopher, or the egotistical exit of a criminal posing as a martyr and philosopher?' (1907, p. 159). Irving would undoubtedly want us to conclude the latter. Perhaps the most vivid example of the remorseless criminal in Irving's writings is Lacenaire, whose words he quotes: 'I kill without passion. Before killing, as after killing, I sleep equally well, and always peacefully. I am about to make an animate being inanimate, that is all. I see a light, I breathe on it, it goes out' (1901, p. 5).

110

Such, for Irving, is the height of criminal genius, which he defines in terms of the criminal's 'moral insensibility', the incapacity of the criminal to enjoy 'altruistic pleasure' (1901, p. 172).[4] But the 'moral insensibility' of the criminal leads us to a paradox in Irving's equation of the criminal and the actor. The criminal is an actor by virtue of his inability to feel, to identify, or to empathise; the actor, according to late nineteenth-century theories of acting, is the ultimate empathist, 'personating' the role through carefully developed powers of sensibility.[5] This paradox is an important one. Let us examine a detail from Irving's biography of Lacenaire: the young murderer-to-be was involved in a duel, the result of which, Irving writes, 'was as fatal to himself as to his adversary. The equanimity with which he found himself able to regard the latter's dying agony, convinced him that he was endowed with a peculiar insensibility to the sight of human suffering' (1901, p. 9). This type of story – a person studying his own emotions dispassionately – is precisely the kind of evidence cited by Diderot in arguing, in *The Paradox of Acting*, that the actor does not actually feel the emotions he is depicting on stage. But William Archer, in his famous nineteenth-century refutation of Diderot's paradox, *Masks or Faces?* (see above, p. 54), uses similar evidence to argue a different set of conclusions. A large number of actors Archer surveyed reported that at moments of great grief, such as a death in the family, they found themselves watching themselves, dispassionately, taking notes on their own emotional expressiveness. This, Archer concludes, is evidence that the actor has a dual, or multiple, consciousness, that actors can at the same instant both experience emotions and monitor themselves.[6] In the case of Lacenaire, dispassionate self-observation was evidence of insensibility; in Victorian acting, dispassionate self-observation is evidence of a dual consciousness, which in turn is proof that the actor is simultaneously sensible and artistically in control.

This concept of dual consciousness was particularly liberating for Victorian actors and actresses. Purveyors of the anti-theatrical prejudice would maintain that actors' identification with their roles rendered them vulnerable to pollution from the vices and flaws of their characters. But the concept of dual consciousness enabled actors to argue that they could 'personate' their roles to the full, while at the same time retaining the moral integrity of their true selves. John Martin-Harvey, a disciple of Henry Irving, even developed a theory that great actors, such as Irving, contain within their souls a multiplicity of selves, any of which could be drawn upon in the act of personation.[7] H. B. Irving agrees with this principle explicitly. He writes:

he [the actor] is as much the master of his fate, the captain of his soul, as the advocate who

111

pleads for the man he cannot help knowing to be guilty, the journalist who has to sustain a
cause against which his inward conviction rebels, or the novelist who throws the full energy
of his genius into the creation of some splendid type of human villainy.   (1906, p. 119)

The criminal has provided the model for Irving to explain the contradic-
tions inherent within acting. With no moral sensibility, he can become a
consummate actor. The actor, by contrast, sustains his mastery of his true
self by acknowledging the duality of his consciousness, the multiplicity of
his selves, the presence within him of both the diabolical and the humane,
both the vicious and the moral, both the anarchic and the artistically
controlled. Theories about the criminal soul, and theories about the
actor's selves, stand at the threshold of late nineteenth-century understandings of the human mind and the human soul.

Let us now look at Irving's work in the theatre, to see how his studies of
criminals may have affected his interpretations, and how the writings may
help us to appraise his acting.

With Eugene Aram and Lesurques and Dubosc he chose to write about
subjects which had already served as the bases for dramas. In addition,
references to literature are plentiful in the criminal biographies. He is sure
to note when leading actors and literary figures attended the trials and
executions of criminals and to tell of the taste of criminals who were
readers or theatregoers. Comparisons of criminals to fictional characters
abound: to those of Shakespeare, Ibsen and Maeterlinck, and, more
significantly, to those of J. Sheridan LeFanu, Edgar Allan Poe, and Robert
Louis Stevenson. These last examples are significant because they indicate
Irving's connection with late nineteenth-century neo-Gothic romanticism. Irving was very careful to distinguish between romanticism and the
modern, scientific tone of his studies in psychopathology: contrasting
Charles Peace with the eighteenth-century criminal Jack Sheppard, he
observes that 'in the nineteenth century the romance of crime has ceased
to be' (1918, p. 96). In fact, however, the neo-romanticism of Poe, of
LeFanu, of Stevenson and others, had rediscovered, and psychologically
modernised, the romantic criminal in line with Irving's 'modern' thinking. The guilt-obsessed criminal living a double life not only appears in
The Bells and 'Eugene Aram', but is the subject of Stevenson's first play,
Deacon Brodie (subtitled The Double Life), an early version of the Dr Jekyll
and Mr Hyde theme. Other contemporary treatments of related themes
included Bram Stoker's Dracula, George du Maurier's Trilby, Wilde's The
Picture of Dorian Gray and Max Beerbohm's The Happy Hypocrite.

As we have seen, theories of dual and multiple consciousness, even of
multiple personality, were central to the new emotionalist theories of

acting. In addition, the practice of multiple casting, in part a product of the self-displaying ambitions of the actor–manager, brought issues of multiple personality and the relation of physiognomy to the soul into prominence. Take, as an obvious example, the dramatic and theatrical premises of *The Lyons Mail*: Lesurques is so physiognomically similar to Dubosc that he is mistaken for the criminal and sentenced to the guillotine; the implication is that beneath similar faces lie two completely different souls. The star actor plays both Lesurques and Dubosc, the implication being that within a single person, within the same soul, lie two antithetical personalities.

H. B. Irving's acting career touched upon this dramatic and theatrical motif in several important ways. After his father's death in 1905, he took over such of his roles as Louis XI, Charles I, Mathias and Lesurques and Dubosc. But clearly these old plays, some of them more than half a century old, somehow spoke to the younger Irving's modern Gothic sensibilities, and gave him, despite their age, vehicles for the exposition of his modern psychological ideas.

Take, for example his interpretation of the double roles in *The Lyons Mail*. His Dubosc was purely malevolent, like his father's; but his Lesurques differed from his father's saintly martyr. According to his son Laurence, H. B. Irving 'represented him as a well-to-do man of the world, sure of his position as a reputable citizen and of the love of his family, scarcely able to believe that such a misfortune could have befallen him, and angrily protesting to the last his sense of outrage that he could be the victim of such fantastic charges' (L. Irving, 1971, p. 113). This interpretation is consistent with Irving's criminological writings and with the other roles in his repertoire. This Lesurques was like a Mathias without a guilty secret, a pillar of the community with a strong sense of self and identity, suddenly finding the parameters of his self erased, the integrity of his identity violated and his true knowledge of himself called into question. Lesurques angrily denies that he has any dark recesses in his soul. Meanwhile, the actor playing the part not only has these recesses but gives them expression in his other role, that of Dubosc.

Irving's portrayal of the dual roles in *The Lyons Mail* can be seen as a rough sketch for his appearance in J. Comyns Carr's adaptation of *Dr Jekyll and Mr Hyde* in 1910. The relation of Jekyll and Hyde to Lesurques and Dubosc is obvious. The two complementary sides of human character, which share the same face in *The Lyons Mail*, here share the same person. It is as though Lesurques recognises, and even cultivates, the presence of Dubosc within himself. In his writings on criminology, H. B. Irving had exploded the notion that morally insensible criminals were bothered by, or even capable of, genuine remorse. And yet Irving had inherited, in such roles as Mathias, a tradition of the remorseful criminal protagonist. Here, in *Dr Jekyll and Mr Hyde*, he could present a truly remorseful man, Jekyll, and a morally insensible criminal, Hyde, inhabiting the same body.

Another dimension of Irving's performance as Dr Jekyll and Mr Hyde deserves mention. His son Laurence described Irving's 'paroxysms' of uncontrollable rage, tantamount to spells of 'brief madness', which would come over him on occasion in private life. Evidently, this hidden side of Irving's personality found an outlet for expression in his portrayal of Hyde. In performance, increasingly as the play's run continued, '"the doors of the prison house" were indeed shaken and from them emerged an evil emanation that inspired terror and revulsion in his fellow players . . . fear, real not illusory, was abroad in the theatre . . . the essence of evil, hitherto an academic study, had been revealed to him with shattering intensity' (L. Irving, 1971, p. 160).[8] He had transformed Stevenson's neo-Gothic territory into an arena for psychological investigation consistent with his studies in criminology.

And so we come to H. B. Irving's interpretations of Shakespeare. Most of Irving's writings on the subject of Shakespeare's characters date from the time of his later criminological writings. The most significant document is the introduction to the *Book of Remarkable Criminals*. Here Irving compares the criminals in the volume (Peace, Holmes, Webster and others) to Shakespeare's criminals: Richard III, Iago, Claudius, Macbeth and Lady Macbeth. Shakespeare's Richard, unlike the historical Richard, who was probably motivated by the political 'exigencies of the situation', is a career criminal completely devoid of moral sensibility (p. 21). Iago, Irving feels, is closest to the criminals he describes in his volumes of biographies, a 'domestic' version of Richard (pp. 21–2). 'In Macbeth and Lady Macbeth', Irving writes, 'the germ of crime was latent; they wanted only favourable circumstances to convert them into one of those career couples who are more dangerous for the fact that the temptation to crime has come to each spontaneously and grown and been fostered by mutual understanding, an elective affinity for evil' (pp. 25–6). Claudius is, for Irving, the supreme political criminal, 'the most successful, and therefore the greatest, criminal in Shakespeare' (p. 22). Claudius' double life, his concealment of any signs of remorse, are virtually complete:

But for a supernatural intervention, a contingency against which no murderer could have been expected to have provided, the crime of Claudius would never have been discovered. Smiling, jovial, genial . . . King Claudius might have gone down in peace as the bluff hearty man of action, while his introspective nephew would in all probability have ended his days in a cloister, regarded with amiable contempt by his bustling fellowmen. (p. 22)

Irving's first Shakespearean roles were at Oxford, where he played Decius Brutus, King John and Boyet. For Ben Greet on tour he played a wide variety of roles: Othello, Benedick and Don Pedro, Leontes, Orlando and Jaques, Berowne, Orsino, Romeo, and ultimately Hamlet. Only when he was a supporting actor for George Alexander in the West End did he play some of Shakespeare's minor villains: Don John, and Oliver, which latter, Bernard Shaw reported, Irving played 'very much as anybody else would play Iago' (1932, vol. 2, p. 270).

In order to examine the relationship between Irving's writings on the criminal-as-actor and his Shakespearean acting, we must look at his performances, not as any of Shakespeare's criminals, but as Shakespeare's revenger-as-actor, Hamlet. Irving's appearances as Hamlet fall into four distinct phases: his performances for Greet, 1895; with the Asche–Stuart management of the Adelphi, 1905; under his own management, from 1908 to 1912; and again under his own management in 1916. Irving's conception of the role changed in each phase, and each related in a different way to his criminological writings.

In his first Hamlet, Irving seemed most concerned with understanding and dealing with the Prince's apparent madness. He visited several lunatic asylums while rehearsing and performing the role on tour, and engaged in an enormous conflict with the director over his conception. Irving claimed that he was not portraying the Prince as someone actually mad; 'but', he wrote to his fiancée during the rehearsals, 'it can hardly be said that Hamlet was a very reasonable man' (L. Irving, 1967, p. 246). Irving deliberately blurs the boundary between Hamlet's actual instability and the spectacle of madness which he presents to the rest of the court. Hamlet is a man carried away by his uncontrollable passions. Shaw noted the insensibility of Irving's Hamlet to his having killed Polonius: while Hamlet tells his mother that, at her age, 'the heyday of the blood is tame . . . And waits upon the judgment', Shaw felt that 'at Mr Irving's age the heyday of the blood does not wait upon the judgment, but has its fling (literally) regardless of reason' (1932, vol. 2, p. 115).

Perhaps it was Irving's experience in playing both Othello and Leontes for Greet that shaped his interpretation, inspiring him to draw a distinction between motivated passion and the mysteries of sudden derangement. Hamlet's sudden shifts from lucidity to passion, from moral qualms to seeming insensibility, are explained not by rational decisions or by concrete stimuli, but by contradictory, deeply felt, emotional attachments, and an almost schizophrenic division within Hamlet's personality. Irving's first Hamlet was not a criminal but a man with such conflicting sides to his personality that moments of anger, hatred and cruelty could erupt with astonishing speed and at a frightening and often dangerous pitch. Hamlet was a man standing at the edge of the abysses of his own personality.

These qualities were taken even further in Irving's 1905 Hamlet. Critics again noted the cruelty of the closet scene, Hamlet's callousness towards the corpse of Polonius and his rapid shifts in mood. This Hamlet was substantially more pathological, 'a man', his son writes, 'at the mercy of impulses that had he not been a Prince might have brought him to the gallows' (L. Irving, 1971, p. 90). This Hamlet was even more of a manipulator, using madness as a means of manipulating the court, and even his charm and sensitivity to manipulate his friends, including the trusted Horatio.

The general trend of Irving's first two Hamlets is followed by a surprising shift in the third. In a lecture at Sydney University in Australia when he was on tour with the role in 1911, Irving presented an analysis of the character of Hamlet. Hamlet is decidedly not mad, though he does briefly cross the borders of sanity in his wild response to the Ghost. It is this sudden explosion of uncontrolled passion that inspires Hamlet to use an antic disposition as a social disguise before the court. Hamlet, for Irving, is now simply a weak man who cannot excape from the 'radical infirmity' of his character; when his mettle is finally tested, by his mission of revenge, he fails, tragically, to rise to the occasion (H. Irving, 1911a, p. 19). Irving's fourth Hamlet was a step further in this direction. Hamlet is again a weak character called upon to be a man of action; but this time, to emphasise the distance between the actor and the desired act, Irving cut the play unconventionally, emphasising the narrative flow, and thereby clarifying the line of action which Hamlet is called upon, and fails, to execute.

Does this shift, from madness to sanity, from near schizophrenia to mere philosophical pusillanimity, represent a retreat from an interpretation based on an understanding of the criminal mind? Perhaps Irving, having played Dubosc and Mr Hyde, no longer thought Hamlet's consuming paroxysms of passion a sufficient explanation for his ability to impel the action of the play forward. Hamlet's temporary insanity, in his scene with the Ghost, lets him stand at the edge of the abyss for one brief moment only. Like Lacenaire observing his reaction to the man he has just killed in a duel, Hamlet's self-reflection, his one brief glimpse into the *terra incognita* of his soul, gives him the ability to become a role-player. He becomes, as an actor, the captain of his soul, even though he cannot become a man of action, truly the master of his fate.

Irving's experience in playing Shakespeare's criminal heroes was limited to playing Iago, in Lewis Waller's production of *Othello* at the Lyric Theatre in 1906. Irving's Iago was written about favourably by critics, who recognised his interest in criminology and detected resemblances to his father's interpretation of the role. From all reports, one can conclude that Irving consciously sought to play, in Iago, the type of morally insensible pseudo-philosophical criminal genius that was his favourite subject in his criminal biographies. This Iago was a self-proclaimed Nietzschean superman, disdainful of all whom he deemed to be his inferiors, placing himself above conventional morality, seeking both personal gain and the sheer pleasure of proving his intellectual superiority; in short, an incarnation of Lacenaire.[9]

Was Irving a great Shakespearean actor? This is difficult to assess. Some critics praised his 'realistic' diction, and felt that his Hamlet was someone one might meet coming around the next street corner; others criticised his inability to speak verse with any musicality, and felt that his Hamlet lacked tragic stature. But H. B. Irving's dubious success as a Shakespearean actor should not discourage us from taking a closer look at his art and craft. It is, after all, no easy task to assess the greatness of an entire generation of Shakespearean actors, those who were the successors of Henry Irving. The classical actors, such as Johnston Forbes-Robertson, Frank Benson and John Martin-Harvey; the debonair walking gentlemen such as George Alexander; the costumed swashbucklers such as Fred Terry, Julia Neilson and Lewis Waller; the modern psychological realists, such as Mrs Patrick Campbell and the Irving brothers; the character actors, such as Beerbohm Tree, Arthur Bourchier and Oscar Asche; and the rising generation, such as Henry Ainley, Lillah McCarthy and others – all these actors were at the crossroads of the drama and theatre of their day, caught between a supposed Shakespearean tradition, a moribund romantic costume repertoire which was becoming increasingly ludicrous and overblown, the fashion for dramas and comedies of modern society, and the new repertoire of social consciousness. To understand the Shakespearean acting of the period, we must see the Shakespearean repertoire as the actors of the day saw it: as a set of characters conforming to particular understandings of human personality and motivations, to be presented on the stage according to an aesthetic of performance which was rapidly changing.

I began with a quotation which had remarkable autobiographical implications. I conclude with another, a remark made by the presiding judge to Henri Charles during his trial: 'You neglected your legal studies for the study of psychology, which seems to have had a disastrous effect on your mind' (1901, p. 220). Perhaps this too applies to H. B. Irving. But Irving's study of psychology resulted in a body of writings on criminology which provide the theatre historian with a valuable document for determining late Victorian and Edwardian attitudes towards character, drama and acting.[10]

NOTES

1 Wainwright was connected to the Irvings in two ways: 'Eugene Aram' was a favourite recitation piece of Henry Irving; and Wainwright himself was a personal acquaintance of Frank Tyars, who became a supporting actor and reliable 'table leg' in the companies of both Henry and, later, H. B. Irving.

2 This lecture was given at the Royal Institution on 1 February 1895, and published in the *Fortnightly Review*, n.s. 57 (1895), 369–79. For responses to Irving's contention, see Ouida, 'Mr Irving on the Art of Acting', *Nineteenth Century*, 37 (1895), 786–97, and Max Beerbohm, 'Actors', repr. in Beerbohm, 1899.

3 The literary and theatrical transformations of the Aram story are described in Tyson, 1983, though Tyson fails to see the connection between Aram and Mathias, whom she mislabels 'the Polish Jew, an agonized, blood-guilty Shylock type' (p. 124).

4 The concept of 'moral insensibility' links Irving to one contemporary school of thought regarding crime and deviant behaviour. The science of 'criminal anthropology', developed in Italy by Lombroso and Ferri, following Darwin (see *The Descent of Man*, 2nd edn, London 1881, p. 137), believed that criminals represented a reversal of evolutionary progress, (a 'degeneracy' or 'atavism'), and meticulously documented the supposed physical and intellectual inferiorities of criminals, such as unusual hair formations, palm spans, cranial slopes and low intelligence. Irving rejected Lombroso and Ferri categorically (see 1918, p. 12), preferring to study the 'instinctive' criminals of extraordinary genius, and citing what Goldwin Smith calls 'the most complete absence of moral sense' (1898, pp. 218–20). For a survey of both the ethical and the anthropological arguments current in Irving's time, see Havelock Ellis, *The Criminal*, 5th edn, London, 1916.

5 The concept of 'personation' is presented by George Henry Lewes, 1875. Several late Victorian discussions of 'emotionalist' acting were collected by Brander Mathews in *Papers on Acting*, repr. 1958. For a modern critical summary and bibliography of the Victorian debate on the art of acting, see D. J. Gordon and John Stokes, 'The References of *The Tragic Muse*', in Goode, 1972.

6 See Archer, 1888; repr. 1957, chs. 6, 10. The specific example of the actor observing his own grief is given by Talma in 1825, in an essay which appeared in English in pamphlet form in 1883 as 'Talma on the Actor's Art' with a preface by Henry Irving (repr. Mathews, 1958). Talma supports the emotionalist position; Coquelin cites Talma's story to support the anti-emotionalist position in 'Art and the Actor' (1880; repr. Mathews, 1958, p. 24).

7 See 'Some Reflections on the Art of Acting', in G[reen]-A[rmytage], 1932, pp. 43–55.

8 Irving had already explored the duality of the soul and the mechanism of guilt and remorse in another Stevenson piece, W. L. Courtney's adaptation of the short story, 'Markheim'. The story is an extended dialogue between a thief who has just murdered a shopkeeper, and a mysterious 'other', who together debate the connection between evil, character and deed. Here, too, Irving was able to represent both criminality and remorsefulness by dividing the psyche into two characters, though for stage purposes Markheim and the Other could not be doubled.

9 Laurence Irving, who played Iago to Beerbohm Tree's Othello in 1912, probably succeeded far better than his elder brother in presenting the Nietzschean criminal, catching a fly during one of his soliloquies and burning it to death in a candle flame. Laurence's contact with Russian literature and philosophy, his attempted suicide, his adaptation of *Crime and Punishment* (as *The Unwritten Law*), his performance as Raskolnikov and his repeated attempts to adapt and stage LeFanu's *Uncle Silas* warrant close scholarly attention.

10 Research for this essay was supported by a grant from the American Council of Learned Societies, and the preparation of this essay was supported by a Summer Research Grant from the University of Pennsylvania.

PART 3

Shakespeare Ancient and Modern

PREFACE

WHAT is widely considered to be the definitive mid-twentieth-century production of *King Lear*, that by Peter Brook in 1962, was much influenced by the ideas of Jan Kott whose *Shakespeare Our Contemporary* includes a chapter entitled 'King Lear, or Endgame'. Accustomed as we are to search for relevance in Shakespeare's plays the Victorians' perception of the relationship between their age and the events and characters depicted in Shakespeare's plays provides an interesting contrast.

A characteristic response is recorded by Queen Victoria herself when she attended Macready's *King Lear* in February 1839. She had visited his previous revival in 1834 and greatly annoyed that social reformer Harriet Martineau (1877, vol. 2, pp. 119–20) by her inattentiveness. This may account for Macready's diary entry for 18 February 1839: 'Acted King Lear well. The Queen was present, and I pointed at her the beautiful lines, "Poor naked wretches".' Clearly this was to good effect for the next day the young monarch recorded in her journal:

Talked to Lord Melbourne of my having seen *King Lear* and its being a fine play; talked of it for some time, of the way in which it was acted now at Covent Garden. 'I always thought him [Lear] a foolish old fellow', said Lord Melbourne. 'It's a rough coarse play . . . written for those times, with exaggerated characters.'   (Esher, 1912, vol. 2, pp. 121–2)

In dismissing *Lear* as 'a rough coarse play . . . written for those times' Lord Melbourne was subscribing to the orthodox view of the play, from Nahum Tate – via Dr Johnson – to 1838–9 and beyond, that the events depicted in it were so monstrous that either they had to be rewritten with a more comforting view of the human condition or placed firmly in an historical context remote from the lives of the present.

The latter approach accorded well with the contemporary enthusiasm for antiquarianism, which was often seen to have an educational function as a means of showing audiences how past ages lived.[1] Dr Bratton – and

121

Professor Carlisle with reference to *Cymbeline* – emphasise the importance that Macready attached to historical setting, a view shared by Irving and Beerbohm Tree, both of whom employed the distinguished academician Alma-Tadema as scenic designer. The question arises as to whether this dominating vogue for antiquarianism (Shakespeare Ancient) precluded any awareness of his relevance to Victorian society (Shakespeare Modern).

Going back to 1838, at least one critic was prepared to concede that even in *King Lear* Shakespeare was depicting 'incidents' which, if not within the experience of the average respectable Victorian playgoer, were possibly within that of his better-travelled contemporary:

> Those, indeed, who can form no other notion of existence than what they see around them, may call these incidents unnatural; but he who can even throw his eyes to the East, not to mention past history wherever society is unsettled, will find no difficulty in matching them.   (*Spectator*, 27 Jan. 1838)

In fact there were examples close at hand. The winter of 1838 was very severe – ice on the Thames – and the press carried regular accounts of the homeless. The same issue of the *Spectator* described more than 400 people huddling together for shelter in Mayhouse Yard: 'it may be that some respectable but poverty stricken people may prefer the clean straw and quiet of the shelter'.

If the problems of homelessness proved as intractable in Victorian Britain as in 'those times', help was at hand for those afflicted with elderly parents of unsound mind:

> Invalids – Imbecility or weakness of intellect. –
> A highly respectable family, occupying a spacious mansion, surrounded with several hundred acres of land, in the most salubrious part of the South of England [Dover?], would be happy to receive for residence a LADY OR GENTLEMAN, who, from bodily or mental infirmity, might require peculiar care and attention with every domestic comfort, Christian kindness, and suitable attendance . . . A suite of apartments, with the use of a carriage, saddle horses, or pony phaeton, for air and exercise abroad, or within the private grounds can be offered.   (*The Times*, 26 Jan. 1838)

The association between Lear's madness and that of King George III was, as Dr Bratton points out, publicly acknowledged between 1810 and 1820, but thereafter any identification between the monarchy and its forerunners in Shakespeare was carefully selected for more patriotic ends. *Cymbeline*, depicting, as it does, Britain's resistance to an imperial power, is an interesting example. Professor Carlisle notes of Macready's production that 'he chose a period somewhat later than Cymbeline's, when British men of rank had begun wearing a simple Roman tunic', indicating that they had partly assumed the mantle of Roman civilisation. However the insistence on national pride is demonstrated by the refusal of this Cymbeline to pay tribute to the Romans.

This ambiguous attitude towards Roman imperialism – partial emulation, partial patriotic resistance – is developed as the century progresses. With Queen Victoria declared Empress of India in 1877 her subjects did indeed have to look back to Rome for comparable imperial grandeur. Thus Dr Bratton, though describing Irving's Lear in 1892 as 'a Viking primitive, inhabiting the ruins of a civilised nation. The sets were Roman palaces in a state of decay . . . ', also points out: 'the Anglo-Saxon period was itself in vogue, a major rediscovery in language, politics and art had jumped very well with Imperialist visions of English history'. Again the imperial Roman inheritance is balanced with the assertion of national history.

By the turn of the century any residual tendency to hark back to the Britain of Roman subjugation was overwhelmed by the powerful identification of the British Empire with its Roman precursor, as Ralph Berry demonstrates. Professor Berry refers to the 'slow-moving volatility' of Shakespearean drama, a process which is illustrated by the way in which the plays under discussion here were variously interpreted during the reign of the Queen–Empress.

NOTE

1 Michael Booth, 'Shakespeare as Spectacle and History; The Victorian Period', *Theatre Research International*, 2 (1976), 99–113.

The Lear of Private Life:
Interpretations of *King Lear* in the
Nineteenth Century

J. S. BRATTON

W HAT follows is an attempt to sketch out the fate of one of
Shakespeare's plays within the pictorial, illustrative stage conditions described by Michael Booth, and to see beyond the effects
of those conditions to a further interpretative level. Victorian productions
of *King Lear* must strictly be said to begin with Macready's staging of the
play, during January and February 1838, for eight nights. This is also, of
course, the first time the Shakespearean text, including the character of
the Fool and excluding all of Nahum Tate's alterations, is recorded as
having been played in England since 1681. But I feel it is not as suitable a
point at which to begin a consideration of the Victorian *King Lear* as it
might at first appear. Theatrical memory is fickle, but not necessarily
short; expectations mould performances, and the position of *King Lear*
critically, as well as in the theatre, for the previous half-century influenced
Macready himself profoundly and shaped the reception of his production.

King Lear was in a peculiarly ambiguous and difficult position when
Macready began his theatrical career. At the beginning of the nineteenth
century it shared with several other Shakespearean plays the situation of
having been comprehensively rewritten and performed in various different
versions for over a century. Garrick, the great restorer and transformer of
texts, was also a great Lear, and he continually tinkered with the play
during the thirty-four years he had performed the role, never restoring
Shakespeare's plot, but perpetually imping out with his poetry the broken
wing of Nahum Tate's verse. On Garrick's relinquishing of the role in 1776
others were free once more to attempt it; but J. P. Kemble, who soon
became the chief possessor, had in this instance none of Garrick's feeling
for the restoring of Shakespearean sense, and played a statuesque old king
in the Restoration version of the tragedy. No one much liked it. His Lear
was his Coriolanus grown intolerably old and gone improbably mad. Leigh

Hunt, for example, reviewing Kemble's revival for *The Examiner* (22 May 1808), spoke disparagingly of Kemble's 'gloomy carelessness' in the role and his inappropriate stiffness and gravity. Of course the great ones of the Regency theatre did not respond to such upstart Romantic critics with automatic acceptance of their views. Kemble was going through considerable difficulties in holding together his traditional theatrical enterprise at Drury Lane, beset as it was by the depredations of the politically ambitious Sheridan and of the rapacious shareholders, as well as by outrageously expensive and antiquated stage and management techniques, violently shifting public taste and appalling physical surroundings. Possessed of the stiff-necked courage which drove him forward in the teeth of these, he was not the man to yield to pressure about his plays from such an upstart and puny lobby as was constituted by cockney critics like Leigh Hunt. So his King Lear staggered on, speaking Tate's text, costumed in false shoulders, lace collar and silk stockings, white moustachios and a feathered hat, interpreted as being in the last stages of a decrepit but dignified old age, and in his madness resembling nothing so much as a 'melancholy mad statue' (Hunt).

Then came the moment which set some sort of final seal on the decline of *King Lear*: the madness of George III reached such a pitch, in the autumn of 1810, that the play was withdrawn from the stage. J. P. Kemble (who retired in 1817) never played it again. And then, with no chance of a theatrical presence to refute them, the Romantic critics produced a statement of their position which effectively wiped not only Tate's version of *King Lear*, but Shakespeare's too, off the theatrical map, and captured it for the closet. Charles Lamb wrote in 1811: 'the Lear of Shakespeare [perhaps as opposed to the Lear of Tate, which Lamb had seen performed] cannot be acted . . . Lear is essentially impossible to be represented on a stage.' He added that the experience of the play, a profound and moving one, is accessible to the imagination only through the page: 'while we read it, we see not Lear, but we are Lear, – we are in his mind, we are sustained by a grandeur which baffles the malice of daughters and storms; in the aberrations of his reason, we discover a mighty irregular power of reasoning, . . . exerting its powers . . . at will upon the corruptions and abuses of mankind'. He thus offered a wonderfully comprehensive Romantic reading of the play, but one which specifically cut it off from the spectacle of 'an old man tottering about the stage with a walking stick' which makes us simply 'want to take him into shelter and relieve him. That is all' (C. Lamb, 1903–5, vol. 1, pp. 97–111).

This was the new intellectualism with a vengeance: it asserted that the theatre of the mind possessed such advantages over the stage as took this particular drama from the tawdry playhouse for ever. Even when the old King died, and the theatre could once again challenge for its possession, Lamb's pronouncement, apparently embodying and justifying all the anti-theatrical pressures of nineteenth-century evangelicalism and middle-class snobbery, hung over the play like a jinx. His lavish praise of King Lear amounted, in fact, to a wholesale condemnation – for if a dramatic poem is not a play able to be staged, then it has already failed, and any attempt to produce it will only demonstrate the inadequacy of author and actor alike. In its ten compulsory years off the stage, King Lear could have sunk out of sight, and remained unacted for the rest of the century. In fact, it did remain on the defensive throughout that time, and never shook off the dead hand of misplaced critical adulation of the Bard outside the theatre.

This was not immediately apparent when the ban was lifted, early in 1820 (George III died on 30 January; the theatres were closed until 19 February). There were managements chafing to get their hands on the play, as the hottest property of the season. At Drury Lane Elliston flung himself, and Edmund Kean, into a production. Essentially a man of the theatre, Elliston was not very interested in the textual purists' arguments for Shakespeare's King Lear. For him Tate's happy ending, the additional scenes for Cordelia, and the added love motif, all made sound box-office sense, and the part of Lear, monstrously exaggerated and isolated into a point-studded vehicle for a virtuoso actor, was just right for Edmund Kean. Elliston had his finger sufficiently on the pulse of the age, however, to feel it necessary to contribute something from the stage management side that would mark his King Lear as a modern production; and, in discussion with Kean himself, he hit upon a single device of staging that would embody the Romantic spirit in which the play was now being read: to match the modern focus upon intense feeling and irrational emotion, they would create a visual correlative for Lear's stupendous madness – they would stage a Romantic storm.

Edmund Kean had wanted more than this. In correspondence with Elliston he poured scorn on Kemble's costuming of the character, his 'Silk Hose an article never seen in this country until the end of the 15th Century – those who wore the Saxon Hosa were equally incorrect Holinshed places the reign of Leir. Anno Mundi – 3105. Nearly 800 Years before the first conquest by Caesar . . . Garrick was equally erroneous in wearing a Hat. Hats were never worn but by Cardinals – till Charles the 9th of France entered Rouen in triumph in 1449' – and so on.[1] But Elliston summoned up the basic theatrical commonsense in the face of pretentious-ness which kept him afloat despite his many wild adventures. He asserted in the Advertisement to the edition of the play which he hastened to publish that 'in such a case [as *King Lear*, full of anachronistic references], to talk of correctness or incorrectness [of period] would be something more than absurd; all that is left is to choose the costume of any period, not too recent, and adhere to it with fidelity, or if any additions are made, to let them be the products of fancy' (Elliston, 1820, p. vi). So much for Holinshed. They used a Saxon setting and fanciful Saxon costuming, as Garrick had done in his later performances.

Garrick had already, of course, felt the stirrings of an interest in theatrical spectacle, as his employment of more, and more distinguished, scene-painters demonstrated; but his designer, de Loutherbourg, had one new trick, the collection of scenic illusions which he called his Eidophusikon, which Garrick had not been able to bring to the Drury Lane stage. De Loutherbourg had built and exhibited it in a small box; now Edmund Kean and some friends of his, claiming expertise as machinists, magnified the thing to full stage size, to produce the storm effects for the 1820 *King Lear*, adding to it the first theatrical use of magic lantern projections. James Winston, the stage manager, was delighted with the effect: 'King Lear revived with entirely new scenes, particularly the storm scene in third act lighted by a new process from the top of the stage. Very successful', he noted;[2] but on the first night the critics were not yet so convinced about such methods applied to legitimate plays. Black smoke rolled unexpectedly and suffocatingly across the first rows; a terrible racket drowned Kean's personal efforts and reduced his performance of the scene virtually to a pantomime. The fullest description is Joe Cowell's:

the hurricane was after the picture by De Loutherbourg called 'Storm on Land', but to give this additional effect, the sea was introduced in the background, the billows, painted after nature, 'curling their monstrous heads and hanging them with deafening clamours' – trees were made to see-saw back and forth, accompanied with the natural creak! creak! attending the operation; Winston had hunted up, *without expense to the management*, every infernal machine that was ever able to spit fire, spout rain, or make thunder, and together [these] were brought into play behind the entrances. Over head were revolving prismatic coloured transparencies, to emit a continual-changing supernatural tint, and add to the unearthly character of the scene [so that] King Lear would one instant appear a beautiful pea-green, and the next sky-blue, and, in the event of a momentary cessation of the rotary motion of the magic lantern, his head would be purple and his legs Dutch-pink.

According to Cowell, who seems to have had something of a grudge against the Drury Lane stage management, the carpenters competed to see who could make the most noise, the packthreads nodding the trees were distinctly visible, and Kean begged Winston to slack it all off a bit for the second night (Cowell, 1845, p. 47). Nevertheless, the production was a distinct success by the standards of Elliston's management, which had not

127

so far contrived to please either the critics or the public, but which achieved the comparatively long run of twenty-six performances in six weeks with this. The hint was not wasted. In the next year Elliston moved steadily away from Shakespeare revived to follow the path to popularity and solvency opened by the successes of stage spectacle.

The success of the Drury Lane *King Lear* was at least partly Edmund Kean's personal triumph, in spite of the special effects; Lear became one of his favourite roles – increasingly so as premature old age and personal detraction made him feel Lear's sorrows with a keen self-identification. At Covent Garden in February 1820 the management was not fortunate enough to have the services of an Edmund Kean. Macready, then only twenty-seven, first accepted the tempting role, then jibbed at essaying it in a hurry and in the old Tate text. He undertook Edmund, and critics used his performance as a stick with which to beat the unfortunate Junius Brutus Booth, who accepted Lear. Macready genuinely possessed the scholarship to which Kean's letters to Elliston pretended, and he was personally influenced by contemporary respectability and abhorrence of the theatrical. He did not even want to be on the stage; but since he was already sufficiently well established there to make his own decisions, he refused to lend himself to such a travesty in ill-considered haste. *King Lear* was very important to him as a symbol of what Shakespeare should be, as opposed to what the theatre had made of the Bard.[3]

His sense of his personal understanding of the play, and its superiority to the vulgarly theatrical, can be felt if one contemplates the copy (preserved in the Forster Collection at the Victoria and Albert Museum) on which, some time in the 1820s or early 1830s, he made cuts and notes towards a performance. It is of course a Shakespearean text, not Tate, and he cuts chiefly to bowdlerise a little and to remove the Fool, whom he did not at first feel could be restored. Thus far the decisions are practical and could be theatrical; but his annotations of the role of Lear are a different matter. They are intensely personal, and concerned with the poetry, with his experience as a reader: creating a performance, certainly, but primarily the performance in the mind, as described by Charles Lamb. They are so private, so removed from, even opposed to, any idea of usefulness to a stage manager, that they are chiefly in Latin, with excursions into Greek. The learned languages are an extremely revealing affectation. He indicates by them that he thinks and writes about the play not simply as an actor, but rather as a scholar, and so 'naturally' chooses to write in the scholarly tongues. It was not until 1834 that Macready agreed to bring this vision into confrontation with theatrical reality – theatricality, indeed, at its very worst, in the person of his *bête noire*, Alfred Bunn, under whose management he performed Shakespeare's text, without the Fool, at Drury

Lane and Covent Garden. He later swept this event so completely under the carpet that he is quoted in the Variorum Edition of *King Lear* (1880) as claiming that the play was not restored until 1838, when he himself staged it as manager at Covent Garden.

Macready naturally plumed himself on the restoration of Shakespeare's text. It was an example of the practical steps he could take in answer to criticism of the theatre – it showed that theatre could be scholarly, artistic, serious, an important intellectual activity, the shrine of a national drama. As a manager he could take other measures to back up that claim; he was able to extend his good taste and learning to the setting of the play. Garrick and Edmund Kean had toyed with antiquarianism in setting; Elliston introduced elaborate stage illusion for the storm; Macready drew these together into the Victorian mode that is the focus of these papers, that of spectacular, illustrated Shakespeare. His 1838 *King Lear* was firmly set in Saxon times, with Druid stone circles, round-capped soldiers, semi-circular arches and all the fuss and elaboration of 'historicist' sets. It is important to stress that the reason for this was extra-theatrical. Macready, not unlike some of his successors in politically and socially orientated companies today, hoped to justify the theatre by making it a living lesson, in this case a lesson in national poetry and national history brought tellingly to life.

Macready's lead was followed by Samuel Phelps in 1845, Charles Kean in 1858, Edwin Booth in 1881 and Henry Irving in 1892, in a crescendo of Anglo-Saxon attitudinising. The historical/scholarly was the central Victorian method of presenting, and defending the presentation of, Shakespeare's plays; it justified the theatrical in anti-theatrical terms. And the Anglo-Saxon period was itself in vogue, a major rediscovery in language, politics and art that jumped very well with imperialist visions of English history. But Elliston's commonsensical pronouncement that 'to talk of correctness or incorrectness' to any period in *King Lear* is 'something worse than absurd' seems to loom menacingly in the background of all these productions; for none of them, with the possible exception of Edwin Booth's, was more than a *succès d'estime*, and in Irving's case it was not even that.

The managers were themselves conscious of the problems in making the spectacular, historical approach stick in the case of *King Lear*. Phelps, perhaps because of his financial constraints at Sadler's Wells, seems to have been extremely sceptical and sensible about it. He relied for the respectability and seriousness of his production upon textual purity, upon closeness to Shakespeare rather than to some impossible historical vision. His text was unique in the period for its genuine fidelity not only to the words Shakespeare wrote, but to the order in which he arranged them:

Macready, Charles Kean and Irving all silently allowed Tate's rearrangement of the events of the action to shape their supposedly restored texts. Phelps's settings, Saxon in inspiration, were mostly carried out in an 'ideal and simple' manner which made his fuller text possible by cutting down the scene-changing time; his chief concession to spectacle was, once again, an uncomfortably naturalistic storm (*Athenaeum*, 8 Nov. 1845).

Charles Kean, whose text G. K. Hunter (1970) has described as '*King Lear* minced', represents the opposite pole. He filled the stage with boarhounds and yule logs and all the antiquarian detail imaginable; but even he, it has been shown by Christopher Murray (*Theatre Survey*, 11 (1970)) was comparatively restrained in his elaboration of *King Lear*, spending far less on the production than was characteristic of him. This must have been partly because it came at the end of an expensive season, but perhaps there was also some sense that no amount of money could, in this instance, merge the play and the historical exhibition. Most critics spoke, in terms of approval, of the subordination of the spectacle to the action. They were presumably not familiar with the thousand or so lines of the play that his staging obliged Kean to cut out.

Henry Irving also economised – for him – on the staging of *King Lear*, in the down-swing from *Henry VIII* in the same year, which had cost £16,500 and been swamped by its sets. For *King Lear* he was still archaeological, but he used simpler constructions, old-fashioned drops and wings. To modern eyes he seems to have made the best possible use of his historical approach, because he seems to have created from a setting in a precise period – 'a time shortly after the departure of the Romans' from Britain – an artistic logic which justifies the spectacle in terms of the play, rather than for its own sake. It gave him a set of images which offer a theatrically very expressive correlative for some of the most important themes of the drama. His Lear was a Viking primitive, inhabiting the ruins of a civilised nation. The sets were Roman palaces in a state of decay, with Lear (and also Albany) inhabiting them as squatters, sharing with the natural world, roots of saplings and festoons of ivy, a temporary lodging whose decay was being hastened by their living presence. These were the works of giants, as the Anglo-Saxon poet had called Roman remains; and they were incomprehensible to giants of a different kind like Lear, whose presence there signalled dissonance and danger. This gave, as one might say, a semiotic polarity on which to build the production, between symbols of grandeur and signs of decay. Lear misused the edifices of civilisation, turned them to self-aggrandisement and a setting for his raw power, making magic within what was once a rational framework; the clash produced lightnings and destruction. Several levels of conflict were embodied in the symbolic opposition. His misuse of political and civil power, bringing the grandeur around him into disarray, was echoed in his misuse of the personal, emotional power of love; and the decay outside mirrored the decay of his mind. Like the palaces, the glorious structure of his reason was invaded by wild things; disruptive natural forces broke the strength of his control and turned it upon itself in collapse and ruin. By the end, the man-made structures were all gone, stripped away, leaving him to die at the foot of a backdrop of Dover cliffs, himself and all his retinue overshadowed by the towering, unchangeable natural world, and dazzlingly lit as if by an indifferent sun (Hughes, 1981, p. 135; Robertson, 1931, p. 169).

Yet even this coherent and magnificent application of Victorian stage methods was not enough to lift the jinx on the play. The public made polite noises about some of these productions, but stayed away from them all. Though Queen Victoria went four times to see it, Charles Kean's eight-week run was far too short to recoup the cost of his production; for Irving the play ran seventy-six nights, but was never revived or toured, and passed into his canon as a disaster (Hughes, 1981, p. 117).

The Victorian failure to come to grips with *King Lear* may be partly explained by the fact that the play resists the urge to set the actor in a solid realisation of an actual period. But looking beyond that obsession, there are, I feel, other aspects of these productions that can be seen to have influenced their reception. In particular, a recurrent interpretation of the play itself that contributed to its failure to take effect. Once again, the key to this aspect of the Victorian *King Lear* can be found in the events of 1820.

When Edmund Kean made his not uncontroversial impact in the play at Drury Lane, the management at Covent Garden persuaded Junius Brutus Booth to compete with him. Hazlitt, determined to be fair and judicious in his own hot-headed way, was not at all sure that Kean won in this round of the competition; he condemned some parts of Kean's performance as 'downright rant' and found things to praise in Booth (*The London Magazine*, May 1820). But this was not the general verdict, and Booth's Lear was not very well received. At the end of the season Booth went off, as he had in 1819, to appear at a minor theatre, the Royal Coburg, during the recess of the patent houses in the spring and summer. Glossop, the manager of the Coburg, was at that moment engaged in defending an action brought against him by the Patentees for putting on *Richard III* in the previous season, for the sake of displaying Booth's talents in the role. The play had been 'melodramatised'; the managers and Booth and the spy who was sent to inform on Glossop argued at length about whether or not the music, necessary to this process, was audible. Glossop had a very good argument, in natural justice, in the leeway which the magistrates had previously allowed him over such pieces; but in fact the law, once invoked, was clearly against him, and he lost the case. While this was going on, he could hardly repeat his offence in his new season, by staging a 'melodramatised' version of Booth's latest legitimate role, King Lear. He commissioned instead, for Booth's first appearance of the summer season, a play entitled (in large capitals) THE LEAR OF PRIVATE LIFE, and (in smaller print) 'or, Father and Daughter, founded on the famous novel by Mrs Opie'. The bill matter – written, like the play, by the house dramatist W. T. Moncrieff, who had also done the *Richard III* rewrite – is interesting. It puffs both Booth and Mrs Opie, the latter for her 'heart-rending fiction' which has 'ever proved a fruitful source of Interest and Tears'. 'If we could convert the tears of Pity to Pearls,' he goes on, in a burst of sensibility, she 'would deserve the richest Coronet that ever was bestowed by the hand of sympathy to grace the brows of Genius'. He then turns to self-praise, asserting 'At a moment when modern Tragedy seems to have forsaken the stage for ever, this endeavour to yield a faint reflection of but a few of her charms as far as the powers of a Minor Theatre will allow, may not be totally unacceptable', and, by way of a climax, drops into verse:

> The Tale each feeling Heart shall thrill,
> Laughter shall hear it and be still,
> And sacred to a Father's woe,
> The Tear of sympathy shall flow.

This stress upon tears, and specifically upon the woes of a father, is, I would argue, the most interesting aspect of Moncrieff's play. He has written it to display the talents of Mr Booth, 'in the Lear of Private Life, the Heart-broken and distracted Father, overpowered with filial tenderness and Parental suffering'. In other words, the significant aspect of the forbidden play *King Lear*, the point for which it is worth creating an ersatz version, is not the richly ambiguous moral overtones of abdication, or the display of evil desires; it is not the ruthless clash of power politics, or the fall of a massive and deluded personality, or the heart-stopping fluctuations of the archetypal struggle between generations – it is none of these: the essential *Lear* is a tale of 'filial tenderness and parental suffering'. So Moncrieff took Amelia Opie's story. In doing so, he made central to the play a relationship which, to judge from the number of successful pieces based upon it during the period, had a special emotional intensity for Victorian audiences and readers. The father–daughter theme was a favourite with Sheridan Knowles, described by Christopher Murray as the Victorian Shakespeare; it is, of course, the subject of his most famous play *Virginius*; Dickens probably had Lear and Cordelia in mind when he created Little Nell and her grand-father. From these and many other examples of successful and popular writing it seems that the Victorians were fascinated by the possibilities of the relationship. Amelia Opie had written several novels in which the father–daughter bond is important; Moncrieff made a shrewd selection when he substituted a story of hers for Shakespeare's *King Lear*.

Opie's story tells of a girl who is seduced by promises of marriage and elopes, only to return with her baby in her arms to her father's home, to find that he fell into a depression after her departure, became bankrupt, and lost his reason. She nurses him devotedly, but on the day he recovers his senses and recognises her he expires; so does she. At the funeral the child is snatched by the father, who happens to be passing, and who has thought both mother and child were long dead. He proceeds to die too, worn out by his vices, bequeathing his fortune to the boy. Opie's focus is upon Agnes, her sin, her suffering and her expiation, and secondarily on the suffering she has brought upon her father and her lover's remorse. It is a tale, as the moral at the end points out, about the irreparable emotional and moral damage that follows the yielding to temptation.

Moncrieff boasts on the bills that he has followed the story closely, and indeed he has, with the usual melodramatic additions such as a comic sub-plot; but he has rebalanced it to focus on the father, and imported what were to him the essentials of *King Lear*. The first of these is the scene in which the returning daughter encounters the deranged father. Opie set this in a forest, and in her writing it is faintly reminiscent of Tate's scene on the heath, where Cordelia wanders in search of her father; Moncrieff underlines this with a storm and with Shakespearean cadences in the father's insane speeches. He gives Booth a further mad scene, in a madman's cell – distinctly reminiscent of Tate's *King Lear*, which ends in a cell, with Lear in chains – but he does not make this the denouement of his play. Instead he changes the climax of both Opie's tale and of *King Lear* by ending with a scene which draws upon both the recognition scene between Lear and Cordelia from Act 4 and the restoration of Hermione from *A Winter's Tale*. The five years of tender nursing which lead up to the deaths in Opie disappear, and at their third encounter father and daughter are revealed to each other and reconciled, to live happily ever after. As the curtain rises the old man is revealed asleep on a couch; he wakes, and is about to relapse into despair, when the doctor draws a curtain and reveals Agnes as a portrait: an early example of a favourite device of theatrical pictorialism. She then plays on her harp the song 'Tears such as tender fathers shed', and he recognises and forgives her as she falls at his feet. The repentant seducer also rushes in and is forgiven, and all live happily ever after.

This melodrama was, it seems, a success, and was repeated every week until the end of the season. If we turn to the productions of *King Lear* itself, armed with it as a model, then an emphasis upon the familial and domestic aspects of the play, and upon Lear as father, rather than as king or as an individual caught in conflicts of passion, is easily detected there too. Moreover, the scene which emerges in production after production as the focus of the play is indeed 4.7, the recognition scene.

Edmund Kean's text was largely unregenerate Tate, but Elliston did restore some of Shakespeare's text: a few lines in the first scene, and, at length, 4.7. Kean, especially in his decline, played Lear all out for sympathy. In Tate's final scene, where Lear physically defends Cordelia against the soldiers sent by Edmund, he made such claptrap of the moment where Lear, exhausted, throws aside his sword, and exclaims 'I am old now', that he evoked an 'hysterical scream' from his audiences (Hillebrand, 1933, p. 311). The *Spectator* critic prefaced his review of Macready's revival (27 Jan. 1838) with the plain statement 'The object of the poet in this tragedy, is to exhibit filial ingratitude and parental anguish', and praised his handling of the recognition scene 'for its touching pathos and histrionic skill'. With Samuel Phelps's Lear, the emphasis on the parental became explicit and the keynote of his interpretation. The reviewer for the *Athenaeum* (8 Nov. 1845) said: 'Mr Phelps's performance of *Lear* may be easily excelled in royal dignity and in physical vigour; but, as a *pathetic* piece of acting, is unrivalled. Mr Phelps never forgets the father.' Indeed, another critic felt 'the king is utterly lost in the father' (Phelps and Forbes-Robertson, 1886, p. 191). Charles Kean did exactly the same. The *Times* review (26 Apr. 1858) noted the significant picture with which his production began: 'Lear himself on his throne, with his three daughters grouped around him, [which is] not only a pleasing picture to the eye, but it serves the purpose of an Euripidean prologue, in introducing to the audience the principal figures of the tale so arranged as to furnish the mind with a starting point. Here are King Lear and his daughters a happy family party, bound together by ties of apparent affection.' This Lear had no grandeur, did not aim at tragic stature, but was at the beginning of the play an 'essentially . . . good-natured and rather stupid old man', an 'easy, passionate, dinner-desiring, joke-loving old man', destroyed by his daughters' unkindness, and restored to 'frantic joy' on recognising Cordelia.

Irving conceived the role in much the same way, as an innocent quite guiltless of his own destruction. The special Irving ingredient, the histrionic exploitation of guilt described by Peter Thomson, was absent from this characterisation. His Lear freely gave and expected love, his world was shattered by the discovery of betrayal, and he was restored to faith and peace by Cordelia. This was, of course, Ellen Terry, who played to him with the utmost sweetness and submission (pl. 19). Irving, as Gordon Crosse reported, 'brought out the human side of Lear, and therefore the pity of his story . . . for example, in his affection for Cordelia' (1953, p. 12). He played the recognition scene up to the hilt for 'heart-probing pathos', and regularly reduced Terry to tears, which he then tasted on his fingers, speaking to her like a wistful child begging his nurse for forgiveness. Sentiment could hardly go further (Hughes, 1981, p. 135).

And yet the play was never really a success. What was amiss? Perhaps some of the terms of the critical response are helpful. Charles Kean,

19. Henry Irving's *King Lear*, at the Lyceum Theatre. This picture from the production's commemorative programme shows the reconciliation scene between Irving as Lear and Ellen Terry as Cordelia

enunciating the respectful, serious, scholarly claim for the superiority of all Shakespeare's productions, spoke of *King Lear* in the introduction to his acting text as 'supreme' – but 'supreme' as 'an evocation of human misery'. Phelps's pathos was highly praised but agreed to be exceedingly painful; and the reviewer for *Black and White* (19 Nov. 1892), who did not like Irving's Lear, said his rendering of the recognition scene made him feel so 'very poignantly . . . the pity of the tragedy', was so 'unspeakably tender and pathetic', that it was 'too heart-breaking, too painful'.

In other words, for these commentators the pain of the play, while it was much admired as a redeeming feature of the piece and not felt to be overplayed or excessive, was nevertheless not satisfactory; it left behind it a sense of distress. We may postulate that this was because it was not resolved and answered within the drama; the tragic pattern does not end on peace, faith and restoration. The temptation was to blame the play for this; and that is what we find has happened in the essentially Victorian critical analysis of A. C. Bradley. All of the introduction to his essay on *King Lear* in *Shakespearean Tragedy* (1904) leads up to this point. He discusses the gap between the critical esteem of the play, as Shakespeare's greatest, and its lack of success on the stage and concludes: '*King Lear* seems to me Shakespeare's greatest achievement, but it seems to me *not* his best play' despite the 'ineffably beautiful scene in the Fourth Act between Lear and Cordelia'. The reason he finally gives for this, after much hedging, is that he must admit that his 'feelings call for [a] "happy ending"'.[4] He is reluctant to say this, of course, because it makes him seem to agree with Nahum Tate, which is a sin against the basic tenet of Victorian Shakespeareanism: a denial of educational Shakespeare, scholarly, correct texts, carefully illustrated on stage – the Bard adored. But it is a statement of deep feeling. The play, as he perceives it, ought not to end as it does: Shakespeare seems to have got it wrong. So Bradley seems to me to embody the problem of the Victorian stage and public in their relationship to *King Lear*. They are caught in a cleft stick. The emphasis that they found most meaningful in the play, the thing that brought its characters and situations home to them, was the pathos of the old man cast out, then restored, forgiven and petted: love denied then granted. What they needed to embody this was either Nahum Tate – unthinkable – or a domestic melodrama – *The Lear of Private Life*, ending as it did upon the restoration scene, which in Shakespeare is only an element of the fourth act.

I would by no means wish to say that Victorian pictorial, historicised, reverential Shakespeare is necessarily unsuccessful. I feel that Irving's *King*

Lear could have been an occasion upon which that theatrical method created something deeply exciting. But I would suggest that in this instance the usual approach could not embody what was really needed from the play, could not deliver a domestic and familial *King Lear* with a happy ending.

NOTES

1 Kean to Elliston, 31 Mar. 1820, quoted in Murray 'Elliston's productions of Shakespeare', *Theatre Survey*, (1970), 112–13.
2 James Winston, *Drury Lane Journal*, quoted in Rees, 1978, p. 84. The information about the use of a magic lantern is given on the authority of this study; Pieter van der Merwe, however, has suggested to me that the device used was rather a revolving construction of coloured transparencies from which light was reflected on to the stage.
3 See Macready, 1912; repr. 1969, vol. 1, p. 175; vol. 2, pp. 17–19, 242.
4 Quoted from the 2nd edn, 1905, pp. 244, 247, 252.

Macready's Production of *Cymbeline*

CAROL J. CARLISLE

I N H I S four seasons of management (Covent Garden, 1837–9, and Drury Lane, 1841–3), William Charles Macready offered performances of *Cymbeline* on six occasions only, two in 1838 and four in 1843; yet his treatment of Shakespeare's romance, particularly his careful revival of 21 January 1843, deserves serious attention. After all, the significance of Macready's productions cannot be gauged by the frequency of their repetition: his famous *King Lear*, for example, was seen only ten times in its first season and only fifteen times in all. His *Cymbeline*, though hardly equal to his *Lear*, was a worthy attempt to bring a strange and difficult play within the realm of early Victorian experience; it was, besides, a notable achievement in acting and staging – one which, despite its short life, was long remembered.

When Macready's assistant prompter, George Ellis (later stage-manager for Charles Kean), raided the Macready materials after his former employer retired from management, he made some fine watercolour drawings of the scene and costume designs used in the 1843 *Cymbeline*, as well as a complete copy of the prompt-book. These materials, which include carpenter's notes for the scenes, are now in the Folger Shakespeare Library. When supplemented by reviews of the performances, they make it possible to reconstruct Macready's production in considerable detail.[1] Space forbids a scene-by-scene description in this paper, but a general account of the production, followed by partial reconstructions of some major scenes, will suggest – with some vividness, I hope – what Macready's *Cymbeline* was like.

Cymbeline had enjoyed one period of high popularity on the stage, and one only, since Shakespeare's own day: from 1761, when Garrick successfully revived it, until 1776, when he retired from the stage. His successors, John Philip Kemble and others, produced it only 'sporadically' (Hogan, 1952–7; Shattuck, 1974, vol. 2). In 1843, when Macready announced the 'revived Play of CYMBELINE from the text of Shakespeare' (Drury Lane playbill, 21 Jan.), there had not been, as far as I know, any production elaborate enough to justify the term 'revival' for about a decade and a half. Macready's reviewers repeatedly mentioned the play's low popularity as a vehicle for the stage or pointed out such impediments to theatrical success as its improbability, indelicacy, and lack of 'dramatic coherence'. Considering that *Cymbeline* offered little chance of enriching the treasury or increasing the fame of the actor–manager (there was no starring role for him), it is astonishing how much careful artistry Macready expended on it.

Literary critics would have given him little help in the interpretation of the play. Notable commentary on *Cymbeline* was relatively scarce, and most of it dealt with the character of Imogen, Shakespeare's 'most perfect woman' (Hazlitt, 1930, vol. 4, pp. 179–86; Jameson, 1833, vol. 2, pp. 50–87). If Macready could have looked forward to our own day, he would have found much discussion of the play's unusual characteristics – its paradoxes, its blatantly artificial devices, its strange blends of tragedy and comedy, its sudden, dislocating shifts in perspective – but considerable disagreement about the meaning and value of these traits. Take, for example, the incongruities that result when an ethereal heroine and an intriguing villain keep breaking away from their proper sphere of romance. Are Imogen's vitality and Iachimo's moments of psychological realism 'destructive' elements which Shakespeare should have kept under control? Or does his disturbing mixture of the improbable and the probable have a validity of its own? For Macready, the problems posed by *Cymbeline*'s eccentricities were not simply aesthetic but very practical.

In general he dealt with the incongruities by eliminating as many as possible. The most glaring improbabilities were either removed or rationalised; realistic character traits were further developed; grotesque effects were softened. Legend was made to seem history, not through the recreation of a particular historical period, but through the suggestion of a familiar kind of past – one where a bachelor party in a Roman *triclinium* and a diplomatic mission in an ancient hall of state were instantly recognisable occasions. There was much beauty in Macready's *Cymbeline*, and at certain moments there was probably a sense of exaltation, but on the whole understanding and emotion were emphasised at the expense of wonder. These general tendencies of the production may be traced in the details of text, staging and acting.

As usual, Macready's idea of faithfulness to Shakespeare's text did not preclude extensive omissions. Some 1200 lines are cut from the play in his prompt-book. Two relatively unimportant short scenes (the Folio's 3.8 and 4.3) and an important long one, the prison scene containing Posthumus' vision (5.4), are left out entirely. The Soothsayer, no longer needed to interpret the prophecy, is omitted, and with him a long passage in the final scene. The importance of the Queen is greatly reduced: many of her lines have disappeared, as have all references to her deathbed confessions. There are predictable cuts for propriety's sake (Posthumus' frenzied diatribe against women is omitted, for example, and Cloten's plans for Milford-Haven do not include the rape of Imogen), but many others can only have been made to save time. (The production ran for three hours and five minutes.) Among the major characters Imogen has lost the most lines, Iachimo the fewest.

In omitting the diatribe, the vision, the Soothsayer, and the Queen's confessions Macready was perpetuating a tradition begun by Garrick and continued by Kemble. Many of his other cuts, however, differ from Kemble's, and his arrangement of acts and scenes introduces some notable changes. Macready occasionally combines two or more of the Folio scenes, but he makes no transpositions (except for adding a few lines from the omitted prison scene to the scene that precedes it) and he inserts no new lines. Two of his act divisions are the same as Garrick/Kemble's: Act 1 ends with the wager scene (the Folio's 1.5) and Act 4 with Imogen's ordeal beside the headless corpse (4.2). His Act 2, however, ends with the original 2.1 (a short scene of Cloten's concluding with the Second Lord's prayer for the protection of Imogen's honour) rather than with Garrick/ Kemble's choice, 2.3 (Imogen's rejection of Cloten and his vow of revenge). This change provides an interval just before the bedroom scene (now beginning Act 3), during which its elaborate set can be put in place. Macready's third act, instead of ending in the traditional manner with the exciting death-letter scene (3.4), goes on through 3.5 and concludes with Cloten's villainous scheme for Milford-Haven. This allows Act 4 to be reserved entirely for the Fidele sequence, a natural unit. As curtain scenes Macready's new choices are relatively quiet, but each sounds a note of apprehension or threat.

For the twenty scenes in his production Macready had eleven sets, at least some of which were probably the work of Charles Marshall[2] – in effect, twelve sets, for one was used to indicate two separate places by different combinations of its parts. They were evidently designed for imaginative effect, not historical consistency: the scene in Rome was obviously classical, but the interior views of Cymbeline's palace predominantly suggested the Romanesque architecture of a later period. Imogen's elegant bedchamber, though incongruous with the fortress-like stateliness of other rooms in the same palace, appropriately mirrored her own rich but delicate charm.

A modern writer on Shakespearean costume, F. M. Kelly, remarks that

Cymbeline 'allows of unlimited freedom of treatment' (1970, p. 106). Many of Macready's contemporaries would probably have agreed. Since Shakespeare himself had mixed ancient Romans with Renaissance Italians and legendary Britons, why should there be a pedantic insistence on the fashions of Augustus Caesar's time? True, the developing trend towards 'historical accuracy' in Shakespearean production had already extended to *Cymbeline*: Charles Kemble in his 1827 production had costumed the Britons in the manner of 'the Gaulish and Belgic Colonists of the Southern Counties of *Britain* before their Subjugation by the Romans' (Covent Garden playbill, 10 May). There had been little critical response, however, and the *Theatrical Observer* of 17 May had even remarked that the antiquarian décor often represented 'an absurd departure from poetical sense'. At the time Macready produced *Cymbeline*, no manager, as far as I know, had followed Kemble's lead.

Nor did Macready do so. If he did consult the authorities, he chose a period somewhat later than Cymbeline's, when British men of rank had begun wearing a simple Roman tunic instead of their former ensemble of pantaloons-tunic-and-cloak, and he disregarded the long, drooping moustaches that were their distinctive feature (see pl. 20). Even then he gave his costumier considerable latitude, particularly in adapting the women's two-layered costume of ankle-length tunic and shorter gown (see Planché, 1881, pp. 9–17). For the Romans he used a knee-length white tunic with short, loose sleeves and a richly coloured cloak fastened on one shoulder – something that looked convincingly classical without evoking memories of *Julius Caesar* or Sheridan Knowles's *Virginius*.[3] For the Britons he evidently wanted costumes that would suggest a people influenced by Rome but maintaining a certain character of their own. The male courtiers wore knee-length tunics, differentiated from those of the Romans by being coloured rather than white and by having long, medieval-style sleeves, puffed above the elbow and straight below it. Imogen's court dress whimsically played upon the idea of an underdress and overdress, without in the least suggesting anything Roman or ancient British: her basic garment of soft pink material had a long, full skirt and split sleeves that dangled like those on a Master of Arts gown; on top of it perched a crisp white dress of hour-glass design. Cymbeline and his Queen looked like story-book monarchs, slightly more exotic than usual because of the veils or draperies attached to their crowns. The outlawed Belarius and his foster-sons, the unwitting princes, wore rude garments of fur and were equipped with hunting horns and spear-tipped poles.

Most reviewers agreed that Macready's production was tasteful, elegant and appropriate, though less brilliant than some of his previous

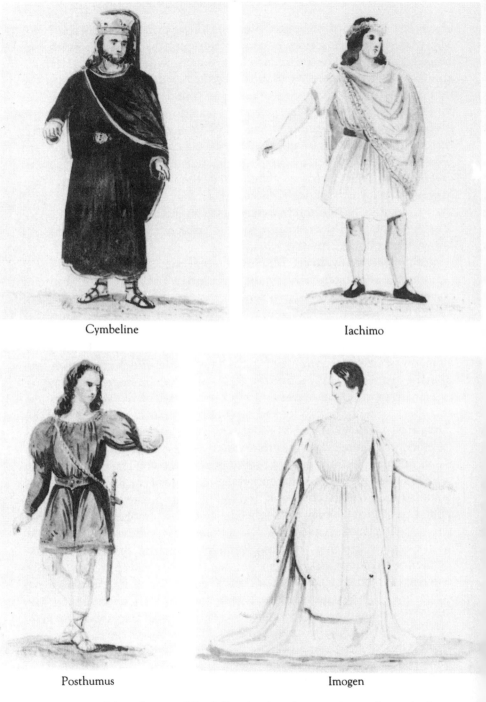

Cymbeline

Iachimo

Posthumus

Imogen

20. Macready's production of *Cymbeline*; drawings showing costume designs for four characters

Shakespearean revivals. The only hostile criticism came from the *Morning Post* (23 Jan. 1843), an old enemy of Macready's, which protested against such breaches of historical accuracy as the 'ultra-barbaric mixture of early Norman-French dress and the classic *toga*'. But even the *Post* critic joined in the journalists' chorus of praise for the splendidly staged wager scene.

The cast was very strong, even in the less prominent parts. Samuel Phelps, always excellent in rough but manly roles, made Belarius a 'full round' character 'with a heart and blood throbbing in it' (*Post*). Edward William Elton was a gentle, subdued Pisanio, blending earnest devotion and delicate feeling (Fletcher, 1847, pp. 106–7); Helen Faucit later recalled him as the best Pisanio of her time (Lady Martin, 1891, p. 160). Henry Compton's Cloten, a 'pompous fop', was praised for its consistent characterisation and its 'gloriously asinine' humour. Critics disagreed about the character itself, however, and thus about Compton's interpretation: some thought a prince, however foolish, should be more refined, but others considered this Cloten too quiet and solemn for Shakespeare's 'bouncing, blustering' fool. The cave-dwelling princes, Guiderius and Arviragus, were played, respectively, by a handsome young actor named Hudson, whose usual line was light comedy, and a singer named Allen. Both acquitted themselves well in their unaccustomed duties, and Hudson in singing Fidele's dirge surprised the critics with a 'full rich tenor voice'. Amid so many good performances Miss Ellis's juvenile-looking Queen was disappointing; the part needed Mrs Warner, but cuts had rendered it too insignificant for this imposing 'heavy' actress. John Ryder, however, made a sufficiently royal Cymbeline, despite his comparative youthfulness.

Of the major characters James R. Anderson's Posthumus was the least impressive, though he had some very effective moments. A good-looking, athletically built young actor with a fine voice, Anderson had become well known in London since 1837, when Macready brought him from the provinces to serve as leading young man at Covent Garden. His Posthumus was described as 'animated and powerful, though occasionally a trifle too violent' (*Morning Chronicle*, 23 Jan. 1843).

Helen Faucit, who played Imogen, had been acting almost constantly as Macready's leading lady (except in 'heavy' parts) since shortly after her London début in 1836. Her reputation as a major actress had now been established, and her brilliant starring career lay just ahead. In her Imogen of 1843 she evidently followed her usual style, balancing the humanly 'real' and the poetically 'ideal', though in later years she allowed her portrayal to become increasingly ethereal. At all times, however, she rejected the conception of a passively sweet Imogen. In writing of her 1843 performance, George Fletcher said that at the outset she established the princess as a dignified, intelligent woman with noble ideals; her strength of character gave additional effectiveness to her normal gentleness of manner and explained her occasional abandonment of that manner (1847, pp. 95, 97). Some reviewers would have preferred a more consistently gentle Imogen – for example, they censured Miss Faucit's denunciation of Iachimo in the temptation scene as too vehement and too unfeminine – but most of them were very complimentary.

Macready, now in his fiftieth year and at the height of his profession, had a well-earned reputation for building his productions around himself, with the other actors revolving like satellites about his sun. His decision to act the villain Iachimo instead of the hero Posthumus, traditional role of Garrick and the Kembles, was therefore a surprise. Perhaps it can be explained by his most recent experience as Posthumus (in May 1837), when he disappointed himself with a 'discreditable . . . undigested, unstudied' performance (1912; repr. 1969, vol. 1, p. 394). As manager of Covent Garden, he had stayed out of the cast when he offered *Cymbeline* briefly in 1838, giving Posthumus to Phelps and Iachimo to Vandenhoff. Macready had acted Iachimo in his early years without producing much effect, but his portrayal in 1843 was the product of fresh study and original thought. Some reviewers considered the innovations un-Shakespearean – for example, the convincing air of frankness instead of the sly, insinuating manner they associated with the character – but nearly everyone agreed that the performance was highly effective. Surprisingly enough, the critic for the *Post* forgot his usual hostility and became the chief advocate of the new interpretation. Iachimo, he explained, is a wealthy darling of society whose naturally good heart has become 'encrusted' with selfishness; he 'grows into a rascal out of circumstances'. Posthumus is so obviously a gull that Iachimo is piqued into betraying him, scarcely realising the pain caused by his own villainy. 'Its result appals him.'

From such reports one may form a reasonably good idea of Macready's *Cymbeline*, but to come closer to an imaginative experience of it one must try to visualise an actual performance. This process will be facilitated, I hope, by the following description of salient details from six major scenes.

The setting for Macready's wager scene was an 'Apartment & Terrace of Philario's House' (pl. 21). The terrace, which formed the background, was suggested by a colonnade of grey marble (painted flats, with cut-out spaces, set in the fourth grooves), between whose columns could be glimpsed a bird's-eye view of Rome (depicted on flats in the sixth grooves). The 'apartment', which occupied most of the stage space, probably had its walls and ceiling indicated in the usual way, by wings and borders. At the centre was a large table, spread with a magnificent banquet and surrounded

21.   The set for the 'wager scene' in Macready's production of *Cymbeline*

(except on the audience's side) by scarlet couches, on which Philario and his eight guests reclined, all crowned with roses. Six pages bearing wine jugs were in attendance. Tripods placed about the scene were flaming with incense. Classical vases and marble figures mounted on pedestals added to the beauty of the appointments (see pl. 22). The whole effect was of 'noble splendour and luxurious ease' – or, if one preferred, of 'the Sybaritish refinement of the decaying empire' (*Morning Post*, 23 Jan. 1843; *Cymb.* 17, opp. p. 13).

Macready's Iachimo, festively garlanded and attired in a golden cloak over his white tunic, gave a tone of 'jocund recklessness' to the whole scene. The other actors, well-trained in their apparent spontaneity, kept up the hilarity very convincingly. Critics were surprised that Macready was capable of so much frivolity, so much ease and abandon. Anderson as Posthumus, handsome in his royal blue tunic, effectively portrayed the

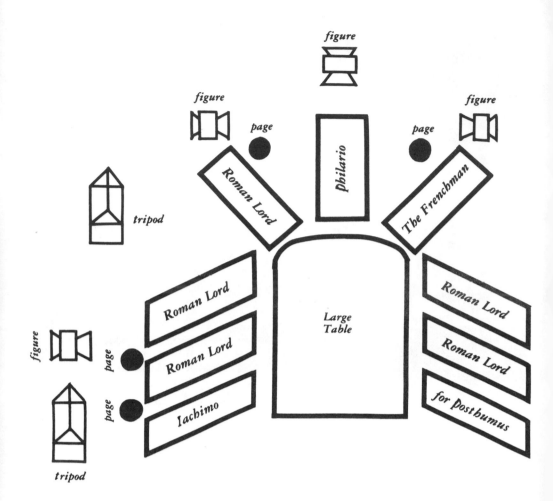

22. Artist's diagram of the 'wager scene' in Macready's production of *Cymbeline*, based on a prompt-book sketch

serious stranger surrounded by jovial, uninhibited Romans: 'he marked out the growing indignation at the levity of Iachimo, carefully managing the curling lip and darkened brow' (*TheTimes*, 23 Jan. 1843).

Several reviewers noticed the effect of this scene of classic festivity on the interpretation of the play: as the *Spectator* pointed out, it threw 'a veil of voluptuous wantonness over the repulsive incident of a man, wagering on the virtue of his wife', making Posthumus 'appear merely a rash boaster, and Iachimo a licentious profligate inflamed with wine, both acting on a hasty impulse'.

For the famous bedroom scene Macready provided a set that enhanced the impression of chaste loveliness to which Iachimo responds in the sleeping Imogen. Ellis's note directing the scene to be 'set up to' the fourth grooves (Cymb. 8) and his statement that the 'Scene itself should be enclosed' (Cymb. 17, opp. p. 33) suggest that in this instance Macready abandoned the usual arrangement of a pair of back flats supplemented by wings and used instead an early type of box-set, with one pair of flats at the back in the fourth grooves and two 'raking flats' set 'along the side of the stage from the front to the back and joining the back flats to form the three sides of a room' (Southern, 1952, pp. 328–9).

The result must have been impressive. Ellis's watercolour drawing shows a spacious, elegant room with slender gilded columns, an elaborately decorated ceiling and ornate gold mouldings. Large blue tapestries are displayed on the walls, and a green curtain at stage left covers a practicable door at the second entrance. Imogen's bed, with its small gilded hood and its tent-like drapery of blue and silver, placed well to the front, dominates the picture. According to Ellis's notes, all the other items of furniture – tables, chairs, lamps, pedestals with vases, etc. – are gilt. An intimate bedtime atmosphere is created by small touches like Imogen's dress hanging over a clothes-rack and her sandals standing on a low footstool beside the bed. At the left centre, handsome but intrusive, stands Iachimo's red and gold chest.

As the scene opened Imogen was discovered in bed, reading. She wore a 'white soft muslin robe trimmed with lace', having a 'high body' and 'long sleeves loose at the wrist'.[4] After she had kissed Posthumus' bracelet and retired, the chest opened and Iachimo emerged into the gloomy half-light of the scene (we know from a prompter's note that the border lights were down). As he crept to the bed and stood contemplating the sleeping Imogen, Macready 'greatly added to the harrowing effect of the situation' by 'suppressing his voice to a whisper'. Unfortunately the chilling sensation was created at the expense of the poetry, for much of Iachimo's language became inaudible.

Skipping now to the scene in which Imogen learns that Posthumus has ordered her death, one shifts from elaborate to simple staging: a carelessly executed painting of a mountainous landscape near Milford-Haven, set in the first grooves, made a perfunctory background for some of the finest acting in the production. According to *The Times*, Helen Faucit's performance here equalled 'some of Rachel's best efforts'. As Imogen read Posthumus' letter, the 'stunning misery of the blow' was evident in the 'staggering and faltering of her eye and voice, in [the] sheer bewildered incredulity' over the accusation of adultery, and, after she came to the part commanding her death, in the 'fainting away of her accents', in the 'trembling which overcame her, and her fall at last on the ground'. When Pisanio revived her, she was hysterical at first, but she evidently regained her self-control before long. Her speech 'False to his bed!' was full of pathos mixed with indignation. When she begged Pisanio to carry out his master's command, she was not a passively obedient wife – her 'tone of pathetic irony' in saying 'A little witness my obedience' made that clear – but a woman whose anguish over the treachery of her idolised husband made life insupportable.[5]

In Macready's *Cymbeline* all the Fidele episodes were combined in a long scene that constituted the whole of the fourth act. For this sequence a 'set scene' was used, comprising a number of separately constructed pieces set up in different parts of the stage. The background of distant mountains was placed in the sixth grooves, thus allowing considerable depth for the scene. At stage left, set, oblique, from the third grooves, was a large piece representing a rocky prominence with the mouth of Belarius' cave at its base. In front of this was a 'double bank' on which the bodies of Fidele and Cloten would be placed in the funeral episode. At stage right a 'ground piece', representing loose boulders and small bushes, screened an opening at the fourth entrance, where a section of the floor had been slid away so that actors could come up by stairs or ramp from under the stage. Behind the opening stood a high piece of scenery painted to look like a rocky mountainside; it was backed by a 'raking platform', whose ramp could be ascended or descended by actors to give the illusion of climbing the mountainside to a higher elevation or coming down from one. The general effect of the scene, as depicted in Ellis's sketch, was a bare, rugged grandeur, softened somewhat by blue haze and blue shadows, a few brown bushes and an occasional patch of dark green moss or bracken.

In the first episode of the fourth-act sequence, Helen Faucit, now dressed as the boy Fidele in a dark green page's costume, amused the audience with her timid approach to the cave. As she slowly drew near it, she called out to its possible inhabitants in a faint, terror-filled voice 'Ho! who's here?' – after which she instantly retreated in 'great trepidation' and shrank behind the nearest bush or rock. At her words 'Best draw my sword' she drew it 'awkwardly underhanded'. Finally she advanced slowly to the cave and entered it, holding the sword straight in front of her (Cymb. 17, opp. p. 77; Lady Martin, 1891, pp. 197–8).

The idyllic passages that followed – with the graceful youth Fidele, the gruff but kindly Belarius, and the lively but gentle Guiderius and Arviragus – were the part of Macready's production where the atmosphere of romance was at its purest. If the young princes were a little too refined for their 'sylvan breeding', as the *Spectator* noticed, they were so much the

148

closer to Arcadian tradition. The sad beauty of Fidele's 'death' cast its proper charm despite some cuts in the poetry and despite the use of not-so-ingenious instruments (violins and violoncellos, according to the prompt-book) to produce the haunting strains of the death-music.

In the Cloten episodes Macready cut out, as much as possible, the grotesqueness of the original play. Guiderius, after killing Cloten, did not offend the audience with the grisly spectacle of a severed head; he displayed the dead man's *sword* instead. In that strange scene when Imogen awakens from her drugged trance to find what seems to be Posthumus' headless body beside her, Shakespeare's nightmare mixture of shocking, pathetic, morbid and comic effects was too much for Macready. The attempt to qualify and temper this mixture is evident both in his text and in his stage directions. For example, the impression of headlessness was softened by enveloping a dummy in a large cloak which Cloten had previously carried on his arm. Of course this would make nonsense of the lines in which Imogen recognises (as she thinks) Posthumus' leg, his hand, 'his foot Mercurial, his Martial thigh' – but then these lines were stricken from Macready's text.

The battle scene was spectacular. According to the *Theatrical Journal* (4 Feb. 1843), it rivalled the 'startling and brilliant gorgeousness' of the opera *King Arthur* as recently produced by Macready. Against a background of distant mountains (sixth grooves) a colourful mixture of British and Roman soldiers could be seen through the large central opening of the 'cut wood' flats (fourth grooves), moving in panoramic style from the right to left as they engaged in close combat. An instrument called a 'Crash' augmented the noises produced by flourishes and shouts. The smoke and dust of battle poured from a machine that the *Morning Post* superciliously dubbed an 'irascible teapot'. At the front of the stage, in close-up view, Posthumus, vulnerably dressed in a peasant's coarse brown tunic, over-came an invincible-looking Iachimo, godlike in golden armour and scarlet cloak. No wonder the humiliated Roman blamed his defeat on a guilty conscience.

For his finale Macready created a 'striking and beautiful picture'. Its central point was Cymbeline's tent, a square crimson pavilion with the hangings looped back; this was flanked by two set pieces – on the right another tent, slightly upstage, and on the left a large tree with drapery strung across it; at some distance behind was a backcloth of the 'British Encampment', showing numerous white tents against a mountainous background. When the scene opened, Cymbeline was seated at the entrance of his tent, with various attendants ranged at each side and before him: twenty-four soldiers in two symmetrical groups, eighteen lords similarly divided, six pages (three on each side of the stage), and four banner-bearers. At the left, far downstage, stood Pisanio, Belarius, Guiderius and Arviragus.

After Cymbeline had called his three 'preservers' forward and knighted them, a colourful procession of Roman prisoners entered from stage right, with two British captains at their head and a dozen British soldiers marching behind them as guards. The captives included Lucius (the commander) with his page Fidele, Iachimo, Posthumus and a representative number of captains and soldiers (six and twelve, respectively). They were all in chains except those who bore the Roman Eagles and other trophies, all of which were lowered to an inclined position as they entered. By my count there were now ninety-three people on the stage – more if the Eagle-bearers were not included among the Roman soldiers.

The seemingly endless series of revelations in this scene, so likely to provoke laughter after a while, was somewhat curtailed by leaving out reports of things the audience themselves had seen. Omissions relating to the Queen's confessions and the prophecy reduced the effect of improbability.

According to reviewers, Macready's impersonation of the guilty Iachimo, 'prostrate beneath the weight of his crime', was 'masterly', and his attempt to do 'manful reparation for an unmanly wrong' invested the character with 'interest and grace'. Anderson, as Posthumus, might have overacted in the 'roar of lamentation' with which he rushed forward upon hearing Iachimo's confession, but an 'outpouring of emotion' was traditional here. Helen Faucit's 'real' and 'ideal' acting were effectively combined in her reconciliation with Posthumus, which was considered both 'charming' and 'sublime'. Her 'divine' Imogen was balanced by a down-to-earth Belarius, whose attempts to reassume the courtly habits of earlier days were constantly 'overpowered by the freedom and lawlessness of his recent life': he roughly thrust aside two lords who were arresting Guiderius at Cymbeline's command, and he 'bawled' the truth about the princes into the King's ears.

In this final scene Cymbeline did not (as in Shakespeare's text) agree to pay tribute to Caesar despite the British victory – that would have seemed unpatriotic as well as irrational to Macready's audience – but he did follow Shakespeare in his generous treatment of the defeated enemy. Translating his magnanimous words into action brought the play to a pageant-like close. At Cymbeline's decree that the Romans be allowed to share in the general happiness, British soldiers went among the prisoners and took off their chains. Then came the elevation of the Roman Eagles, signifying that the vanquished had been restored to equal status with the victors.

Finally, when Cymbeline commanded that 'A Roman and a British ensign wave/Friendly together', the actors formed a procession across the stage, with men from both countries intermixed, and a Roman trophy and a British banner carried side by side. On this emblematic picture of harmony restored the curtain came down.

Had Macready continued his management of Drury Lane, as he fully intended to do, he would probably have repeated *Cymbeline* during the following season; as things turned out, its last performance was on 16 February 1843. But his impressive revival, however short-lived, must have enhanced the reputation of the play, both critical and theatrical. Certainly it encouraged a long-term interest in it by two members of the cast: Helen Faucit began acting Imogen as a starring part in 1844 and later described her as Shakespeare's 'masterpiece' (Lady Martin, 1891, p. 158); Phelps produced *Cymbeline* with much success at Sadler's Wells in 1847 and repeated it on several later occasions (Allen, 1971, pp. 107–8, and Appendix I). There were more direct and tangible influences, too. About 1850 Charles Kean was planning a virtual reincarnation of Macready's production at the Princess's Theatre, using the same prompt-book and scenic designs (Shattuck, 1965, pp. 83–4, items 10–13, 15), but for some reason it never materialised. In the autumn of 1864, however, twenty-one years after Macready had given up management, a revival of *Cymbeline* was mounted at Drury Lane which strongly recalled the one of 1843. Phelps, who had been Macready's Belarius, now acted Posthumus, and Helen Faucit resumed her old part of Imogen. When the play was repeated in the spring of 1865, with Miss Faucit but without Phelps, James R. Anderson, another of the 1843 cast, had Macready's role of Iachimo – and even attempted his stage whisper in the bedroom scene (*Examiner*, 11 Mar. 1865).

Most critics were charmed by the visual beauty of the new production – the *Morning Post* (19 Oct. 1864) described the furniture of Imogen's bedroom as 'one of the most elegant and effective specimens of stage upholstery' the theatre had yet produced – and most of them admired the performances as well, particularly Helen Faucit's subtle but eloquent Imogen.[6] The Drury Lane *Cymbeline* of 1864, though it took second place to a spectacular *Macbeth* starring the same actors, was an important event: there would be no revival of comparable significance until Irving's production thirty-one years later (Hughes, 1981, p. 205). Both the *Sun* and *The Times* (18 Oct. 1864), remarked that the admirable staging was in the tradition of Macready. The sense of *déjà vu* was no accident. Evidently the scenery *was* Macready's: after being stored at Drury Lane for two decades, it seems to have remained in good condition, only requiring some touching up by William Beverley (*The Times*, 28 Oct. 1864). Macready's production of *Cymbeline* had cast a long shadow – one that could not always be distinguished from the substance.

NOTES

1 In discussing Macready's production I use the following materials from the Folger Shakespeare Library: PROMPT. Cymb. 17 (the prompt-book); PROMPT. Cymb. 8 (the scenes); PROMPT. Cymb. 9 (the costumes). Reviews from the following journals (all published in 1843) are used: *Observer*, 22 Jan.; *The Times*, 23 Jan.; *Morning Post*, 23 Jan.; *Morning Herald*, 23 Jan.; *Morning Chronicle*, 23 Jan.; *Athenaeum*, 28 Jan.; *Spectator*, 28 Jan.; *Examiner*, 28 Jan.; *Theatrical Journal*, 28 Jan., 4 Feb. George Fletcher's critique, first published in the *Athenaeum*, 15 Apr. 1843, was republished in Fletcher, 1847, pp. 95–108; my references will be to the latter.

2 Marshall, who was Macready's chief scenic artist, must have had a hand in a revival with so many new sets, but he was probably not responsible for all of them. Macready sometimes listed the artists in his playbills, but often he did not; in this case no artist is mentioned in either playbills or reviews. Perhaps Marshall and Tomkins shared the work on *Cymbeline* as they had done on *The Two Gentlemen of Verona* in the previous season (see Downer, 1966, p. 228).

3 One costume had a specific claim to authenticity: the armour of a Roman general (worn by Iachimo and, for a short while, by Posthumus), which, according to Ellis's note, was based on a bas relief in Florence.

4 Ellis's brief description of Imogen's 'second dress' is in the Index to PROMPT. Cymb. 9. He does not provide a sketch of this costume. The phrase 'high body' is puzzling. At first I took it to mean 'having a high bodice', but Marion Jones (for whose expert advice I am grateful) has convinced me that a garment with separately constructed bodice would have been unduly elaborate for nightwear in 1843 and would also have been wasted on the bedroom scene since Imogen is never seen at full length here. I am afraid 'high body' may mean 'high-necked' (as a decorous nightdress ought to have been), but in that case – how did Iachimo see the mole? Helen Faucit later eliminated this problem by striking out all references to the mole. (See her prompt-book, PROMPT. Cymb. 2, Folger Shakespeare Library, pp. 37, 48.)

5 See *Morning Post*; Fletcher, pp. 100–2; *The Times*; *Observer*; *Spectator*. Macready did not allow Imogen to speak the lines surmising that some 'jay of Italy' had seduced Posthumus, but Helen Faucit may have let some of their bitterness colour her speech. She later restored this passage in her own acting version (PROMPT. Cymb. 2, p. 60). For her comment on this passage, see Lady Martin, 1891, pp. 191–2.

6 For a few of Miss Faucit's many enthusiastic reviews in 1864, see *Morning Post*, 19 Oct.; *Morning Herald*, 19 Oct.; *Sunday Times*, 23 Oct. For a different point of view, see *Spectator*, 29 Oct.: the reviewer acknowledged Miss Faucit's excellence in her own style of acting but thought she made Imogen too ideal. I know of only one writer who disapproved of the production: E. W. Godwin, in 'Theatrical Jottings', *Western Daily Press* (Bristol), 2 Nov., ridiculed the scenery and costumes for their historical inaccuracy and deplored much of the acting. (I am grateful to Dr Kathleen Barker for this reference.) Even Godwin, however, was complimentary to Helen Faucit.

The Imperial Theme

RALPH BERRY

I N March 1900, Winston Churchill, then a war correspondent in South
Africa, wrote from Ladysmith to his friend Pamela Plowden in
England:

Pamela,

Here is an idea; and I think you can help me to turn it into fact.

I will write a play: scene South Africa: time: the war. A play of the Drury Lane autumn
drama class; only this should be produced by Tree at H. Majesty's theatre in the autumn. It
will be perfectly true to life in every respect and the scenic effects should be of such a novel
and startling character that the audience will imagine themselves under fire. Local colour
will be perfect throughout and I should hope to show several of the real Dutch and Colonial
types. Of course the piece would have to be largely spectacular but I believe that with my
name, and a good deal of assistance from a skilful playwright a great success might be
obtained. Ask Tree about this and if he likes the idea, I will get to work.

(Churchill, 1967, vol. 1, p. 1159)

No more is heard of this imperial epic. It vanishes into limbo, Churchill's
drama of the Boer War. I quote the letter because it identifies so well some
key aspects of Tree's reputation, in the public mind as in Churchill's.
Those aspects are the spectacular, allied to the literal and realistic, the
patriotic, and the imperial. The spectacular was central to Tree's work,
and needs no illustration here; but the patriotic/imperial might be cited,
as in Henry Arthur Jones's *Carnac Sahib* (a drama of the Indian Mutiny)
which Tree put on in 1899. Tree was later to make a great success with
Louis N. Parker's *Drake* (1914) and *The Man Who Was*, a play by Kinsey
Peile based on Rudyard Kipling's short story of the same title (1903, and
again in 1912). (It was of this drama that Hesketh Pearson wrote: 'As he
lay dead under the Union Jack while the Last Post was being sounded, he
blew up the flag from his face with every breath he expelled, the rest of the
company doing their best to appear unconscious of this uncorpselike
proceeding' (Pearson, 1956, p. 141)).

The imperial/patriotic is a manifest presence in Tree's work, as in so much art of the period. Less obvious are the ways in which the imperial consciousness imbues the major productions of Shakespeare's Roman plays. This was a theatrical development which Tree guided and promoted, but with which Irving's *Coriolanus* can conveniently be linked. Hence I want to consider certain aspects of Tree's *Julius Caesar* (1898), Irving's *Coriolanus* (1901), and Tree's *Antony and Cleopatra* (1906). It is not my purpose to analyse these productions in their entirety, but to stress those aspects which promote a common theme. The main linking theme is that Rome was perceived (by the British audiences of the day) as the direct analogue to imperial Britain.

In tracing this theme, I make an assumption about Shakespeare's plays with which, I think, there will be general agreement, but which I ought to make explicit. It is that Shakespearean drama exists in a state of slow-moving volatility, and not as a repertory of chemically stable objects. They are coloured by the issues, the preconceptions, the personalities of the day. We know, for instance, that eighteenth-century Americans found in *Julius Caesar* a model of Republican virtue overthrowing tyranny, that the Parisians of 1934 saw in *Coriolanus* a right-wing denunciation of a corrupt centre–left government, that Peter Brook found in *Antony and Cleopatra* (1978) a set of private games from which public issues were all but excluded. The plays are plastic – not infinitely so, but readily conforming to the perceptions and obsessions of the times. At the end of the Victorian era, and during the Edwardian years, the three great Roman tragedies yielded up to the director elements which were presented to the audience as recognisable facets of the imperial situation.

Queen Victoria's Diamond Jubilee was celebrated in June 1897. The event had been rehearsed ten years earlier, as the Golden Jubilee; and 1897 saw the apogee of imperial splendour, with troops summoned from all parts of the globe to march in procession through London. London was the stage for imperial theatre that summer. This spectacular demonstration of the imperial principle contained the genesis of Beerbohm Tree's *Julius Caesar*. It was during the summer of 1897 that Tree re-read *Julius Caesar* carefully, while enjoying a yachting holiday off the Isle of Wight (Pearson, 1956, p. 104). Tree customarily used his summer vacations to plan his major campaigns, and that summer he determined the major castings and lines of his *Julius Caesar*. He himself was to take Antony: 'For the scholar Brutus, for the actor Cassius, for the public Antony' (Pearson, 1956, p. 119). Alma-Tadema would be responsible for the sets. All was to be gorgeous, spectacular, authentic. First performed in January 1898, Tree's *Julius Caesar* became a staple of the repertoire at Her Majesty's Theatre (later His

Majesty's), and with a single exception was produced in every one of his Shakespeare Festivals up to 1913. This production, so often revived, was enormously successful, much more so than the other two plays to be considered here. For the entire Edwardian era and its adjacent years, Tree's was *the* production of *Julius Caesar*.

Its guiding conception was laid down in the Souvenir Programme. Tree located his scene in

> the heart of an empire, Rome. At Her Majesty's it is not the historic band of conspirators that strikes the key note of the play. It is not even the mighty figure of *Caesar* treacherously brought low. It is the feverish, pulsing life of the imperial city.

As is well known, Tree's three-act design had as its centrepiece the Forum scene. The 'feverish, pulsing life of the imperial city' was actualised in a crowd of a hundred. We can see what that crowd looked like in a photograph reproduced in Pearson's biography. No one today can see anything remotely approaching that crowd, for economic reasons habitually restrict stage crowds to perhaps a dozen, if that. The size, the orchestration of that crowd was the production's most memorable effect. It was a standard observation of the reviewers that the crowd was the main personage in the drama; and for the Coronation Gala of 1911, Tree put on a special performance of the Forum scene in which the numbers were raised to around 250 (*Daily Telegraph*, 26 June 1911). This species of giantism was current; it was later in 1911 that Reinhardt staged his *Miracle* at the Olympia, London, with a cast of 2000. On Tree's Forum scene, *The Times* commented:

> The Forum crowd has always been wonderfully life-like at His Majesty's, and there was no perceptible difference in the total impression last night. And, to our thinking, Sir Herbert's usual setting of the scene, in which the crowd – the real protagonist here – occupies the stage, the orators being on one side, is better than Mr Barker's strictly symmetrical arrangement. But the whole affair, the rhythm and movement, and cumulative force of it, was a triumph. (28 June 1911)

The Forum scene is what Tree's *Julius Caesar* is remembered for, but the undertones of his production are worth eliciting. The Roman/British analogue sets up what looks, in the programme, like veiled social criticism:

> Rome was the pleasaunce of the aristocracy. Its life, no less than its palaces and temples, reflected their boundless wealth and indescribable extravagance . . . The once hardy, abstemious mode of living soon degenerated into grossness and sensuality . . . These carpet knights, these leaders of society in the saloons and circus, the party of property and privilege, met their Waterloo on the plains of Pharsalia; and a picture of their camp, when Caesar's legions fell upon it, still survives. Houses of turf had been built for the languid young lords. Trailing ivy masked the entrances to shade their faces from the summer sun. Cushioned couches invited a delicious repose after their expected victory. Tables were

spread with plate and wines, and the daintiest triumphs of Roman cookery. It was thus that they faced the hardships of war. What picture could be over-coloured of their pursuits and haunts in the piping times of peace?

If Rome is luxurious and decadent, Caesar is a benign reformist and sorely needed dictator:

Rome was a hot-bed of profligacy and corruption. It was Caesar's aim to reform it altogether. And it is of the essence of the tragedy that a luxurious Rome, fin de siècle, over-civilized and decadent, shall always be visible: quickening the nobles to greed of the spoils being hourly wrested from their hands, and deepening the resolution of the great Dictator to rescue from their clutches the soil of Italy and to ensure the happiness of millions of mankind.

This is not a concept we are well used to. It is true that in stage history it is rare to find the extreme thesis, that Caesar is a fascist dictator. Orson Welles did it, famously, in his Mercury production of 1937; and Trevor Nunn repeated the thesis in his RSC production of 1972 (Ripley, 1980, pp. 222–37; Houseman, 1972, pp. 285–321; David, 1978, pp. 150–5). But usually Caesar is presented as a flawed human being, one about whom the production is itself ambivalent. Tree saw Caesar in a much more favourable light. It is curious that in the same year (1898) Shaw was writing his *Caesar and Cleopatra* (not produced until 1906) with its idealised and Shavian picture of the benevolent despot. Were idealised dictators in the air at this time? Certainly the Caesar of Tree's opening production sounds not a league away from Shaw's:

'The Caesar of Mr. Charles Fulton is dignified, and dignity is all important', wrote the *Times* reviewer; but without sacrificing his essential stateliness, Fulton did 'laudable justice to the gentleness and affability', the genial humanity, of Caesar as well. Even Caesar's egoistic flights, which often seem mere braggadoccio, Fulton managed to convey with 'a resolute coolness and reserved force' which left Caesar's distinction unmarred.

(Ripley, 1980, p. 175)

It might be just, if facile, to suggest that Tree, who took Antony for himself, needed a Caesar to whom he could decently be loyal. Shaw puts the matter with more verve: 'When it was announced that Mr Tree had resolved to give special prominence to the character of Caesar in his acting version, the critics winked, and concluded simply that the actor–manager was going to play Antony and not Brutus' (Shaw, 1932, vol. 3, p. 299). At all events, Tree presented a sympathetic and reformist Caesar ruling over a great imperial city.

Julius Caesar, then, was spectacular, realistic, urgently suggestive of analogues:

A month after the ending of Queen Victoria's jubilee the British were conscious of the analogy of their Empire with that of the Roman world and many of them equated those virtues of the stoic father and the Roman matron with those of their own race. If the Roman mother saw her sons leaving for the frontiers of Gaul or Britain, the British matron saw her sons leaving for the North-West Frontier, or darkest Africa. (Bingham, 1978, p. 98)

All such possibilities rest on the basic equation of London and Rome. It is that which makes the play, in the programme's words, 'actual as though the Curia were at Westminster, the Forum no farther than Trafalgar Square, and *Caesar's* murder the last sensation of the hour'.

If, as Shaw wrote of *Julius Caesar*, 'The real hero of the revival is Mr Alma Tadema' (Shaw, 1932, vol. 3, p. 302), that hero was little less prominent in Irving's *Coriolanus*. But this was no sudden piece of opportunism. Irving's *Coriolanus* had been planned since 1879, when Alma-Tadema was commissioned 'to make designs for the play and to superintend its production' (Stoker, 1906, vol. 2, p. 65). Alma-Tadema 'started to investigate Etruscan remains in order to set the play correctly in the Rome of about 1500 B.C.'.[1] The production was conceived as a classic late Victorian exercise in the spectacular, founded on the archaeologically correct. As it happened, *Coriolanus* was not put on until April 1901, a few months after Queen Victoria's death. How far this event contributed to the production's failure is impossible to guess. It sounds, from contemporary accounts, as though this *Coriolanus* was muted, lacking in energy and definition in its major gestures. Irving was evidently too old for Coriolanus, notwithstanding the junker-like force he projected in his part. Ellen Terry was miscast as Volumnia. The crowd was well drilled, but with fifty supers did not compete with Tree's. The tribunes were comic rather than threatening or repellent. Still, it is the crowd that locates the focus of interest for us, and on which we can pause briefly.

The crowd is the co-protagonist with the title-role in *Coriolanus*. In it is contained much of the play's political energies; and this fact is well represented in the very stage directions, which are thought to be by Shakespeare himself. The first stage direction reads '*Enter a company of mutinous citizens*'; later there is, simply, '*enter Plebeians*'; but also '*enter a rabble of Plebeians*'. The stage directions vary from the neutral (and by implication respectful) to the abusive. This catches the political problem nicely. Are the Roman citizens a deserving body of people, unjustly oppressed by the fascist beast Coriolanus, or are they a dangerous and unstable mob whom he is quite right to discipline? The evidence is all there, in the text. But it is for and against, and a production will have to make up its mind. Here, though, we come to an historical fact about English productions of *Coriolanus*: they have tended to back off from the political issues, as defined in sub-Marxist terms. It is all very well for critics to agree, as we all do, that *Coriolanus* is 'the most exclusively political play by Shakespeare' (Palmer, 1945, p. 250). In practice, England has tackled the political element much more gingerly than has the continent. A revolutionary mob is potentially the most alarming of theatrical spectacles, but Irving was bent on banking the fires.

This emerges plainly from Alan Hughes's account:

> The significance of the 'political' plot was also reduced. The Lyceum mob was neither an idealized proletariat nor a debased rabble: they were costumed as honest tradesmen, and were not very tumultuous until aroused by Marcius' contempt. Some observers found them sympathetic, and all agreed that Irving grouped and individualized his fifty supernumeraries as never before.
>
> (1981, p. 167)

As for Coriolanus himself, there seems some doubt as to the direction of his playing. Dickins has an interesting commentary:

> It seems doubtful, too, whether [Irving] was wholly in sympathy with the character. For Caius to interest and move an audience the part must surely be approached from the point of view of the Patricians, and Irving appeared to view it from the standpoint of the Plebeians. He conveyed an idea of his fearlessness, of his pride, and of his superior intellect, but he did not present a man who would have been beloved even by his fellow nobles.
>
> (1907, p. 98)

Setting aside the question one would love to ask – where on earth did Irving find the evidence for Coriolanus's 'superior intellect'? – it seems likely that there is a basic hesitancy in this treatment of the role and text. Even the not very distinguished production by Benson that preceded Irving's by a few months did, in Oscar Asche's Sicinius Velutus, offer a genuine Hyde Park demagogue. But here we have an assembly of actors of whom all are insufficiently dislikeable.

If my reading is correct, then, Irving avoided the politico-social aspects of the text and instead played for the old values of spectacle and splendour. But of this – notwithstanding a fine 'Ovation' scene, Coriolanus' return from Corioli – there is not enough. So the production offered a very quiet footnote to Irving's Shakespearean career.

For Tree's *Antony and Cleopatra* (1906), it is unnecessary to offer a general account. The production is covered in Margaret Lamb's stage history (1980) and while she is not especially sympathetic to Tree the production undoubtedly failed to register major success. The reasons, I think, are located in the *Zeitgeist*. On paper, Tree's *Antony and Cleopatra* sounds fine. Another Roman–oriental spectacular, with Joseph Harker taking over from Alma-Tadema: hugely opulent scenes of the landing stage of Cleopatra's Palace in Alexandria, and of Caesar's house in Rome, for instance: a voluptuous and striking Cleopatra in Constance Collier (even if she were burdened with three onstage children, insisted on by the capricious Tree); all the devoted technical excellence of a production at His Majesty's. And yet, something went wrong. The opulence seemed overblown, the evening too long (even with a third of the text shorn off), the production itself verging on self-parody. The unease with spectacular, pictorial Shakespeare that led to the Barker revolution is much in evidence in the press reviews. The text, of course, poses its problems at all times. James Agate wrote, years later, 'If ever a Shakespearean play calls for music, processions, and Tadema-like excesses in bathroom marble, *Antony and Cleopatra* is that play' (1943, p. 176). That view, I think, still cannot be discounted, whatever the prevailing theatrical fashion. Tree, inevitably, chose the spectacular route to this play. But what lay at its heart?

A. B. Walkley of *The Times* has an enlightening analysis:

In every one of his Shakespearean revivals Mr Tree has gone straight for the all-important thing, unity of impression. . . . It is in the passion-*motif* of Cleopatra and Antony, there and not elsewhere; and it is upon that *motif* that Mr Tree concentrates the whole force of his stage. Hence the scenes in 'Caesar's House' are cut very short indeed. Hence the passionate duologue between Cleopatra and Antony is given all the advantage of scenic magnificence and orchestral illustration – Egypt, not Rome nor Athens nor Misenum, becomes the 'hub' of the play.   (*The Times*, 28 Dec. 1906)

The 'passion-*motif*', of which Walkley speaks, offers the 'conception of Antony for the most part as an amiable and charming, but essentially weak epicure' (*Daily Chronicle*, 28 Dec. 1906). What emerges from the reviews is a highly Anglocentric view of the love affair, in which the Roman code is inherited by English public schoolboys. Thus, 'but always this latest Antony was a soldier, lovesick, uxorious – for surely Cleopatra was his only "wife", a man whose vigour and whose better nature are sapped by sensuality and free living' (*Standard*, 28 Dec. 1906). And then, from the same review, 'We see the soft East subdue the virile West.' At last the true genre of this *Antony and Cleopatra* stands revealed. It is an Anglo-Indian amour, out of Kipling: a *Plain Tale from the Hills* with all the trimmings.

To this concept Constance Collier's appearance added materially. As she tells us, 'I looked very beautiful in this scene, the contrast of the silver and my dusky brown skin making a wonderful picture' (Collier, 1929, p. 186). This is not, I think, standard practice today. My impression is that Cleopatras are invariably white-skinned: this is certainly true of the last four Cleopatras I happen to have seen (Margaret Leighton, Janet Suzman, Glenda Jackson, Helen Mirren). In other words, modern productions play up the straightforward psychological aspects of the relationship between

Antony and Cleopatra – they are simply people living together, endlessly bickering about the mistress's status as non-wife – and play down suggestions of a cultural or ethnic divide. Tree, in following the text ('a tawny front') chose to play up this Roman–Egyptian cultural clash. And that points to a field, where the imperial representative encounters the sexual temptations of the natives, which has been extensively tilled by Somerset Maugham, Joseph Conrad, Edgar Wallace and many others.

Let me try to draw together the threads of this paper. The imperial experience is complex, many-faceted, but in Victorian theatrical terms was grounded in the pomp and circumstance of imperial Rome, a succession of superb opportunities for the scenic art of Alma-Tadema and Harker. On that foundation, Tree developed his analyses of government and insurrection, of proconsular weakness; Irving marked, but did not pursue, the class conflict of patrician and plebeian at the centre of imperial greatness. Critics have often thought that Shakespeare used Rome as a means of exploring contemporary politics without penalty; and the same, I believe, is substantially true of the Roman plays in this as in other eras. Tree, whose artistic intuition marched, I suspect, with political prescience, knew that the era was drawing to its close, and the Elgarian note recurs time and again in his productions. It is perhaps not too fanciful to include his *Tempest* (1904) as a codicil to the Roman plays. That production suggested a myth of decolonisation, one that ended in the experience of parting and loss. Famously, Tree chose to show the ship departing from the shore, leaving Caliban to rule his isle. The prompt-book, now at the Folger Shakespeare Library (Temp. 15) gives the following conclusion to the stage direction:

Meantime, Caliban has entered from his cell, climbs rocks, and watches the ship disappearing in the distance . . . At this moment Caliban, who has been watching the departing ship, hearing the voice of the Lark, points in the direction from which the sound is coming; thus forming picture at which the curtain descends.

The picture is described thus:

Moonlight – Cal discovered, crouching on rock with arms uplifted, bidding farewell to the ship, which is dimly seen in the distance.

The imperial theme leads ultimately to abdication and withdrawal, and Tree's art in symbolic form traces this pattern.

NOTE

1 Sybil Rosenfeld 'Alma-Tadema's designs for Henry Irving's *Coriolanus*', *Shakespeare Jahrbuch*, 71 (1974), 84–95.

PART 4

Shakespeare as a Contemporary

PREFACE

I T is the nature of Shakespeare's legacy that he was not only a creative genius in himself, but the cause that other men aspire to such heights. Leaving his interpreters in the theatre aside, Shakespeare inspired Victorian dramatists, poets, composers, painters, artists and craftsmen of all kinds to emulate, imitate or celebrate their mentor.

David Scott, the Pre-Raphaelites and Singer Sargent have already been cited as painters inspired by Shakespearean subjects. Christopher Smith in 'Shakespeare on French Stages' enumerates operas by Rossini, Verdi, Berlioz and Gounod based on Shakespeare plays, and Arthur Jacobs summarises the Shakespearean scores of that quintessentially Victorian composer Arthur Sullivan. Prior to the abolition in 1843 of the Patent Theatres Monopoly, which restricted legitimate drama to Covent Garden, Drury Lane and the Haymarket, minor theatres had often introduced music as a way round the ban on their performing Shakespeare's plays. Even after 1843, the necessity removed, the traditions of 'melodrama' were so ingrained that musical accompaniment for Shakespeare's plays extended way beyond settings for his songs. These were popular in the concert hall too. Sims Reeves had many Shakespearean songs in his repertoire, including settings (for instance, 'Take! Oh, Take!' from *Measure for Measure*) by the indefatigable composer and conductor Alfred Mellon, married to actress Sarah Woolgar, and successively musical director at the Haymarket, the Adelphi and Covent Garden theatres.

Dr Stedman also refers to the importance of music – by Clay for James Albery's *Oriana* and by Alfred Cellier for Albery's *The Spectre Knight*. She shows how the appeal of *A Midsummer Night's Dream* and *The Tempest* extended to other Victorian dramatists including Planché, H. J. Byron and Robert Reece, who used these source plays for generally comic purposes. The mention of H. J. Byron recalls the popularity of burlesques in the Victorian theatre; and Stanley Wells has collected together five volumes of Shakespeare burlesques, including examples 'by authors with independent reputations as comic writers for the stage' (1977, vol. 3, p. ix).

As Dr Wells points out, many of the burlesques were aimed at particular contemporary performances, those of Charles Kean being, not surprisingly, a popular target, as, for example, in *Perdita; or, The Royal Milkmaid* by William Brough in 1856. The close relationship between stage performances of Shakespeare's plays and new drama has been illustrated by Dr Bratton with reference to W. T. Moncrieff's adaptation of Mrs Opie's *Father and Daughter* as *The Lear of Private Life*. Likewise Christopher Murray, detecting a similarity between Sheridan Knowles's heroines and certain of their Shakespearean counterparts, notes that the same actresses – Fanny Kemble, Ellen Tree and Helen Faucit – played female leads in plays by both dramatists.

The roll-call of 'serious' dramatists working in what Dr Ernest Reynolds has called the 'neo-Elizabethan' vein is lengthy – from Byron, Browning, Bulwer Lytton and Tennyson, whose reputations are assured by their non-dramatic writing, to Sheridan Knowles, Richard Hengist Horne, John Westland Marston, Charles Jeremiah Wells, Sir Henry Taylor and others, who, though much lauded by their contemporaries, are now relegated to the supporting cast of dramatic annals. The recruitment of writers of stature was a conscious attempt on Macready's part to enhance the theatre's reputation, but by definition such men had no experience of the practicalities of playwriting and they reached out to Shakespeare as a blueprint for dramatic method. Bulwer Lytton was at least aware of the differences between Shakespeare's theatre and that of the 1840s. He wrote to John Forster about a notion for 'an Historical Pageant' in three or five acts: 'All this in a story of the Epic form – or even in a Drama, long and loose like Shakespeares or Schillers. Historical plays might tell – But for our close and hard compact Theatrical Necessities it would be feeble – & I renounce it. – tho' with regret' (Shattuck, 1958, p. 221).

Here Lytton recognised the essential difference between the Elizabethan theatre ('long and loose') and the Victorian ('close and hard compact'). It was the recurrent practice of Victorian actor–managers to compress, cut and reshape the 'Epic form' of Shakespeare's plays for a theatre which specialised in the compact and the localised. That a dramatist whose plays required such wholesale revision to be accommodated on the contemporary stage should be adopted as an apt model by so many Victorian would-be dramatists is a measure of his stature and their lack of theatrical sense.

Not surprisingly these dramatists often met the same fate as Shakespeare at the hands of actor–managers. Ernest Reynolds (1936, p. 114) writes of Swinburne's *Bothwell* (1874), 'that monstrous drama which drags its slow length along for six hundred closely printed pages', yet the author 'was surprised to find, when he interviewed Irving about a performance, that the actor was not enthusiastic'. Tennyson fared somewhat better. Nevill Coghill described Tennyson's *Becket* as 'in many ways the most successful piece of sham-Shakespeare ever written: he seeks to follow his master almost exactly'. Coghill catalogues the Shakespearean characteristics: chronicle form; sub-plot; all classes of society; blank verse for high-ranking characters; comic-prose for the lower orders; a five-act structure; each act consisting of several scenes in different locations.[1]

It is not surprising that when Irving finally staged *Becket*, in 1893, the year after the poet's death, he meted out to it the same kind of large-scale rearrangement and compression as was his custom with Shakespeare, thereby reversing Tennyson's choice of dramatic model. But with Tennyson, unlike Shakespeare, Irving's alterations were improvements, as Henry Arthur Jones observed:

Becket owed everything to Irving's arrangement and performance. never was an author more indebted to an actor than was Tennyson to Irving in Becket, not merely for the acting of the chief part but for the shaping, arranging, and direction of the play.[2]

Jones was writing in 1912, by which time a dramatic form had been created, of which he was a leading exponent, and which was in tune with, indeed partly created by, current theatre practice. Now it was Ibsen who provided the blueprint; and when William Archer, his advocate and translator, wrote *The Old Drama and the New* in 1923 the battle over dramatic form was, for the time being, lost and won.

NOTES

1 Eliot, 1965, pp. 151–7.
2 Jones, 1931, p. 62; quoted by Peter Thomson in 'Tennyson's Plays and Their Production', in D. Palmer, 1973, p. 246.

James Sheridan Knowles: The Victorian Shakespeare?

CHRISTOPHER MURRAY

J AMES Sheridan Knowles, whose father was a first cousin of Richard Brinsley Sheridan, was born in 1784 in Cork, where he spent the first nine years of his life. The family then removed to London, where James received an informal education and was tutored, coached and befriended by Hazlitt and Lamb. He was writing plays at the age of twelve, and he early abandoned a promising medical career in the Jennerian Society in London in order to go on the stage. Subsequently he took up his father's profession of schoolteacher, in Belfast and Glasgow, but the lure of the stage kept him scribbling even after a thirteen-hour day. Once *Virginius* was staged at Covent Garden, in May 1820, he was launched as a playwright, and thereafter lauded as a 'modern Shakespeare' – a description now worth reassessing, especially since few people today, outside devotees of the nineteenth-century verse drama, have read a line of Knowles.

He was the author of eighteen plays, apart from various fragments, and perhaps four or five of these held the stage until the age of Irving. In *The Spirit of the Age* Hazlitt called him 'the first tragic writer of the age'; Lamb found *Virginius* inferior only to Shakespeare.[1] The comments of reviewers tended to inflate Knowles's reputation along these lines. 'His genius as a dramatic writer is the greatest and most undoubted that the world has seen since the age of Elizabeth', said one such reviewer in 1833 (Knowles, 1872, p. 98). Critics were not as a rule willing to equate Knowles *with* Shakespeare, but they had no hesitation about granting him equal rank with Shakespeare's contemporaries, expecially with Massinger. In America, it is true, the hesitation was far less pronounced. In a 'Memoir' for *The Dramatic Works of James Sheridan Knowles* in 1838 (just inside the Victorian period), R. Shelton Mackenzie remarked: 'He is inferior only to Shakespeare. He equals him in originality of thought and expression. It is no hyperbole to say that, since Shakespeare, no dramatist save Knowles, has written so much *from* and *to* the heart!' We may be forgiven for

23. *James Sheridan Knowles*; an engraving by W. Finden of the drawing by
T. Wageman, 1840

thinking, after all, that this *is* hyperbole; but, as we shall see later on, the
emphasis on the heart contains the clue to Knowles's hold over the
imaginations of his audience.

More interesting than Mackenzie's misplaced Bardolatry was the critical
view which saw Knowles as both Shakespearean and contemporary.
Sometimes the critic was unable to deal with the ambivalence, as

happened when R. H. Horne addressed the question in *A New Spirit of the Age* (1844, p. 90). But others, such as the critical biographer in the *Dublin University Magazine* for October 1852, understood the point better: 'adopting the style of the elder dramatists, he has had the courage to think for himself' (p. 435). Thus was Knowles perceived both as 'bringing again the theatre of Shakespeare' – to anticipate Yeats's phrase – and as a peasant poet, warbling his native woodnotes wild, heard, presumably, on the outskirts of Cork. The latter view, specifically relating Knowles to Burns, was vigorously promoted by the *Athenaeum* in 1847 and found its way into the 'Advertisement' to the two-volume edition of Knowles's *Dramatic Works* in 1856. As this edition was prepared by Knowles himself, who revised his plays for the occasion, it must be supposed that he rather favoured the unlearned than the Shakespearean description. But his (second) wife, Emma, thought otherwise. In 1872 she published a fragment of an early play, *Leo; or, The Gypsy*, in which Kean and Knowles had acted together about the year 1810: 'Two masterminds', she calls them; 'the actor second only to Garrick, the author second only to Shakespeare' (1874, vol. 1, p. 46). The introduction to the next two-volume edition of the *Dramatic Works* (1883) accordingly carried a correction, first made in 1859, of the earlier reference to Knowles's lack of education. The alternative myth of a natural talent, an early nineteenth-century O'Casey risen from the slums, was officially squashed by a dutiful widow.

The broad question of Knowles's Shakespeareanism takes into its ambit the issue of poetic drama, theory and practice, in the nineteenth century. As George Rowell has said in *The Victorian Theatre* (1978, p. 38), the real trouble with the Romantic poets was that they were unwilling to come to terms with the contemporary theatre. Knowles may, indeed, have been too willing to collaborate with the stage conditions of his day. Macready said, in praise, that Knowles was 'open to conviction' from himself (Macready and Pollock, 1876, p. 230), and it is quite clear that Knowles allowed his early plays to be altered and revised by Macready in order to ensure the best results. It may be said that this pliability was more the mark of humility than of weakness, however. Knowles trusted Macready and the consequence ratified his trust. Between them playwright and actor struck the right chords in the public mind, so that two of these early plays, *Virginius* and *William Tell*, proved long-lasting successes on the British and American stages. But once Knowles returned to the stage as actor, after 1830, both in his own plays and in Shakespeare, the friendship with Macready cooled. Macready saw him as getting above himself, as ungrateful, and so on – the way only Macready could see such matters.

James Sheridan Knowles

Knowles's return to the stage certainly signifies his total commitment to the theatre of his day; consequently the plays he wrote thereafter, eleven in number, are far less vehicles for a star actor and more in tune with the contemporary interest in melodrama on the one hand and comedy of manners on the other. Uninhibited by the burden of tradition, or at any rate showing himself able to offset this burden with the claims of a nightly audience to be entertained, Knowles persisted until 1843 in offering the London theatres five-act tragedies and comedies in verse, so successfully that, although he made little money out of them,[2] he won much acclaim. It is significant that at the time of Wordsworth's death in 1850 Knowles was recommended for the positions both of Poet Laureate and of curator of Shakespeare's birthplace. The fact that he secured neither position does not diminish the scope of his achievement as a poetic dramatist. He had proved that to be a full-time writer for the theatre was far from being a disgrace.

Looking more closely now at the relation of Knowles to Shakespeare and what this tells us of Victorian taste and understanding, I should say that insofar as Knowles was a good dramatist he broke away from the centuries-old slavery of imitative writing. But it would have to be conceded that he did fall at times into echoing Shakespeare, not so much in his language as in his plots. *Caius Gracchus* recalls *Julius Caesar* in its mob scenes and *Coriolanus* in the demeanour of its hero. *The Wife* is reminiscent of *Othello*:[3] parts of *The Hunchback* and *Woman's Wit* recall *Julius Caesar* and *Cymbeline*.[4] And so on. No great importance attaches to such echoes: they are never more than faint, and they serve to contrast rather than to align two quite different points of view.

Among the features which lent Knowles's plays their reputation were his language, his use of comedy, his characterisation of women and his emphasis on domestic situations, a quaint phrase which has to be retained for want of a better. These might loosely be termed his Shakespearean features. Against these can be placed his contemporary features, which include his fondness for a well-made structure, his use of melodramatic situations and his moral idealism. These two areas overlap, but they serve to indicate that there was a dichotomy in Knowles's work and that it illuminates the Victorian view of Shakespeare. In other words, Knowles's contemporary features correspond to some degree with the manner in which Shakespeare was then interpreted and staged. The writers were thus inversely rather than directly related.

In referring to the Shakespearean features I must be very brief here. Coleridge had emphasised in his *Biographia Literaria* the organic nature of Shakespeare's imagery. In his plays Knowles too showed himself capable of using language so that the images related to the theme and meaning symbolically. For example, when Virginius tries to refute Appius' claim that Virginia is not his daughter he says:

> The lie
> Is most abortive then, that takes the flower –
> The very flower our bed connubial grew –
> To prove its barrenness!　　　　(1856, vol. 1, pp. 99–100)

Here the relationship between 'abortive', 'flower' and 'barrenness' is essential and revealing: Appius' 'lie' would seek to deny the natural process, something Virginius cannot be party to. The description of the eagle in *William Tell*, 1.2, offers another good example, since the eagle symbolises freedom, the main theme of that play; later, the villain Gessler refers to Tell's son as 'this fine eaglet' whom he will use to trap bigger game. Likewise in *The Wife* the image of 'enmeshing' is used thematically. But it would be foolish to suggest that Knowles wrote like that habitually. On the contrary, he seemed so aware of the dangers of 'fine writing' (something he warned against as a lecturer) that he tended rather to avoid than to cultivate ornament in his plays.

His language, indeed, inclines towards colloquialism, for which Knowles was faulted in his own day. One gets this sort of thing, for example:

> [She]　I'll see you to your horse.
> [He]　What, with that face?
> [She]　Will you not see your boy before you go?
> [He]　I saw him, Sweet, as I came in.
> [She]　Well, Caius,
> 　　　　Farewell!
> [He]　Now, that's my own Licinia!
> 　　　　　　　　(*Caius Gracchus* (1856, vol. 1, p. 14))

Knowles nods like this in several plays – my own favourite is a passage which includes the word 'dentifrice' in blank verse – but on the whole he seems to be in pursuit of a colloquial speech not yet at that time accepted as worthy of tragedy. He pushes beyond blank verse in the same direction that Browning pushed in the dramatic monologue but failed to do in the theatre.

Thus quite often Knowles provides verse thin by Shakespearean standards but naturalistic when compared with the traditional blank verse still favoured by critics and closet dramatists. One further example must serve here. In *The Hunchback*, 4.2, the eponymous hero shows his ward Julia around the house of her new fiancé, whom she has chosen in preference to her impoverished lover. He pauses in front of a tapestry:

James Sheridan Knowles

> The story's of a page who loved the dame
> He served – a princess! – Love's a heedless thing!
> That never takes account of obstacles;
> Makes plains of mountains, rivulets of seas,
> That part it from its wish. So proved the page,
> Who from a state so lowly, look'd so high; –
> But love's a greater lackwit still than this.
> Say it aspires – that's gain! Love stoops – that's loss!
> You know what comes. The princess loved the page.
> Shall I go on, or here leave off?   (1856, vol. 1, pp. 268–9)

The use of irony here, defined in *Love* as 'but a laughing truth', is bound up with character (the speaker is really – unknown to her – her father) and situation (he really wants to teach her a lesson). The flexible use of the line was something Knowles could manage very well. The end of Act 4 of *Love* and the delightful scene in *The Love Chase* where the sixty-two-year-old widower tries to persuade himself and his friend how youthful his appearance is (1856, vol. 2, p. 7) supply other examples. It looks as though Knowles, however unsurely, aspired to realism, but was held back by the conservatism of the age. Consequently, his plays are suspended between Shakespeare and realism.

Knowles's use of comedy was fairly conventional. From *William Tell* on he combined a serious with a romantic and/or farcical sub-plot, always taking pains to relate the two. In one of his lectures he complained that Shakespeare had dissipated the potential of *The Merchant of Venice* by making the Bassanio–Portia plot so strong as to rob the audience of any real knowledge of Antonio. As a result, the trial scene suffers: 'I think he [Shakespeare] had a glorious climax here, of which he has made nothing' (Knowles, 1873, p. 124). In his own serious plays the comic material is quite subservient and would strike us today as mere padding, though for the Victorians the comic relief was obviously essential. In the comedies proper, which dominated his later work, Knowles made use of the traditional romantic material of disguise, mistaken identity, and recognition scenes revealing long-lost sons, daughters and parents. Recently Robertson Davies, unsympathetic to the tragedies, praised the comedies, finding there 'a depth and certainty of touch that marks Knowles as a man of uncommon gifts' (Booth, 1975, p. 224). It would seem from such plays, however, that comedy was not to be related to real life very forcibly. It was artificial; it was mechanical; it was fundamentally joyous. There was no such thing as dark comedy. Jack must have his Jill at the end, or better still, three Jacks (as at the end of *The Love Chase*) have the right Jills.

The plots themselves often turn on the unacknowledged love of compatible characters divided by social class ('The princess loved the page'). In spite of the artificiality a moral realism underpins the plot which is only Shakespearean in that it is humanist. It is heard once again in Knowles's last (and unsuccessful) play, *The Secretary* (1843), where Knowles's spokeman is a 'providential' figure called Colonel Green (played by Macready). He informs the secretary of his true identity, which causes the latter to cry out in anguish at the reality to which he has been awakened; to which Colonel Green replies (1856, vol. 2, p. 451):

> Reality! There's none, boy, but the thought
> Of doing right! He grasps who holds to that!

It may not be entirely fanciful to relate this secretary to another confidential clerk, just as Eliot's attempts to marry verse drama and the popular stage are not without relevance to Knowles's almost lifelong efforts. In any event, a fairly intense but unobtrusive evangelical spirit permeates Knowles's comedies, the work of a man who abandoned the theatre to become a Baptist preacher after 1843.

Knowles's characterisation of women, it follows, was highly idealistic. In later years, when he was congratulated by a woman on behalf of her sex for the view of womanhood he had offered in his plays, he replied, somewhat nauseatingly, 'What else could I have done, my dear madam? . . . God bless you, I painted them as I found them.'[5] There is a striking parallel between Knowles's heroines and the Shakespearean characters beloved of the Victorians: Juliet, Rosalind, Ophelia, Desdemona and Cordelia. The same actress often played both Knowles and Shakespeare – for example, Fanny Kemble, Ellen Tree and Helen Faucit, although Emma Elphinstone created several of Knowles's leading roles after 1834.[6] Knowles was thoroughly Victorian in his depiction of women. The counterpart of this is to be seen in Mrs Jameson's *Shakspeare's Heroines*, where 'the angelic refinement' of Desdemona, or Imogen as 'the angel of light', or a Cordelia 'too sacred for words' is to be found. But then even Henry Morley could speak of the 'womanly perfection' of Imogen.

The domestic theme follows logically from this point. Perhaps the best-known quotation on the topic is Horne's complaint about *Virginius* in *A New Spirit of the Age* (p. 87): 'We have Roman tunics, but a modern English heart, – the scene is the Forum, but the sentiments those of the "Bedford Arms".' In play after play by Knowles, the plot hinges upon a father–son or father–daughter relationship, with the wife–husband relationship coming next in importance. It is easy to take this for granted in his work. As Horne said, 'The age is domestic, and so is he.' Or, as Coleridge put it in his *Table Talk* (27 Sept. 1830) 'every one wished a Desdemona or Ophelia for a wife'. It is easy to see Knowles as merely exploiting a contemporary predilection. Yet the domestic ideal was a conviction carrying almost mystical fervour in his work, so that one must consider that he expressed the feeling of the age by expressing his own conviction. Whether he shaped taste in this matter it is impossible to say, but it became a basic melodramatic theme of the nineteenth century. Moreover, side by side with the various father figures in Knowles's plays, Macready's acting of such roles as Prospero, Lear or Leontes provided much emphasis on domestic values. There is thus a parallel between Knowles's domesticity and the contemporary fondness for interpreting Shakespeare's roles in the terms that the Bedford Arms might appreciate.

Knowles went very far in *Caius Gracchus* in the direction of upholding the home over all other values, even at the cost of depicting the wife, Licinia, as very un-Roman and pacifist. In a key speech she describes herself as 'Consummate happy in my world within' (1856, vol. 1, p. 10) only when her husband is at home with her. She anticipates O'Casey's Nora Clitheroe in the scene (5.1) where she tries to drag her husband home from dangerous involvement in political action. In *Alfred the Great* Knowles tried to balance the claims of family and country – a preoccupation also of *John of Procida*, where the patriotism of the eponymous John costs him the life of his son. And of course in *William Tell* these same claims provide the heart of Tell's dilemma, far clearer in the play's revised form.[7] The world without, then, is a terror to the world within in Knowles's plays, as if he were forever rewriting *Othello*, with Iago cast as the leader of a foreign power. In such a scenario, the only alternative, indeed the pole, to the melting mood was jingoism. And that was the domestic theme writ large – or, in the case of *Brian Boroihme*, writ larger than life, for that piece was the Celtic *Indiana Jones* of the 1830s. (It was not included in the definitive *Dramatic Works* of 1856.)

The mystical side of the domestic theme forms part of the metaphysic which replaces the older, Shakespearean world-view in the nineteenth century. Fatherhood in Knowles is divine, a source not only of authority and order in a frightening world but a symbol of transcendental love. This is rather hard to take today, used as we are to the realism of Arthur Miller and Eugene O'Neill in their treatments of the family as tragic arena. Yet we must try to understand the Victorian concept if we are to appreciate what Victorians saw in Lear or King Henry IV for example. Knowles provides a very strange and yet gripping treatment of his ideas about fatherhood in a play entitled *The Daughter*, a psychological melodrama. But the philosophy, if one can call it that, is probably best expressed in *The Maid of Mariendorpt*, where the dutiful daughter who is prepared to sacrifice all for her condemned father says what filial love means:

It is worship –
Although no lip be moved, no eye be strain'd,
No hands be clasp'd –   (1856, vol. 2, pp. 129–30)

As to the contemporary aspect of Knowles's work, insofar as that is relevant here it is best approached through a consideration of his own lectures. For many years from about the mid-1820s Knowles was a successful touring lecturer on drama, poetry, oratory and elocution. His lectures on drama (privately printed in 1873 as *Lectures on Dramatic Literature*) offered an indirect account of his own concept of what constitutes a good play, as well as presenting his views on Shakespeare, the Greeks and some few moderns (such as Byron and Maturin). He put much emphasis on structure and on the value of what later came to be known as the well-made play. He faulted *Hamlet* for its deficiencies of form and action, its lack of 'progress of the plot', finding its power to be 'rather the effect of isolated parts than of a continuous whole'(p. 93). 'Herein', he deduced, 'if I am not deceived, we detect the difficulty of constructing a successful acting drama. Everything must be to this purpose; nothing, or as little as possible, must be from it: nothing digressive, nothing superfluous' (p. 95). *Macbeth* was his ideal play; he devoted two full lectures to it. Since the great aim of the tragic dramatist was 'to excite suspense' (p. 37), *Macbeth* was supreme as tragedy. In his analysis Knowles pointed out Shakespeare's skill in maintaining suspense, enthusing most of all over the climax, where Macduff undermines Macbeth's sense of invulnerability: 'Here was the dramatist. Here was perception of the use of situation and incident' (p. 40). It is somewhat amusing to note that Rita's appreciation of Macbeth in Willy Russell's *Educating Rita* centres on this same climactic moment (1981, p. 28). There was, to be sure, something comparably unspoiled about Knowles's response to Shakespeare. He concluded: 'One word and no more. "Macbeth" is the most melodramatic tragedy in the whole range of the drama, and it is to the credit of Shakespeare that it is so' (p. 41). This tells us a great deal about Knowles's dramatic values and reminds us that the popular theatre was for him the standard of excellence. Reciprocally, of course, the performance of Macready in *Macbeth* at this time was constantly referred to as melodramatic, a term by no means as pejorative as he himself seemed to think.

Apart from structure, Knowles stressed the passion in Shakespeare's tragedies. The point is an important one since it relates to his own work fundamentally. William Archer, in his attack on post-Shakespearean verse drama in *The Old Drama and the New*, condemned passion as an obscurantist feature. Passion was to be equated with bombast and stood at the opposite pole from nature. Archer thus faulted Knowles's drama for what he termed 'robustious un-nature' (p. 171). But it is clear from Knowles's lectures that for him passion *was* nature, and the very life-blood of great drama. As he put it:

The grand ingredient of the drama, that which contributes most to the impression which a play produces upon an audience, is passion; because passion is univerally understood. This is the lightning which melts the diversified assembly into one mass, so that they become but one man and have but one heart. (1873, p. 140)

Here, as elsewhere, Knowles seems to echo Hazlitt, whom he called his 'mental father' (1872, pp. 10–11) and who in his essay 'On Shakspere' stressed the 'force of passion' in Shakespeare's plays.[8] Knowles had in fact no sympathy with the bombast and artificiality which Archer attributed to him. What he admired in Shakespeare, moreover, he endeavoured to put into practice in his own plays. Thus a favourite touchstone for him was the quarrel scene in *Julius Caesar* where the dialogue was 'so true that it resembles something that had occurred in real life' (1873, p. 122). Archer, scoffing at one of Knowles's plays, *The Hunchback*, tells us that one scene in it became material for elocution classes as a comic counterpart to 'the quarrel scene between Brutus and Cassius' (1923, p. 245). This surely indicates that Knowles was capable of practising what he preached.

Frequently the interpretation which Knowles gave to Shakespeare's plays in his lectures was mediated by stage performances. For example, whatever his misgivings about *Hamlet* as a well-made play, the effect of it when acted (by Kean) was 'successively to arouse, to amaze, to appal, to melt, to awaken every chord of the human heart into thrilling, exquisite vibration' (p. 94). This is the language of nineteenth-century evangelism, no doubt. He wrote in similar terms about Mrs Siddons's Lady Macbeth; of the sleepwalking scene he remarked: 'I could pity a murderess who should look upon that scene . . . the chill of the grave seemed about you while you looked on her.'[9] But he also said: 'This tragedy is from first to last an impressive, convincing, luminous, moral lesson. And so is every good tragedy in the language' (p. 197). 'Luminous' is the key word here, just as in defending Shakespeare against Puritans he talked of the light that beams from Shakespeare's pages, 'the light of philosophy and Christianity – the light of natural and revealed religion harmoniously and invigoratingly blending' (p. 86). The light comes from the thrill; the thrill from the performance, or from a correct reading. In another typical passage in the lectures Knowles described a visit to Shakespeare's birthplace and burial place, where he experienced religious feeling, 'thrilling by the grave, and gazing on the monument, of Shakespeare' (p. 202). That the idealism underpinning such sentiments is ridiculous to our way of thinking is no matter: Knowles speaks for his time, and this is borne out by the fact that, when Irving first acted Macbeth in a totally new way, Knowles's conception of the play was brought forward by one harsh critic as the traditional view which had been shared by Kean and Macready (*Sheridan Knowles's Conception* . . . 1876, p. 7). Thus we cannot discuss either Knowles's own plays or the interpretation of Shakespeare's in the first half of the nineteenth century without taking into account that trembling, religious fervour which makes open-hearted fellows like Knowles appear at once risible and inflamed.

My final area of exploration is the question of why Knowles enjoyed such a high reputation in his own day. The obvious point with which to begin an answer is the spirit of the age. I have already quoted Horne, 'the age is domestic, and so is he'; this seems to me now glib. We need, I think, to keep alive in our minds the awareness that in the nineteenth century old certitudes were crumbling and old securities yielding to new terrors. Knowles was one of those writers – Dickens was another – who tried to combine wholesome entertainment with cultural sustenance. Matthew Arnold's contention that poetry in its widest sense had to take the place of religion in people's lives was not born *ex nihilo* in the 1860s. Its genesis can be dated to the early decades of the century. 'Be in earnest', was Knowles's firm advice in *The Elocutionist* to all would-be orators; it is implicit in his plays as well. It was an imperative much believed in by Macready as actor; it was something which, as Walter E. Houghton (1957, pp. 218–62) has shown, was a vital part of the Victorian 'frame of mind'. Knowles's plays offered the sort of exhortation which Victorians took as felt life. If the domestic form became, as Michael R. Booth has claimed, 'the backbone of Victorian drama' (1969, vol. 1, p. 23) it was because it provided a stay against the anarchy inherent in nineteenth-century progress. It soothed, consoled and assuaged.

Weighed against Shaw or Ibsen, Knowles is decidedly conventional. He mirrored a conventional age. When that age passed, or was transmuted into Arnold's age of sick hurry and divided aims, Knowles ceased to articulate the 'sentiment' of an audience. But before Knowles is condemned for failing to speak out in a voice that might be heard at the end of the century two things must be conceded. One concerns the official censorship of his day, moral and political. In spite of its severity, Knowles wrote many lines in *Virginius*, *Caius Gracchus* and *William Tell* which were considered too radical to be spoken on stage at the time.[10] His conformity was thus a qualified one. Shakespeare too was forced to conform at this time: many of the comedies were kept off the stage, and Bowdler's *Family Shakespeare* reflected the aims of middle-class culture. Secondly, what

Knowles's plays exhibited above all, as the *Athenaeum* (27 Feb. 1847) noted, was 'heart'. Hazlitt's word in the *London Magazine* (July 1820) was 'nature', but it is clear he meant the same thing: 'Our unpretending poet [Knowles] travels along the high road of nature and the human heart.' Imaginative sincerity was for Hazlitt the criterion of excellence in art, and this in turn was the basis of Knowles's style. Therefore he was popular because his plays caused a glow in the hearts of his audiences, for these were non-intellectual times (Park, 1971, pp. 167–8).

A more telling reason for popularity was Knowles's theatricality. Perhaps somebody like Archer, all zeal for the new form of drama, could justifiably be impatient with Knowles's style, which it was part of Archer's mission to declare obsolete. But more sympathetically looked at Knowles's plays are the work not of a charlatan but of a man steeped in the theatre of his day. He was, after all, an actor–playwright, a rare animal in the early nineteenth-century legitimate theatre.[11] In his early days he had been on the Irish circuits with Kean, who encouraged him to write. How invaluable this experience was to him is borne out by his lectures on drama and oratory, where the live theatre is never far from view. His return to the stage as actor in 1832, for ten years or so, again stamped him as a man who, if he was never more than a mediocre actor, mastered the craft sufficiently to win plaudits in his own plays on both sides of the Atlantic. An interesting contrast would be with Robert Browning, perhaps the most promising of the would-be playwrights who were mainly poets. Browning was always at the mercy of Macready and the critics; he never could develop the drama towards which he groped. Knowles overcame such servitude and learned to use the conditions of the stage to his advantage. His plays were so written as to provide good scenes, good situations, well varied, within well-structured tragedies or comedies. If the situations strike us as trite or unreal they did not strike contemporary audiences so. The corollary is signified by the 'points' style of acting Shakespeare. Knowles's plays are full of areas inviting acting display, within the context of early nineteenth-century conventions. Theatre history acknowledges the degree to which Macready, in particular, reaped the benefits of these opportunities; but so also did Charles Kean, Samuel Phelps, Edwin Forrest among the men and, among the women, Fanny Kemble, Helen Faucit, Ellen Tree and Charlotte Cushman. In America Knowles's plays were, for various reasons, more popular than in England, and *Virginius*, for example, was acted over two hundred times on the New York stage during the eighty-five years between its première and the time Eugene O'Neill's father played in it (Meeks, 1933, pp. 174–5).

Fanny Kemble, who created the role of Julia in *The Hunchback*, said that the great merit of it as an acting play covered all its defects, and added something which might be applied to many another Knowles play: 'it is a very satisfactory play to *see*, but let nobody who has seen it well acted attempt to read it in cold blood' (Marshall, 1977, p. 59). Samuel Phelps could make even the least promising parts in Knowles seem powerful. His villain Almagro in the première of *The Rose of Arragon* in 1842 was described by the *Sunday Times* as being 'as magnificent a piece of acting as we have ever beheld'; and of a similar role in Knowles's last play, *The Secretary*, it was said: 'The character would have been intensely disagreeable, but Phelps's excellent acting was apparent more than ever in this part.' By naturalistic standards, perhaps, the excellence of the acting *should not* have been apparent, but that merely defines for us the style then in vogue. In a word, then, Knowles's plays gave scope to actors and actresses vocally, emotionally and creatively, so that audiences could be, to use one of his favourite words, thrilled.

A final aspect of Knowles's dramaturgy which requires attention is his pictorial sense. In commenting on *Virginius*, Hazlitt said:

Besides the merits of Virginius as a literary composition, it is admirably adapted to the stage. It presents a succession of pictures. We might suppose each scene almost to be copied from a beautiful bas-relief, or to have formed a group on some antique vase . . . But it is a speaking and a living picture we are called upon to witness. (*London Magazine*, July 1820)

Yet the scenery for this production, Hazlitt makes clear, was all wrong. The pictorialism was thus in the conception and in the staging. What might be termed Knowles's melodramatic sense served him well in providing tableaux in all of his plays, as the acting versions make clear. Far more is told on this point by George Scharf's famous drawings for Macready's 1838 productions of *Virginius* and other plays. The great climax of *Virginius*, the Forum scene, was graphically captured by Scharf (pl. 24). Alan Downer faulted Knowles for leaving Virginius '*utterly at a loss what to do*' in this scene, until his eye falls on a butcher's stall bearing a knife which he takes (1966, p. 67). But Scharf's picture makes plain that the scene of the sacrifice must be a total surprise, for all the power is on the side of the villain Appius. The actor had to create this climactic situation by rising from confusion to certitude. In the picture, in spite of the mob of soldiers and the lictors, there are really only three characters: Virginius, about to kill his passive daughter, and Appius, rising in disbelief from his chair as if to prevent what he himself has brought about. The non-involvement of everybody else, their virtual indifference, gives a primal tragic form to the sacrifice. Such was the pictorialism that Knowles's drama at its best achieved.

In *William Tell* there is a moment which declares the nature of this pictorialism. In Act 4 Gessler is depicted as a hopeless coward as well as a cruel tyrant; he castigates his soldiers for fleeing from one man, Tell, while he trembles as Tell is brought in in chains. As his men try to force Tell to his knees Gessler sits and comments on this struggle. His role here is to mediate the valour and nobility of Tell, to focus the audience's attention on the moral meaning of the scene. Touches like 'Behold!' and 'They gaze on me' (1856, vol. 1, p. 158) make plain the tableau form in which the scene was played. Making the villain the interpreter of the scene indicates the degree of audience involvement Knowles required. The technique is a form of anti-naturalism; the proscenium stage is used as a moral focus. Another example is provided by the opening of Act 5 of *Alfred the Great*, where a curtained recess stage is used. We see at such moments what was inherent in Victorian pictorialism. Victorian staging of Shakespeare precluded ambiguities and offered clearcut, vivid interpretations. Knowles agreed with this method. Commenting in his *Lectures* (1873, pp. 150–1) on the cavern scene in *Macbeth* (4.1) he said: 'What a picture should it suggest! . . . Let not a word be spoken, till the audience have had time to

24. *Virginius*, by James Sheridan Knowles, 4.2: the death of Virginia. Drawing by George Scharf jun. of Macready's production of the play, 1838

study the picture.' His own plays rarely got the careful production lavished on Shakespeare, but it remains true to say that Knowles wrote his plays in such a way as to correspond to the growing trend in theatrical illustration.

By the time of his death in 1862 Knowles had long given up 'all such sinful thoughts and pleasures' as the theatre affords (Meeks, 1933, p. 53). Coincidentally, the time between his abandoning the stage for the pulpit and his death spans the management career of Samuel Phelps at Sadler's Wells. It is interesting to observe what this new era, ushered in by the 1843 Theatre Regulation Act, meant for Knowles's plays. Of the various contemporary playwrights staged by Phelps, Knowles was the most popular (Allen, 1971, pp. 275–6, 316, 319). No fewer than six of his plays formed a regular part of the repertory, and in addition the highest number of performances for a single play (to borrow the jargon of the prize-givers) went to Knowles's adaptation of *The Maid's Tragedy* entitled *The Bridal*. It can perhaps be said, then, that Knowles shared in Phelps's enterprise of bringing poetic drama to new audiences.

In 1862, moreover, the year both of Phelps's retirement from management and of Knowles's death, the critic Henry Morley commented on the continuing popularity of Knowles's plays in such a way as may serve here for conclusion. *The Hunchback* and *The Love Chase* were at this time playing at the Princess's Theatre, under the new lesseeship of Lindus, and of these Morley wrote:

There is a bad imitation of Elizabethan manner in the language and some clumsiness of invention in the plot of these plays, but they are immeasurably better entertainment than the extravagance of scenic melodrama by which alone many managers are now tempted to think that the public can be charmed.   (Morley, 1891, p. 237)

The Shakespearean comparison may finally be dispensed with, as it has no real basis. Yet, with the success of Phelps at Sadler's Wells and Kean at the Princess's, Shakespearean production was shown to be potentially every bit as colourful and lively as the more popular forms of theatre, and in that regard Knowles and Shakespeare moved towards each other from opposite directions. For a brief while it looked as if they actually coincided, as they seemed to occupy the same ground. But this was only an illusion, one more expression of a Victorian ideal.

NOTES

1 'With wonder I/Hear my old friend (turned Shakespeare) read a scene, /Only to *his* inferior in the clean/Passes of pathos', 'To J. S. Knowles, on His Tragedy of "Virginius"', quoted *Dublin University Magazine*, 40 (1852), 428.
2 Archer, 1923, p. 245 implies otherwise. At a banquet in 1842 Knowles said: 'I stand

before you a poor man, after having produced fifteen plays, all of which, if I might judge from their reception and criticisms upon them, have been successful.' Quoted Watson, 1926, p. 250.

3 In the epilogue, written by Charles Lamb, the eponymous heroine says: 'I dream'd each night, I should be Desdemona'd . . . /But my Othello, to his vows more zealous–/ Twenty Iagos could not make him jealous!' (Knowles, 1856, vol. 1, p. 343). Hereafter this edition is used for all quotations from Knowles's plays.

4 Knowles, 1856, vol. 2, pp. 96–7. Lewson, the tool of the villain Lord Athunree, enters the ante-chamber of Hero's room at night and describes the setting. The Victorian touch is also worth noting: 'Is this her chamber? No, her dressing-room' (p. 96), a delicacy often found in Knowles's plays.

5 Quoted in 'Our Portrait Gallery', Dublin University Magazine, 40 (1852), 435.

6 Crabb Robinson saw and admired her in The Maid of Mariendorpt at the Haymarket in 1838: 'She will become a distinguished actress I have no doubt.' (She became Knowles's second wife instead.) See Robinson, 1966, p. 160.

7 In the original, acting, version there was an Act 5, which was later (in 1856) dispensed with. At its climax Tell storms Gessler's castle, where his son Albert is threatened with death if he advances. Totally against the spirit of Acts 3 and 4 Tell's response is: 'I see him not!–/I see my country, Verner, not my son!' (p. 86). In the revised form the play ends shortly after Gessler's death and this contradiction disappears.

8 The essay is included in Knowles, 1832, pp. 58–61. The quotation is on p. 59.

9 Lectures, p. 167. When Edwin Forrest once asked Knowles what Mrs Siddons was like in the sleepwalking scene, he replied, 'Well, sir, I smelt blood! I swear that I smelt blood!' Forrest was much impressed. See Meeks, 1933, p. 52. Knowles's response to Charlotte Cushman's Romeo in 1846 was equally typical. He compared her scene with Friar Laurence (3.3) with Kean's Othello in Act 3: 'It was a scene of topmost passion. I listened and gazed and held my breath while my blood ran hot and cold.' Quoted Watson, 1926, p. 312.

10 Hazlitt referred to the cuts in Virginius in his review for the London Magazine (July 1820). 'This is the case almost uniformly wherever the words "Tyranny," or "Liberty," occur', he commented. Macready said that after Virginius was passed by the Lord Chamberlain the text was requested by the Prince Regent just before performance and was returned with pencil marks through some lines in the part of Appius on tyranny (See Macready, 1876, p. 159). Cumberland's acting version bears this out. Caius Gracchus shocked the Lord Chamberlain by its 'liberal sentiments', according to the Life, p. 70 (Meeks, 1933, pp. 140–1). Again, Cumberland's acting version shows many cuts in passages that might cause a political response in the audience. The 'Remarks' of D–G prefacing William Tell in Cumberland's acting edition make clear (p. 5) that politics was to be treated with caution as dramatic material.

11 The prologue to The Wife, apparently by Charles Lamb, implies that Knowles's taking up acting was socially disastrous: 'A poet once, he found–and look'd aghast–/By turning actor, he had lost his caste' (Knowles, 1856, vol. 1, p. 292). Shirley S. Allen says that Knowles was the 'one notable exception' to the general rule that five-act plays were written either by amateurs or by those with reputations in other forms of literature, (1971, p. 273).

Victorian Imitations of and Variations on
A Midsummer Night's Dream and
The Tempest

JANE W. STEDMAN

I N every way the nineteenth century was indeed a *cabinet des fées*: from
Benjamin Thompson's ill-fated *Oberon's Oath* (1816) to J. M. Barrie's
enchanted wood of second chances in *Dear Brutus* (1917); from
Fuseli's grotesque wing-things and Paton's *Reconciliation of Oberon and
Titania* to Arthur Rackham's Kensington fairies; from Mendelssohn's
incidental music for *A Midsummer Night's Dream* to Sullivan's for *The
Tempest*; from Hans Christian Andersen's tales to Oscar Wilde's. Marie
Taglioni's tragic sylph danced across Europe, and playwrights depicted the
lost pleiad as a fallen fairy. In fact, when Mr Rochester called Jane Eyre his
fairy, elf, sprite, sylph, mustard seed, and changeling, he unconsciously
ran through the cast of nineteenth-century plays, romantic, pathetic,
pastoral, comical, fantastical and instructive.

Victorian dramatists, especially the writers of extravaganzas, chose
plots, characters, and scenic images from the collections of Perrault and
Madame D'Aulnoy, while pantomime turned to the less elegant tales of
the Brothers Grimm. Eighteenth-century moralised fairy-tales, such as Dr
Johnson's *The Fountains* and Madame Genlis's *Le Palais de Vérité*, the
acknowledged source of W. S. Gilbert's *The Palace of Truth*, were easily
available. There were native English fairy traditions, of course, with their
Renaissance elaborations by Spenser, Jonson, Herrick, and others (Briggs,
1959). All this and Shakespeare too! – for *A Midsummer Night's Dream*
and *The Tempest* exerted a continual influence on nineteenth-century
drama, both in themselves and as transmitted through the German poet
C. M. Wieland's eighteenth-century fairy epic *Oberon*, in William
Sotheby's 1798 translation. So useful, indeed, were Shakespeare's fairy
plays that W. Phillips's choice of scenes from *A Midsummer Night's Dream*
and *The Tempest* to decorate the new Vaudeville Theatre in 1870 seems to

represent both an acknowledgement of theatrical indebtedness and a hope for reflected lustre.

The prestige of such imitative glory was, in fact, one of four closely related elements which made Shakespeare's fairy comedies popular with serious Victorian dramatists writing for an adult audience. Other elements were spectacle (including music), plot construction, and theme.

The possibility of prestige had an obvious attraction for stage writers conscious that their craft was not currently venerated, but that Shakespeare had long been idolised – as witness the elder Thomas Hood's long poem *The Plea of the Midsummer's Fairies* (1827). This adulatory work tells how Shakespeare's shade saved Titania, Puck, Ariel and other clustering fays from the deadly clutch of Giant Time. Hood's fairies, like Shakespeare's, are nature spirits and encourage lovers, but, like the much later Tinkerbell, they are dependent on 'the fickle faith of men'. Shakespeare has hitherto kept them alive, and finally, unable to destroy his august ghost, Time goes baffled away, while the fairies pay pretty homage to the haloed Bard:

> 'Nod to him, Elves!' cries the melodious Queen.
> 'Nod to him, Elves, and flutter round about him. . . .
> Plant in his walks the purple violet . . .'   (Hood, n.d., pp. 219–20)

As 'Time's famous rival till the final date', Shakespeare thus presented a standard of immortality to aim at, although a Victorian dramatist knew that he himself would inevitably fall short. But if he could not hope to create another Hamlet, he might save a fairy or two with a variation on *A Midsummer Night's Dream*. At worst – or best – he might have a *succès d'estime* and win the coveted title of poet rather than playwright. The *Era* (26 Feb. 1871), for instance, described the dialogue of Robert Reece's *Perfect Love; or, Oberon's Triumph* as characteristic of a highly poetical mind; and when James Albery's *Oriana* proved unstageworthy, Joseph Knight (*Athenaeum*, 22 Feb. 1873) advised him to publish and be read, for his merits would then be recognised and his reputation as a verse writer enhanced.

Unfortunately, however, Reece, Albery and their fellow-dramatists, in attempting to be poetic, produced an archaic, image-ridden blank verse, neither Shakespearean nor dramatic, although approved and praised by critics, and therefore prestigious. Imitating Shakespeare also called for profundity, since he had been wise on every subject from youth to age.[1] Consequently, dramatists often inserted reflective passages such as the wise fool's speech in *Oriana*:

> Oh! what a monster's popularity!
> Love and respect of laws, of art or prudence,
> Unless they wear the colour of the time,
> Change or go out of fashion like a cloak.
>
> (Albery, 1939, vol. 1, p. 432)

Elsewhere, elevation was sought through quasi-allegory: metaphors and personifications which seemed to mean more than they really did, but which had not been developed in a continuous symbolic line. Even W. S. Gilbert, less willingly Shakespearean than his colleagues, could write in *Broken Hearts*:

> Why, silly child, believest thou that Time
> Will see the fruit that ripens on those cheeks,
> And note the dainty banquet of those lips,
> And not preserve such rich and radiant fare,
> For his own feasting in his own good time?
> Trust the old Epicure! (Gilbert, 1881, p. 7)

Furthermore, in *un embarras de richesses* serious imitators did not forgo reminiscences of other Shakespearean plays any more than Victorian burlesque writers did; for, if F. C. Burnand's travesty of *Richard III* (1868) punned on lines from *Macbeth*, *Hamlet* and *Henry IV*, Albery's *Oriana* echoed *Julius Caesar*, *The Merchant of Venice*, *Henry V* and *Romeo and Juliet*. Burnand produced a comic patchwork, one function of burlesque being to dismember, and other writers, such as H. J. Byron in *Princess Springtime* (1864), used a *mélange* of Shakespeare quotations to convey comic rage or madness; but Albery's eclecticism was a means of enriching his poetic texture, and *The Times* (20 Feb. 1873) pronounced it the result not of deliberate copying, but of inspiration derived from Albery's love of Shakespeare's works.

The spectacle which accompanied these fine thoughts and this elaborate language was, of course, encouraged by Charles Kean's productions of Shakespeare and by William Beverley's designs for Planché's extravaganzas. It was appropriate, therefore, that when *Oriana* failed, Frederic Clay told its author not to revive it except in the lavish style of Kean's *Sardanapalus*, which Clay remembered from his boyhood (Albery, 1939, vol. 2, p. 804). Scenic display and marvellous machinery were means by which serious verse drama might be made palatable to a general audience, and as late as 1900 St John Hankin, reviewing Beerbohm Tree's *Midsummer Night's Dream* (*Punch*, 9 May), gave Prospero–Tree a speech explaining that

> The things the British Public really like
> Are cloud-capp'd towers and gorgeous palaces

And solemn temples, triumphs of the art
Of that egregious wight, the scene painter.
Poor SHAKSPEARE'S insubstantial puppets fade.
Only the *scenes* remain.

Albery's imitation of A *Midsummer Night's Dream*, therefore, begins with directions for a scene near the Happy Isles:

At L. 2 E. is a dripping well, into which water slowly pours; at L. 3 E. and L. 4 E. some steps lead to Hymen's Temple, above which there is a row of golden bells; at R.C. is the King's stone, the place where the kings are crowned, behind which is a statue of the king armed. From R. 3 E. to back is an avenue of trees; all backed by a distant view of the 'Happy Isles' stretching far away into the sea. A dull mist is hanging about; and the back is dimmed by 3 gauzes. (1939, vol. 1, p. 400)

Reece's *Perfect Love*, billed as 'A Spectacular Fairy Play' and derived from Wieland as well as Shakespeare, included a shipwreck by thunderbolt and a valley of palms which changed to Oberon's Bower, whence the Fairy King descended on a glittering star. Costumes in these plays were gorgeous, 'medieval' and /or fantastic.

Music was a particularly important part of Shakespeare imitation. Planché had turned Wieland's poem into a libretto for Weber's opera, *Oberon; or, The Elf-King's Oath* in 1826, at Covent Garden. Clay composed music for *Oriana*, and Alfred Cellier set Albery's *The Spectre Knight* so melodiously that the audience refused to let Albery take a curtain call without him (*Lloyd's Weekly*, 10 Feb. 1878). *Perfect Love* included music by Beethoven, Reece himself, Mendelssohn, Weber, Schubert, Sterndale Bennett, and Handel. Its theme-song, written by T. Thorpe Pede, was available from the composer, post free, for twenty-four stamps. Having earlier composed a *Tempest* fantasia, Tchaikovsky in 1892 made a one-act opera, *Yolanta*, out of Henrik Hertz's idyllic play *King René's Daughter* (1845) with its Miranda-esque blind princess.[2] (Hertz's play had already been adapted for the English stage by Theodore Martin and by W. G. Wills.)

The third element which encouraged imitation of Shakespeare's plays was their construction. Here magic was paramount in multiple plots, which combined the effects of high seriousness and low comedy, thus suiting the Victorian taste for mixed modes. Magic in comedy is the equivalent of providential coincidence in melodrama and just as useful for complication and resolution; so Shakespeare's little purple flower, whose juice scrambles and unscrambles lovers, became a philtre in the communal teapot of *The Sorcerer* and the magic ring of *Oriana*.

To Shakespeare's plot in which disharmony in fairyland affects the natural world, those nineteenth-century dramatists who embraced Wieland as well added the complication that disharmony in fairyland can be resolved only by mortals. In the 1760s Wieland had translated both *A Midsummer Night's Dream* and *The Tempest* into German, and had staged the latter while he was director of the Evangelical Theatrical Group in Biberach (van Abbe, 1961, pp. 75–6). His epic, drawing upon Shakespeare and upon folk and medieval literature, describes a quarrel between Oberon and Titania. Reclining on a bank of flowers with their train of sportive fays, they observe an old man with his faithless young wife. Oberon takes the husband's side, Titania the wife's, exclaiming, 'Is liberty your lot, and patience ours alone?' (Wieland, 1844, p. 142). Anger and estrangement ensue, and Oberon banishes his Queen until he finds a pair of lovers faithful unto death. These prove to be Huon of Bordeaux and Rezia, the Caliph's daughter.

The episodic story of these mortal lovers, their sexual indulgence, consequent trials, fidelity and rescue from death at the stake may be read as a Christian allegory of temptation, fall and redemption (van Abbe, 1961, p. 143). But Wieland also recognised, in his preface to *Idris* (1767), that 'Amusement is the Muses' first of duties, but in their playing they yet do teach most lastingly' (van Abbe, 1961, p. 181). Consequently, there is much of the marvellous in his fairy poem, including Huon's horn, which sets its hearers dancing, a device repeated by the English playwrights.

Like Shakespeare's, Wieland's Oberon walks by day (but bitterly delights in tormenting lovers). Titania fulfils one of her mythological functions as childbirth goddess by assisting Rezia to bear Huon's child. Oberon has a favourite, but nameless, fairy, who flies on his bidding swift as a beam of light. When Planché dramatised Wieland's poem he restored Puck's name and developed Fatima, Rezia's maid, as a kind of Blonde, who is paired with Sherasmin, Huon's squire. English adapters had already turned Sherasmin into a broadly comic character; so there were now three pairs of lovers whose fates were intertwined: the supernatural pair, the heroic/romantic pair, and the comic pair. Since the theme of these fairy plays is constancy in love, the fairy couple initiates the action, the romantic couple carries it on, and the comic couple comments upon it and provides relief. At the end, Oberon as fairy *ex machina* tidies things up – almost like the ending of a pantomime, especially since Wieland's Oberon transports the dramatis personae to his magic castle for a happy ending.

Planché's plot came from Sotheby's translation, but dialogue and lyrics were his own – with Shakespeare's assistance in such lines as

> Merrily, merrily dance we here
> Over the sands by her light so clear.
>
> (Planché, [1865?], p. 35)

or

> That's my good goblin!
>
> (p. 9)

or

> Hie thee back, Spirit, over land and sea,
> Swifter than thought, till thou dost meet with them;
> Cast a deep sleep on both, and bring them hither
> Before the breath be cold that bids thee.
>
> (p. 9)

As in Wieland and Hood, imitative Shakespearean flower imagery is everywhere, so much so that Weber had to explain gently to Planché that lines such as 'Like the spot the tulip weareth/Deep within its dewy urn' could not be developed dramatically in music (Planché, 1901, p. 53). Still, the opera had a great, though evanescent, success on its first production, in spite of being handicapped by a cast in which the actors could not sing and the singers could not act – except for Madame Vestris as Fatima, who, happily, could do both.[3]

In fact, despite the attraction of faithful love combined with supernatural spectacle, none of the early variants of *Oberon* proved to be popular successes. For nearly four decades after Weber and Planché's opera, Shakespeare's influence was felt chiefly in burlesques and extravaganzas such as the Broughs' *Enchanted Isle* (1848) and Nelson Lee's *Romeo and Juliet; or, Harlequin Queen Mab and the Land of Dreams* (1853). Meanwhile, in 1838 Macready staged *The Tempest* with an almost completely authentic text, a flying Ariel and a huge, storm-tossed ship; two years later Madame Vestris produced *A Midsummer Night's Dream* at Covent Garden with an enchanting last scene of dancing fairies and twinkling lights, devised by Planché. In the 1850s Charles Kean mounted both plays, as did Samuel Phelps at Sadler's Wells.

When Victorian playwrights began again to imitate rather than parody Shakespeare's fairy plays, they and their audiences were still attracted by the theme of faithful love, but now they took an increased interest in that of Miranda-like innocence in its first response to a new world – a theme which, together with the character of Ariel and Gonzalo's speech on the commonwealth,[4] seems to have been what Victorians derived from *The Tempest*. Nineteenth-century 'Mirandas', therefore, include the blind princess Iolanthe, whose eyes open on love and her own paradisal garden; Gilbert's just-animated statue; or Frederic, the male Miranda of *The Pirates of Penzance*, who has never seen a young woman before.

Miranda's naïveté could be treated satirically, as in *Pygmalion and Galatea*, where Galatea's brave new world cannot function in her truthful presence; it could be treated lyrically, as in Iolanthe's response to the voice of Count Tristram; or it could be treated playfully, as in Albery's *Spectre Knight*, where Viola gurgles with teenage delight at seeing boys for the first time.

The plot of *The Tempest* is also a prototype of what I have elsewhere called the Gilbertian invasion plot – that is, an action in which an outsider or group of outsiders enters an isolated society and affects it (in Gilbert's plays adversely) – and may, in turn, be affected by it. For example, when the tempest wrecks him on Prospero's island, Alonso learns to regret his old treachery, Miranda learns love and Caliban, who has also seen a brave new world in Stephano and Trinculo, learns that those who seem goodly creatures may not be so. In Gilbert's *Broken Hearts*, Vavir, too, learns love, but Florian learns compassion too late. Elfinella in Ross Neil's play of that name learns to prefer a mortal life with love to an immortal one without it. *Elfinella*, however, first produced in Edinburgh in 1875, belongs to a different line of serious fairy plays which depict the often unhappy loves between mortals and supernatural beings. Nevertheless, intrinsic to *Elfinella* as to all serious invasion plots, are themes which give it and them the effect of rites of passage and initiation.

These, then, are the main elements which I think attracted imitators – and variators – to Shakespeare's fairy plays: the prestige of the Bard, the opportunities for spectacle, the multiple plots and mixed modes for which Shakespeare gave example and warrant and the themes of fidelity, innocence and, to a lesser extent, polity which lent significance to the plays.

In the early 1870s a new impetus was given to verse drama by W. S. Gilbert's fairy comedies, beginning with *The Palace of Truth*, which opened the decade. In 1871, Reece's *Perfect Love* was performed at the Olympic, and Gilbert created his first Miranda in *Pygmalion and Galatea*, followed in 1873 by his *Wicked World* at the Haymarket and Albery's *Oriana* at the Globe, and in 1875 by Gilbert's last fairy play, *Broken Hearts* at the Court Theatre. *Elfinella*, *The Sorcerer*, and Albery's *Spectre Knight* were performed in 1878, and in 1880 Ellen Terry and Henry Irving appeared in Wills's *Iolanthe* at the Lyceum. Of these, the plays by Reece and Albery, together with *Broken Hearts*, demonstrate in some detail the range of Shakespeare's influence.

Robert Reece, whom G. R. Sims described as a scholar, poet, musician, and punster (1917, p. 297), dedicated *Perfect Love* to Planché, 'To whose influence/And example/I am so much indebted/For what grace may be in my work' (1871, p. 1). Reece was therefore using Wieland's *Oberon* plot, but at one remove and with Planché's and his own more closely Shakespearean fairies and imagery.

Avoiding the 'grossness' of Wieland's argument (as did all English adapters), Reece makes the quarrel in fairyland arise when Oberon is late for his own anniversary party and Titania is angry at being kept waiting. There is a touch of the pantomime dame in the Fairy Queen's vindictive temper, especially when Puck whispers that she uses rose petals for rouge. She and Oberon each insist that his or her own sex is more constant in love, until, at Puck's suggestion, they choose Huon and Rezia[5] for the usual Job-like experiment, testing them by hardship, each fairy unfairly helping his or her respective protégé. Titania, for instance, raises the requisite tempest. Puck meanwhile casts a love spell on Sherasmin and Fatima, exclaiming, 'Love, fools! and make of constancy a jest,/And your romance a living parody/Upon this fairy wager!' (1871, pp. 14–15). This the comic couple proceeds to do, replaying Huon and Rezia's farewell in a serious but fundamentally burlesque style. Puck proclaims the contest a draw; Titania and Oberon exchange forgiveness, and the play ends with a 'Grand Burst of Music' – its theme-song – and tableau.

Although the *Illustrated London News* (26 Feb. 1871) described Reece's blank verse as musical, and the *Era* thought it characteristic of a highly poetical mind, it is really rather wooden – more like stilted Gilbert than stilted Shakespeare. In fact, the *Era* praised Reece for following Gilbert's example in substituting blank verse for the more conventional couplets. Yet Reece's tone is archaic, his vocabulary thee-and-hast-ish, his set similes long and unexciting. And, as in every variation on A *Midsummer Night's Dream*, there is considerable floral imagery of 'sturdy mallows and the dainty ferns,/The dandy honeysuckles and wildbriar' (1871, p. 4). Titania flies in a bat-drawn chariot with lantern-flies as couriers. She addresses Puck with a 'How now, mad spirit, here?' Sherasmin, waking bewildered, exclaims:

> Oh, I have dreamt
> Such things! that could they but be written down,
> Would make a poet's fortune;   (p. 10)

And so on.

There is some satire, directed mostly against women, whom Oberon calls 'pantherous creatures' that delight in 'little tortures, which would shame a man'. Other passages dealing with the relation of the sexes recall the definition of loving in As *You Like It*, 5.2, and Katherine's speech in *The Taming of The Shrew*, 5.2. When Fatima urges constancy, Sherasmin replies that it is a virtue for a couple alone on a desert isle: ''Tis a fact/That two are constancy, but three are not!' Commenting on human nature, he observes that 'so many virtues shine/By mere compulsion; and, throughout

187

this life,/Fear is the mother of Morality' (p. 19). E. L. Blanchard told his diary that *Perfect Love* was a funny drama: 'very fair' (1891, vol. 2, p. 394). Two years later, he dismissed the more inventive *Oriana* as a queer, dull piece (1891, vol. 2, p. 422).

Yet, as Blanchard said in his *Daily Telegraph* review (17 Feb. 1873), rarely had the announcement of a dramatic novelty drawn a more brilliant audience. Albery had subtitled his play 'A Romantic Legend', and the full house had been attracted by the expectation of literary quality and the earlier success of the author's Robertsonian comedy, *Two Roses*. *Oriana* was now his *Preislied* and his challenge to Gilbert, with whom most reviewers compared him.

Albery's triple plot, in which mortal love determines fairy happiness and a gross politician leads a rebellion, is loosely connected by Peep, a crippled fairy with bound wings. Having vindictively poisoned the Fairy King's favourite hound, Peep has been banished until mortal King Raymond loves his Queen again. That Queen Oriana is of ladies most deject is made clear in her Shakespearean exchange with Solon, the Court Fool. He asks her why she weeps:

> Oria.   I have
>   More cause to weep than you to ask the cause.
> Solon.   You've every comfort that the world can give.
> Oria.   I have no comfort that the world can take.
> Solon.   You are a queen, beloved by everyone.
> Oria.   I am a queen forsaken by the king,   (1939, vol. 1, p. 406)

King Raymond has taken up with a throng of Bacchantes, led by his favourite Moth, who hail him as 'Red-lipp'd Raymond! Kissing King!' Forgetting his Queen and luxuriating in sensuality and leopard skins, he sings, 'Soft but mighty/Aphrodyte,/Be our goddess evermore' (p. 413). (The licence copy title was 'Naughty King Raymond'.)

Peep intends to reunite Raymond and Oriana by means of a magic ring, a love charm obtainable only by a virgin who sits all night alone beside a magic well. But, as usual, the charm works contrary to intention, for the virgin, a coarse milkmaid named Chloe, puts on the ring and is immediately and besottedly loved by King Raymond. Chloe is a kind of Audrey, complete with characteristic raw turnip and down-to-earth lines such as her reply when Raymond wonderingly asks if she is mortal: 'No, I am not mortal; nor do I know who she is. I am Chloe Beantop; and old Beantop is my father, and has been ever since I was born' (p. 421).

The ring then passes through successive hands, causing Raymond next to love a fat high priest ('My divine is my divinity'), and then, in a frenzy of narcissism, himself, while Oriana temporarily is infatuated with Oxeye, the people's orator and rabble-rouser. At last the charm works properly; Peep regains wings and freedom, and Raymond puts on true kingship after defeating Oxeye in single combat. In another part of the sub-plots, Oriana dons her husband's armour to quell the rebellion and uses Malcolm's Birnam Wood trick to make her forces seem larger: her ten Knights of the Spotless Shields (emblems of truth) hang their shields on trees to seem to reflect a multitude of knights.

Under its fanciful embellishments and picturesque stage effects, reviewers recognised, and generally praised, *Oriana*'s indebtedness to *A Midsummer Night's Dream*. Peep is Puck by plot, but Ariel by temperament, singing, 'Oh! how happy I shall be/In my dear home, whole and free!' (p. 415). There is the usual flower imagery, as Peep invokes her companions:

> Wake, elf and fairy, sprite and fay,
> Oriana comes this way.
> Quick, my sweet companions, come,
> With merry chirp and drowsy hum.
> Lovingly each footstep trace,
> And with a daisy mark the place.
> Spill the cups you've filled with dew,
> Lest they wet her dainty shoe.
> 'Twixt your hands the rose-buds squeeze,
> And cast their fragrance on the breeze.
> Leap from chestnut into may,
> And scatter blossoms in her way. (p. 405)

The comic yet sinister agitators, Oxeye, Broom and Sinapis, are Albery's attempt at rude mechanics, although with their shouting mob they seem to have dropped in from *Julius Caesar*. The *Athenaeum* observed that Shakespeare's low comedians fit into his play, but Albery's do not fit into his: 'Cloth of gold and cloth of frieze have been unhappily joined.'

Oxeye's first long speech recalls the rhetorical patterns of the more famous ones of Shylock and of Claude Melnotte (in Lytton's *The Lady of Lyons*):

I cannot have these things because I am not a king. And why? Can I not sit on this stone as well as he? Will this head not carry a crown as well? It is harder and thicker, and will carry ten times the weight. Can I not eat and drink as much? Can I not love beautiful women as well? Why! I have quite a gift that way. Why, then, should a man be forced to be virtuous and temperate, just because he is poor? I could be as bad as King Raymond is, if I had the chance. (p. 402)

Albery scattered so many bits of Shakespeare through the dialogue ('thou art as witty as thou'rt beautiful'; 'This hour men yet unborn shall name'; 'I fear this sudden folly', etc., etc.) that the *Daily Telegraph* felt compelled to

189

warn him he had 'greatly over-calculated the value of poetic diction as adequately supplying the place of dramatic action'.

Indeed, Albery went far beyond Reece in trying to reproduce a Shakespearean style. To a groundwork of blank verse, he added inter-polated songs, couplets, a sonnet, prose for common characters, plays on words, conceits and reflective passages, including his own version of 'All the world's a stage' – until *Punch* (1 Mar. 1873) objected that an artistic whole could not be expected from such a mixture: '*Oriana*, to be enjoyed must be read, not seen, and then the comic part must be skipped.' However, Albery derived at least one shrewd speech from his Shakespearean mixture:

Oxeye. How can I love you in prose? It is not enough that King Raymond has the earliest intelligence, and the latest hours; the finest clothes, and the coarsest jests; the longest credit, and the shortest temper; the dampest dungeons, and the dryest wines. He and his courtiers have all the poetry: blank verse, and versing verse; metaphors and similes; and we plebeians have nothing but prose; but prose is good for one thing.
Chloe. What, dear?
Oxeye. For revolutionary speeches. Dull prose is good for that. I can emancipate my country in stupid prose. (p. 404)

Unfortunately the cast of *Oriana* was not up to the pressure of the music. Clement Scott thought that H. J. Montague (Raymond) and Rose Massey (Oriana) should never have appeared in fantastic opera (Blanchard, 1891, vol. 2, p. 422n.), and while Carlotta Addison's Peep was praised by most reviewers, there were objections to a crippled fairy as being an anomaly: 'The very essence of the idea associated with fairies is a painless existence', wrote Joseph Knight.

Other points against Albery were the length of his play, the political satire, which his audience took more specifically than he intended, the unconscious homosexuality of Raymond's epithalamium to the High Priest, which included such choruses as 'Happy arm that shall be placed/ Round that slender subtle waist!' and Raymond's assertion that Helen's face did not wear a sweeter smile 'When Paris' hand was on the door'.[6] This love song, said the *Daily Telegraph*, must have seemed harmlessly funny when Albery imagined it, but proved disagreeable on stage. Nevertheless, other critics praised Albery's grace and delicacy and his ambition towards a 'higher' sort of drama.

Albery was more fortunate in his second imitation of Shakespeare: *The Spectre Knight*, a one-act operetta, performed at the Opera Comique in 1878 as a curtain-raiser to Gilbert and Sullivan's *The Sorcerer*. Its plot was necessarily less diffuse, and its cast, which included Rutland Barrington and Richard Temple, was completely at home with Alfred Cellier's music.

The Spectre Knight is a combination of *As You Like It* and *The Tempest*. A banished Grand Duke, his daughter Viola, his Lord Chamberlain and two ladies-in-waiting live in a haunted glen. The Duke has concealed his daughter from the world for fear he will lose her little fortune if she marries. Unlike Shakespeare's Duke, Albery's does not enjoy the rustic life; part of the eccentricity he imposes on his tiny court is the pretence that the menial tasks which they really do for themselves are performed by servants. Young Duke Otho, having overthrown the usurper who banished Viola's father, arrives, disguised as a friar, to inspect his fair cousin,

> who has never seen
> A man beside her father, and the old
> Lord Chamberlain who waits upon him still;
> Now I will see this maid, and, if she's fair,
> And all I hope to find her, I shall win
> A bride, not made of padding, stays, and paint,
> But a pure girl. (1939, vol. 2, p. 159)

Viola warbles of birds and flowers and would like to see a *young* man. When the 'friar' promises to send her one, she innocently speculates, 'I wonder now if he will have a beard/ . . .? If he's a beard/The colour of my hair, I shouldn't mind it' (p. 166).

The court sings a generic Shakespearean song:

> Too-whit too-woo, too-woo too-whit;
> The owl has ta'en her flight;
> The bats are out,
> The moths about,
> 'Tis time to say good night.
> Good night, good night. (p. 168)

All retire but Viola, who lights candles and waits. Otho, now disguised as the spectre, appears and woos her. With his song about 'A well-behaved ghost of high degree' all resemblance to Shakespeare ends, but Albery ties up everything in fairy tale fashion with new robes and choice viands for the court. Otho confesses that his disguises have been 'a mere mid-summer jest', and Viola concludes: 'If what I feel is love's sweet power,/I never loved till now.'

This pleasant little operetta was very well received: 'full of fancies, which are original, amusing, and often poetical' was the verdict of the *Illustrated Sporting and Dramatic News* (16 Feb. 1878), whose reviewer pronounced Viola a delicately and poetically conceived heroine.

If Albery was the playwright most persistently and self-consciously influenced by Shakespeare, W. S. Gilbert was surely the one least so. He did not like Shakespeare; he did not like the way Shakespeare was acted and cut – especially by Henry Irving; and he did not like the adulation of Shakespeare, which he considered ill-founded in a modern age. Yet *Broken Hearts* is his *Tempest*, albeit an unhappy one, a work which he considered one of his most personal and best. It was *Broken Hearts* that caused Joseph Knight to say that Gilbert's fairy plays 'form the most important contribution to fairy literature that has been supplied by any dramatist, or, indeed, any writer, since the commencement of the seventeenth century' (*Athenaeum*, 18 Dec. 1875). In *The Wicked World*, Knight wrote, Gilbert is a satirist; in *Pygmalion and Galatea* he is a humourist; but in *Broken Hearts* he is a poet.

Gilbert's blank verse, however, is not very poetic, its regularity, neatness, and practicality being more French than English. Moreover, he avoided the mixture of forms which *Punch* so disliked in *Oriana* and contented himself with only one interpolated, unimitative song – an appropriately sad one for his heroine to sing.

To the medieval, tropical island of Broken Hearts comes a group of ladies, all unfortunate in love except Vavir (played by Bessie Hollingshead), the youngest, frailest and most unworldly. Vavir has accompanied her sister Hilda (played by Mrs Kendal), who has loved Prince Florian from afar and fled to her island sanctuary after he has been lost at sea. The local Caliban is Mousta, who looks like Quasimodo and talks like Shakespeare's witches as he reads a love-spell:

> Take scammony and rue,
> With henbane gathered in a fat churchyard –
> Pound in a mortar with three drops of blood,
> Drawn from a serpent's tail at dead of night.
> . . .Take pigeon's egg
> Wrapped in the skin of a beheaded toad. (1881, p. 3)

In Gilbert's draft scenario, Mousta was the original proprietor of the island, but in the finished play the ladies have brought him as their servant because 'by reason of my face and form/I do not count as man'. Nevertheless, Mousta considers himself more human than the ladies, each of whom has chosen to love some inanimate object, which she anthropomorphises. Hilda loves a fountain, Vavir a sundial.

Prince Florian (Mr Kendal) approaches these 'virgin shores' in a little boat. Not drowned after all, and equipped with a veil of invisibility, he hears Vavir address her sundial:

> I'll weave a bower of rose and eglantine
> To place above thy head at eventide,
> When the full moon's abroad. (p. 11)

Impulsively, Florian tells Vavir that he is a spirit imprisoned in her dial:

> I am but one of many. This fair isle
> Teems with poor prisoned souls! There's not a tree –
> There's not a rock, a brook, a shrub, a stone,
> But holds some captive spirit who awaits
> The unsought love that is to set him free! (p. 14)

Florian also impersonates the spirits of Hilda's fountain and of Melusine's mirror. Both Vavir and Hilda fall in love with him, but he loves only Hilda. Mousta steals the veil and uses it to speak to Hilda so eloquently that she plights her troth to this noble 'spirit', only to discover in horror that he is her deformed servant. Furiously she winds the veil around herself and disappears, this garment having produced the same complications as Shakespeare's little purple flower. There is, however, no antidote, and the resolution must come through character, not magic.

Gilbert's *Tempest* ends with the death of its Miranda, carelessly deceived by Ferdinand–Florian, who, finally realising what he has done, treats her more gently. Hilda offers to give Florian up to Vavir, but her sister fades away beside her faithful dial, saying 'My sun has set. Good night!' For, unlike Planché, Reece and Albery, but like Shakespeare in his bitter comedies, Gilbert depicts love as a destructive force.

Blanchard recorded in his diary that he was charmed with Gilbert's play: 'a perfect fairy poem, admirably interpreted' (1891, vol. 2, p. 454). The *Era* (12 Dec. 1875) praised it as 'more of a poem than a play'. Yet there was some critical debate over the propriety of the shriek with which Mrs Kendal threw herself on Miss Hollingshead's corpse – a shriek as out of place, complained the *Athenaeum*, as a clang of cymbals would be at the end of Mendelssohn's overture to *A Midsummer Night's Dream.*

Broken Hearts ran for seventy-eight performances; L. J. Sefton toured it in the provinces with Florence Terry as Vavir, and for more than a decade it was occasionally revived at professional or special matinées, sometimes to display young actresses such as Julia Neilson. At one of these, Lewis Waller played Florian, and at another Gilbert himself substituted for the injured Kyrle Bellew. The piece was 'well-suited for a morning performance', said a reviewer, but 'not quite robust enough for the taste of the average playgoer in the evening bill'.[7]

This was the abiding difficulty with Victorian verse plays, a problem intensified (but partly surmounted) in Gilbert's case, since he had not used spectacle to attract an unpoetic public. Nevertheless, *Broken Hearts* ran longer than *Oriana*, which died in three weeks, perhaps because Gilbert had a stronger sense of plot and a greater independence of Shakespeare than the others did. Such may also be true of English adaptations of *King René's Daughter*, which was revived intermittently for some forty years, because Iolanthe offered a delightful role to Mrs Stirling, Mrs Kean, Helen Faucit and Ellen Terry. Albery's *Spectre Knight*, less pretentious than *Oriana*, enjoyed two runs of six and ten weeks respectively, and would have run longer had Albery been more prompt in delivering it to the Opera Comique management (Albery, 1939, vol. 2, pp. 823–34).

Most imitators of *A Midsummer Night's Dream* and *The Tempest*, however, achieved only a transitory prestige. They were not, alas, Time's rivals till the final date. Why did they not have runs commensurate with their high intentions?

Setting aside the imponderables of cast and such misfortunes as the death of Weber, who lived less than two months after the première of *Oberon; or, The Elf-King's Oath*, certain deficiencies – or superfluities – occurred in almost all these plays.

First, except for *Broken Hearts*, *King René's Daughter* and *The Spectre Knight*, they were too long and involved. Secondly, characters, although elaborated, were undeveloped psychologically except by Hertz and Gilbert, and even then were not really complex. Thirdly, most of these playwrights rarely perceived that what seems ornament in Shakespeare is almost always dramatically or psychologically relevant. Moreover, with the resources of scene-painter and stage machinist, who could depict banks of wild thyme and sinking vessels, Victorian dramatists still insisted on imitating the lines in which Shakespeare, of necessity, described scenes which his bare stage could not show. Imitators, therefore, made the mistake which *Punch* accused Albery of making – that is, of substituting poetic diction for dramatic action – and thus failed to organise their multiple plots clearly enough for audiences to follow. This was an even greater problem in plays which imitated Wieland's overflowing epic. Finally, Shakespeare's English was to his admiring imitators no longer a truly living language but an artificial poetic diction which they assumed for elevation but could use only self-consciously, and therefore awkwardly, often imposing a barrier between themselves and their audiences.

Playwrights such as Planché, Reece and Albery had elsewhere demonstrated felicity of utterance and command of their craft, but Shakespeare was too much for them. They wanted to get everything into their verse plays, and audiences unfortunately got too little out of them. Fancy, which they could copy, was not enough, and Shakespeare's imagination was beyond them. Yet the Victorian imitators of Shakespeare accomplished something; they had great if unfulfilled expectations, and, while we cannot say of them, 'renowned be thy grave', we can perhaps adapt an epitaph from Ovid:

> And if they did not drive the horses of the sun,
> At least they fell in a magnificent dare.   (*Metamorphoses*, book II)

NOTES

1 'From that mind issued views, maxims and references time can never destroy . . . on upwards of five hundred subjects' *The Mind of Shakespeare* (Morgan, 1860, pp. ix–xii). This was only one of many books which catalogued Shakespeare's universal wisdom.

2 Tchaikovsky knew Hertz's play through a Russian translation. *Yolanta* was first produced in St Petersburg on 18 December 1892, doubled-billed with *The Nutcracker*, also being premiered. Neither work was a complete success, although *The Nutcracker* eventually became so (Warrack, 1973, pp. 253–61). Hertz's immediate source was a story by Hans Christian Andersen.

3 Mary Anne Paton was Rezia and John Braham Huon. Braham insisted on having a *scena* which included the lines 'Oh! 'tis a glorious sight to see/The charge of Christian chivalry'. The future Mrs Keeley sang the Mermaid's song but had no spoken lines. Since Weber did not live to revise his opera, other musicians, including Sir Julius Benedict, have at times attempted to rearrange it for him. Most musicologists agree that the fault for *Oberon*'s rapid fall from favour is Planché's. Still, it was revived in 1843, 1861 and 1863, the last time with Sims Reeves, Santley, Trebelli, Alboni and Titiens.

4 Gonzalo's speech is often referred to in connection with Gilbert's equality comedy in *The Gondoliers*.

5 Reece spelled his heroine's name 'Reiza' instead of 'Rezia'; I have regularised the spelling.

6 Licence copy, Lord Chamberlain's Deposit, British Library (quoted by kind permission of the British Library Board). Other lines describe the Priest as more attractive than Cressida, Hero, Semele and Cleopatra.

7 Unidentified press cutting in the Theatre Museum. The review must have been written in early July 1884.

Sullivan and Shakespeare

ARTHUR JACOBS

FROM Schubert's three songs to Verdi's three operas, from Berlioz's 'dramatic symphony' on *Romeo and Juliet* to Tchaikovsky's well-known 'overture–fantasia' on the same play, composers of the nineteenth century turned to Shakespeare for works of many different kinds. In England, no composer was so closely associated with Shakespeare as Arthur Sullivan (1842–1900). He contributed incidental music to five of the plays in six productions by important managements, and independent musical settings came from his pen too.

It was indeed with Shakespeare (and not with W. S. Gilbert, whom he had not yet met) that Sullivan became famous overnight before he was twenty-one. As Britain's first Mendelssohn Scholar, he had proceeded from the Royal Academy of Music to study at the Leipzig Conservatory, where his graduation exercise was a suite of incidental music to *The Tempest*. Returning to London and befriended by George Grove, he expanded it to twelve vocal and orchestral numbers, in which form it was given at the Crystal Palace (where Grove was secretary, i.e. administrator) on 5 April 1862. Among enthusiastic reviews from influential pens may be cited Henry F. Chorley's in the *Athenaeum* (12 Apr. 1862):

It was one of those events which mark an epoch in a man's life; and, what is of more universal consequence, it may mark an epoch in English music, or we shall be greatly disappointed. Years on years have elapsed since we have heard a work by so young an artist so full of promise, so full of fancy, showing so much conscientiousness, so much skill, and so few references to any model elect.

Music from this score was used by Charles Calvert for his Manchester production of the play two years later – an event which, strangely, went unmentioned in Grove's own entry on Sullivan in the first edition (1879–89) of his *Dictionary of Music and Musicians* and has remained unmentioned in all subsequent editions. The list of Sullivan's Shakespearean productions is as follows:

	Title	Year	City	Theatre	Management
1	*The Tempest*	1864	Manchester	Prince's	Calvert
2	*The Merchant of Venice*	1867	Manchester	Prince's	Calvert
3	*The Merry Wives of Windsor*	1874	London	Gaiety	Hollingshead
4	*Henry VIII*	1877	Manchester	Royal	Calvert
5	*Macbeth*	1888	London	Lyceum	Irving
6	*The Merry Wives of Windsor*	1889	London	Haymarket	Tree

To these must be added, in the present context, Sullivan's incorporation of lines from *The Merchant of Venice* in his so-called masque (actually a concert work) *Kenilworth* (1864) and his settings for voice and piano of five independent songs to Shakespearean texts. These, dating from 1863 to 1864, are:

'Orpheus with his lute'	(*Henry VIII*)
'Willow Song'	(*Othello*)
'From the east to western Ind'	(*As You Like It*)
'O mistress mine'	(*Twelfth Night*)
'Sigh no more, ladies'	(*Much Ado About Nothing*)

A study of the use made of Sullivan's music in actual theatrical production might be doubly fruitful in revealing how the composer considered his music in theatrical terms, and how managements actually handled it. But such an assessment still awaits a prior stage of theatrical research. We need to know how musicians were engaged for theatres, how they 'doubled' on different instruments, how the musical director consulted with the manager in his capacity as stage-director, in what fashion 'ready-made' pieces were used alongside new music, and what freedom was observed in cuts and repetitions to fit the timing of the action. Such information has hardly begun to be sorted from memoirs, press reviews and any play-scripts, sheet music, letters and pay-slips surviving from theatre libraries. Frequently the musical components of a production must have been short, improvised at rehearsal, changed at short notice and never published. An undated note from Irving to Sullivan, evidently written during preparations for *Macbeth*, gives a hint or two:

Trumpets and drums are the King's (Duncan's) behind scenes.
Entrance of Macbeth, only drum. ('A drum, a drum, Macbeth doth come.')
Distant march would be good for Macbeth's exit in 3rd scene – or drum and trumpets as you suggest.
In the last act there will be several flourishes of trumpets. ('Make all our trumpets speak, ' etc.) and roll of drum sometimes.

197

Really anything you can give of a stirring sort can be easily brought in.
As you say, you can dot these down at rehearsals – but one player would be good to tootle-
tootle, so that we could get the exact time.[1]

In a period which laid stress on historical correctness of scenery and costume, the desire to have new, specially written music might need to be reconciled with the propriety of 'historical' music. Thus Charles Calvert, in the published edition (1871) of his version of *The Merchant of Venice*, noted:

The music that occasionally accompanies the action is chiefly old Italian, excepting that termed 'the Lorenzo masque', which is the composition solely of Mr Arthur Sullivan –

and immediately went on to make the general point:

Correctness and completeness of illustration is surely the office and function of the theatre, and in proportion to its faithful use the highest and most valued form of literature (the dramatic) is nurtured and rendered fruitful for good.

Sullivan himself, however, by no means wrote imitation 'old' music: the music to the masque actually includes such an anachronism as a waltz. But his theatre music, if not 'historical', is always 'characteristic' as understood in the nineteenth-century sense – that is, with picturesque touches (whether of rhythms, melodies or harmonies) to suggest a suitably unusual scenic location or period, sometimes by means of dance. For 'the Lorenzo masque', occurring at the end of Calvert's first act (after Lorenzo's line 'Our masquing mates by this time for us stay'), Sullivan provided not only a suite of dances but a song to newly written Italian words, 'Nel ciel seren', in the barcarole rhythm particularly associated in the nineteenth century with Venice – with precedent from Chopin, Mendelssohn and others.

For *The Merry Wives of Windsor*, produced in 1874 at the Gaiety Theatre by its famous manager, John Hollingshead, there was similarly an interpolated song (this time by Swinburne), given to Anne Page in the final act. It is of some interest that it was Hollingshead and not Sullivan who approached the poet. (The lyric 'Love laid his sleepless head' was afterwards published separately and survives as the only collaboration between Swinburne and Sullivan.) A letter from Sullivan (17 Dec. 1874) to his friend, the music critic Joseph Bennett, indulges in a playful confusion between his own music and Mendelssohn's and makes it clear that even an 'original' score might be expected to be combined with other composers' work. In this case an overture – whether Nicolai's or not – would have had to be chosen by the theatre's musical director:

I was rather dismayed when I first got the commission to do *The Merry Wives* for I could see no opportunity for music. However in the last act I have been able to do a little, and it will I hope be bright . . . I wouldn't write an overture, because I did not care about competing with the very pretty one of Nicolai.

Your masterly judgement, my dear Joseph, will at once enable you to see that as the fairies are not *real* fairies (if such exist) but only flesh and blood imitations, I have endeavoured to indicate this, and have not written music of the same character as I wrote for *The Midsummer Night's Dream*, or that Mendelssohn wrote for the third act of *The Tempest*. I have only had three weeks to do the whole thing in . . . All the music is new, but (and this is not necessarily for publication) if you remember a ballet called *L'Ile enchantée* which I wrote for the Italian opera, Covent Garden, many years ago, you will recognize two of the themes.[2]

For *Henry VIII* (Calvert, 1877) Sullivan again included an interpolated item – the song 'Pastime with good company' to words which are thought to be by King Henry himself. Again the music displays the 'characteristic' rather than the strictly historical manner: in a nineteenth-century context the beginning would have sounded suitably Tudor-ish. Only four numbers from the music to *Henry VIII* were published.

It is the music to *The Tempest* and to *Macbeth*, the first and almost the last of Sullivan's Shakespearean play settings, that may most repay our interest. The score to *The Tempest* represents, as it were, a composer's idealised theatre. On the analogy of Mendelssohn's music to *A Midsummer Night's Dream*, it presents an integrated response to the play – though a slightly incomplete response: curiously, there is no tune for Caliban's 'No more dams I'll make for fish'. We find orchestral music to precede individual acts, songs and dances required by the text, and 'melodramatic' music in the strict sense (music as purposeful background to the spoken word) for passages of supernatural or other unusual significance. In place of a theatrical cast the 1862 concert presentation used a single speaker who delivered a specially written narration (by Chorley). The *Macbeth* score for Irving's production at the Lyceum is similarly integrated (that is, there is a musical relationship between the numbers). The considerable documentation of this occasion – reflecting the interest aroused by the conjunction of Irving and Sullivan, the undoubted leaders of their professions in England – allows a closer inspection of the theatrical process than is available with the other works.

In the music to *The Tempest* it might seem odd that an 'overture' precedes a middle movement instead of the first. Apparently Sullivan, like Verdi, made a distinction between an *overture* as formally observing 'sonata-form' or something like it, and a *prelude* or *introduction* as a less strictly organised musical structure, perhaps depicting a single mood. The scheme for *The Tempest* is as follows, the musical text referred to being that of the full score (London: Novello, 1891). Sullivan's numberings and headings are as given in the left-hand column. The description in the right-hand column is my own.

As the music following No. 11 is quite separate from that number and belongs to a different scene of the play, I have thought it advisable to recognise it as a separate, unnumbered item.

No. 1 [1.1], Introduction

No. 2 1.2 (melodrama, with sections each a few bars long, separated by pauses, the first section being cued at Prospero's 'Come away, servant'; the music cued at 'So, slave, hence' leads to setting for soprano, offstage chorus and orchestra of Ariel's 'Come unto these yellow sands'; the dialogue begun during the postlude ('Where should this music be?') leads to the setting of 'Full fathom five' for the same musical combination)

No. 3 2.1 (melodrama, beginning with Ariel's 'Solemn music' after 'five weeks without changing'; resuming with Ariel's entry after 'O, but one word', Ariel later changing from speech to song for 'While you here do snoring lie . . . Awake, awake!')

No. 4 Act 3, Prelude

No. 5 [3].2 (melodrama for Ariel's entry after 'I will stand, and so shall Trinculo'; later, piccolo and tabor for 'Ariel plays the tune on tabor and pipe'; later, after dialogue ending 'I say tonight, no more', orchestral passage for 'solemn and strange music', leading to next number)

No. 6 [3.3], Banquet Dance (dance for the 'Shapes'; later, at 'Enter Ariel, like a harpy, claps his wings upon the table, and with a quaint device the banquet vanishes', melodrama for Ariel's 'You are three men of sin . . . and a clear life ensuing'; then repeat of dance as 'Enter Shapes again and dance about with mops, etc.')

No. 7 Act 4, Overture

No. 8 4.1 (orchestral music for the masque, after dialogue ending 'No tongue; all eyes; be silent'; Iris and Ceres speak during the music; after music, Juno enters and speaks, leading to next number)

No. 9 [4.1] 'Honour, riches, marriage blessing' (setting for two sopranos, mixed chorus and orchestra of this song for Juno and Ceres)

No. 10 [4.1] Dance of Nymphs and Reapers (orchestral, after dialogue ending 'encounter every one in country footing')

No. 11 Act 5, Prelude

[unnumbered. 5].1 [headed:] 'Dialogue ends (PROSPERO) 'But this rough magic I here adjure [sic]' (reprise of some material from Prelude to the act, as melodrama for dialogue ending 'Ariel, fetch me my hat and rapier in my cell')

No. 12 [5.1], Air 'Where the bee sucks' (setting for soprano and orchestra of Ariel's song, with the variant 'there lurk I'; later, after dialogue ending 'I drink the air before me, and return or e'er your pulse beat twice', a three-bar orchestral fragment evidently for Ariel's exit; later, after dialogue ending 'Please you, draw near', melodrama for Prospero's epilogue, again alluding musically to the Prelude to the act)

200

Musically, the particular interest is that one theme represents Ariel's carrying-out of Prospero's magic skills – a theme which has a particular chromatic step (in the key of C, the step is F, F sharp, G). It is first heard in No. 1 with minor-key harmonics in slow time, but later is ingeniously transformed into the grotesque, jolly, major-key theme of the 'Banquet Dance' (No. 6), when Ariel deceptively entertains Alonso, Antonio and Sebastian ('Enter several strange shapes, bringing in a banquet'). When the banquet disappears and Ariel denounces the villains ('You are three men of sin'), the theme resumes its original contour. This musical process of 'thematic metamorphosis' is one which Sullivan was to employ with equally striking effect in the *Overtura di Ballo* (1870) and *Iolanthe* (1882); but only *The Tempest* adds to the effect by the use of melodrama (speech against music).

Unlike that for *The Tempest*, Sullivan's music for *Macbeth* was never published, except for the overture, and the composer's autograph score of the whole work has not been placed on public access by its anonymous American owner. But the existence of a manuscript copy of the score in the hire library of Sullivan's publishers Chappell & Co., has permitted a keen study of the music by David Russell Hulme.[3] This Chappell manuscript, a photocopy of which is in the BBC Music Library, is also the basis of the present study.

Irving's edition of the play (1889), published in connection with the performance, gave Sullivan a prominent place on the title-page. In his preface, the first point discussed by Irving is that of the propriety of the two songs 'Come away' and 'Black spirits and white' – the first lines only of which are given in *Macbeth* itself, the complete verses being found in Middleton's *The Witch*:

These songs have now been set to music by Sir Arthur Sullivan, to whom I am greatly indebted for composing the whole of the incidental music for this production.

The only lines, therefore, introduced into this stage-arrangement of *Macbeth*, from Middleton's *Witch*, are the four lines of the song, 'Black spirits and white,' and the ten lines of the song, 'Come away, come away,' which latter I have ventured to transpose from the fifth scene of the first act (in the original) to the end of the first scene of the fourth act in this version.

Sullivan provided a full-length overture to the play; perhaps unexpectedly, it does not anticipate the tragic outcome but ends with confident martial swagger. Irving having re-grouped the usual Acts 4 and 5 into three acts, Sullivan provided orchestral music to precede each of the six acts and for use in a number of other scenes. 'Melodrama' was used at salient points for the appearances of the Witches and for the scene with Banquo's ghost, but the anonymous review in *The Times* (cited by Hulme) praised Sullivan as much for what he did *not* do:

His music for *Macbeth*, in consequence, if not very profound or intensely dramatic, is singularly appropriate. It is never in the way when not wanted, never out of the way when required; and the composer deserves praise for what he has left undone no less than for what he has accomplished. Let us cite a case in point. It has been said that some poems in themselves are so musical that they do not require, and, indeed, lose much of their beauty by the addition of an actual melody. Such a poem is the sleep-walking scene as seen by Miss Ellen Terry . . . An aspiring composer might here have discovered one of the changes aforementioned and would probably have spoiled the effect impression by some 'slow music' of the approved pattern. Sir Arthur Sullivan knows better than this; not a sound is heard in the orchestra, and the voice of the actress is the only music which breaks the silence. (31 Dec. 1888)

The phrase 'the approved pattern' gives a hint of what might have been the theatrical treatment, at the hands of a resident musical director dipping into his stock of mood-pieces.[4]

The copyist's score of *Macbeth* contains the material listed below. The two non-choral numbers of Act 4 (other, that is, than the two Middleton songs) are bound *after* the prelude to Act 5, the correct dramatic order of the music being as follows. The items are unnumbered, but the headings used by Sullivan are as in the left-hand column. 'Introduction' (in place of 'prelude') here apparently denotes music which passes straight into dialogue without formal close. Once again, the right-hand column gives my own description.

Overture

1.1, Introduction	(after eighteen bars, 'Curtain up'; later, 'dialogue begins'; ends with cornet fanfare 'behind the scenes', i.e. melodrama for all the Witches' scene, ending at entry of Duncan, etc., sc. 2)
1.3 and 4	(restatement of martial theme from the overture; evidently meant to *precede* sc. 3)
1.3	(fourteen introductory bars, then 'dialogue begins', i.e. melodrama; later cues given, 'A drum, a drum, Macbeth doth come' and 'the charm's wound up')
1.6	(nineteen introductory bars, with two horns 'behind the scenes' answering two in orchestra; then 'dialogue begins', i.e. melodrama)
Act 2, Prelude	(at nine bars before final close, 'Curtain [up]', but no overlap into dialogue)
Act 3, Prelude	(in lively, rather grotesque orchestral style, beginning in 5/4 time! At nine bars before final close, 'Curtain [up]', but no overlap into dialogue)
3.2, 'In the banquet scene'	(At cue, 'May't please your highness sit', four bars of eerie

music on muted strings and piccolo, recalling Prelude to Act 2, i.e. music for appearance of ghost of Banquo)

4.1, Introduction   (thirty-one introductory bars, then 'dialogue begins', i.e. melodrama)

4.1 [headed]   'How now, you secret, black and midnight hags! What is't ye do?' (melodrama in short sections – first two bars cued as 'a deed without a name', next two bars as 'Come high or low; thyself and office deftly show'; further short sections cued 'thou shalt harp [sic] my fear aright', 'more potent than the first', 'and sleep in spite of thunder', 'shall come against him', 'seek to know no more', 'deny me this', 'Show! show! show!', etc.)

4.1, Chorus of Spirits in the Air   (setting for three-part women's chorus, with orchestra, of 'Black spirits and white', with words much repeated)

4.1, Witches' Dance   (headed, as cue, 'our duties old [sic] his welcome pay')

[4.2] Chorus of Witches and Spirits   (setting for two-part women's chorus, with orchestra, of 'Come away, come away, Hecate, Hecate, come away!', etc. – see Irving's preface, quoted above. The scene consists *entirely* of this musical number)

Act 5, Prelude   (N.B. this act begins with the usual 4.3: Malcolm and Macduff. The music, not marked by a curtain-up point, plainly evokes Macduff's grief at the news of his family's slaughter. Irving's text omits the preceding scene, the usual 5.1 now following as 5.3.)

Act 6, Prelude   (This act comprises the usual 5.2–8. The music brings back the martial main theme of the overture. No curtain-up is indicated)

Flourishes, drum-beats, etc., which would certainly have been required are omitted from this copyist's score. Was anything else omitted? It seems odd that no formal music is stipulated to conclude the play (the ending is much truncated in Irving's version), leaving the martial theme of the *fortunate* Macbeth as the last music to strike the audience's ears.

Additionally, items from Sullivan's scores of *The Tempest* and *Henry VIII* were pressed into service as entr'actes for the production. (In this case, they were merely music for passing the time during intervals, not for leading directly back into the drama.) There is, as Hulme notes, a discrepancy between the listing of these additional items in *The Times* (advertisement, 29 Dec. 1888) and in the programme the same night.

The jarring nature of some of these interpolations struck the *Times* reviewer (31 Dec. 1888), but nothing seems to have disturbed Sullivan's first-night pleasure. An unusually jocular entry in his diary tells the story:

We left at 7.15 for
The production of *Macbeth* at the Lyceum Theatre
Words by Shakespeare.
Music by Sullivan.

Produced by Irving.
        Great Success!
Author, composer and stage-manager called enthusiastically.
Only the two latter responded.[5]

Sullivan's non-theatrical Shakespeare settings may be more briefly dealt with. *Kenilworth* (with text by Chorley, who apparently saw no inconsistency between collaborating with the young composer and praising him in the press) was a festival cantata based on an episode from Scott's novel of that name. An entertainment presented for Queen Elizabeth is supposed (not in the novel) to have included the famous love scene for Lorenzo and Jessica in *The Merchant of Venice* – a scene which, incidentally, was to be excerpted by Vaughan Williams for his *Serenade to Music* (1938). Chorley's selection of lines beginning 'In such a night' is most effectively set by Sullivan as a soprano and tenor duet with orchestral accompaniment: this number was often heard on its own at later concerts in Sullivan's lifetime and well deserves revival. Chorley's solecism in changing 'Such harmony is in immortal souls' to 'in immortal sounds' could be corrected.

Of the five early songs for voice and piano, 'Orpheus with his lute' may be recognised as an inspired essay in transferring the idiom of the Schubert *lied* to an English context. (The song has been splendidly recorded by Janet Baker with Gerald Moore's accompaniment.) Indeed Schubert's own Shakespearean setting of 'Who is Sylvia?' seems to have been a direct model for Sullivan's use of a little motto-theme in the piano part of this song. The other songs are less striking, though not insignificant, the one from *As You Like It* being an oddity: in the play the lines are part of a spoken poem, not a song.

In Sullivan's output such 'art-songs' are to be sharply differentiated from his many popular, money-earning 'ballads' such as *The Lost Chord*. He composed a few more art-songs late in life but no more to Shakespearean texts. The *Macbeth* overture, however, was one of the few substantial, autonomous (that is to say, wordless) works of his later years, and may rank as among his major compositions, though marred by its jaunty coda where something as grand as the end of Wagner's *Meistersinger* overture seems called for. The youthful *Tempest* score, thoroughly original despite its flavouring of Mendelssohn and Schumann, may today impress as even better. Indeed, with the current modest revival of Sullivan's non-Gilbertian works, it must be held that the time is ripe for Sullivan's *Tempest* music to be heard in full again.

Sullivan and Shakespeare

NOTES

1 The theatrical memorandum from Irving to Sullivan is in the Gilbert and Sullivan collection (the chief source of Sullivan material) at the Pierpont Morgan Library, New York.

2 In the Pierpont Morgan Library.

3 Published 1984 in Nos. 18 and 19 of the magazine of the Sir Arthur Sullivan Society.

4 On this, see Mayer and Scott, 1983.

5 The diary excerpt is from the composer's manuscript diaries at the Beinecke Rare Book and Manuscript Library, Yale University. These sources are further discussed and excerpted in Jacobs, 1984.

PART 5

Shakespeare as a Foreign Dramatist

T
HE European country with which Britain was most closely associated during Queen Victoria's reign was, of course, Germany. As
George Rowell has pointed out (1978, p. 47) Prince Albert 'was
bound to contrast the flourishing Court Theatre at Coburg with the total
absence of such an institution in a country as rich and influential as
England'. The court theatricals inaugurated at Windsor in 1848 were a
conscious attempt at emulating the theatrical patronage exercised by the
rulers of several German states.

Of these the most celebrated was George, Duke of Saxe-Meiningen, a
family into which Queen Victoria's granddaughter Princess Charlotte
(eldest daughter of Princess Victoria and the Emperor Frederick) married
in 1860. Duke George's company, not established until 1874, enhanced
its reputation for a carefully integrated ensemble, lavish historical costumes and well-drilled crowds through extensive foreign tours, including
London in 1881. The impact of the Saxe-Meiningen Company's eight-
week London season, during which they performed *Julius Caesar* (sixteen
times), *Twelfth Night* (two) and *The Winter's Tale* (seven), has been
assessed by Michael Booth. Like Muriel St Clare Byrne before him,
Professor Booth observes that many of the Saxe-Meiningen Company's
alleged innovations had been anticipated by Charles Kean, whose production of *Richard II* Duke George had seen in London in 1857.[1]

The traffic was definitely two-way. In May 1859 the normally cautious
Samuel Phelps made his one and only foray overseas, taking his Sadler's
Wells company to Berlin and Hamburg with an extensive repertoire of
seven Shakespeare plays including *King Lear*, which received the most
favourable reception (Allen, 1971, p. 153). Sometimes the contact was
scholarly as well as theatrical, and Jan McDonald has noted the influence
of Ludwig Tieck's theories about the Elizabethan stage upon Ben Webster's
The Taming of the Shrew in 1844 and 1847 (in Richards and Thomson,
1971, pp. 157–8). As Dr Fowler suggests, David Scott's *Queen Elizabeth*

Viewing the Performance of the 'Merry Wives of Windsor' in the Globe Theatre was also part of this first wave of reconstruction of Elizabethan theatres.

Ludwig Tieck's versatility extended to completing Schlegel's translation of Shakespeare and creating his own of Ben Jonson. As Simon Williams demonstrates, Tieck's theories and experiments were furthered by Karl Immerman at the Dusseldorf Theatre and Jocza Savits at the Munich Court Theatre, where William Poel was greatly impressed with a production of *King Lear*, 'the most stimulating performance of the tragedy I have ever seen' (1929, p. 92; Speaight, 1973, pp. 107–8).

The rapport and interchange between English and German Shakespeareans during Queen Victoria's reign excelled anything enjoyed between other nations, but French and Italian actors became increasingly aware of the attractions of the leading roles. Inevitably translation was a problem, and both Dr Smith and Professor Richards point out that Italian acting editions were often based on French versions of the originals. Even these were sometimes the work of non-English-speaking 'translators', whose abiding vision tended to be shaped by the classical principles of dramatic construction which Shakespeare had so consistently flouted, but to which the French theatre attached such importance. Nevertheless, as Dr Smith argues, these 'creative adaptations' stand comparison with much that was happening on the contemporary English stage.

It was in the sphere of acting (rather than production) that France and Italy made their greatest contributions to the presentation of Shakespeare. Dr Smith reveals that for all its apparent absurdity Sarah Bernhardt's Hamlet was a serious and creditable performance, involving the preparation of a new translation. 'The Divine Sarah' presented her Hamlet in London in 1899, by which time metropolitan audiences were accustomed to foreign actors visiting the capital in search of the final, authoritative stamp of approval on their Shakespearean performances.

Amongst these foreign thespians were three Italian players of exceptional quality: Adelaide Ristori, Ernestino Rossi and Tommaso Salvini. All three combined a native Italian temperament with a refreshingly original approach to Shakespeare's plays, free of the accretion of tradition which burdened English actors. Not surprisingly they were happier in some plays than others, with Salvini's Othello being generally regarded as outstanding.

As the European nations colonised the world, the lot of performing Shakespeare to emigrants who retained their mother language often fell, as Professor Richards shows, to non-English players. Indeed in performing Shakespeare at all foreign actors were in a sense helping to extend the influence of England. Patriotism – or chauvinism – was never entirely absent in the increasingly international world of the theatre. Charles Fechter, whose Hamlet was so widely acclaimed in London in 1861, withdrew from the Shakespeare tercentenary programme in Stratford-upon-Avon largely because of increasing resentment that a foreign actor should play the leading role in honouring a national hero. The young French actress Stella Colas, who enjoyed a fleeting success as Juliet, agreed to take part in the celebrations only on the condition that in the event of public hostility the committee should make known the reluctance of her acceptance (Foulkes, 1984, pp. 15–16).

G. H. Lewes was dismissive of the hapless Mlle Colas: 'With regard to Mlle. Stella Colas, bad as our actors are, they have nothing to learn from her' (1875; repr. 1952, p. 151). But such was certainly not the case with other foreign players, whose influence upon the ever-changing process of Shakespearean acting and production cannot be denied.

NOTE

1 Muriel St Clare Byrne, 'Charles Kean and the Meiningen Myth', *Theatre Research*, 6.5 (1964), 137–53; Michael R. Booth, 'The Meiningen Company and English Shakespeare', *Shakespeare Survey*, 35 (1982), 13–20; Koller, 1984.

The 'Shakespeare-Stage' in Nineteenth-Century Germany

SIMON WILLIAMS

THROUGHOUT the nineteenth century, in the German theatre the plays of Shakespeare were treated primarily as opportunities for spectacle, often of the most lavish and detailed kind. From the opening decade, during which August Wilhelm Iffland staged Shakespeare, along with several contemporary historical dramas, at the Berlin Royal Theatre in a fashion more suited to the presentation of grand opera than to the more intimate spoken theatre, to the closing years of the century in which the productions of the Meiningen company were widely admired and imitated, grandiosity and largeness of scale were the rule. Germany was not, of course, unique in this. Parallel lines of development can easily be established in the history of the English theatre and in that of other continental theatres. The tendency towards spectacle and a corollary concern with historical accuracy to the minutest of details did not, however, go unchallenged. In various countries, critical voices could be heard objecting, with varying degrees of vehemence, to the unremitting emphasis placed upon the visual elements of theatre. In Germany, these voices were, perhaps, more persistent than elsewhere, and, given the closer ties that existed there between the theatre and scholarly or critical writing, occasionally resulted in practical attempts to stem the tide of spectacle. The focus of such efforts was mainly on the production of Shakespeare's plays. These, some theorists and practitioners maintained, were unsuited to the demands of the illusionist stage of spectacle. Their enquiries subsequently led them to reconstruct, as far as contemporary theatrical conditions and the current state of knowledge allowed, approximate replicas of the Elizabethan stage. Such undertakings anticipated by some years experiments in England and France, conducted by William Poel and Aurélian Lugné-Poë at the end of the century.

The genesis of this interest in the Elizabethan stage has been attributed to the publication, early in the nineteenth century, of Schlegel's translations of several of the plays of Shakespeare (Nussel, 1967, p. 22). For the first time, there were made available to the public the plays as they actually appeared in the First Folio, without the omissions, contractions and radical alterations that had marked all productions and publications of Shakespeare during the last decades of the eighteenth century. Schlegel's translations revealed in the originals previously unacknowledged aspects of Shakespeare's work: frequent changes of scene, seemingly disruptive oscillations between the pathetic and comic modes, and an apparent demand for awkwardly large casts. These were well-nigh impossible to realise in the relatively narrow confines of the illusionist stage and led some to rule out entirely the possibility of the originals being produced. Goethe, for example in his famous essay 'Shakespeare und kein Ende' ('Shakespeare without End', 1815), argued that Shakespeare was a dramatist by default alone, that he appealed not to the eye, but to the 'inner sense', the 'picture world of the imagination'.[1] Reading Shakespeare was, therefore, more satisfactory than seeing him performed. 'In reading', Goethe argued, 'all . . . things pass easily through our minds, and seem quite appropriate, whereas in representation on the stage they strike us unfavourably and appear not only unpleasant but disgusting.' No attempt to revive original stage conditions would work, he claimed, as the Elizabethan theatre represented 'the childlike beginning of the stage, a scaffolding, where one saw little, where everything was *signified*'. Goethe had diminished confidence in the expressive power of the bare stage; furthermore, he found theatrical moments in Shakespeare rare, 'scattered jewels, separated by much that is untheatrical'. In appearing to champion the dominant move towards a more literal stage realism, Goethe advocated the continued use of the old eighteenth-century adaptations.

Goethe's views were not, however, shared by Romantic writers closely associated with the theatre, particularly not by Ludwig Tieck, who, from the early 1790s through to his death in 1853, published regularly editions of Elizabethan plays and essays on them that argued consistently for a return to the original performance conditions as a prerequisite for successful production. For Tieck, Shakespeare's plays were remarkable because of the playwright's ability to summon up a world of fantasy that the audience experienced as if it were in a dream. In an early essay, which introduced his translation of *The Tempest*, 'Shakespeares Behandlung des Wunderbaren' ('Shakespeare's Treatment of the Marvellous', 1793), Tieck demonstrated a broader, more generous view of the potential of the theatre than Goethe would do later, finding Shakespeare above all other dramatists fulfilling this potential. 'Perhaps no other writer', he wrote, 'has so well calculated theatrical effect in his works of art as Shakespeare, without resorting to empty *coups-de-théâtres* or providing entertainment through wretched surprises'.[2] Especially remarkable for Tieck was the completeness of Shakespeare's fantasy world. This challenged the performer to maintain entire the illusion, 'so that the mind [of the spectator] is never transferred to the normal world and the illusion broken'. Tieck considered the conventional theatre of his time – and he was particularly antagonistic towards the arch-illusionist, August Iffland – to be inadequate. Its actors were too precise and dry, while its concern with impressive spectacle stood between the audience and the play. So that Shakepeare's plays could be performed in a manner that allowed the audience to participate fully in their world, Tieck argued for a stage that allowed the actors closer proximity to the audience than was possible in the early nineteenth-century theatre with its broad orchestra pit. Furthermore, their stage should not be encumbered with heavy, realistic scenery, but should be arranged so as to allow for swift transitions from one scene to the other. This non-scenic stage would, by its very nature, not presuppose the unity of tone implied by the conventional perspective stage, but would be an ideal environment for the 'variety, episodes, and juxtapositions of the comic with the tragic' characteristic of Shakespearean drama. Naturally, the Elizabethan theatre provided a model for this stage, and Tieck did much pioneering research into the conditions in which Shakespeare's plays were first performed. In addition to several publications on the Elizabethan dramatists and their theatre, in 1836 he completed, with the help of the architect Gottfried Semper, a reconstruction of the Fortune Theatre. This was not entirely accurate. Instead of the stage thrust out into the audience, indicated by the Henslowe contract, he provided a broad, shallow, relief stage, and from this he had two conspicuous flights of stairs leading up to a substantial balcony stage. But, despite its inaccuracies, this reconstruction demonstrated the possibility of staging Shakespeare in an alternative way to that of the illusionist stage.

In more practical spheres, Tieck was less successful. As dramaturg to the Dresden Court Theatre between 1825 and 1841, he did much to advance the cause of Shakespeare in the theatre, sometimes influencing the way in which his plays were staged.[3] But a faithful reconstruction, or even anything remotely approaching it, remained purely within the realm of his literature. In his novel *Der junge Tischlermeister* (*The Young Master Carpenter*, 1828), Tieck described an imaginary production of *Twelfth Night*, staged by amateurs in the hall of a large mansion, on a stage that ran down the length of the hall. In the centre of this long, narrow stage stood 'the upper balcony or gallery . . . supported by free-standing pillars, the ionic capitals of which were elegantly gilded. Below was the smaller, inner stage, hidden by curtains of red silk. The steps [to the inner stage] were also designed with colourful coverings, so that the stage could be itself, whatever one wanted.'[4] For Tieck, it was the lack of any definite locale that was the key appeal of such a stage. Not only did its sparseness not 'contradict the poet's work'; it also gave the spectator the right to imagine whatever space was represented in it. The all-encompassing illusion Tieck asked of the stage was enhanced rather than destroyed by the non-illusionist presentation and, owing to the uninterrupted performance, described by Tieck, the audience were free to enter into the imaginative world of the play.

Tieck's researches into the Elizabethan theatre bore more immediate practical fruit in the work of Karl Immermann, who, as intendant of the Düsseldorf Theatre between 1834 and 1837, trained a company of actors whose standards of ensemble playing were to become a yardstick for the German theatre in the middle years of the century (Fellner, 1888). Immermann was a disciplined man, who favoured economy in the theatre for artistic as well as financial reasons. For him, the essence of theatre was in the spoken language rather than the spectacle. 'Like all poetry', he wrote, 'dramatic poetry should attempt to attain its effect by *audible* signs. The visual, the mimetic must come to the fore, but only as a supplementary means. The pure basis of performing art remains speech; beautiful recitation is primary and most important.'[5] This somewhat limited view of the actor's art led Immermann to adopt simple settings and to strive to find means of lessening the distance between the actors and their audience. On one of his travels, he visited Tieck, who introduced him to both Greek and Elizabethan theatrical forms. In these theatres, Immermann realised, 'human action remains the main point of the drama', and any scenic decoration, which he described as a 'lifeless' element, fulfils a purely supportive function.

During his intendancy at Düsseldorf, Immermann was unable to attempt any reconstruction of the Elizabethan stage, but in February 1840, using amateur actors, he produced *Twelfth Night* for the Fasching celebrations. For this production, Immermann did not have a regular theatre at his disposal. Instead he used a large hall where, with the help of a Professor Wiedmann, he constructed a stage that was not an exact replica of the Elizabethan. Nevertheless, using both the model from *Der junge Tischlermeister* and certain Elizabethan and Italian Renaissance elements, he provided an effective and flexible setting for the play. The forestage, which was long, narrow and not in the form of a thrust, was backed by four entrances and a central playing area. This area was an inner stage with walls arranged in perspective, framed by pillars and a triangular portico and raised two steps above the mainstage. Here took place those scenes of a private, intimate nature, in contrast to the more public scenes set in the streets, the garden and the palace. For these, the undifferentiated area of the mainstage was used. On each side of the inner stage, next to these two archways, were two doors, behind which perspective scenery was placed. Following possible ancient Greek precedent, one of these archways led to the harbour, the other to the town. On each side of the mainstage were two further entrance points. The whole structure faced the audience. Immermann, who was aware of the unhistorical nature of his stage, all the same considered it to be an effective solution for the performance of Shakespeare's play.

Shakespeare, among all poets [he wrote] is least tolerant of the admixture of modern pettiness. He always deals with greatness, wholeness, the unvarnished fates of the world and humanity; everything illusory, operatic in design, falls from his limbs like bad lacquer from a beautiful statue; he must be brought into the most intimate proximity with the listeners, when the secrets that flow forth from the heart of his people will be understood.[6]

With this stage, Immermann had achieved the necessary intimacy, the audience's attention being fixed almost solely on the actors. Furthermore, the flexibility of the stage – including a curtain at the back of the inner stage, there were seven entrances – allowed Immermann to achieve unusual effects in blocking. Its bareness enabled him to work at placing the characters with an eye to how this could reflect relationships between them; in this way he clarified the action. In particular, as he describes the manner in which he arranged the first visit of Viola to Olivia's house, it is clear that, using skilfully both the mainstage and the inner stage, he satisfactorily represented simultaneous actions and achieved an interesting contrast between Olivia and Viola before they met, something quite impossible on the illusionist stage.

Immermann died a few months after his production of *Twelfth Night*: any further experimentation was left to the now ageing Tieck. This opportunity occurred in 1841, when he received a summons to join the Berlin Royal Theatre as dramaturg. His first experiment in presenting a play in a style approximating its original performance conditions was with Sophocles' *Antigone*; but in 1843, with the aid of the stage designer J. C. Gerst, he produced *A Midsummer Night's Dream*. Like Immermann, Tieck did not attempt to reconstruct precisely the Elizabethan stage, though in the context of the proscenium stages first of the Potsdam Court Theatre, then of the Berlin Royal Theatre, he incorporated some of its principles, especially in the use of vertical space. This he had already exaggerated in his reconstruction of the Fortune. Gerst's permanent set consisted of three storeys that included 'visible flights of stairs and several playing areas, a forestage and side-steps behind the proscenium, covered by carpets' (Kindermann, 1964, p. 28). The multiple playing areas enabled Tieck to present the action with a fluidity unique to the time. But the popularity of this production – it was given more than forty times, a considerable number for those days – must have been dependent partially upon substantial concessions being made to audience taste for realistic illusion and spectacle. The galleries at the back were so constructed as to allow realistic backdrops to be lowered into each partitioned space. In this way, a particular area at a particular point in the action was localised. Moreover, the workshop of the mechanicals, which could not be accommodated in one area of the permanent stage was realised through lowering, in front of the galleries, a realistic backdrop as specific as anything in the conventional theatre. Also, this was the production for which Mendelssohn wrote his popular incidental music to A *Midsummer Night's Dream*, which meant that considerable portions of the performance included ballet, performed among attractively designed woodland scenery lowered from the flies. This served to disguise the architectural nature of the permanent set. Unlike Immermann, Tieck settled for a compromise between conventional theatre and the non-illusionism of the Elizabethan stage. While this was a highly successful venture (especially as the audience, helped by Mendelssohn's music, became deeply involved in Shakespeare's fantasy world), it did not fulfil to the letter Tieck's ambition to reproduce a staging as sparse as he considered that of the Elizabethans to be.

In the latter half of the nineteenth century critics and practitioners continued to demonstrate an interest in the Elizabethan theatre. No further practical experiments took place until 1889, when the intendant of the Munich Court Theatre, Karl von Perfall, commissioned one of his directors, Jocza Savits, and the resident designer, Kurt Lautenschläger, to construct a stage that allowed an approach to Shakespearean production different from that of the by-then ubiquitous Meiningen company, which took realistic spectacle to its ultimate limits. Perfall was prompted in this partially by an essay by the theatre historian, Rudolf Genée, 'Die Natürlichkeit und die historische Treue in den theatralischen Vorstellungen' ('Naturalness and Historical Accuracy in Theatrical Performances'), published two years earlier. In this essay, Genée took up and expanded at length those themes concerning the relationship between design and inner action that had previously been touched upon by Tieck and Immermann. He posited the possibly dubious equation that standards of acting fell in direct relationship to the increasing emphasis placed upon spectacle – a process he saw as endemic to all theatrical activity in contemporary Germany. This, he claimed, violated the very essence of dramatic art, for drama is wholly dependent upon 'symbolic' action, upon the suggestion rather than the manifestation of reality. For Genée, the purpose of theatre was to give internal experience an outer form. 'The dramatist', he wrote, 'has done enough when he awakens in us the impression of inner truth, when he knows how to express the inner being by the symbolism of appearance, so that we survey the whole by means of concentrated images, from whose accumulated lines the picture is assembled'.[7] Recognising the earlier efforts of Immermann and Tieck, Genée called for a theatre in which artistic effects were achieved solely through the words of the poet and the performance of the actor. Like Immermann, Genée considered the spoken word to be the single most important element of the performance; all gesture and movement should be solely to give external form to the 'inner truth' expressed by the word. In the severely restricted theatre conceived by Genée scenic decoration had only one function, to support the actor. It was at its most successful when the audience was least conscious of it, as their whole attention should be focussed on the actor. If scenery were reduced to a necessary minimum, then the plays of Shakespeare would be played in a manner that would allow the symbolic nature of the action to unfold. Like Tieck, Genée argued that this would give the audience freedom to exercise their imagination.

Genée's essay and Perfall's reaction to it initiated the most extended attempt in nineteenth-century Germany to evolve a means of playing Shakespeare without encumbering him with 'the heavy, exceedingly complicated apparatus and mechanism of the modern stage'.[8] To solve the problem of distance between the stage and the audience, Savits and Lautenschläger built a forestage over the wide orchestra pit of the Munich Residenztheater, leaving only a narrow gap between the front of the stage and the first row of the stalls. There was sufficient room within this gap for a flight of stairs leading from the pit to the stage. The broad, empty forestage extended back behind the regular proscenium arch of the theatre to an elaborate proscenium wall, decorated with Romanesque arches. In the centre of this wall was a square archway, eight metres in width, which framed a substantial inner stage, raised three steps above the forestage. The whole structure, though it had the appearance of great solidity, was remarkably mobile and could be constructed or dismantled in two hours (see pl. 25).

Savits and Lautenschläger's solution seemed strikingly simple. By retaining a sizeable and clearly visible inner stage, they were able to create the interaction between public and private spheres of action that Immer-

mann had prized, while the extremely open forestage, which was never to
be cluttered with props, was an ideal platform for the actor who wished to
draw audience attention solely to the role he was playing. But, like Tieck
before him, Savits compromised the original severity of his conception.
While the oppressively decorated proscenium wall and the walls at the side
of the forestage remained constant throughout any performance, the inner
stage contained scenery, arranged in conventional perspective style,
which was changed regularly in the course of performance. For example,
during the opening production of *King Lear* on 1 June 1889, an over-
complicated, even fussy, use of the relationship between the forestage and
the inner perspective stage was adopted. The start of the performance was
announced by a trumpet call, whereupon the main curtain, which covered
the whole structure including the forestage, went up, and Gloucester,
Edmund and Kent entered on to the forestage. At the end of their

25. Jocza Savits' production of *King Lear*, at the Royal Theatre, Munich, 1889

217

conversation, a curtain which hid the inner stage parted to reveal Lear on his throne, surrounded by courtiers. His daughters, accompanied by their husbands, entered through doors on each side of the inner arch, and the court formally arranged itself on the forestage, with men to the left, women to the right. At the end of the scene, the curtain in front of the inner stage closed, only to open a few minutes later to reveal a room in Gloucester's palace with Edmund discovered. He then left the inner stage to deliver his monologue on the forestage. Such interchange between the two stage areas occurred throughout the production, there being twenty-three different scenes on the inner stage.

Some attempt was made to indicate the difference between outdoor and indoor scenes. Whenever the inner stage represented a scene outdoors, characters entered on to the inner stage directly and, when using the forestage, entered only from the doors on the extreme sides; this gave an impression of greater space. For indoor scenes, they used the doors to the side of the arch in the scenic wall and moved in more constricted patterns than in the outdoor scenes.

The primary flaw of Savits' new Shakespeare stage and his use of it was the mixture of the techniques of open and illusionistic staging. Given contemporary audiences' unfamiliarity with any style of theatre that did not attempt to realise the stage world realistically down to the minutest detail, there were several complaints that the emptiness of the forestage detracted from rather than added to the impact of the play's action. In particular, several critics commented on the contradiction between the heavy scenic wall on which Romanesque arches were graphically painted and the inner stage, especially when outdoor scenes were shown. Because of these two negative reactions, while the Shakespeare-stage continued to be used, both for Shakespeare and for other plays from the classic repertoire, progressive attempts were made to neutralise the two stages, so that by 1890, for a production of Goethe's *Götz von Berlichingen*, the arch was framed with an elaborate surrounding of foliage to soften the severe lines of the original. Furthermore, plays were staged so as to ignore the difference between the two stage areas. Ultimately the whole structure was treated as little more than an illusionist stage with a peculiarly large forestage.

In order to accomplish a revolution, changes effected should be radical and complete. This Savits admitted only after the Shakespeare-stage, which was used periodically at the Residenztheater until 1906,[9] had finally been abandoned. The 'innere Regie' ('internal direction') he wished to achieve could be accomplished only on a stage where scenery and spectacle had been reduced to an absolute minimum, so that the audience focussed solely on the unity between words and gesture in the actor's performance. The Munich Shakespeare-stage, he felt, had made too great a concession to the desire for realistic illusion. As a result, those in the company who opposed the conception – and these included the actor Ernst von Possart, who was promoted to intendant on Perfall's retirement in 1892 – could all too easily adapt it to more conventional purposes. Even Savits, one suspects, while he was directing on the stage could never entirely free himself from a lingering taste for overt theatricalism. For example, in a production of *Macbeth* in November 1891, staged with the leafy cover over the inner arch, he had the Witches perform behind gauzes and employed an elaborate dumb-show in which Duncan displayed the trust he had in Macbeth while Macbeth himself was delivering down on the forestage the soliloquy in which it becomes clear that the Witches' prophecy is working on him. Later in the play there was liberal use of thunder and other sound effects to augment the dramatic impact. Clearly this was not a theatre in which the actor was the sole medium. But because of its deliberate lack of technical sophistication, the Shakespeare-stage failed to provide a satisfactory alternative to the fullness of spectacle normally expected of theatre.

Nevertheless, the wide spaces of the forestage did allow for some experimentation, which was to foreshadow later developments in play direction. In particular, stage plans that have survived of the productions indicate that Savits explored with much accomplishment the potentiality of blocking to express the play's action. In *Julius Caesar* (produced in December 1897), for example, instead of the crowd being at the centre of the play, as had been the case with the Meiningen productions, Caesar himself became the pivotal point of the action. The assassination was accomplished with particular effect, the space of the forestage being used to underline the motives of the characters, the effect being achieved by groupings of the conspirators in which their physical distance from Caesar's body reflected their personal relationship to him (Durian, 1937, p. 69). At such a moment, Savits seems to have discovered on his stage what Immermann had discovered on his, the possibility of arranging actors in 'clear lucid groups' (1971, vol. 1), so that their thoughts, impulses, and motives could be simply realised as part of the whole play.

In a long and often bitter retrospective account of the Munich Shakespeare-stage, Savits attributed its ultimate demise to several causes. First, as already mentioned, he recognised his mistake in catering to the desire for spectacle and illusion. There was considerable support for his stage from the audience, he claimed, but he blamed the critics who attacked his work for being unwilling to allow the stage to return to something approximating its elemental form — an accusation not totally justified, as several critics discussed seriously and responsibly his efforts at reform.[10] He also blamed the actors, many of whom said they were uneasy on a stage that was almost entirely free of the usual clutter of props. The exposure so produced hindered them in their attempts to achieve freedom of expression, as if this could be found only when an easy escape could be made to the security of stage furniture. But above all Savits realised that, whatever the purity of his ambitions, he was incapable of reversing an accelerating trend in the theatre towards spectacle. In order to do this, he claimed, a revolution within the institution of the theatre itself would have to take place, requiring the actors to perform constantly on his open stage, with no option of returning regularly, as they did, to the conventional illusionist stage. The very mobility of his stage structure militated against its lasting effectiveness. Throughout his efforts he was hampered, he insisted, by the crippling spirit of the conventional theatre of his time:

> It is as if there reside in the mind and soul of both artist and spectator, out on the stage and in the auditorium, tedious, malicious sprites and goblins, demons of ostentatious scenery, nesting in all angles and corners. They play a thousand tricks on the new [theatrical] dispensation that offends them . . . Against them, in the [old] theatre the memory is defenceless.
> (Savits, 1908, p. 229)

Savits retired from the theatre a disappointed man, defeated by the 'malicious sprites and goblins' of spectacle. History has not subsequently raised him to a high rank as a reformer; indeed, the whole history of the German Shakespeare-stage has remained distinctly peripheral in the history of the theatre. This has been due, no doubt, to what many contemporaries and later commentators have seen as the irremediable academicism of his efforts and of the efforts of Immermann and Tieck. Although it has been argued with some persuasiveness that all were concerned first and foremost with practical problems of staging plays that were dramaturgically unsuited to the scenic arrangements of the time (Nussel, 1967, pp. 164–72), it must be admitted that there was a strongly antiquarian impulse behind their work. Moreover, in the writings of Genée and Savits, there is a tone of elitism, which suggests that they were producing a theatre from which all but those who were like-minded should be excluded. This is paradoxical, as both claimed that in their search for an appropriate stage for Shakespeare they were striving to realise a 'popular' theatre, appealing to the broadest possible cross-section of society. The model they developed, however, was unlikely to engage the interests of a wide spectrum of the population, since it rejected rather than incorporated those aspects of theatre that created and sustained the support of the nineteenth-century theatre.

The 'Shakespeare-Stage' in Germany

The Shakespeare-stage did have some influence on later theatrical developments: the 'relief stage' of the important Munich Artists Theatre (Stahl, 1947, p. 505) was a direct outgrowth of Savits' work at the Munich Court Theatre, and this did much to simplify the increasingly complex manner in which the classic drama was produced on the German stage. Its influence was also more durable than that of Savits' Shakespeare-stage. But the most effective forces of change on techniques of staging in the modern theatre came from practitioners whose vision of an alternative theatre was more cogent and better adapted to contemporary taste. Savits used illusion in order to sweeten the bitter pill of non-illusion. The more influential theoreticians and designers of the time, such as Adolphe Appia, Edward Gordon Craig, Alfred Roller, and Ernst Stern, did not deny illusion: rather, they simplified it, reducing detail to a minimum but maintaining the framework with which their audience was familiar. Their boldly conceived, progressively more abstract sets were, in most cases, devised with intentions similar to those of Savits, as they too worked to release the imagination of the audience from quotidian concern with real things in order to focus their attention on the world of the actor. Their scenery provided, in a necessarily indirect way, intimations of the inner life of the characters represented on stage. But unlike Savits they transformed the current mode of theatre rather than half-heartedly refuting it. The principles of Shakespeare's stage were once again examined a few decades later by Bertolt Brecht. This was done, however, in order to achieve an aesthetic more radical and complete than any that had been devised by the nineteenth-century reformers – and, of course, in a society where values were radically different. Nevertheless, in a period when theatrical performance was subject to a notably uniform style of presentation, Immermann, Tieck and Savits kept alive an awareness that an alternative to this uniformity was available. Like William Poel in England and Aurélian Lugné-Poë in France, their experiments with variations on Shakespeare's stage served to relieve the monotony of a theatre given almost wholly to spectacle. They were not leaders of change, but they prepared the way for it.

NOTES

1 Goethe, n.d., p. 288. Goethe's essay is available in English translation under the title 'Shakespeare ad Infinitum', in LeWinter 1970.
2 'Shakespeares Behandlung des Wunderbaren' (Tieck, 1848, vol. 1, pp. 38–9).
3 In particular his ideas had some influence on the staging at the Dresden Court Theatre of *Macbeth* in 1836: see Kindermann, 1964, vol. 6, p. 27.
4 'Der junge Tischlermeister' (Tieck, n.d., p. 418).

5 'Über das Theater zu Düsseldorf im Winter 1832–1833' (Immermann, 1971, vol. 1, p. 679).

6 'Zur Afführung von Shakespeares Lustspiel *Was ihr Wollt*' (Immermann, 1971, vol. 1, p. 691).

7 'Die Natürlichkeit und die historische Treue in den theatralischen Vorstellungen' (Genée, 1889, p. 67).

8 Karl von Perfall's memorandum to the Munich Court Theatre; quoted Stahl, 1947, p. 493.

9 The Shakespeare plays produced on the Shakespeare-stage were *King Lear, Macbeth, Romeo and Juliet, The Winter's Tale, Julius Caesar, Cymbeline, Twelfth Night, Richard II, Henry IV Pts. 1 & 2, Henry V, Henry VI Pts. 2 & 3 and Richard III*. Productions of *Hamlet* and *Othello* were planned. See Durian, 1937.

10 For a sympathetic assessment of Savits' work, see Alfred Mensi von Klarbach, 'Die Shakespeare-Bühne im Jahre 1898', *Shakespeare-Jahrbuch*, 35 (1898), 362–75.

Shakespeare on French Stages in the Nineteenth Century

CHRISTOPHER SMITH

'I CANNOT, on my heart, take Sarah's Hamlet seriously.' So wrote Max Beerbohm in 1899 (1924, vol. 1, p. 61), valiantly endeavouring to make it plain that, while others might once again be succumbing to enthusiasm for the French actress appearing at the Adelphi, he had kept an exemplary cool head and his incomparable waspishness. Nowadays it is perhaps difficult to resist the temptation of sharing a smile with him at the thought of Madame Bernhardt in her ripe fifties gallivanting to Elsinore clad in a fur-trimmed tunic with leg-of-mutton sleeves and with black tights over her none too shapely thighs (pl. 26). Yet the phenomenon warrants serious attention, and not just as a performance in its own right. That performance, in fact, as regards its most immediately striking feature, was perhaps not too surprising, for in the nineteenth-century theatre, even more in France than in England, there was a distinct tradition of ladies of mature years in breeches playing the roles of callow youths. So Sarah Bernhardt's Hamlet should not be regarded as entirely untoward, albeit a female Romeo might well have caused less comment, quite apart from any argument that a performer's sex is hardly more relevant than age or several other factors in the creation of theatrical illusion. What matters here, though, is not a question of acting conventions, but a problem in the history of the theatre. In this context, Sarah Bernhardt's decision to play Hamlet in a specially prepared translation of the play provides striking evidence about the status of Shakespeare on the French stage at the very end of the Victorian era; or rather, since the accession and demise of the Duke of Kent's daughter can hardly be said to have marked epochs in the annals of drama in Paris, at the end of what may fittingly be called the Romantic century.

Up until that *Hamlet*, Sarah Bernhardt's career in Shakespeare (if in little else) might appear to have been fairly orthodox.[1] At the appropriately early age of twenty she had scored one of her first major successes as Cordelia, when *King Lear*, in Jules Lacroix's translation, was performed at the Odéon in 1868. Ten years later, at a benefit performance for Bressant, she had played Desdemona opposite Mounet-Sully. For this performance of *Othello* at the Comédie-Française, Aicard's translation was used; the reception accorded to the play despite a distinguished cast, seems not to have been regarded as sufficiently warm to justify its inclusion in the repertory for any reasonably long period. In 1884, just before the reprise of Lacroix's *Macbeth* at the Odéon, Sarah Bernhardt starred at the Théâtre de la Porte Saint-Martin in a version of the play which had been prepared by her current lover, Jean Richepin. This production, in which Philippe Garnier took the male lead, met with little success, though that did not discourage Sarah Bernhardt from essaying it at the Gaiety when she came over to London in June of that same year. Next, in 1886, came a free adaptation of *Hamlet* in which she played Ophelia. Though there was perhaps nothing especially unusual about Sarah Bernhardt's Shakespearean appearances up to this point, it is worth observing that her roles in Shakespeare had, in fact, come at quite widely spaced intervals and that, after a first triumph, she had been denied the successes which she might well have hoped for. Furthermore, many of the Shakespearean parts which a leading English actress might have expected to have the opportunity of interpreting – Juliet, of course, in her younger days, Portia and the heroines of the romances, and, in her more mature period, Cleopatra – never came her way. She had, moreover, always played Shakespeare in versions substantially refashioned for use on the French stage.

When Sarah Bernhardt decided to play Hamlet she was not simply staking a claim to a great role; in the enterprise there was, in fact, something of a pioneering spirit and an effort to reveal to the French public, as if for the first time, all the richness of the text and the complexity of the hero. The context of Sarah Bernhardt's revival of *Hamlet* is significant. Alfred de Musset's *Lorenzaccio* is generally regarded as the most genuinely Shakespearean of all the French Romantic dramas; and so great was the influence of Shakespeare on its dramatic technique that it was regarded as unstageable and was never performed during its author's lifetime. It was not until 1896 that Sarah Bernhardt put on at the Théâtre de la Renaissance Armand d'Artois's adaptation of the play (de Musset, 1898), finding in the title role a part that suited her well. The Romantic combination of passionate emotional involvement and a temperamental incapacity for action seemed to her – and to her audiences, it must be granted – to be aptly expressed when the male tragic hero was played by a woman. Long admired, but at some remove from theatre, *Lorenzaccio* attracted great attention when Sarah Bernhardt played it. The case is similar, though not exactly the same, with *Hamlet*. Known for gener-

MME. SARAH BERNHARDT AS "HAMLET."

Lafayette
LTD.

COPYRIGHT.

LONDON, DUBLIN, GLASGOW,
MANCHESTER & BELFAST

26. Sarah Bernhardt as Hamlet

ations, it had been played in France for decades, but only in a variety of adaptations which had introduced distortions far more substantial and grievous than those which were inevitable when such a difficult text as Shakespeare's was translated into a foreign language. By comparison with earlier versions, the *Hamlet* in which Sarah Bernhardt appeared was remarkable for its fidelity and its completeness. Doubtless it would be mistaken to suppose that the actress was inspired solely by scholarly considerations. She was naturally anxious to ensure for herself yet another major theatrical success in the sort of role she had discovered suited her well. Criticisms that her *Lorenzaccio*, however great its merits, had been unfaithful to Musset's original may have stung her too. Whatever the balance of motives, the upshot was that the *Hamlet* which she mounted at the end of the nineteenth century was intended to be more authentic than any that had been seen in French before. Accordingly she sought a new translation; it was provided by the youthful Marcel Schwob and Eugène Morand.

In the preface (Schwob 1928, vol. 6) there are a number of remarks which seem designed especially to satisfy Sarah Bernhardt; after some discussion it is, for instance, gravely concluded that Hamlet should no doubt be portrayed as being between twenty and twenty-five years old and that 'fat' should not be interpreted in the sense that the uninitiated might suppose. It is, however, more important to note the claim that this is a genuine and full translation of the complete text, not an adaptation. That that point should have needed stressing at so late a date is remarkable indeed. The translation was, it should be added, in prose, which allowed a flexibility and width of vocabulary that even then, it appears, would not have been compatible with French verse habits. It had taken the Naturalist revolution and, probably more pertinently for Sarah Bernhardt, the example of *Lorenzaccio* to make it possible to abandon the alexandrine. Now, at last, Sarah Bernhardt would be able to follow up her success in Romantic drama by a triumph in a similar role in Shakespeare. Next would come, in 1900, *L'Aiglon*. Specially devised for her by Edmond Rostand, it dramatised the anguished existence of Napoleon's only son, the Duke of Reichstadt, and it gave Sarah another breeches part which we should resist the temptation of calling a travesty of acting since so many were deeply moved. Later on she was to speak with pride of her good fortune in being able to interpret before the public three Hamlets: Rostand's 'white Hamlet', the Hamlet from Musset's Florence and the black Hamlet of Shakespeare, in a new play, in a play which had never before been performed and in a play which in France had hitherto been misinterpreted.

Though misinterpreted, *Hamlet* had certainly not remained unknown or undiscussed in French literary or theatrical circles. So Sarah Bernhardt's revival of *Hamlet* invites us to ask what the French Shakespearean revival really had meant up to then. Some clearer idea of what was involved may emerge from consideration of an article which Maurice Bouchor contributed to the *Revue de Paris* in 1895.[2] What is most striking about it is that, apart from a number of references to contemporary productions and to the names of living writers and actors, it is written in a spirit and with a manner and tone which might almost have been as apt in 1795 as a century later. Bouchor is inspired by twenty years' devotion to Shakespeare, and he has familiarised himself with his plays not just by reading the texts in the original but by regularly attending the latest productions in London as well as in Paris. He does not approve of everything he has seen on English stages, but finds that Shakespeare productions are invariably far worse in France. In fact he is worried that his criticism may seem utterly damning, and feels obliged to add that he would not wish at any price to discourage theatre managements from doing what they can to give French audiences a better idea of the English dramatist he so much admires. He notes that a new production of *King Lear* at the Théâtre-Libre under Larochelle has been announced; he is glad about this, yet cannot suppress misgivings about what will be forthcoming. He knows too that the Comédie-Française puts on plays ascribed to Shakespeare, yet he feels that the author of *Hamlet* is only tolerated, and not loved, at the *Maison de Molière*; and what applies to the leading French theatre holds good for the French public more generally.

After toying with the paradox that Shakespeare transcends theatrical production yet is fully comprehensible only when performed on stage, Bouchor finds four main reasons why Shakespeare has not succeeded in France. First, he complains that the available translations, which had perhaps better be called adaptations, are generally unfaithful to the letter of the original and sometimes cruelly distort its spirit. He knows well what great efforts have already been made to translate Shakespeare into French, yet he can only judge the enterprise to have been in vain so far; at best, the French versions sound more like Victor Hugo than Shakespeare, which is an intriguing criticism, given that Hugo aspired to the role of prophetic bard that he thought had been Shakespeare's. Bouchor's considered recommendation is that prose should be used for Shakespeare's blank verse as well as for his prose, with French verse reserved for the passages in which rhyme is used in the original and for songs. Next Bouchor complains about the fashion for mounting spectacular Shakespeare productions in which the scene-changes take so long that much of the text has to be sacrificed if the performance is not to be intolerably protracted. On this score the

27.   Mounet-Sully as Hamlet

Lyceum does not 'scape whipping, but Bouchor gives English producers credit for making greater efforts than their Parisian counterparts to keep the action moving along, though he would prefer a return to Elizabethan pace. As for production style, he asserts that the French theatre has not yet acquired any real skill in handling crowd scenes, while the portrayal of violence and of ghosts can still provoke hilarity all too easily. The actors are generally ill at ease in Shakespeare too; they are uncomfortable at any mixing of genres, because it conflicts with their fondness for indulging in oratorical sublimity, which they expect to be greeted with salvoes of illusion-shattering applause. In a judgement fully endorsed by Clement Scott (1900; repr. 1969, p. 41), Bouchor grants that at the Comédie-Française Mounet-Sully is an impressive Hamlet (pl. 27), yet he finds that the rest of the cast is evidently not at home in a style which it finds alien to its concept of drama and to its traditions of acting. There has been, as Bouchor well knows, a century of efforts to bring Shakespeare before the French public, despite the persistent coldness of certain critics, yet still the task of revealing to the mass of the French public the depth of his psychological penetration, the consummate skill of his stagecraft and the beauty of his language remains to be accomplished. First, he declares roundly, Shakespeare must be recognised by all and without reservation or cavil as 'one of the three or four greatest poets that have honoured the human race'; then there must be a willingness to accept his drama just as it is, without any surrender to the ever-present temptation to adapt and, as if that were possible, to improve his works to make them more acceptable to French taste.

It might be possible to discount Bouchor's opinions as simply the typical attitude of a critic who feels the need to decry all previous endeavours and argue for a fresh interpretation, which must, of course, be based on a new reading of the original text. But the views he put forward were not without justification, and neither the tenor nor the tone of his article was inappropriate. It was a remarkable comment that, after more than a hundred and fifty years of fitful effort to come to terms with Shakespeare, at the end of the nineteenth century there was still much pioneering work to be done. The name of Shakespeare was revered, but reverence stopped short – even out of respect, it was averred – of presenting his works unadapted on the stage. Philippe van Tieghem (1961) concludes a magisterial survey of the evidence by pointing out that, though Shakespeare's classic status, after being hotly contested for generations, was widely admitted in France from about 1850, and though his influence was found everywhere from then on, particularly in prose fiction, it was only towards the end of the century that complete performances of some of his plays were risked on the stage in Paris. In accounts of the reception of Shakespeare in France emphasis is naturally placed on ignorance and aesthetic chauvinism. Misplaced enthusiasm for merely a few aspects of his achievement and supposed character, however, perhaps caused just as much damage; and though there has grown up almost a tradition of disparaging the more or less free adaptations of his works that were set before the public, it could well be that it was because these were successful enough in combining the novel with the familiar to satisfy the public that translators and theatre directors were inhibited from risking something closer to the original.

English troupes toured France in Shakespeare's day, and Louis XIII was struck by a scene from *Henry VI*, but that was long before he reached the age of discretion.[3] After that, there is scant evidence that Frenchmen, even when in London, took any interest in Shakespeare during the seventeenth century. Occupied with the enterprise of fashioning their own species of drama from the classical heritage, French playwrights turned, when they felt the need for alternative traditions, to the Spanish Golden Age. While the climate was favourable, it was from the south-west, not the north-west, that the wind blew, and the triumph of classicism spelt the rejection even of Spanish seductions. It was only in the third decade of the eighteenth century, when English thinkers were already to some extent fashionable in intellectual circles on the continent, that Frenchmen who for one reason or another found themselves in London turned to Shakespeare, with curiosity tinctured by superciliousness. By then classicism, hailed on all sides as a towering product of high civilisation, had passed its peak and the century-long search for renewal both within the tradition and outside it had already begun. The major name in this context is, of course, Voltaire's. But in his *Lettres philosophiques* Shakespearean drama is only one of several aspects of English life to which he refers, and he is far more reserved in his comments on Shakespeare than in those on many other topics. The constant implication of his observations is that they order these things better in England than in France, but he cannot bring himself to go so far with regard to Shakespeare. The playwright has genius, to be sure, but no education, no taste and no knowledge of the great tradition in drama; from him something may be learned, but only if due caution is exercised, for he can never be accepted wholeheartedly as a model by any writer whose ambition is to please the polite and cultivated public of Europe. There is no need to trace here the phases of the waxing and waning of Voltaire's attitudes towards the dramatist he claimed, with less than total justification, to have brought to the attention of his compatriots, or the impact of Shakespeare on his own dramas. In his ambiguous response he did, however, inaugurate a misconception that was destined to be long-lived. The formulation that Shakespeare was a barbarian of genius was not just cagily double-edged; it also launched the persistent, pernicious and quite groundless notions that

Shakespeare was a purely natural genius whose vision was not mediated, indeed was not vitiated, by being expressed through any aesthetic or cultural tradition, and that any imitation of his plays must be circumspect.

The next important step, after the account given by Voltaire, was the publication in London in 1746 of the first volumes of Pierre-Antoine de La Place's *Théâtre anglois*. In a prefatory discourse on English drama, La Place starts by referring to Pierre Brumoy's translations of Greek plays, which had appeared some fifteen years earlier. These translations, he says, naturally made an immediate appeal because the original plays formed the basis of the great drama of modern times; but, in drawing attention to the fact that those of his contemporaries who professed reverence for the ancient paradigms had virtually forgotten what they were really like, he placed his finger on a weakness in classicism. Like the new interest in Homer, which Kirsti Simonsuuri (1979) has explored, fresh information about the ancient dramatists added a new dimension to the *Querelle des Anciens et des Modernes*, contributing to the emergence of neo-classicism, in its restricted sense, and then to the later development of Romanticism. La Place does not, for his part, make excessive claims on behalf of Shakespeare; he prefers to approach his works in what was at the time the fashionable spirit of anthropological relativism in order to discover what he can about this dramatist whose reputation is high in a land so close to France yet whose dramatic method appears totally alien when judged by French criteria. Unaware of Shakespeare's debt to English predecessors and contemporaries, and (what is perhaps less understandable) failing to appreciate his relationship with Renaissance high culture generally, La Place follows Voltaire in ascribing all the dramatist's merits to his genius, which enabled him to copy nature so persuasively. But next comes the caveat: genius is unreliable, and, as French classical poetics always warned, it is dangerous if educated taste and reasoned restraint are not employed to shape inspiration.

In view of these considerations, La Place felt that offering a complete translation of Shakespeare would serve only to expose the English dramatist to ridicule, and he took the view that there could be no thought of performing these patently uneven plays. Accordingly, he offered versions in rhymed alexandrines (for at the time no other verse form for serious drama was thinkable) just of the main scenes of the plays, which he read in Pope's edition of 1728. He also provided prose connecting passages which summarised developments which in his judgement were peripheral to the main plot or else in such poor taste as to be likely to cause offence. One might smile at this aesthetic bowdlerisation, were it not for the thought of what was being done to Shakespeare in eighteenth-century

England. It can also be said in justification of La Place that he was able to offer a coherent defence of his form of presentation and that he did much to bring Shakespeare to the attention not only of French readers, but of the European cultured public in general. Soon something was known of *Othello, Romeo and Juliet, Henry VI, Richard III, Hamlet* and *Macbeth*; and, of those, four were to remain the most popular of Shakespeare's works on the continent for more than a century and a half. Generally the comedies and romances were found too problematic, while the histories, with the exception of *Richard III*, were doubtless too parochial. As for the Roman plays, appreciation of them was cramped by comparisons between *Julius Caesar* and works in the classical tradition.

In 1776 Pierre Le Tourneur began to bring out his full translations of Shakespeare. The subscription list has been taken as evidence for the quite wide demand for a text more reliable than La Place's. Re-editions are testimony to the merits of Le Tourneur's work, which, with some refurbishment, continued to be consulted throughout the nineteenth century. It was not, however, conceived as an acting edition, any more than were those provided by Jean-François-Victor Hugo (the son of the poet) between 1859 and 1865 and by many other nineteenth-century scholars. The idea that Shakespeare is worthy of respect and study yet that his plays cannot be performed without revision is not, of course, without parallels in England in either the past or the present; but the divide was far more strongly marked in France. The major difficulties arose over the sprawling action, which implied a flouting of the unities, the problem of finding for the dialogues a suitable metre, the earthy concreteness of the language and the mixing of genres.

It was Jean-François Ducis who first, apart from some relatively insignificant efforts, brought Shakespeare to the Parisian stage.[4] He has been denied the credit that is his due because French Romantic writers, led by Sainte-Beuve, were wont to belittle his achievements. Alexandre Dumas had been quite bowled over by a performance of Ducis's *Hamlet* at Villers-Cotterets, but he had little gratitude for the man who had fired his enthusiasm for Shakespeare. It was, too, a general source of annoyance that Ducis's versions held the stage while Romantic plays and new adaptations of Shakespeare did not. Ducis was an earlier Bardolator who had been in contact with Garrick when he visited Paris and performed excerpts from Shakespeare in salons. He lacked, it is true, what seems to be the *sine qua non* for his self-appointed role as the apostle of Shakespeare to the French, for he could not read English. But he knew his public and he possessed a gift for what may fittingly be called the creative adaptation of foreign masterpieces. As well as an *Œdipe chez Admète* which ranks as a major contribution to neo-classicism, he devised a version of *Hamlet* in 1769, to be followed by *Roméo et Juliette*, *Le Roi Lear*, *Macbeth*, *Jean sans terre* and *Othello*. Everything is arranged to suit French taste, with five acts of rhyming couplets for declamation, plots shorn of digressions and purged of indelicacies and humour, and the number of characters drastically reduced. The possibility of happy endings, in Garrick's fashion, was envisaged too. In the course of time awareness that these plays were merely based on Shakespeare's would lead to the demand for versions that were more faithful. What needs to be stressed first, however, is the fact that these plays, apart from *Jean sans terre*, caused a stir in their day, showing that Shakespeare could be performed, albeit in disguise, on the French stage even before the Revolution. Furthermore, Ducis's plays, especially his *Hamlet*, continued to be performed during the Restoration, the July Monarchy and even later. Talma said in irritation that he wanted Shakespeare and was given Ducis, yet he went on playing him, as did the early interpreters of French Romantic drama at the Comédie-Française.

There is nothing easier than being lofty about Ducis and his filleted Shakespeare. It is, however, only fair to recall what was being done to Shakespeare in England at the same time, and Ducis does not come badly out of the comparison. In the late eighteenth century and throughout the first half of the nineteenth century, neither a conservative public nor the senior actors who held such power at the Comédie-Française would have swallowed Shakespeare whole, and theatre is an art that depends for its effect as well as for its finance on its ability to win the support of the audience before which it is played. It is to the credit of Ducis that he judged to a nicety the degree of novelty that would be acceptable in his time, and he made Shakespeare a theatrical reality to French audiences, not a literary curiosity, leaving in his versions enough of the original to inspire, if not to satisfy, the coming generation.

It was through eighteenth-century French enthusiasts for Shakespeare that the Italians too came to know him. The debt was amply repaid when Salvini visited Paris in the mid-nineteenth century, for his performances were found as electrifying there as in London. We should not, however, overlook the impact of Shakespearean opera which, after stirring elsewhere, became one of Italy's cultural exports to Europe generally and helped to fix, though not perhaps to create, some highly Romantic images of Shakespeare's tragic heroes and heroines.[5] The impact was particularly strong in Paris, where opera was always in close contact with other forms of drama, even to the extent of often sharing the same theatres. Germany, it is true, led the way. France soon followed, with *Tout pour l'amour; ou,*

Roméo et Juliette performed in 1792 in the Salle Favart, in Paris, to music by Dalayrac and words by Jacques Boutet de Monvel, and the highly successful *Roméo et Juliette* at the Théâtre de la rue Feydeau the same year, with music by Daniel Steibelt and words by J. A. P. de Ségur. Then it was the turn of Italy, where L. Caruso's *Amleto* and L. Marescalchi's *Romeo e Giuletta* had already been performed in 1789; Niccolo Zingarelli's *Giuletta e Romeo*, with a text by G. Foppa had its première in 1796; Nicola Vaccai wrote an opera, with the same title but on a libretto by F. Romani, which was first performed in Naples in 1825 and, like Bellini's *I Capuleti ed i Montecchi* of 1830 (also with a libretto by Romani), was well received when first produced shortly afterwards in Paris. Meantime, Rossini in 1816 had composed his *Othello*. Though none of these composers, who set libretti based on a variety of late eighteenth-century and early Romantic sources, concentrated on Shakespeare to any marked degree, the cumulative effect of these presentations of his tragic situations must have contributed to the moulding of taste. The tradition was to be continued by Verdi, who was as much at home in Paris as in Italy and whose *Macbeth* came, of course, far earlier than his *Falstaff*; by Thomas, whose *Hamlet* was highly regarded for a time; by Berlioz, who through Harriet Smithson had especial reason to be mindful of the Shakespearean heritage; and finally by Gounod.

In milieux less pretentious than the opera house, the Odéon and the Comédie-Française – that is to say in the theatres on the boulevard and even at the Théâtre Olympique – Shakespeare continued to make his way in rather different guises.[6] Louis Henri, for instance, made *Hamlet* into a tragic pantomime interspersed with dances as early as 1816, finding in its reception encouragement to conjure a spectacular melodrama out of *Macbeth*. Cuvelier's *Othello* (1818) for the Cirque Olympique, which the Franconi family conducted on the lines of Astley's Circus, treated the plot of Shakespeare's play rather after the manner of Voltaire's *Zaïre*, adding topical interest by giving Desdemona a brother who is imprisoned by the Turks, escapes and on returning sets up another motive for the Moor's jealousy. After a few words of dialogue to introduce scenes and situations, the main emotions are expressed in dumb-show, and the plot is primarily developed to justify spectacular effects. Violent though the play is, Cuvelier baulks at the suffocation. So Desdemona withdraws from sight, is stabbed with a poignard and utters a piercing cry, which satisfies simultaneously the demands of classicism and of Romantic melodrama.

It was, then, only after Shakespeare had been known of, if not truly known, for three or four generations that these famous visits to Paris by the English actors took place: the first, which was in most respects a failure, in

1822 at the Théâtre de la Porte Saint-Martin, the second, which was something of a triumph, in 1827 and 1828. The details have been fully recorded. What remains moot is the significance of these visits. The relatively minor point that Penley's company was a victim of anglophobia need not be taken too seriously, for at a date closer to the defeat of Napoleon, Ducrow in military uniform had won friends in equestrian displays. It must be added that the performances by the British actors and their choice of repertoire, far from revealing something yet undreamt of, tended rather to confirm the image of Shakespeare that had been prevalent in France since the time of La Place. It is true that it was around this time that the second generation of French Romanticists was beginning to discover Shakespeare, but only in the sense of young men making personal discoveries, and there is no reason for imagining that they had found something no one else had had an inkling of before. Similarly their attacks on classical theatrical practice, for all their vehemence, are little more that amplified echoes of complaints that had been voiced a generation and more earlier. Furthermore, despite a new enthusiasm for Shakespeare which was expressed with verve by Stendhal in *Racine et Shakespeare* (1823) and by Hugo in the *Préface de 'Cromwell'* (1827), and which is reflected in de Vigny, Musset and Dumas, in Delacroix, Daumier and Berlioz, this period does not in fact witness the production either of authentic translations of even the relatively restricted canon of plays by Shakespeare familiar to Frenchmen at the time or of original works unmistakably and thoroughly Shakespearean in conception. It is hardly too much to say that Shakespeare remained for the French Romantic writers what he had been for Ducis, an astounding dramatist from whom much could be learned about humanity but whose theatrical manner could be copied only with diffidence. It is not without its irony that *Lorenzaccio*, now recognised as the most Shakespearean of the plays of the period, was not, like the other French Romantic plays, intended for immediate performance in the theatre.

Unlike Hugo and Dumas, who did not know English, Vigny was quite well qualified to translate Shakespeare, and after an early attempt at *Antony and Cleopatra* he turned to *Othello*.[7] His version was performed at the Comédie-Française in 1829 and may be regarded as a respectable achievement. But after a reasonably good run during its first season it was played no more, apart from an abortive revival in 1862, whilst a three-act adaptation of *The Merchant of Venice* was not played at all. Vigny's *More de Venise* was nearer to *Othello* than earlier versions had been, though the structure of the original was altered and the language, in alexandrines, was made more refined and conventional. The very modest success of this relatively scrupulous treatment of the play was not sufficient to encourage further developments along similar lines.

The history of the Dumas–Meurice *Hamlet* shows how slowly change came.[8] It was not until 1840 that Dumas suggested to the Comédie-Française that there was need for a replacement of the Ducis text. Conscious that the time was not ripe for a full translation, he offered a version of the play which he had prepared in collaboration with Paul Meurice. The Comédie-Française was quite impressed but demanded further changes; meantime it continued to play Ducis's *Hamlet*, which remained in the repertory until 1851. In some dudgeon Dumas decided to go his own way, and in 1846 his *Hamlet* was first played at Saint-Germain-en-Laye and then transferred to his Théâtre Historique in Paris in December 1847. Though later critics may be surprised at the number and extent of the changes introduced, the new play was acclaimed for its superiority over any version of Shakespeare that had previously been available on the French stage. The High Renaissance costumes appear to have been based on pictures of scenes from *Hamlet* by Eugène Delacroix, and the lead was played by the dark-haired Philibert Rouvière, who also took the role at the Odéon in 1855 and in subsequent revivals and on tours. In 1864 Meurice judged the time right for a more authentic version; he brought back the Ghost in Act 1, for instance, and accepted the tragic ending which had appeared too bleak twenty years before. At last the Comédie-Française was tempted, despite misgivings over the heavy expense involved, and it was in the revised Meurice version, still in alexandrines, that Mounet-Sully was to make a great impression as late as 1886, in a part he played more than two hundred times. Meantime, however, in 1886 at the Théâtre de la Porte Saint-Martin, as we have already seen, yet another adaptation of *Hamlet*, by Cressonnois and Samson, was being played in medieval costume, with Sarah Bernhardt as Ophelia. It was probably this *Hamlet* that Lucien Guitry, a powerful figure with moustache and trim beard, played at St Petersburg, though he seems not to have tried the role in Paris.

What is as striking as the dedication to Shakespeare shown by some of those discussed here is the clear evidence that it was always felt that something new and daring was being attempted; and the question of the need to adapt the English dramatist for presentation to French audiences continued to be debated with some heat. This was not simply healthy controversy about production styles and interpretation, but something more fundamental. In the 1820s Dumas had hailed Shakespeare fervently; twenty years later, he was offering the French public an adaptation of *Hamlet* which seems nowadays barely more than a travesty of the original.

Though it might be argued that he had felt obliged to tone down the play to make it acceptable to the Comédie-Française, that consideration hardly applied once he had decided to produce the play on his own account. It seems clear that Dumas, who had more practical experience of the theatre than any other French Romantic author, judged that the public would not yet accept a complete *Hamlet*. From a man who had not shrunk from controversy and innovation, this hesitancy is significant, even if it is true that Dumas was the last man to be held back by anything like scholarly scruple. A footnote on Dumas's attitude to Shakespeare is provided by his *Kean*, in a revival of which Sarah Bernhardt appeared as Anna Danby. The excerpts from *Romeo and Juliet* mangled by a drink-sodden barn-stormer can have done little to dispel Gallic prejudices about the relationship between *génie* and *désordre* in English drama and its interpreters.

Though Shakespearean productions continued fairly frequently in nineteenth-century Paris, there was always something tentative about them. George Sand took *As You Like It* to the Comédie-Française in 1856, for instance, and argued that the French had been mistaken in valuing only the tragedies. Yet, though she declared that she would like to reveal Shakespeare in his entirety, she concluded that this simply could not be. She went on to write a free adaptation, which in fact pleased only for a short while. Falstaff, as a character with similarities to Corneille's Matamore, attracted the attention of Auguste Vacquerie, who, like Dumas, was happy to collaborate with Meurice; and *A Midsummer Night's Dream*, with Mendelssohn's music and a text, once again, by Meurice, was given at the Odéon in 1869.

More or less isolated productions, often on benefit nights when novelties were tried out and character parts attracted ageing stars, continued throughout the century. There was, however, one rather different development which is worth exploration. In 1888 a translation of *The Tempest* was published by Maurice Bouchor, to whose article dated 1895 reference was made at the outset and who, like Meurice, had a life-long devotion to Shakespeare. His *Tempest* is virtually complete, and he scrupulously mentions his omissions in his preface, defending them with the argument that Shakespeare is invariably cut when played in England. His text is in prose, except for the songs. What is remarkable about this translation apart from its conscientiousness, is that it was intended not for actors, who apparently could still not be expected to take to such a play, but for performance by Henri Signoret's marionettes in the Petit Théâtre in the Galerie Vivienne, just behind the Bibliothèque Nationale.[9] The production was included in one of Signoret's early seasons, in the course of which he aimed to present a series of unfamiliar old plays in idioms quite different from the French classical tradition. Care was taken over sets and the carving of the puppets' heads, poets and good actors spoke the text offstage, and, for *The Tempest*, there was music specially composed by Ernest Chausson for singers and small orchestra – including the celesta, which had been invented by Auguste Mustel only in 1886. Critics such as Anatole France responded enthusiastically to Signoret's productions, which contributed something to the development of Idealism. Even as the nineteenth century was ending, then, the development of a Shakespearean play could still appropriately be included in a programme of theatrical novelties and still, equally interestingly, act as a spur to fresh creativity.

Discovered, at least in the more obvious senses of the word, in the early days of the Enlightenment, Shakespeare was adulated by French Romantic writers, perhaps to some degree because he remained a shadowy figure who could take on whatever mythic significance might be ascribed to him by dazzled votaries. Among the host of foreign influences that fertilised French culture in the nineteenth century, Shakespeare always occupied a place apart, as a corrective first to the routines of classicism, then to the rigours of realism. Sarah Bernhardt's *Hamlet* has a certain notoriety because her decision to play the lead looked to some like the extravagant whim of an ageing actress. The production and the full text prepared for it stand, however, as testimony to the problems still experienced over the assimilation of Shakespeare into French cultural traditions. Just a few years before *The Rite of Spring*, there was still much that was novel in his infinite variety.

NOTES

1 Sarah Bernhardt, 1923 and 1907; Baring, 1933; Geller, 1933; Richardson, 1959; Taranow, 1972; Beryl Turner, 'Sarah Bernhardt dans les grandes tragédies de Shakespeare', unpublished MA dissertation, University of Birmingham, 1954.

2 Bouchor was a minor poet of the time, with a great interest in poetic drama: Bouchor, 1888 and 1896; see also his articles: 'Le Petit Théâtre des marionettes', *Revue de Paris* (Sept. 1895), 174–97.

3 F. Baldensperger, 'Esquisse d'une histoire de Shakespeare en France', *Études d'histoire littéraire*, 2 (1910); Gilman, 1925; Green, 1935; Hedgcock, 1912; repr. 1969; Horn-Monval, 1963; Jusserand, 1898; van Tieghem, 1961; Besterman, 1967.

4 Ducis, 1826; repr. 1839. See Sylvie Chevalley, 'Ducis, Shakespeare et les Comédiens français', *Revue d'histoire du théâtre*, 16 (1964), 327–50, and 17 (1965), 5–37; Charles-Augustin de Sainte-Beuve, *Causeries du lundi*, 6 (1853), 372–86; Peter V. Conroy, 'A French Classical Translation of Shakespeare: Ducis' *Hamlet*', *Comparative Literature Studies*, 18 (1981), 2–14.

5 Barzum, 1982; Hartnoll, 1964; Weinstock, 1968 and 1972.
6 Baldick, 1959; Borgerhoff, 1912; Leathes, 1959; Wicks, 1950–79.
7 de Vigny, 1955–8; Sessely, 1928.
8 Bassan and Chevalley, 1972; Jean Jacquot, 'Mourir! Dormir! . . . Rêver peut-être: Hamlet de Dumas–Meurice, de Rouvière à Mounet-Sully', *Revue d'histoire du théâtre*, 16 (1964), 407–46; Joannidès, 1901; repr. 1970; and 1917; Mounet-Sully, 1917; Ross, 1981.
9 'Les Marionettes de M. Signoret' (France, 1926, vol. 6, pp. 464–6); Jules Lemaître, 'Théâtre des marionettes', *Impressions du théâtre*, 4 (1890); Margueritte, 1888; de Neuville, 1892.

Shakespeare and the Italian Players in Victorian London

KENNETH RICHARDS

T HE Italian theatre was late to discover Shakespeare. Throughout
the eighteenth century Italian literature and drama were dominated
by French neo-classical principles, and Shakespeare was known
primarily through the negative view of Voltaire. The occasional comments of some dramatists, like Goldoni and Gozzi, were sympathetic – but
they were certainly not well informed; a few of the plays were translated,
and one or two were even performed – but in versions taken from French
adaptations and thus at a far remove from their originals.[1] Even during the
period of Romanticism, when translations were made direct from the
English, when the cultural climate was more congenial and Shakespeare
had become a subject of vigorous literary debate engaging the interest of
writers like Alfieri, Monti and Foscolo, the conservative and traditional
Italian stage remained firmly resistant. The stage discovery of
Shakespearean drama was thus slow and intermittent. Increasing approval
of the English dramatist's work in literary circles undoubtedly helped, and
treatments of Shakespearean tales in the musical theatre, however
liberally handled, did something, even if only in a small way, to
acclimatise audiences to the plays themselves.[2] The discovery depended
greatly on the initiative of individual actors, and was achieved in the face
of much hostility and indifference.

The major tragedies were the first to be taken up. Between 1810 and
1820 versions of *Othello* were given by Carlo Cosenza and Francesco
Lombardi, and in 1842, in a notoriously controversial production in
Milan, the same play was done by the great reformer of the Italian stage,
Gustavo Modena.[3] In 1849 Alamanno Morelli acted Macbeth and in 1850
Hamlet, and adaptations of *Macbeth*, *Othello* and *Romeo and Juliet* may
have been given in or before the 1840s.[4] It was not until the middle
decades of the nineteenth century, however, that a few of Shakespeare's
plays, mainly the tragedies, began to appear with any regularity, and from
fairly respectable texts, in the repertoires of leading Italian players.

Perhaps the date that signalled significant change was 1856. In that year two of the most distinguished young actors of the age performed for the first time in Shakespeare: on 16 June Ernesto Rossi acted Othello at the Teatro Re in Milan, and fifteen days later he played Hamlet; again in June, although possibly after Rossi had appeared in the part in Milan, Tommaso Salvini played Othello at Vicenza.[5] In the next few years both actors added other Shakespearean tragic roles to their repertoires, and they were joined by the leading Italian actress of the day, Adelaide Ristori, who took on the role of Lady Macbeth. It was these three players who in due course were to introduce English Victorian theatregoers to the very distinctive ways in which the Italians understood and interpreted the tragedies of Shakespeare.

That La Ristori, Rossi and Salvini came to play Shakespeare in Italian before London audiences was largely thanks, first, to the growth, particularly in the latter half of the nineteenth century, of an international market for the talents of outstanding 'star' performers of the 'straight' as well as of the musical theatre; secondly, to the special and adverse conditions which pertained for much of the century in the Italian theatre itself. Opportunities for international touring by leading 'straight' theatre players were opened up by a number of factors, including the rapid development of rail and steamship lines, an increase in literacy that made 'classic' drama more familiar, the spread of information, and thus curiosity, about other cultures, and the existence in major cities on several continents, particularly the Americas, of sizeable immigrant communities. Italian players of ability were readily disposed to seize these opportunities. The economic and cultural stability of Italian 'straight' theatre companies was notoriously precarious: prose theatre enjoyed little regional, let alone national, support, audience tastes differed markedly the length and breadth of the peninsula, and the competition presented by dialect and musical theatre was, at least for the finances of the 'straight' theatre, generally debilitating (Knepler, 1968). Of all the touring 'stars' in the century, from Rachel to Duse, the Italians were the most relentlessly peripatetic, travelling to many parts of Europe, to North Africa, and to North and South America, often spending a year or more away from a homeland that on occasion became little more than a resting-place between international forays. The spread of Shakespeare's reputation internationally coincided with his discovery in Italy. Ristori, it is true, played only Lady Macbeth abroad, and Duse only Cleopatra; but the corner-stone of the international reputations of Rossi and Salvini was their playing in a handful of Shakespearean tragic roles.[6] For the most part they won success in these roles most triumphantly and unreservedly in Europe and in Latin America, in countries where the translated and adapted texts they performed proved less of an impediment to unconditional acceptance. North American audiences and critics were more demanding. But the accolade of achievement in Shakespeare was finally to be won only by approval in London. This La Ristori, Rossi and Salvini essayed in various ways, over several decades, and with varying degrees of success. To review all their London appearances in detail is beyond the scope of a short paper, and the most that can be attempted here is brief comment on some aspects of their performance and reception.[7]

The first Italian to play a lead role in a version of Shakespeare on the London stage was Adelaide Ristori, who between 1856 and 1882 made seven visits to Britain.[8] Born into the profession, a lead actress while still in her teens, and long associated with the foremost Italian acting company, the Reale Sarda, La Ristori began her international career only a year before her first visit to London, when, with Rossi as her leading man, she appeared in Paris and was acclaimed by French critics as superior to the great tragedienne, Rachel. It was probably during this Paris engagement that she conceived the idea of undertaking Lady Macbeth, although according to her own account it was London friends who during her 1856 visit urged her to consider the role. It was part of her repertoire when she returned to London, in June 1857, and was keenly awaited, for La Ristori had established a formidable reputation there with her non-Shakespearean repertory, above all in a version of *Medea*.[9] The English, like the French, thought her acting style innovative: she eschewed more traditional formal and studied declamation in favour of the familiar and domestic, without sacrifice of authority or dignity, and established the psychology of the characters she played by the accumulation of pertinent detail in business and the careful choice of emphases in movement, gesture and delivery (Hingston, 1856). Her view of Lady Macbeth was forthright but somewhat simplistic: 'a creature worse than a wild beast, colossal in her perfidy, dissimulation and hypocrisy' yet not wholly an arch-villainess, for Ristori brought out too Lady Macbeth's personal and domestic motives, such as her love for Macbeth and her willingness to subordinate herself to his ambition (Ristori, 1887). Macbeth in this staging was mentally and physically dominated by his wife's implacable resolve, a reading Ristori neatly underscored by a much admired piece of stage business which recurred in her London performances: on the final lines of the first interview scene she slowly pushed her husband from the stage, 'her hands on his shoulders, her eyes on his, her head nodding slowly at him, and a smile of determination on her face' (*The Times*, 5 July 1882; Field, 1867).

From that point on Macbeth was wholly under her control, Ristori demonstrating authority by every look, gesture and movement in the aftermath of the murder, where she feigned humiliation and confusion at the disgrace brought on the house of Macbeth while all the time watching over her timorous husband with a 'warning and anxious eye' until confident he had regained his composure. But undoubtedly the high point of Ristori's performance was the sleepwalking scene, which she 'rendered with an appalling truth and terror' (pl. 28). It was a *tour de force* in which every detail was calculated for its psychological truth and stage effectiveness, and in which 'every motion, every gesture was instinct with meaning, and every word seemed the revelation of an agonised heart' (*Observer*, 6 July 1857). Lady Macbeth became one of La Ristori's stock parts.

Although La Ristori returned to London several times in the sixties and early seventies, no other Italian player was tempted there until Tommaso Salvini in the spring of 1875. About Salvini it is signally difficult to write in brief. The most perceptive critics of the age, from George Henry Lewes to Henry James, from Gautier to Piccini and Bernard Shaw, thought him one of the greatest tragic actors they had ever seen. William Poel was similarly impressed, as was Stanislavsky (1924). Salvini was forty-six and at the peak of his ability and career when he appeared in London for the first time. Trained in his early teens by Gustavo Modena, he long played lead roles in major Italian companies, and with the most distinguished actresses of the day, including La Ristori, before embarking on an international touring career with a visit to Spain and Portugal in 1869. From then until his retirement at the end of the century, his progress was almost monotonously triumphant through the principal cities of Eastern and Western Europe, the United States and Latin America, punctuated by seasons in his homeland and periods of semi-retirement in his villa in Florence for study and preparation of parts. Shakespeare's major tragic roles were prominent in his touring list. As early as 1863 he had considered making a visit to Britain, but despite La Ristori's success there judged the London theatre to be 'an inaccessible world' (C. Salvini, 1955). What finally brought him was an invitation from the manager of Drury Lane, James Mapleson, who hoped to capitalise at his theatre on the enormous advance reputation Salvini had acquired from his recent and highly successful first American tour. There was possibility of profit too in setting up Salvini in London as a rival to Irving, whose *Hamlet* was still running at the Lyceum: Mapleson insisted that the Italian include the play in his season. Salvini opened on 1 April with *Othello*. His performance is recorded as one of the most stunning, if controversial, interpretations of the century: 'about the greatest ever witnessed by an English audience', judged one reviewer (*Illustrated News*, 10 Apr. 1875) (see pl. 29).

Since first giving the role in Italy nearly nineteen years before, Salvini had progressively refined his performance to draw out, by carefully paced playing, by look, gesture, movement and 'business', and by every modulation of his richly resonant voice, the savage and elemental passions beneath Othello's veneer of civilisation (Mason, 1890). As depicted in Salvini's portrayal, those passions, lying deep and dormant and scarcely known to the Moor himself, but gradually roused by guilt and fed by suspicion, carried the tragic hero relentlessly to his doom in a denouement of wild destruction that shocked critics and audiences alike in its uncompromising barbarity: Desdemona was seized by her hair, dragged to the bed and strangled 'with a ferocity that seems to take delight in its office'; Othello slashed his own throat with a scimitar, 'hacking and hewing at the flesh, severing all the cords, pipes and ligatures that there meet, and making the hideous noises that escaping air and bubbling blood are likely to produce' (*Sunday Times*, 11 Apr. 1875). It is said that strong men in the audience blanched and women fainted; but the acting profession called for a special morning matinée and Irving, unable to attend that, crept in to a later performance, describing it as 'a thing to wonder at' (C. Salvini, 1955, p. 288). Inevitably, the final scenes provoked great controversy: 'a step backwards towards gladiatorial shows', thought one critic; 'the effect on the audience is repellent to the last degree', wrote another (*Sunday Times*, 11 Apr. 1875; *Athenaeum*, 10 Apr. 1875). But the authority, subtlety and unity of the interpretation as a whole could not be gainsaid. The reading was intelligent and imaginative and realised by an actor endowed with exceptional resources of which he was in total command: a magnificent physique, superbly rich and flexible voice, mobile, expressive face, and grace of movement and gesture. Othello was the key role in Salvini's touring career, and although he was admired for his performances in non-Shakespearean plays, like *Il gladiatore* and *La morte civile*, it is the part for which he is best remembered. Henry James (1949) condensed the opinion of the majority when he wrote later: 'the depth, the nobleness, the consistency, the passion, the visible, audible beauty of it, are beyond praise'. Some weeks later, in June, Salvini acted Hamlet, having first fought shy of a role that in London seemed the preserve of Irving; but a visit to the Lyceum production convinced him, by the time it had reached the closet scene, that he need not fear adverse comparison. His performance was admired for its detail and perfection of method and for the ways in which it brought out the emotional rather than the intellectual sides of

28.   Adelaide Ristori as Lady Macbeth: the sleepwalking scene

29. Tommaso Salvini in *Othello*; from a drawing by Hugh Thomson

Hamlet, but it never excited the public imagination to the extent of his Othello, not least perhaps because the production was exceedingly slow: although the text was substantially cut the play ran for nearly four hours.[10] Like *Othello*, *Hamlet* was a stock play in Salvini's touring repertoire. Unfortunately, these two plays were all of Salvini's Shakespeare that London audiences were to see for some years, as his return visit in May 1876 misfired: he fell sick and by the end of the month had departed, cancelling his announced *Macbeth*. Poor attendance at the Queen's, a less prestigious theatre than Drury Lane, may well have contributed to his going, as may the limited publicity he received, for most reviewers were content merely to remark his return and to refer readers back to their earlier notices. It is possible too that by late May 1876 English theatre-goers had had a surfeit of Italians in Shakespeare as Salvini had been preceded to London by his main Italian rival, Ernesto Rossi, who had moved there, via Brussels, after a triumphant five-month season in Paris which had been extensively reported in the British press (*Sunday Times*, 12 Mar. 1876).

Rossi was the same age as Salvini, and like him a product of Gustavo Modena's training. Even before Salvini played in London, readers of the English theatrical journals had been made aware of this second Italian tragic actor whom some judged to be Salvini's equal and, at least in versatility, perhaps his superior. A former leading man to Ristori, an inveterate tourer, and with the reputation of having introduced Shakespeare to the Italian stage, he was keenly awaited. He opened at Drury Lane on 19 April with *Hamlet* (pl. 30) – but not altogether happily, for the English weather had seized his voice, prefatory excuses for which had to be made from the stage. Both this and his second piece, *King Lear*, were mildly controversial. Some English critics insisted that he misinterpreted both plays by over-emphasising madness: he seemed to think that Hamlet's madness was real, not feigned, and played Lear for mad from the very start of the play. The criticisms stung enough to prompt Rossi to write a letter to the press defending his readings.[11] Both admiration and dispute were excited too by his enthusiasm for introducing novel 'business'. In *Hamlet*, at the end of the play scene, he threw himself on to the King's throne with 'boyish glee', clasped his hands above his head and wheeled about 'in an ecstasy of delight'; in the closet scene he tore the miniature of Claudius from Gertrude, hurled it to the ground and stamped it to pieces. When later he did *Romeo and Juliet* he used a version based on Garrick's adaptation in which Juliet awoke before Romeo was dead, providing Rossi with a theatrically effective opportunity fearfully to approach his mistress, recognise her, embrace her and fall dead. In *Macbeth* he added a touch to the end of the banqueting scene: 'Rossi treads on his mantle, and turns in alarm as if to see again the spectre. He seizes his sword to defend himself, but it drops from his trembling grasp, at the same time that his crown falls from his brow.'[12] While these interpolations and modifications of the traditional offended purists, they pleased in the theatre and a number of reviewers grudgingly acknowledged the Italian's 'ingenuity'. But in no single play was Rossi's reception uniformly favourable. His Macbeth and Romeo impressed more than his Hamlet or his Lear, and although most agreed that his versatility was remarkable and some ranked him as 'one of the most illustrious artists that have visited our shores', he did not establish an enduring reputation. When he returned, for a brief and unsuccessful visit in June 1882, one commentator expressed what was probably the general view: he was respectfully appreciated, but had not gained the same acceptance as Salvini (*Illustrated London News*, 17 June 1882). How true that was was demonstrated two years later, when from 28 February 1884 at Covent Garden, Salvini made his farewell London appearances. In addition to Othello and Hamlet (the first as powerfully impressive as when he gave it in 1875, the second continuing to divide critical opinion) he now gave Macbeth and King Lear. Of the two roles, Lear was thought the more striking, and an interpretation on which the actor had evidently bestowed profound study. For some this was 'Shakespeare's Lear . . . a very obstinate, passionate, wrong-headed old man, somewhat arrogant, somewhat vain'. It was questioned, however, whether pathos fell wholly within his range, and whether the very power and authority of his great physical presence undercut his ability to convey 'subtle indications of madness'.[13] Salvini's interpretation of Macbeth was for many more conventional than they had anticipated, and where it persuaded it did so more by the sheer brilliance of the actor's playing than by the truth of the conception (*Observer*, 9 Mar. 1884; *The Times*, 10 Mar. 1884). But both his Lear and his Macbeth were manifestly major performances by a great tragedian, and perhaps no foreign actor, and certainly not his rival, Ernesto Rossi, left Britain with a more substantial reputation than did Salvini at the end of his last tour.

30.   Ernesto Rossi as Hamlet

However, to be just to Rossi it must be said that the failure of his 1882 London engagement was caused less by the inadequacy of his playing than by the unfortunate experiment he attempted: a version of *King Lear* in which he acted in Italian, while the rest of the cast (a 'scratch' company of London actors) performed in English. He announced his intention to do other works of Shakespeare in the same manner if this attempt with *King Lear* met with approval. It did not. Particularly awkward was the difficulty the English actors found in picking up their Italian cues, and to involve them Rossi had frequent recourse to gesticulation and grimaces. Even when cues were no problem, many exchanges verged on the grotesque:

Lear.   Ola, chi sei tu?
Kent.   A man, sir.
Lear.   Che vuoi?
Kent.   To serve.
Lear.   Chi?
Kent.   You.
Lear.   Mi conosci amico?
Kent.   No, sir.

Parts of Rossi's interpretation impressed, as they had on his first visit; but the experiment tended, if anything, to point his limitations: he was felt to lack dignity and bearing and to be wanting in declamatory power and any real intellectual insight.[14] The experiment did his reputation no good, and it was curious that he tried it, for a similar and earlier venture in the United States had met with little support. But such undertakings were then rather modish: Salvini had done *Othello* in America in the same fashion. La Ristori went much further. At the end of her 1873 London engagement she did the sleepwalking scene from *Macbeth* in English, and a few weeks after Rossi's ill-fated Lear she played the whole part in English with a London troupe. She got a better reception than Rossi, but most critics preferred her to act in Italian.[15]

These various ventures indirectly point up, of course, certain of the problems encountered by the Italian international touring 'stars' when acting Shakespeare in English-speaking countries: the language barrier, and the quality and validity of the Italian texts they used, not just in performance, but for their understanding and preparation. The first was the lesser problem, notwithstanding these occasional sallies into English or two-language performance. The appeal of the foreign 'stars' lay in their novelty value and in the histrionic personality and skills they brought to the interpretation of familiar roles. It is a measure of the drawing power of players like Ristori and Salvini that, although few English spectators understood Italian and most were not culturally starved of 'quality' theatre (as audiences in Cairo, Caracas or even Philadelphia might have been said to be), the Italian 'stars' won substantial followings not just in London, but also in the major cities to which they toured throughout Britain and Ireland. Although some theatre managements supplied enthusiasts with dual-language versions of the adaptations (and reviewers drew on these occasionally to make fine points about textual omission or interpolation), performance in the Italian language was a readily acceptable *donné* of the occasion. Reviewers and audiences seem to have been tolerant too of the Italian translations and abridgements. Even a radically truncated text, like Ristori's version of *Macbeth*, was accepted with little demur as long as it fulfilled its stage purpose (*Athenaeum*, 11 July 1857; *Illustrated London News*, 11 July 1857). Yet the Victorian attitude to such acting versions did not lack discrimination. A Shakespearean text was not sacrosanct, and it could be accommodated to 'star' emphases, but many expected it to be treated as something more than a mere dramatic vehicle for the 'star'. A certain 'decorum' was looked for in the way professional theatre needs were balanced against the supposed requirements of the text. Rossi's stage versions were the most strongly criticised, for these were felt too frequently to sacrifice Shakespeare's apparent intentions to mere theatrical effect or, worse, to provide readings which distorted the interpretation of the whole. Use of extraneous 'business' and the play on the hero's madness, rather than inadequacies of text, were what primarily provoked objections to Rossi's *Hamlet*, but his acting text of *King Lear*, an abridgement and adaptation of Rusconi's prose version, was vigorously condemned by some as a misleading mutilation that falsified the character of the play's protagonist. [16]

Translation of Shakespeare was of course accepted as an unavoidably reductive practice in which verbal subtlety and complexity were inevitably lost. A direct consequence of that loss was the simplification of character and motive that many felt to be characteristic of the Italian interpretations. The loss was all the more pronounced for some in Shakespeare's 'Northern plays', such as *Macbeth* and *Hamlet*. *Romeo and Juliet* and *Othello*, on the other hand, seemed to fall more easily within the Italian translator's grasp – not least because in action and mood they were felt to be closer to the temperaments, habits and attitudes of the Italian national character. The ways in which the Italian players might distort Shakespeare's supposed intentions were thus seen to lie much deeper than the foreign language and the staging carpentry: Romeo was considered a part within the compass of Rossi's instinctive understanding in a way that Macbeth was not, and some thought King Lear more 'within the scope of Southern vision' than the manifestly Nordic Hamlet. Naturally Othello was accounted the Shakespearean role most accessible to an Italian actor, attuned by temperament to jealousy and 'Southern fire'. Salvini's triumph in the part was hence not unconnected with his ability, in the early stages of the play, to discipline his Italian temperament, to pace out and only gradually unleash the terrible force of his Latin passion. When he played Macbeth, on the other hand, many felt that in key scenes he fell into emotional hysteria and redundant gesture. Such excess was thought ever latent in Italian acting. The disposition of the Italians towards pantomimic playing was frequently remarked, invariably with admiration when the actor's look and gesture bespoke subtlety of character delineation. But often the admiration was qualified by a fear that in Italian acting the bound between persuasive pantomime and unacceptably extravagant movement, gesture and 'business' was a narrow one: Salvini, it was felt, fell to excess, and he was reproved for beating his head with his hands to show Othello's anguish; on her first London performance of Lady Macbeth, La Ristori, it was thought, was forced in some scenes into melodramatic extravagances by the wild over-playing of her Macbeth (Athenaeum, 11 July 1857; Sunday Times, 7 May 1876; James 1949, p. 53).

But in the interpretation and playing of all three Italians much more frequently questioned, at least during their earlier appearances in London, was the new realistic approach they introduced. The method of the concluding scenes of Salvini's Othello excited the most comment, but the inclination of his choices and emphases in this play was recognised as common to the Italian school: 'tendencies in the direction of this kind of so-called art were seen in Ristori and marred her marvellously artistic impersonations', noted the Athenaeum; 'his action', said the Sunday Times of Rossi, 'belongs to the ultra-realistic school, which is characteristic of Italian art' (Athenaeum, 10 Apr. 1875; Sunday Times, 23 Apr. 1876). Not all critics denied the claims of this new realism, but many questioned its appropriateness to interpretation of Shakespeare, and some thought it an unwarranted transference to the stage of a style and tone of representation unhappily emerging in certain contemporary schools of continental painting. In Rossi's performances the new realism was detected in the vigour and vitality of his playing, in the particulars of his ingenious 'business', and in his liking for strong, affecting death scenes. In the work of Ristori and Salvini a feature of the new realism much admired was their ability to develop, through the accumulation of significant detail, psychologically truthful characterisation. The new realism disturbed when it appeared to shed all trace of a romantic and idealistic conception of character and action: the players' inclination to underscore the disagreeably physical and even the horrific prompted one critic to dub the new style and approach 'morbid realism'. Interestingly, by the 1880s, when all three players gave their final performances in London, the strong realism of Ristori and Salvini was accepted with equanimity, while that of Rossi already seemed rather *passé*.[17]

How great an impact the Shakespeare of these Italian players made on later English productions of plays such as *Macbeth*, *Hamlet* and *Othello*, is hard to calculate. Irving's attempt at Othello in 1876 was certainly prompted by Salvini's success in the role the year before, and his comparative failure was in part the result of a deliberate attempt to avoid the Italian's approach. Forbes-Robertson was probably not unmindful of Salvini's performance when he prepared his own Othello, an interpretation that was to restore to the English stage a more romantic, chivalric Moor. Certainly Salvini's Othello and Ristori's Lady Macbeth remained for several generations the definitive performances of those roles. Rossi left no comparable legacy, although his stage brio and delight in novel 'business' may well have helped to liberate some players from constricting traditions. But his and Salvini's visits to London were too few and far between for their example to have been much attended in the English theatre, and Ristori, although she played more regularly in London, confined herself to the one Shakespearean part. All three were admired, but at a distance, and perhaps less, ultimately as interpreters of Shakespeare than as great players, touring 'stars' unexampled for their prodigious globe-trotting, who at once exploited and contributed to Shakespeare's burgeoning international appeal. After all, La Ristori actually played not in *Macbeth*, but in *Macbetto*, and Ernesto Rossi not in *Hamlet*, but in *Amleto*. Even the great, apparently unchallengeable performance of Tommaso Salvini was in a play called *Otello*. His interpretation was powerful, original, intelligent and excitingly controversial, but for all the comparisons with Edmund Kean it was not, as so many critics pointed out, Shakespeare's Othello – but then what was?

NOTES

I am grateful to the Leverhulme Trust for a grant towards research in Italy.

1 The eighteenth-century translations are discussed in detail by Crinò, 1950. See also Collison-Morley, 1916; and Pastore, 1950.
2 For an excellent short account of Shakespeare and Italian criticism, see A. Lombardo, 'Shakespeare e la critica italiana', *Sipario*, June 1964.
3 Although it was long supposed, largely on the authority of Ernesto Rossi, that audience protests broke up Modena's production of *Othello* at the end of the first act, it has recently been shown that the play was given in its entirety. For this episode, and a useful account of the major nineteenth-century actors, see Gatti, 1968. For a valuable

history of *Othello*'s fortunes in Italy, see particularly Busi, 1973. Modena had also studied *Hamlet* (like *Othello*, in Michele Leoni's translation) with a view to producing it, but the opposition his *Othello* met with, for all that the play was done in an adapted and conservative version in the hope of making it palatable to the Milanese audience, deterred him from going ahead.

4 A difficulty with early productions is in deciding if they can reasonably be called versions of Shakespeare. There is a fair amount of information about early productions of Shakespeare in Italy, both known and possible, in Bragaglia, 1973, but unfortunately it is scattered, ill documented and not always reliable. M. Corsi gives a good, short overview in *Il Drama*, 1 Jan. 1949, and another is to be found in the relevant volume of the *Enciclopedia dello spettacolo*.

5 Rossi's performances are discussed by Gatti and Busi (see above, n. 3.). In their autobiographies, both Rossi and Salvini write in general terms about their work: Rossi, 1887; T. Salvini, 1895. A version of this last appeared in English: T. Salvini, 1893. Both actors wrote extensively on Shakespeare's plays and dramatic characters. Rossi translated *Julius Caesar*, playing Antony and, later, Brutus.

6 Rossi, for example, spent a long period between 1871 and 1873 touring in South America and from the autumn of 1874 to the spring of 1876 acted in several European cities. To these players we should add the name of Giovanni Emanuel, a fine Othello, who never performed in London but travelled as far as Latin America, where he won great success. Like Henry Irving, he abandoned the traditional Moorish costume for Venetian dress. Emanuel prepared his own translations and, in addition to Othello, played Hamlet, Lear, Romeo and Shylock. The Sicilian actor, Giovanni Grasso, was another powerful Othello who took the role on tour, but his London visit of 1910 falls outside the scope of this brief survey. An indication of the importance that Shakespearean roles held in the repertoires of these travelling 'stars' is provided by the returns listed in *L'arte drammatica*, 4 Feb. 1882, for Salvini's performances the previous December in Alexandria and Cairo:

Zaira	L. 995,62
Morte civile	L. 401,87
Amleto	L. 1494,37
Saul	L. 752,25
Otello (benefit)	L. 6722,00
Otello	L. 1152,38

7 For the same reason comment has been confined to the three players who first introduced the Shakespeare of the Italians to London in the 1860s and 1870s. Not discussed here are the few performances of Cleopatra that Eleanora Duse gave in London in 1893. She had not been successful with the part in Italy and fared no better in London. The opening was postponed a week, allowing the *Times* critic to express a widely held opinion: it would have been better for her reputation if it had not been given at all (21 June 1893).

8 Ristori's seven tours are discussed in detail by Cristina Giorcelli, 'Adelaide Ristori sulle scene britanniche e irlandesi', *Bollettino del Museo Bib. dell'Attore*, 5 (1977).

9 For Ristori's account, see her autobiography (Ristori, 1887). Ristori being the first major Italian actress to appear in London for decades, her success was in part, of course, occasioned by the novelty of the event. Some informed observers were unimpressed: Macready tartly observed that her style was essentially 'a melodramatic abandonment or lashing up to a certain point of excitement'(Macready, 1875), and when 'Little'

Robson burlesqued Ristori in Robert Brough's comic version of *Medea* at the Olympic
Charles Dickens thought him wickedly perceptive in bringing out 'what she might do
and does not'; quoted Sands, 1979.

10 See C. Salvini, 1955, pp. 281–3. There are interesting accounts of this visit to Irving's
Hamlet in Jarro, 1908, and in T. Salvini, 1893, where Salvini remarks of Irving's
performance that he 'seemed to me to show mannerism, and to be lacking in power,
and strained' (p. 166).

11 *Illustrated London News*, 22 Apr. and 6 May 1876; *Sunday Times*, 7 May 1876;
Observer, 7 May 1876; *The Times*, 5 May 1876. *Illustrated London News*, 13 May 1876,
carried a comment on Rossi's letter, and the Italian actor's interpretation of Hamlet
was strongly, and perceptively, defended by a correspondent to the *Sunday Times*, 7
May 1876.

12 *The Times*, 12 May 1876; *Sunday Times*, 28 May 1876; *Illustrated London News*, 20 May
1876. Joseph Knight's pieces, mainly from the *Athenaeum*, were gathered in *Theatrical
Notes*, 1893, and give a good overview of Rossi's performances. Italian champions of
Salvini tended to play down Rossi's success in England; the London reviews of his
Hamlet, while critical, do not justify Jarro's charge that it excited 'sdegno e critiche
veementi' (1908, p. 294). Rossi also acted, though not in England, Coriolanus,
Richard III and Shylock.

13 For a good overview of his Othello at this time, see *Illustrated London News*, 8 and 15
Mar. 1884; for his Lear, see *The Times*, 3 Mar. 1884; *Observer*, 24 Mar. 1884. Early in
his career Salvini also undertook Romeo and, shortly before he retired, Coriolanus, but
he did not give either in England.

14 *Illustrated London News*, 17 June 1882; *The Times*, 14 June 1882. On one or two
occasions Rossi attempted some of the later portions of the play in English, and this was
preferred to the performance in mixed tongues (*Observer*, 18 June 1882).

15 The quality of her spoken English in both the single scene and the full part was much
admired. According to *L'arte drammatica* (15 Apr. 1882) Ristori had previously
performed abroad not only in Italian, but in French and Spanish. The same journal (17
June 1882) reported rather disarmingly to Italian readers, that Rossi had successfully
done *King Lear* with English actors. When it commented on Salvini's similar
experiment with *Othello* in Philadelphia (25. Dec. 1880) it acknowledged that the
combination of English and Italian was far from pleasing; Salvini's sheer authority in
Othello carried the experiment.

16 *Sunday Times*, 7 May 1876; *Illustrated London News*, 6 May 1876 and 17 June 1882;
Joseph Knight, *Theatrical Notes*. For a detailed discussion of Ristori's version, see the
article by Caretti in Caretti, 1979. Rossi's tendency to use Shakespeare for his own
theatrical advantage has been strongly criticised by some Italian commentators: see, for
example, Zanco, 1945. Also see Frank Archer, 1912.

17 *Athenaeum*, 10 Apr. 1875; *The Times*, 5 May 1876; *Observer*, 4 Apr. 1875; *Observer*, 18
June 1882.

PART 6

Shakespeare in the Provinces

PREFACE

IRVING's professional career started in Bulwer Lytton's *Richelieu* at the New Royal Lyceum Theatre, Sunderland, in 1856; it – and his life – ended after a performance of Tennyson's *Becket* at the Theatre Royal, Bradford, in 1905. For all the glories of the Lyceum years, Irving bowed out in the provinces, but during the intervening half-century theatres outside London had undergone an even greater transformation that those in the capital.

In the 1850s provincial theatres were still operating as stock companies as they had in the eighteenth century. The companies were at least semi-permanent, based in a town, a city or a regional circuit. True, guest actors came and went, Macready's *Diary* chronicling the perils of such a system: a Lady Macbeth in Salisbury on 16 March 1835 who belonged to the old school and was better suited to Dollabella (in *Tom Thumb*); another in Lincoln on 14 June 1836, elderly, by no means word-perfect, much given to mauling her Thane, but cutting 'I have given suck' as too horrible. Such experiences demonstrate one of the attractions of Shakespeare in the provinces: his plays – or rather some of them – were so familiar that actors were able to play together with very little rehearsal.

However, Macready's comments draw attention, by implication at least, to the distinction between the metropolitan and the provincial style of acting – a distinction which, whatever other changes came about, never completely disappeared. Kathleen Barker's account of Charles Dillon's career demonstrates the lot of the provincial tragedian; and even Frank Benson, a graduate of Oxford and the Lyceum, remained essentially a provincial actor – *vide* Max Beerbohm's devastating review of Benson's 1900 *Henry V* (Trewin, 1960, pp. 110–11): 'It was simply what critics call "adequate", meaning "inadequate".' Small wonder that many an actor preferred the relative obscurity of the provinces, away from the deflating scrutiny of London critics like Shaw and Beerbohm.

Nevertheless the barriers between London and the provinces became

255

less pronounced, principally because of the advent of the railway. Arnold Hare refers to the significance of the opening in 1841 of Brunel's London–Bristol railway, which was, of course, matched by similar networks all over the country. Immediately the swift transport of actors and, even more significantly, of scenery became practical. For the Shakespeare tercentenary in 1864 George Vining's complete production of *Romeo and Juliet* played in London on Tuesday night, in Stratford-upon-Avon on Wednesday and back in London on Thursday. The large-scale touring of productions became common practice during the last quarter of the century, with the railroads a hive of activity each Sunday as companies shuttled from theatre to theatre. A spate of theatre building took place, with C. J. Phipps and Frank Matcham as leading architects (Glasstone, 1975).

The trend was obviously towards uniformity, with more theatres buying in productions rather than mounting their own, but the importance of local characteristics must not be overlooked. This is to be seen in the cases of Bath and of Leicester. Bath, a popular spa in the eighteenth century, had a long theatrical tradition reinforced, alternately, by rivalry and by partnership with Bristol. However, by Victorian times Bath no longer attracted so many visitors and the theatre had to rely more on residents of the town and its vicinity. By contrast, Leicester had virtually no theatrical tradition – a state of affairs fostered by Nonconformism and the absence of resident gentry.

It is ironical, therefore, that it was in Bath that the theatre attracted the virulent criticism of the Reverend John East, whereas in Leicester Unitarian ministers consistently upheld the works of Shakespeare as morally improving for their congregations. Jeremy Crump's account of the Shakespearean Chartist Association provides a vivid example of the way in which Shakespeare and his work were seen as an accessible means of self-improvement for the masses.[1] Although this movement was sometimes separate from the theatre, the status of Shakespeare as a national poet, especially after the celebrations in 1864, was often an important attraction for managers who wished to gain acceptance and approval amongst the local city fathers.

The city fathers were not impervious to such arguments, for, although municipal theatres were a long way off, civic pride took many forms. Manchester was eulogised as 'the very symbol of civilization, foremost in the march of improvement, a grand incarnation of progress' (Briggs, 1963; repr. 1968, p. 88). The Art Treasures of the United Kingdom Exhibition of 1857 was a conscious effort to establish Manchester as a civilised city, not merely a commercial and industrial centre. Prominent amongst the promoters of the exhibition were the Agnews, already purveying fine art to the successful entrepreneurs of the locality. Between 1859 and 1875 Charles Calvert established managements at Manchester's Theatre Royal and Prince's Theatre, which George Rowell has aptly described as 'almost certainly the leading Shakespearean ensemble outside London' (1981, p. 134). Furthermore it was Calvert, as Arthur Jacobs has shown us, who first commissioned the young Arthur Sullivan to compose music for a Shakespeare play. It was to Manchester that Annie Horniman repaired in 1908, towards the end of her patronage of the Abbey Theatre, Dublin, and at the Gaiety she engaged William Poel to direct *Measure for Measure* in the Elizabethan style.[2]

Each provincial town can point to its own theatrical history – much like any other town's in many respects, totally distinctive in others.[3] That each town had its own particular chemistry is indicated by the success of a manager such as Dillon in Sheffield and his relative failure elsewhere. But for the Victorian actor the theatre was an ever-expanding sphere, and ultimately his main concern was to find audiences who would pay to watch him perform, preferably in Shakespeare. In the pursuit of this end actors pushed back the frontiers of the theatre-going world. By Queen Victoria's reign theatrical tours to America were commonplace (Shattuck, 1976), and more adventurous spirits journeyed to the Antipodes. Thither went Charles Dillon; Charles and Ellen Kean, whose letters home (Hardwick, 1954) constitute such a revealing record of their experiences; and Gustavus Brooke, who was drowned *en route* for a return visit in 1866.[4]

NOTES

1 Richard Foulkes, 'Adult Education and the Theatre: The Early Years', *Studies in Adult Education*, 11.1 (1979), 30–41.
2 Richard Foulkes, '"Measure still for Measure": Miss Horniman and Mr. Poel at the Gaiety', *Theatre Quarterly*, 10.39 (1981), 43–6.
3 Kathleen Barker, 'Entertainment in Five Provincial Towns 1840–70', unpublished Ph.D. dissertation, University of Leicester, 1982.
4 See Denis Bartholomeusz, 'Shakespeare on the Melbourne Stage, 1843–61', *Shakespeare Survey*, 35 (1982), 31–41.

Shakespeare in a Victorian Provincial Stock Company

ARNOLD HARE

M Y deviation from the general brief to consider Shakespeare in the Victorian Theatre concerns time. Because my purpose is to illustrate what happened to one of the best of the Georgian stock companies during the nineteenth century by examining the changes in its attitude to Shakespeare, I need to concern myself with almost as many years before the accession of Queen Victoria as after: indeed, some of the changes to which I wish to draw attention are already clearly discernible in the Regency period. Since the stock company I am dealing with is that of the Theatre Royal, Bath, and since that company moved into its new and still working building in 1805, I therefore propose to start my account from the opening of the new theatre; while, because the last of the resident stock companies disbanded in 1884, after which the theatre became predominantly a house for touring productions, that year inevitably becomes my closing date. If this choice of time-span enables me to throw some useful light on the later history of the Georgian theatre, as well as on the heart of the Victorian period, I hope this will be considered a proper bonus.

During those seventy-nine years of theatrical history there were four main phases. From 1805 to 1817 the resident company was the Bath–Bristol company, which had worked the two theatres since 1778. This arrangement broke down in 1817, and for the next twenty-eight years Bath was operated as a separate concern, under successive managers. From 1845 to 1868 there followed the second Bath–Bristol company (or, as I prefer to think of it, the Bristol–Bath company, indicating the changed centre of gravity). This company was at first managed by Mrs Sarah Macready, and after her death in 1853 by her son-in-law, James Henry Chute. He survived the Bath theatre fire of 1862, opening a rebuilt interior the following year; but after the building of his new Park Row theatre (later the Prince's) in Bristol in 1867, Chute extricated himself from the toils of Bath in 1868. During the fourth phase, from then until

1884, various stock companies eked out their unpredictable existences, the last of the four unsuccessful company managers being Frederick Neebe, who also ran the theatre in Exeter.[1]

In 1805, the Bath theatre was recognisably a Georgian one. The manager was William Wyatt Dimond, who had been a member of the company since 1774, and in sole managerial control since Keasberry's death in 1795. During the fifty-five-year history of the Orchard Street Theatre from 1750 to 1805 certain of Shakespeare's plays had been a staple part of the repertory, and a quick reference to the *Calendar* of those years indicates which they were.[2] *Hamlet, King Lear, Macbeth, Othello, Romeo and Juliet, Richard III, As You Like It, Much Ado About Nothing, The Merchant of Venice, Henry IV* and *Cymbeline* (plus, of course, other plays from time to time, and occasional excerpts such as *Catherine and Petruchio,* or *The Sheep Shearing.*) These eleven plays were revived regularly over the half-century, and – what is more significant – were staged by the resident company alone. They might only be played two or three times in a season, and not all of them in any one season; but they were an essential part of the company repertoire.

By the 1850s this pattern had changed radically. Shakespeare's plays were still performed, but rarely by the stock company, except as supporting cast for some visiting 'star' actor or actress. Such outside visits first began to filter into the programmes in the late 1790s – to begin with usually as special return visits by players, such as Sarah Siddons and Jane Wallis, who had been popular members of the company but had since gone on to higher things in London. With the turn of the century, star visits became more popular and more frequent. George Frederick Cooke, in the first nine years of the century made eight visits before his departure to the United States of America; and these were so successful financially that after one of them Dimond voluntarily increased his contract fee from £260 to £300. Sarah Siddons, John Philip Kemble, W. H. (Young Roscius) Betty, Charles Mayne Young, J. S. Munden, Mrs Jordan, Elliston, Inceldon, Edmund Kean and later Charles Kemble and Charles Kean, all made visits, some regular and repeated; for many of them several at least of their leading roles were Shakespearean. Thus Betty played Hamlet as well as Young Norval, Mrs Siddons Lady Macbeth as well as Mrs Beverly, Kemble Lear as well as Rolla, Cooke Richard III and Shylock, as well as Sir Pertinax Mac-sycophant and Sir Giles Overreach. At the beginning these specials were in addition to company performances; later they almost completely replaced them.[3]

In 1805–6, for example, in the first season of the new theatre, there were performances of *Richard III, Othello, As You Like It, Hamlet, Romeo and Juliet*, *Twelfth Night*, *Macbeth* and *The Merchant of Venice*, with, additionally, two performances each as Richard III, Macbeth and Shylock by Cooke and as Hamlet by Betty. A decade later there were still company performances of *A Winter's Tale*, *Romeo and Juliet*, *Hamlet*, *Henry IV* and *Richard II*; but four of these were deliberately designed for a young actor, learning his craft in the tradition of earlier company members like John Henderson and Sarah Siddons – a young man by the name of William Charles Macready. Later in the season a remarkable young actor named Edmund Kean made his first guest appearance in Bath and in the week of 8–15 July played Shylock, Othello, Richard III and Macbeth. There could be no doubt that Shakespeareans were still well provided for, and they knew it, and happily discussed details of the performances in the local newspapers.

The rarity of that season was *Richard II*, which W. C. Macready was allowed to put on in a version prepared, it seems, by his father and himself. (Dr Kathleen Barker discussed this production in an article in *Shakespeare Quarterly*, 23.1 (1963), 95–100.) For our present purposes, three sentences from the contemporary *Bath and Cheltenham Gazette* (1 Feb. 1815) are significant. The writer had his reservations about the play, finding it greatly inferior to many of Shakespeare's works; nevertheless it is

pregnant with very emphatic moral reflections and elevated sentiments, and abounds in natural imagery beautifully expressed . . . Still, however, [Shakespeare] appears to have sported with the dialogue; how else could a writer, so justly celebrated for giving the strongest appearance of reality to his expressions of feeling, have indulged in so fanciful a fabrication of prose and verse? Certainly, verse is not the language of *feeling*; to close a tale of distress with a couplet, or make rhymes whilst giving the parting pressure to the hand of one we love, is like touching a cold key with a flat third to it at the end of a piece of music which has called forth our affections . . . [Nevertheless] the extreme rarity of its appearance must alone render it an object of curiosity, and dull must be the heart that is not delighted and improved by its performance.

'Pregnant with very moral reflections and elevated sentiments', 'verse is not the language of feeling', 'to close a tale of distress with a couplet . . .' – these reactions have an ominous ring for the future. By contrast, a long report on Kean's Shylock (*Bath Herald*, 15 July 1815) records a number of his 'points', and then says:

His readings were frequently a fine comment on his author's text, and his countenance and attitudes often formed a study for the artist. Nothing could surpass the picture of ferocity he assumed when exclaiming '*A sentence – come, prepare*'; and we must not omit noticing the effect he imparted to – '*I am – content.*' The last word he gave as if almost choked with its utterance; & '*content*', like Macbeth's '*Amen*', appeared '*stuck in his throat*'. On the whole we think Mr Kean an actor of uncommonly vigorous talent; and though his *Shylock* did not strike us as a complete masterpiece of the art, his peculiar bursts of real genius are such as deservedly place him in the first rank of histrionic fame.

Here is a playgoer clearly responding to the theatrical experience. So far, then, whatever reservation we may have about audiences' taste and reactions, with regard either to company productions or to a distinguished visitor with company backing, Shakespeare is still being well served.

Two decades on, however (in 1836–7), the picture is very different. The only totally company production in that season was *As You Like It* (a *Macbeth* and a *Merchant of Venice* were announced but never played – the unnamed lady who was to have performed Lady Macbeth and Portia was first said to be 'indisposed' and then 'indisposed indefinitely' – and we can easily read behind the lines of that statement!). In February and March Charles Kean arrived and played the usual Richard III, Othello, Hamlet, Macbeth, Shylock, Lear; Dowton played Falstaff for one night for his son's benefit (Dowton jun. was a member of the company), and Butler from Covent Garden, on a four-night engagement, played Coriolanus and Hamlet. Again, a not unreasonable ration of Shakespeare, we might be inclined to think. But in the following season (1837–8, the very first season of the good Queen's reign) the visitors were significantly different: there was W. J. Hammond, proprietor of the New Strand Theatre, to give his popular portrayal of Sam Weller; Dunn, the celebrated 'Jim Crow' with his black-faced parts (ending up rather like Danny La Rue with a demonstration that he was not quite what he seemed); Sinclair, the singer from Covent Garden and Drury Lane; and Mme Celeste from the Paris Grand Opera, who had a role as Madeleine which she could play 'in French and English' in Bernard's *St Mary's Eve – a story of the Solway*, (which she played five times in a week) and a non-speaking part as Maurice, the dumb boy in Planché's *The Child of the Wreck*.[4] In April the celebrated Hungarian Singers appeared, to be followed by a special engagement of the 'Real Bedouin Arabs'. During the whole of that season, the only Shakespeare was a single company performance of *Macbeth*, the announcement of which makes a great point of the male Witches and the vocal parts. Looking at the whole repertoire of that particular season, the popular successes are Fitzball's *The Lord of the Isles*, Lover's *Rory O'More*, *Guy Mannering*, Collier's *Kate Kearney* and Fitzball's *The Maid of Cashmere*. We are undoubtedly being told something significant about the changes of taste in the early Victorian theatre.

And, indeed, from then on company productions of Shakespeare become increasingly rare, so that Chute's two productions in 1858 and 1863 of *A Midsummer Night's Dream*, for instance, have in a different way the prestige status that previously belonged to a Siddons or a Kean appearance. The special visitors still appear from time to time – Mr and Mrs Charles Kean in 1862, for example, with *Richard III*, *Othello*, and *Much Ado About Nothing*; the Herman Vezins in 1864, with *Romeo and Juliet* and *As You Like It*. But when, in the last year of the stock company in 1883–4, Mme Ristori appeared as Lady Macbeth, our interest has less to do with Shakespeare than with a local critic's reaction to the staging of the performance.

When the 'star' system began at the turn of the century it is not difficult to see its initial attractions for management. The main provincial circuits and their theatres were now well established, but with purpose-built theatres to be looked after, and actors on salaries, not sharing profits, the management's financial burden was much greater; and it was not always easy to cope with the cash-flow problems of the dog-days, when audiences had tired of the familiar actors and repertory and voted with their feet. In the earlier days of the circuit system, this was when the tight-rope walkers, the specialist dancers, the Phantasmagoria, the Bands of Hungarian Silver Miners could bring back the bottoms to the benches; and it was in this context that the star visit was first welcomed.

But it soon became clear that there were unsuspected problems. Members of the stock companies disliked the new system, for it took away from them fat parts they would have liked to play themselves, devalued them with their audiences, and (they thought) affected their benefits. As early as 1809–10 Miss Marriott, a regular member of the Bath company, referred publicly to this, complaining after her benefit of the few opportunities she had had of late, because of what she called 'the constant succession of auxiliaries', and announcing that because of this, 'so mortifying and injurious to those performers who are stationary', she would be leaving the stage.[5] But poor Miss Marriott had trouble with audiences, too. In the previous season she had advertised *Measure for Measure* in her benefit bills, but was firmly told that it was an indecent play, and she had to change it for – of all things – *The Provoked Husband* (Genest, 1832, vol. 9, p. 156).

The auxiliaries, too, soon found the drawbacks. Apart from the incessant and extremely uncomfortable travelling involved, the conditions for rehearsal and performance were by any standard outrageous: possibly four different major plays in a week, to be played with a company of whom none, perhaps, had been previously acquainted with the leading actor, and on one rehearsal only – even though some of the company actors might have been learning and playing their parts for the first time. No wonder Macready at times found the life a nightmare.

A Victorian Provincial Stock Company

The record in his *Diaries* (1875, vol. 1, pp. 211–12) of his Bath visit in January 1835 shows the depression and anger it caused him. Though houses could still be crowded and enthusiastic, the could also be unsympathetic, and sometimes very barren indeed (perhaps too many 'star' visits were devaluing even their own attractiveness); and Macready was very unhappy with some of his fellow-players and their inadequacy in both rehearsal and performance.

What it felt like from the company point of view we learn from John Coleman, who was a member of the Bristol–Bath company in the late 1840s and left a record of working with Macready on one of his later visits (Penley, 1892, p. 147; *Bath Herald*, 21 Mar. 1835).

Macready kept us day after day from ten to four o'clock, following every situation, every scene, every line, every word of the text, with an interest as eager and unabated as if he had been acting each play for the first instead of the last time. It was true that he flurried, and worried, and bullied us, but his petulance was peppered with brains; his irascibility arose more from dyspepsia than bad temper, and everything he touched was irradiated with the sacred fire of genius. *Hamlet*, *Othello*, *Macbeth* (the latter with music) were rehearsed letter perfect, words and music, with only one rehearsal, but for the other plays we had two. . . . I acted Othello, Macduff, and the Ghost before; but Ulric, Icilius, de Mauprat, Edgar, and the Prince of Wales were all new parts, which involved sitting up half the night with wet towels on my head, and strong coffee in my stomach. It was a matter of honour to be letter perfect in these great works, and indeed, the imputation of being imperfect in the text was considered a grievous [sic] stigma upon an actor's professional reputation in those days.

But if, in those conditions, being letter perfect was honoured more in the breach than the observance, who could wonder?

Local management, too, found the high fees increasingly demanded by the visitors an additional burden which defeated the major purpose of the exercise. (There was a complaint by Hooper, the manager from 1843 to 1845, that visitors were now demanding not half but the whole receipts from their nights.) (Penley, 1892, p. 142).

In the twenties, thirties, and forties, there were some very difficult seasons in Bath. On 5 April 1823 the *Bath Herald* recorded:

Our managers have been most zealously employed through the season, in their multiform endeavours to suit the taste of the public; good farces and good plays have in their turns been performed; Shakespeare and Sheridan have been produced – but often to barren benches; other specimens of the 'legitimate drama' have been revived for a night or two, but have met with sudden deaths through their chilling reception in the late cold winter; ventriloquism has been tried, but in vain – for the voice of the celebrated artiste reverberated through every corner of the almost deserted house. Thalia's smiles and Melpomene's tears have been disregarded, and even melodrama has lost much of its influence! At last a lucky hit has been made – the managers engaged the undoubted Champion of the Fistic Art, Mr. Neate, with one of his compeers in that fashionable science; and on Monday last they displayed their sparring gymnastics at the Theatre Royal Bath, before an audience *crowded to an overflow* in Gallery, Pit – aye, and in Boxes!!!

And in the 1829–30 season only the special appearance of an elephant drew crowded houses.

There were a number of reasons for this, of which the devaluing of the stock company and the visiting players were only two. Bath was no longer the leading social centre during the winter months that it had been, and the theatre was no longer the fashionable amusement – even the adoption of a later hour for dinner worked against it. Taste clearly was changing, as we have seen, and the supporters of the traditional classic repertoire were ageing, if not dead, and even if surviving unlikely to take kindly to the romantic melodrama and the domestic sentimentality that were becoming the vogue. In the thirties, too, there were political and economic problems, of which the agitation over the Reform Bill and the Bristol Riots of 1831 may stand as symbols. Moreover the moral climate in parts of Bath society was turning strongly against the theatre. We have already noted Miss Marriott's problems over *Measure for Measure* in 1809. In the 1840s there was a further outburst of Puritanism when on 7 January 1844 the Reverend John East, Rector of St Michael's, preached a sermon violently attacking the theatre: 'The character of the theatre', he thundered, 'is strongly marked, and marked with almost every variety of evil . . . therefore, in proportion as it is adapted to the intellectual character of man, and as it is calculated to interest his passions, and to make a deep impression on his heart, it is a dangerous enemy to his virtue and happiness.' The literature and performances of the stage he saw as 'hostile to the doctrines and morals of Christianity, degrading to the professors of the art, and destructive of the present and eternal happiness of man'; and, though he could accept that Shakespeare was an 'unequalled genius', and that 'his writings contain passages of sublimity and beauty seldom or never excelled' yet even *Hamlet*, 'perhaps the very fairest' specimen of his work, 'abounds in the most horrid and blasphemous imprecations, with which the walls of theatres have rung a thousand times, and in the grossest obscenity of language, *some* of which, at least in our times, a player dare not repeat'. And to those of his hearers who had in the past crossed the doors of a theatre he urged a sense of repentance: 'go to the fountain open for sin and for uncleanness, to wash away the stain of precious time so vainly and so guiltily spent'.

This sermon was subsequently published, and started a pamphlet war, from which at least six different specimens have survived – though in the view of Penley (1892, pp. 143–4), writing forty years later, the campaign misfired, proving in fact the best advertisement the playhouse could hope for, and sending audiences flocking back into it.[6]

But that was only a brief interruption to a predominantly sad story. The theatre had had to close early in the season of 1832, and, while a subscription system started up by a group of prominent citizens enabled it to reopen, Bellamy, who had been manager since 1827, abandoned ship in 1833, subsequently moving to the less fraught task of managing the Assembly Rooms. His successor, Barnett from Reading and Newbury, lasted one season. Woulds, who then ran Bath (alongside Swansea and Cardiff) and for a time had W. C. Macready's interest and backing, went bankrupt in 1840. Davidge from the Surrey Theatre lasted less than a full season in 1840–1, and in May of the following year Hay, of Exeter and Plymouth, defaulted leaving salaries in arrear and no assets. However, in January 1843 the optimistic Hooper from the St James's reopened the theatre and survived two seasons till his collapse in March 1845, when Mrs Sarah Macready brought her company over from Bristol to play one or two benefit nights for members of the abandoned company.

Her visit had far-reaching consequences. Having run Bristol successfully for eleven years, later in 1845 Mrs Macready took over Bath in addition, and for the next eighteen years the second conjunction of Bristol and Bath restored some kind of continuity and repute to Beauford Square.

After Mrs Macready's death in 1853 she was succeeded by her son-in-law, James Henry Chute, who for the next decade was to prove the best manager since William Wyatt Dimond. Chute could not, of course, hope to restore the theatre to the national reputation it had then, but he did the next best thing: to quote Penley (1892, p. 150), who had direct experience of his regime, he 'kept the theatre open every year throughout a full season, provided an excellent stock company, produced new and attractive pieces, and revived others of genuine merit, and frequently introduced London stars and Metropolitan attractions'. But there was a difference. In 1841 Brunel's London–Bristol Railway had been completed, and it was now possible for the star not only to go on the road, but to take his company – and later even his scenery – with him. Thus in August 1854 Chute brought down Mme Vestris and Charles Mathews with the principal members of the Royal Lyceum Company, and later that month Charles Kean and twenty-seven members of his company from the Royal Princess's. Even when, in January 1862, the Charles Keans came primarily to lead the stock company in *Richard III*, *Othello* and *Much Ado*, they brought with them three other members of the Princess's company to play major roles. The system of touring companies, which before the turn of the century was to oust most of the old provincial stock companies, was already beginning.

It is not necessary, here, to go into great detail about Chute's achieve-ment as a manager – it has already been authoritatively recorded by Dr Barker in her history of the Bristol Theatre Royal (1974, pp. 135–67), but two important consequences of the development of the touring metropolitan companies should be noted: first, the much higher quality of performance possible for a company that had rehearsed and worked together for long periods – so that one-day improvisations of the stock companies could no longer be tolerated – and, secondly, the greater sophistication of scenery, lighting and presentation. This clearly had an effect on some of the productions Chute mounted with his own companies.

Penley (1892, p. 153) records that in Chute's time 'the scenery possessed by the theatre was abundant and excellent both in design and execution, while its wardrobe and library ranked among the best in the kingdom'. Even so, on some occasions an extra special effort was clearly made.

One such was Chute's production of A Midsummer Night's Dream in November and December 1858. Scenically it was based on Charles Kean's London production at the Princess's, with the designs of the London artists; and the playbill begins with a long programme note by Kean himself explaining what he had in mind. What the playgoer saw is recorded in the Bath Express (4 Dec. 1858):

When the curtain draws up a view of Athens presents itself in the period of its highest splendour. To make the scene more striking, the actual topography is departed from . . . Athens is here made to stand on the very edge of the waters, which flow in front of the city, and wash the very base of the Acropolis. This liberty taken with fact is, of course, excusable, and makes a more effective picture. The marble palaces and the purple ocean in immediate juxtaposition produce a most entrancing effect. This scene does great credit to Messrs W. and George Gordon . . . Scene 2 represents the workshop of Quince the carpenter, the furniture and workmen's tools being copies from discoveries at Herculaneum. Such is the truthful and artistic spirit which Charles Kean has carried into all his revivals. The past is no longer a cold ideal, but glows with life and colour under his magic touch. Act 2 opens with a view of a wood near Athens, the fairies' haunt by moonlight. Here Oberon and Titania appear with their fairy trains, some score nymphs most gracefully attired. The effect of moonlight here produced is a perfect marvel. It seems to be managed by some side reflectors, and the illusion is complete. The shadow dance, where the fairies chase their own shadows, is an enchanting scene . . . To the mystic radiance of moonlight succeeds a thick fog, caused by Puck, which soon disperses, when we have another dance of the fairies. The palm of poetical beauty certainly belongs to the moonlight scenes, but for magnificence, Titania's Bower is unequalled. Its appearance was greeted with a burst of applause. But every successive scene was more or less thus received, and the whole drama was a march of triumph from first to last. A moving diorama is a novelty in dramatic representation, but here it was resorted to. The scenery of the fifth act is by Lennox, and brings before us an apartment in the palace of Theseus and closes with a view of the galleries and illuminated gardens. This is most gorgeous, and the kindling of the fires enhances the effect to the utmost verge of scenic possibility. The closing tableau was the climax of magnificence.

After the disastrous real fire which gutted the theatre on Good Friday 1862, it was this production that was appropriately revived in C. J. Phipps's new stage and auditorium to reopen the theatre on 4 March 1863. This time the Titania was a promising young actress called Ellen Terry,

whose elegant and refined interpretation of the part was received with evident pleasure. We are not surprised at the popularity which this young lady has gained. There are a winsomeness and an *espièglerie* in her style that are irresistible . . . She was a charming 'Titania', and the Fairy Queen herself, however vain she may be, could not have wished for a more fascinating representative.

Thus the *Bath and Cheltenham Gazette* (11 Mar. 1863), with a compliment neatly turned. But however much he may have loved his production, Chute was a hard-headed businessman, too. At the end of the week, coinciding with the marriage of the Prince and Princess of Wales, *A Midsummer Night's Dream* gave way to *Aladdin*. He knew what filled the seats.

Two years later, in 1864, Bath celebrated the Shakespeare tercentenary; and the 147 magnificent column-inches of the *Bath Chronicle* (28 April) which record the two festive days are a detailed and sometimes unintentionally hilarious account of a festival which did not always go according to plan. Sadly, the theatre's part in it was hardly central. A week earlier it had brought in Mr and Mrs Herman Vezin to lead the company in *Romeo and Juliet* and *As You Like It*, but the *Bath Chronicle* (21 Apr. 1864) was not very enthusiastic about the performances. It preferred Mrs Vezin's Rosalind to her Juliet, and found her husband as Romeo manly but melancholy. And when, a week later, the theatre was crammed for the festival itself, it mounted not a prestige performance of one of the great plays, but a pot-pourri in which the forest scenes from *As You Like It* (without the Vezins), the fairy scenes from *A Midsummer Night's Dream*, the quarrel from *Julius Caesar* and Chute himself appearing as the Falstaff of *The Merry Wives of Windsor*, were but a prelude to a 'serio-comic apropos-sketch or masque' styled '*Shakespeare at Home*', which brought together the shade of Shakespeare and 'a comic man, one Mr *Verona Chopkins*, who had come down to Stratford to see the Tercentenary celebration . . . and who met with the poet's ghost while sleeping in the birthplace'. Finally, there was a 'Grand allegorical tableau, in which Fame, Time and the Muses, were represented paying homage to Shakespeare' (*Bath Chronicle*, 21 and 28 Apr. 1864).

It seems all rather chapfallen. Granted there had been forty-eight hours of pomp and circumstance, a good Bathonian day in the open air had been had by all – especially the artisans, who got an unexpected holiday – and some honour had been done to the Bard. But the amateur reading of *A Midsummer Night's Dream* at the Assembly Rooms was a failure, the Grand Procession something of a shambles, the platform for the distinguished persons at the dedication of the Votive Altar in Victoria Park collapsed under them, and the projected Scholarship Fund raised only £18.9s. And in the playhouse, Shakespeare's own workshop, they were soon back to the Peeps of Day, the Secrets of Lady Audley, the Black Flags, and the Tickets-of-Leave-Men of the stock company, and later to the more distinguished visits of the English Opera Company (with Italian operas) and the D'Oyly Carte Company (with *Iolanthe*, *Patience*, *The Pirates of Penzance* and *HMS Pinafore*). Perhaps, indeed, it was appropriately symbolic that for its part in the tercentenary the theatre should have mounted, not a major production, but an anthology and a comic masque. Shakespeare was no longer in the mainstream of the theatre repertoire.

To describe the remaining twenty years of the Bath stock company would be a melancholy task. After Chute's retreat from Bath in 1868, there were seven changes of management in seventeen years. Increasingly the theatre became the home for touring companies, and a poor stock caucus was augmented for its occasional home productions. The last stock company disintegrated with the premature end of Neebe's management in 1884.

During that final season, in October 1883, Mme Ristori made one of the last of the star visits to the company, to play Lady Macbeth. Both she and the production were received somewhat coolly and critically by a writer in the *Bath and Cheltenham Gazette* (3 Oct. 1883):

Of Mme Ristori's personation of Lady Macbeth I have no intention to speak, beyond suggesting that I do not quite see the propriety of the stage 'business' in the sleep-walking scene. The murderer's wife, whose remorse has been so grandly developed by the poet, walks in her sleep and is spoken of as a sleep-walker. But Mme Ristori (like every other actress I ever saw), having come on the stage, stands in front of the footlights, and hardly moves from one spot till she makes her exit. There is no sleep-walking – no pretence at it. But this by the way. The object of this note is to protest against the management of the light in the performance of the tragedy. Surely the witch scene should be gone through in almost total darkness, or in darkness relieved by little beside the flame of the cauldron. But the stage was positively illuminated with the limelight! Actors and managers are very slow to learn how obscurity appeals to the imagination. Take, for instance, this scene with a darkened stage, the characters hardly visible even in outline, the words of the incantation issuing from obscurity; then the spectator's feelings are profoundly impressed. But light up the stage, and the cave is represented by some villainously painted canvas, the witches become three second-rate male actors, very shabbily costumed, and the apparitions, with the procession of kings, stand out a wretched make-believe that annihilates the 'witchery' of the scene. Some great critics (notably Charles Lamb) have questioned the propriety of presenting Shakespeare's tragedies on the stage at all. I do not accept this belief; but would infinitely prefer to read the witch scene, than see it under the glare of the limelight. The over lighting of this scene is, I know, the common practice, – therefore I must give the stage manager who arranged the representation of *Macbeth* all the more credit for having devised a novel sort of annoyance. Everybody knows that one of the points of Macbeth's part is the dagger soliloquy, and that it is spoken in a darkened scene, – and invariably so, for if there were much light the Scottish thane would be in no doubt whether he were looking at a real dagger, or one coined by his imagination. This darkness was too much for the manager on this occasion. He could not with any regard to propriety turn up the stage-lights, so he put Macbeth under the full glare of the limelight! As a result, there was a darkened stage, with one very bright flare directed on Macbeth, and as he moved about, so moved the round spot of light, reminding me of an *ignis fatuus*, or a magic lantern slide. The scene was dense as midnight, while Macbeth was mouthing, posturing, and declaiming in a little circle of apparent sunlight. I have seen many absurdities on the stage, but no absurdity greater than this, for though the actor was fairly intelligent and effective, there was nothing so transcendentally grand in his effort, that the stage sun should run about after him, lest any of his attitudes or grimaces should be lost on the audience.

That particular evil was a long time dying; the moving limelight was still surviving in some provincial theatres as recently as the late 1930s. But behind the writer's comments one senses a new critical climate emerging. Just as in the 1830s we have seen tastes changing, ushering in the heyday of melodrama and sentimentality, so in the 1880s we can detect the beginnings of a reaction against the over-indulgence of theatricality, and a plea for greater realism. *Shakes Versus Shav* is just around the corner.

Of course it was not the end of Shakespeare in the Bath Theatre. An actor by the stage name of Irving had already appeared with the St James's company in 1867, and was to appear again with greater distinction later; since then touring companies of many sorts and qualities have brought their productions to Beauford Square, and no doubt will continue to do so. But it *was* the end of the Bath company, and so nearly the end of my story.

In essence, as I have tried to show, it is a tale of the decline of a provincial stock company – a decline accentuated by the star touring system, moved away by changes in taste to little more than lip-service to Shakespeare and dependence on romanticism and sentimentality, finished off by the rise, in the seventies and eighties, of the touring company. It is not a tale peculiar to Bath, though Bath's previous pre-eminence may make the fall seem more dramatic: it could almost certainly be paralleled in every Victorian city that had inherited a playhouse from the eighteenth century. And so I come back to the Georgian Theatre where I began. Perhaps in one sad sense the history of that theatre might truly be extended as far as the 1880s. For the story of what happened to the plays of Shakespeare in Victorian Bath might equally well be sub-titled, in Gibbonian phrase, the 'Decline and Fall of the Georgian Theatre'.

NOTES

1 Genest, 1832; Penley, 1892, chs. 16–25; Hare, 1977; Barker, 1974, pp. 121–64.
2 Calendars of these years, because of the chance survival of information, must be treated with caution, and should not be used as detailed statistical data; but the number of surviving entries can often be used reasonably safely to infer general trends. See A. H. Scouten, 'The Increase in Popularity of Shakespeare's Plays in the 18th Century', *Shakespeare Quarterly*, 7 (1956), 189–202.
3 Hare, 1980, pp. 155–6 and chs. 10, 11 and 12 *passim*. The sources for all programme details after 1805 are the Playbill Collection in the Bath Reference library (some 4000 bills) and the columns of the *Bath Journal*, *Bath Chronicle*, *Bath and Cheltenham Gazette* and *Bath Herald* for appropriate years, held in the same Collection.
4 Mme Celeste in fact became a regular favourite in Bath and Bristol. She returned regularly, and was still appearing twenty-five years later in March 1862.
5 Penley, 1892, p. 105; see also Holbrook, 1807, pp. 33–4.
6 East, 1844b; A Churchman, A *Temperate Answer to the Sermon*, Bath, 1844; A Resident, *The Bath Theatre Vindicated*, Bath, 1844; Rev. J. P. Bartram, *The Drama*, in *Bath Herald* (in Bath Reference Library folder 'The Bath Theatre 1844'); East, 1844; A Visitor, *The Theatre – Observations on a Recent Pamphlet*, 1844.

The Popular Audience for Shakespeare in Nineteenth-Century Leicester

JEREMY CRUMP

THE history of Leicester's Theatre Royal in the mid-Victorian period was marked by the efforts of successive lessees to re-establish its social standing by restoring the legitimate drama to a central place in the repertoire. In a town which lacked any resident gentry or aristocratic interest in its affairs, and whose dominant bourgeois elite was preponderantly Nonconformist and ill disposed towards the theatre, promoting the legitimate drama was beset by difficulties. Such persistent demand for theatre as there was came largely from a working-class audience whose vociferous presence in pit and gallery provided further evidence to the middle class that the theatre was not for them. Yet, despite social aspirations to the contrary, managers and actors ignored the popular audience at their peril, and the most successful lessees of the Theatre Royal, which had fourteen between 1847 and 1885, excluding summer seasons, were men such as Henry Gill (1847–53) and George Owen (1857, 1860–8) who were able to reach an accommodation with popular taste.[1]

Shakespeare had a strategic importance in efforts to reconcile contradictory demands on theatre managers. Entrenched in British theatrical tradition, Shakespeare was self-evidently legitimate theatre. The use by the directors of the Leicester Theatre Company, formed in 1847 when the Theatre Royal was in danger of closure, of a bust of the dramatist on their seal represents an attempt to identify themselves with that tradition.[2] Leicester's actor–managers prided themselves on their ability to act major Shakespearean roles, and their Shakespeare seasons unfailingly won the approval of local theatre critics. The ability to play the major tragic roles was an important criterion for success with critics and audience alike; George Owen in particular was welcomed as a 'celebrated tragedian', and was complimented for lavish stagings of Shakespeare (*Leicester Journal*, 21 Jan. 1857 and 26 Mar. 1858). The familiarity of the plays made them ideal vehicles for touring stars to work with the stock company. Ira Aldridge's *Othello* in 1857 was described as 'the drama as it should be' (*Leicester Journal*, 27 Mar. 1857).

The established place of certain Shakespeare plays in the stock company repertoire should not be taken as a sign that all productions were equally prestigious though. The *Era*, remarking on a well-prepared *Macbeth* by Owen in 1863, noted:

> Unfortunately, managers have been accustomed to 'do' Shakespeare here on the off nights, without regard to proper scenery, appointments and effects . . . the lukewarmness exhibited has too often originated with the actors, who have been preparing, by rehearsal, for some 'thrilling' drama, and coming before the public with Shakespeare neglected, unlearned and unstudied.   (*Era*, 4 Oct. 1863)

Even in Owen's 1865 *Macbeth*, an undesirable contrast was observed between Duncan's robes, 'become musty with his advanced years' (*Era*, 22 Oct. 1865) and the new costumes of Macbeth and his wife, played by Mr and Mrs Owen. Yet until the advent of Boucicault's sensation plays in the 1860s and the rise of comedy, especially as performed by touring companies, from the 1870s, the major theatrical occasions in Leicester were performances of Shakespeare or of more recently written dramas such as *Ingomar*, *Richelieu* and *The Lady of Lyons* by eminent Shakespearean actors, notably Charles Dillon and James Anderson. Even after the decline of the stock company, Shakespearean productions by touring companies led by Henry Irving or Alexander Marsh remained a major attraction.

Shakespeare was a vital element in the reforming zeal of the gentleman amateur Jonathan Townsend, formerly MP for Greenwich and manager of the Theatre Royal for a disastrous season in 1859. The plays were also that part of English dramatic literature which was most acceptable to Leicester's Nonconformist middle class. A number of the more liberal rational recreationists and ministers of religion advocated the dissemination of Shakespeare as a means of popular education. George Stevenson, a solicitor who was mayor in 1869 and a member of the town council from 1858 until 1891, the Reverend J. Page Hopps, minister of the Unitarian Great Meeting, and Joseph Dare, Unitarian domestic missionary from 1846 until 1873, were amongst those who asserted the need to make available the uplifting literature of the legitimate drama in ways which were free from the disreputable associations of the stage. Such efforts provided would-be reforming managers John Windley (1869–74) and Eliot Galer (1874–7) with a rhetoric of theatrical improvement which bolstered their activities at the Theatre Royal and won influential support for Galer's building of the Royal Opera House as Leicester's second legitimate theatre in 1877.[3] Yet when respectability and a middle-class audience returned to Leicester theatres in the 1880s, it was to see the new light comedy rather than the old legitimate drama.

Shakespeare in Nineteenth-Century Leicester

The practice of popular theatregoing, involving markedly different conventions of audience behaviour and rejecting certain forms of the drama – notably eighteenth-century comedy – challenged attempts to make the theatre 'respectable'. Yet Shakespeare remained extremely popular. The *Era* (2 Nov. 1862) remarked that 'whenever Shakespeare's plays are put up for Saturday, the house is sure to fill'; this state of affairs lasted until the 1880s. Such enthusiasm for Shakespeare has been observed elsewhere and explained in terms of the ease with which the plays could be assimilated to popular dramatic forms. Drastically reduced versions of the plays given by travelling showmen, many of whom performed at Leicester's May and October fairs (Boase, 1979) and statements recorded by Mayhew from East End audiences, such as that by a costermonger who thought that '*Macbeth* would be better liked if it was only the witches and the fighting' (Mayhew, 1861, p. 15), have been taken to suggest that the popular response to Shakespeare was of the most superficial order, with productions butchering the text in order to provide as unbroken as possible a flow of sensational, violent and supernatural events. Michael Booth has commented on the melodramatic nature of some of the plays, notably the nineteenth-century favourites *Macbeth*, *Hamlet* and *Richard III* (Booth, 1965, pp. 40ff.). More recently, though, Douglas Reid has warned against a wholly dismissive view, conceding that parts of the audience may have gone wholly for melodramatic thrills, but that there were also members of pit and gallery for whom Shakespeare was part of an intellectual, radical culture, an aspect of the eclectic autodidacticism of a significant minority of the nineteenth-century working class (Bradby, 1980).

What follows in this essay is an examination of the interest which the popular audience in Leicester had in Shakespeare. It goes beyond the confines of the auditorium to look for other aspects of the cult of the Bard before discussing reaction to performances at the Theatre Royal.

In 1841, the journalist and ex-shoemaker Thomas Cooper formed a breakaway branch of the Leicester Chartist Association which was known as the Shakespearean Chartist Association, Cooper's organisation representing those Chartists least willing to compromise with the town's middle-class radicals over the reform issue (Patterson, 1954, p. 324). Amongst its productions was the Shakespearean Chartist Hymn Book, containing verses by Cooper and other local Chartists. The society prospered for over a year, achieving a peak membership of about 3000 and dominating Chartism in Leicester. The association has been described by Martha Vicinus as 'the best-known conjunction of literary education and

Chartist principles' (1974, p. 109) and by David Vincent as a direct link between the intellectual liberation of autodidacticism and the political liberation sought by the radical movement. Vincent claims:

The writings and in most cases the personalities of Byron, Shelley, Bunyan, Wesley, Milton and Shakespeare were incorporated into a lively new radical culture which played an important part in uniting and sustaining the world's first mass working-class movement.

(1981, p. 193)

The extent to which Shakespeare was central to radical culture in Leicester should not be exaggerated. The name of Cooper's association was derived from the Shakespearean room of the Amphitheatre, a large wooden structure on Humberstone Gate built in 1839, where meetings were held. It is not of itself evidence for Chartist allegiance to the dramatist. Nevertheless, it must have appeared as a happy coincidence to Cooper, who was a lifelong devotee of Shakespeare. For his own intellectual self-training, undertaken while still a shoemaker in his early twenties in Gainsborough, he had set himself the target of memorising seven of Shakespeare's plays as well as *Paradise Lost*, at the same time studying Latin, Greek, Hebrew, French, algebra, geometry, religious evidences and modern literature. This proved too exacting, and after he had memorised *Hamlet* Cooper's health broke down before he could start on *King Lear* (Cooper, 1872, p. 57). Cooper's adult classes at the Amphitheatre

were similarly wide-ranging, and he recalled that unless there were some stirring local or political topic, I lectured on Milton and repeated portions of the *Paradise Lost* or on Shakespeare, and repeated portions of *Hamlet* . . . or I recited the history of England . . . or I took up Geology, or even Phrenology, and made the young men acquainted, elementally, with the knowledge of the time. (Cooper, 1872, p. 169).

Cooper's influence was apparent in December 1842 when the society's dramatic section was busy getting up a performance of *Hamlet*, with Cooper in the title role. It aimed to raise money to pay for Cooper's legal defence against charges brought against his political activities in the Potteries at the time of the Plug Plot earlier in the year (*Northern Star*, 3 Dec. 1842). According to Cooper, the hall, which held 3000, was full to capacity, but the venture was not successful in raising funds, as the other actors demanded payment (Cooper, 1872, pp. 228–9).

Although individuals may have received a lasting impression from Cooper's teaching, as did the young Alfred Mundella, in later life MP for Nottingham and a successful hosiery manufacturer, the Shakespearean Chartist Association left no institutional legacy. The adult classes did not survive the worsening of the depression in the hosiery trade in 1842, and although neither adult education nor radical politics became extinct, no specific links seem to have been made later between Chartism and the cult of Shakespeare.

In 1852, the Leicester Domestic Mission's men's class presented the first celebration of Shakespeare's birthday, starting a custom which was to last until the mid-1870s, when the retirement of the missionary, Joseph Dare, marked the end of the mission's activity in the All Saints area of the town. The purpose of the annual festival of recitations and music was overtly didactic. Dare had expressed his belief in the value of the legitimate drama in his report for 1848, but regretted that the inhabitants of his area, one of the poorest in Leicester, preferred what he called 'the monstrosities of the strolling player or the more horrid orgies of the back room of the tavern' (*Leicester Domestic Mission Annual Reports*, 1848) or what would now be seen as the precursors of the music hall. Shakespeare was offered as 'a more improving kind of entertainment', a counter-attraction which would help do away with the need for singing saloons. According to Dare, current working-class reading habits were degrading, restricted as they were to such things as *Black Highwaymen*, *Dick Turpin*, *Tales of Demons and Spirits* and *Police News*. The adult class offered in the course of its annual programme readings from Shakespeare alongside lectures on popular science and issues of public health, and the annual celebration was soon one of the mission's great social occasions. Dare hoped that celebrations of the anniversaries of Shakespeare, Milton, Burns and Eliza Cooke would serve as rational calendar customs, substituting English worthies for saints' days.[4]

The celebration retained the same form throughout its twenty-year history. A tea-meeting preceded an evening at the All Saints' Open Rooms or, in 1853 and 1854, the much larger New Hall, at which up to a dozen extracts from Shakespeare would be read, interspersed with appropriate music, such as Locke's for *Macbeth*. Press reports do not give occupations of performers, but in 1864 and 1873, the *Leicester Chronicle and Mercury* reported that all reciters were from factory or workshop. It is likely that one function of the celebration was to give members of the mission's elocution class the opportunity to perform in public. Audiences were overwhelmingly from the working class according to the press, and with few exceptions large. Over 300 sat down to tea in 1853 and the New Hall, with a capacity of over 1000, was filled for the performance. Study of lists of pieces chosen suggests that, with the exception of the frequent choice for recitation of Henry IV's invocation to sleep, they reinforced the limited canon of Shakespeare as performed on the stage.

At first sight, these celebrations seem far removed from the activity of the Shakespearean Chartist Association. They were promoted by a missionary who served as an agent for some of the town's wealthiest employers, those who attended the Great Meeting, of which one aim was 'to diffuse a spirit of industry and order, of contentment and religion, throughout the community' (*Leicester Domestic Mission Annual Reports*, 1855). Indeed, the mission was established in 1846 partly as a response to middle-class fears of political disorder created by the Chartist unrest. Dare prided himself on the tendency of the discussion class to take the edge off the radical sentiments of working men who joined it. Class conciliation, not political equality, was its aim. But Dare could not dictate to his students, for whom the door was always available, and just as a later Leicester radical, Tom Barclay, found the men's classes of Canon Vaughan, the Vicar of St Martin's, a source of political education, so did many of Dare's students (Barclay, 1934, pp. 41ff.; Allaway, 1962). In tracing the origins of the Leicester Secular Society, F. J. Gould referred to a group of 'thoughtful young men', including ex-Chartists, who met in the 1840s 'for the debate of religious and social questions'. These moved from the Owenite Social Institution via the Mechanics' Institute to the adult class of the Leicester Domestic Mission. There they enjoyed the right of free speech, discussing teetotalism, the Charter, secularism, frame rents in the hosiery trade and popular education (Gould, 1900, p. 8). It was in such a milieu that the Shakespeare celebration took shape.

Vincent (1981, pp. 164ff.) identifies as a contradiction within the movement for working-class self-education the fact that it shared some of the goals of the philanthropic schemes of the middle class at the same time as it asserted working-class harmony. Its adherents appeared to be in danger of assimilation into the ranks of subordinates of middle-class radicalism, even if this was not in fact the case. The Shakespeare celebrations, with their tea-meetings and glee-singing, were a rejection of the drink-dominated culture of large parts of the working class. But it should not be assumed that participants thus surrendered dignity and independence. The democratic implications of learning were not buried beneath the philanthropic trappings of the mission. In 1866, a working man, A. Garland, introduced the celebration with a prologue he had written himself, in which he declared:

> I have a right, a kindred right I claim,
> Though rank nor titles gild my humble name,
> Tis from his class, the class the proud discard,
> For Shakespeare was himself the people's bard.
>
> (*Leicester Chronicle*, 28 Apr. 1866)

Similar attempts to appeal to popular interest in Shakespeare were made at the Working Men's College, founded in 1862 (Allaway, 1962, p. 7) and at the Working Men's Club (formed in 1866). A Leicester publisher and bookseller, James Hunter, attracted the largest attendance of the club's first year for a reading of his own *The Story of Hamlet Condensed and Interspersed with the Text of Shakespeare's Tragedy, in Three Parts* (1866). It consisted of three twenty-minute readings, with music in the intervals, and was offered by Hunter as a model of how the well educated, of any class, could help to achieve civilisation by entertaining their neighbours. Hunter hoped that the more gifted working men would read it aloud, and included for their benefit 'A Short Practical Essay on the Art of Reading Aloud'. He recommended practice in front of a mirror with passages from the Bible, Cowper, Milton and Shakespeare, works which 'improve the mind, elevate the moral character, and invigorate the style of composition, both for public speaking and writing' (Hunter, 1866, p. vi).

While there does not seem to be evidence of any further so thoroughly planned Shakespearean entertainment, readings from Shakespeare remained an element in improving entertainments and clubs and institutes for working men. As late as 1883, a lecture at the Working Men's Club on Wolsey was illustrated with extracts from *Henry VIII* (*Leicester Daily Post*, 10 Nov. 1883). Such readings were still part of ILP Saturday evening entertainments in the 1900s.

The potential audience for Shakespeare at the theatre thus included many who were acquainted with his works from various institutional contexts which led to a more serious engagement with them than that offered by the travelling showman. Beyond that, individuals could approach Shakespeare less formally on their own behalf. Tom Barclay recalled borrowing Dick's shilling edition of the plays from a neighbour, Jem Dillon, who, like Barclay, was an Irish inhabitant of the impoverished courts off Belgrave Gate in the 1860s. Barclay later borrowed copies from the Municipal Library, which opened in 1869 (1934, p. 15). The writer of the 'Lounger' column in the ILP paper, *The Leicester Pioneer*, recalled how at twelve years of age, he had seen Charles Kean's revival of *Henry V* at the Princess's Theatre. The experience led him to buy Dick's Penny Plays of Shakespeare, which he read when back in Leicester while waiting for cricket matches to begin on the Old Pasture, a popular resort of the Leicester working class (*Leicester Pioneer*, 30 May 1908). Signs of discernment among the crowd are thus to be expected, and are not difficult to find.

As with plays by other authors, there were many instances in which Shakespeare was played to full gallery and pit while the boxes remained sparsely attended (*Leicester Chronicle*, 30 Nov. 1849; *Leicester Daily Post*,

1 Oct. 1895). Occasions when the popular parts of the house were empty were due to the coincidence of rival attractions, such as Sanger's circus, or to prices being higher than usual. The evidence does not support the view that Shakespeare was seen as just another writer of sensation plays, or that the text was unimportant. In 1862, for example, *Othello* was announced for fair week and drew a big crowd. Non-arrival of a costume for the leading actor, John Coleman, meant that the play could not go on, and the assembled audience was offered instead *Rube the Showman*, which had already played that week. A demonstration ensued, the pitites hissing, stamping and groaning while the gallery threw apples at the stage (*Era*, 19 Oct. 1862).

The crowd frequently applauded key speeches by leading performers – a mark of their appreciation of a certain kind of oratory. In 1850, James Anderson's *Hamlet* drew applause for many of the soliloquies, and the same happened to Irving twenty-eight years later. On the latter occasion, the *Leicester Chronicle*'s correspondent regretted that 'Both pit and gallery are given to applauding mere sentiment without reference to the playing, as if they were listening to stump oratory.' They laughed at the 'pathetic humour' of the Gravediggers' scene as if it were burlesque. Such comments imply a conflict between critic and popular audience over how Shakespeare was to be appreciated, although they were unanimous in liking the performance. It seems that the Leicester audience responded to the great set pieces of the play, notably the soliloquies, and if anything preferred their Hamlet acted in a mannered, dated way; but that is not to deny their interest in the text of the play rather than in the effects or the pageantry (*Leicester Chronicle*, 7 Sept. 1878). Even closer attention to the text is implied by the need of Charles Dillon to apologise for the absence of the Player King during a performance of *Hamlet* in 1878, and for the consequent need to omit part of the play – an interruption which was well received by the audience. This may have been an astute means of buying time on the part of an actor confronted with the embarrassment of the non-appearance of a character, but it also hints at respect for the audience's knowledge of the play. Finally, Charles Billson gives an account in his *Leicester Memories* of a sweep, William Kelley, who occupied a regular seat at the front of the gallery for performances of Shakespeare and corrected actors who made mistakes. This suggests a knowledge of the plays comparable to Cooper's (Billson, 1924, p. 112).

There were nevertheless cases of disorder at some performances. Reid (in Bradby 1980) has found that Saturday and Monday night performances of Shakespeare in Birmingham, especially those with ghosts, were the most unruly. Youths in particular came to see the effects without understanding the play. There is no such regularity in the Leicester material. Incidents were most often precipitated by factors, also found in Birmingham, such as overcrowding in the gallery, which was always likely on Saturdays (*Era*, 2 Nov. 1862), bad managerial decisions such as the *Rube the Showman* incident, or poor performances. Conversely, Henry Powell's summer season in 1863, when he presented excerpts from *Hamlet* and *Richard III* and the whole of *Macbeth*, was considered so good that even Saturday nights were not unruly (*Era*, 19 July 1863). An exceptional disturbance took place in 1841; the last theatrical riot in Leicester in which there was considerable physical danger to the crowd. A perform- ance of *King Lear* was attended by 'disgusting oaths', fights in the gallery and bottles thrown into the pit. No explanation of the cause of the brawl was given in the press, although overcrowding for Charles Dillon's performance may have been responsible, as might the unfamiliarity of what remained in Leicester a rarely performed work. There may also have been disappointment that Dillon was suffering from a cold which weakened his delivery and forced him not to appear in the afterpiece (*Leicester Chronicle*, 2 Oct. 1841).

By 1900, W. Scarff was able to write in his *Leicestershire and Rutland at the Opening of the 20th Century* that 'farcical comedy is on the whole more attractive than Shakespearian tragedy' (1902, p. 50). Melodrama was still popular at the Theatre Royal, but the financial implications of theatrical production, based on touring companies, favoured comedy rather than Shakespeare at a time when the latter was receiving the most elaborate productions (*Leicester Pioneer*, 28 Aug. 1911). Shakespeare had flourished under the stock company, which, at its best, established creative familiarity between actors and audience. The appeal of Shakespeare throve on repeated performance and engendered a taste for seeing established local actors, such as Owen, and touring stars such as Dillon and Aldridge, give virtuoso performances of well-known roles. In this respect it was out of step with the late nineteenth-century theatre's desire for continual novelty, which touring companies and national circuits alone could satisfy.

By 1910, a local theatre critic could speculate that the bulk of the audience for Alexander Marsh's week of Shakespeare plays at the Opera House was not even familiar with the plots of the plays (*Leicester Pioneer*, 20 Aug. 1910). In the same year, Bransby Williams successfully repeated two of his 'Shakespearean studies' at the Palace Theatre of Varieties, the biggest local music hall, although the crowd preferred his Dickensian characters (*Leicester Daily Post*, 31 May 1910). His portrayal of 'an old-

Table 1
Productions of Shakespeare in Leicester, 1860–95

	1850	1860	1865	1870	1875 ThR	1880 ThR	Opera	1885 ThR	1895 ThR	TOTAL
As You Like It	1				1	1		1		4
Hamlet	1	3	1	2	3	2			1	13
Henry V							1			1
Henry VIII		1								1
Julius Caesar	2									2
King John		1								1
King Lear	1			1						2
Macbeth	2	2	2	1	1	1				9
Merchant of Venice		(1)		1	2	2	1			6(1)
Much Ado					1			2		3
Othello	2	1	1	2	1	2				9
Richard III	1	3	1(1)		2	1				8(1)
Romeo and Juliet	2	2		1	1	1		1		8
Taming of the Shrew							1			1
Winter's Tale		1								1
TOTAL	12	14(1)	5(1)	8	12	10	5	2	1	69(2)

Figures in brackets = performance of part of play
Sources: Leicester Journal, 1850; Era, 1860–85; Leicester Daily Post, 1880, 1895.

time showman impressing the crowd with the merits of his Hamlet show and giving them a foretaste of its dramatic possibilities' was given as an encore. It is tempting to see in the popularity of such a turn a resonance of the earlier enthusiasm for Shakespeare which had then been on the wane for thirty years. It is not easy to account for the transformation in taste which had taken place. The Leicester Pioneer lamented that theatregoers had been 'Daily Mailed' and 'School Boarded into preferring Mr Hall Caine before the late William Shakespeare' (20 Aug. 1910) and the replacement of autodidacticism by public education seems a plausible factor making for change in working-class reading habits and taste in drama. The use of Shakespeare in elocution classes may also have given his work associations repugnant to those who, for whatever reason, did not choose to be associated with the culture of self-improvement and ostentatious respectability.

Up until the 1880s, some patrons of the Theatre Royal were attracted by the spectacle, or by the opportunity for disruptive exhibitionism, but the

Table 2

Extracts Read at Leicester Domestic Mission Anniversaries, 1853–73

	1853	1863	1865	1866	1868	1873	TOTAL
As You Like It	—	/	—	—	/	—	2
Hamlet	—	/	—	/	/	/	4
1 & 2 Henry IV	/	/	/	/	/	/	6
Henry V	—	—	/	—	/	—	2
Henry VIII	—	—	/	/	/	—	3
Julius Caesar	—	/	—	—	/	—	2
Macbeth	—	/	/	/	—	/	4
Merchant of Venice	/	—	/	—	—	/	3
Midsummer Night's Dream	/	/	—	—	—	—	2
Much Ado	—	—	—	/	—	—	1
Othello	—	—	/	—	—	/	2
Richard II	—	—	/	—	—	—	1
Richard III	—	—	/	—	—	/	2
Romeo and Juliet	—	/	—	/	—	—	2

Most Frequent Performances		Most Frequent Readings	
Hamlet	10	Henry IV	6
Macbeth	8	Hamlet	4
Othello	7	Macbeth	4
Richard III	7(1)	Henry VIII	3
Romeo and Juliet	6	Merchant of Venice	3

evidence assembled here suggests that there was a genuine appreciation of the plays by a large part of the audience which went beyond the taste for melodrama. For this audience, there was nothing incongruous about a programme which included both *Macbeth* and Douglas Jerrold's *Black Ey'd Susan* (*Era*, 22 Oct. 1865). It was one for which Shakespeare and the legitimate drama represented fixed standards of theatrical performance. George Owen, Leicester's most successful theatrical entrepreneur before 1880, appealed to it in 1864 by providing

a multitudinous variety of entertainments, including Shakespeare and legitimate drama, sensational novelties, pieces of a merry and brilliant description, and farces of which broad humour is the speciality.   (*Leicester Journal*, 18 Sept. 1864)

Chartists, philanthropists, rational recreationists and restorers of theatrical respectability all sought to influence popular taste, and no doubt affected individual responses to Shakespeare. But there remained in mid-nineteenth-century Leicester a popular enthusiasm for Shakespeare and Shakespearean acting which defied institutional containment and was considerably more widespread than the intense autodidactic culture represented by Thomas Cooper.

NOTES

1 The history of the Theatre Royal, Leicester is discussed from an architectural point of view in Richard Leacroft, 'The Theatre Royal, Leicester, 1836–1958', *Transactions of the Leicestershire Archaeological and Historical Society*, 34 (1958). For the history of its management and standing in the town, see Jeremy Crump, 'Patronage, Pleasure and Profit: A Study of the Theatre Royal, Leicester 1847–1900', *Theatre Notebook*, 38.2 (1984), 77–87.

2 Examples of the seal are to be found among the Theatre Company's papers in the Public Record Office, BT 41/354/2023.

3 Stevenson, 1864; *Leicester Domestic Mission Annual Reports*, 1846–73. On Dare, see also Jack Simmons, 'A Victorian Social Worker: Joseph Dare and the Leicester Domestic Mission', *Transactions of the Leicestershire Archaeological and Historical Society*, 47 (1971). Page Hopps's views are given in a sermon reported in *Leicester Chronicle*, 23 Feb. 1878. On Windley, see Thomas Windley, 'The Advances in the Provision of Higher Recreative Amusements', *Leicester Commemorative Exhibition Catalogue*, Leicester, 1897.

4 This presumably reflects Dare's antipathy to the Roman Catholicism of the small, but, in his view, all-too-influential Irish community in Leicester. Information about the Shakespeare celebrations is drawn from *Leicester Domestic Mission Annual Reports*, 1848, 1852, 1864 and 1868, and from *Leicester Chronicle*, Apr./May 1853 *passim*.

Charles Dillon: A Provincial Tragedian

KATHLEEN BARKER

NATURE abhors a vacuum, as much in the theatre as elsewhere. Complain as provincial managers might, and did, about the star system, by the middle of the nineteenth century they were so dependent upon it that when the supply of London stars, especially performers of the so-called 'legitimate drama', fell off sharply, it was essential to find substitutes. Concurrently, many aspiring players discovered that the opportunities of engagement at a major theatre in London were as restricted as ever, despite the passing of the Licensing Act, and that careers were more readily built outside the capital. And so, out of common need, developed the Provincial Tragedian.

By no means all of them came of theatrical stock: Barry Sullivan, G. V. Brooke and George Melville, for example, seem to have been the first of their families to take to the stage. But, given the strength of familial tradition within the Victorian theatre, it is not surprising that many were descendants of actors. Charles Pitt and Mary Scott-Siddons were cases in point; so also was Charles James Dillon, whose career may be taken in many respects as typical of a phenomenon which lasted effectively less than thirty years, but which during that time was a major factor in the survival, and later revival, of the theatre outside London.

Charles Dillon was born at Diss in 1819 of theatrical parents called Church; he took the surname of Dillon when his mother transferred her allegiance to Arthur Yates Dillon, successively minor actor, dog-trainer and theatrical agent. From at latest the age of nine, his ambience was the fringe theatres of London, in which his parents played; he is credibly said to have stage-managed for John Douglass at the Westminster in Tothill Street when only fourteen or fifteen.

It was most usual for the fortunate aspiring tragedian to be taken up by a provincial management and, having secured a local following, to be employed to lead in those revivals which it was hoped would establish the respectability of the theatre concerned. Sullivan, Brooke and Melville all took this route. Less typical, though by no means unique, was Charles Dillon's career, made in the minor theatres of London (principally the City of London and the Marylebone) between 1835 and 1845. His grounding over this formative decade was thus primarily in melodrama, whether original, adapted or translated – indeed, he contributed a substantial number of such hack works himself; Shakespeare was for benefits or for stars.

There was consequently imprinted on Dillon's theatrical persona a lasting ambivalence in choice of repertoire; to the end of his life, *Don Caesar de Bazan* and *The Three Musketeers* were as regular a part of his programme as *Othello* and *Macbeth*. On the one hand this left him open to the charge of being 'merely' a melodramatic actor, but on the other it meant perhaps that he was more receptive than most to the possibility of fresh vehicles, in Shakespeare or in new plays.

Some of the youthful Shakespearean parts Dillon did have a chance to essay in the Minors were Bassanio, Romeo and, of course, Hamlet. At the Marylebone, according to an unidentified cutting in the Theatre Museum, 'in some of his scenes he quite astonished the audience'. But for a real opportunity he had to go to the provinces, in a quasi-managerial venture in Leicester during the autumn of 1841. Here he played Lear (at the age of twenty-two), Hamlet and Richard III, as well as producing three of his own pieces. In Shakespeare, not uniquely, the supporting company was totally inadequate. 'There, really, is no-one to second Mr Dillon', said the *Leicester Journal* (8 Oct. 1841). Nevertheless, the personal success, and the responsibility, must have whetted the actor's ambition.

Marriage to Clara Conquest, stepdaughter of Benjamin Conquest, then of the Garrick Theatre, doubtless encouraged this ambition; from 1844 onwards she joined him in several managerial essays in Nottingham and Windsor, in between London seasons. In mid-September 1845 Charles joined a travelling company headed by T. D. Davenport and his ex-Infant Phenomenon daughter Jean, in Holland. Though brief, the engagement gave Dillon the chance of playing a sequence of juvenile leads in Shakespeare, Sheridan and Sheridan Knowles, a good notice in the *Nieuwe Amsterdamsche Courant* (25 Sept. 1845) and an excuse to bill himself later as 'from the Continental theatres'.

After further ventures at Windsor, and officially stage-managing for David Prince Miller at the Glasgow Adelphi, Dillon returned briefly to the Marylebone at Easter 1846, but this seems to have been the point at which, according to various biographical notices, he

resolved to leave London, and return no more till he had starred successfully in every city and town of any importance in Great Britain; and by these Provincial triumphs reach the highest point in his profession. (*Era*, 25 June 1881)

Dillon had already had a taste of being his own master, and he may well have felt he had grown out of the theatre of the London Minors, which nevertheless had influenced him more than he then realised. It is very noticeable that, when eventually he made a name in the London West End, biographical accounts generally ignored his earlier appearances in the capital.

In pursuit of his aim, therefore, though he did not turn down starring engagements, usually with his wife, Dillon spent most of the next six years as a provincial manager in the northern and eastern areas of England, where a number of sizeable towns were open to bids. Sheffield, Wolverhampton, Hull and Norwich occupied him for most of this period.

In all these towns Dillon was well received, but in Sheffield in particular he became the idol of the pit and gallery. For such an audience the fare had to be varied, classical revivals being spiced with the repertoire of the Marylebone. But the overall support of the Sheffield public, and a gradual improvement in the box attendance, encouraged Dillon to produce *The Tempest*, as what he called on the playbill '*a crowning effort* to the close of a *most successful season*'. Ariel was the popular singing actress Emily Grant, whose prompt-book is in the Shakespeare Centre at Stratford and shows a creditably faithful text. The scenic effects, announced the playbill, were lavish and complicated; but they were decidedly erratic in their working, and *The Tempest* ran only five nights. The effort is, however, typical of the need felt by provincial managers to promote respectability by elaborate productions of Shakespeare.

At this stage of his career Dillon's greatest assets were well summarised by the Sheffield *Iris* in a notice of 15 October 1846: 'a well formed and elastic figure, a varied and melodious voice, and his action . . . always round and unconstrained'. In the great Shakespearean parts he was naturally uneven as yet, though allowances must be made for the stress of directing actors unaccustomed to playing in the classics – he had once, for example, to prompt Horatio throughout their important scene in Act 1 of *Hamlet*. But already there can be found tributes to his 'originality', for example in his Richard III, which part he clearly played in a less intensely villainous manner than was the convention. The *Iris* notice quoted above describes how

the personator threw over [the part] the colouring of a disposition, which could smile, and smile, and murder while it smiled, in a manner which evinced the careful analyzer and the successful illustrator.

In the summer of 1849 Dillon had his first engagement at the Queen's, Manchester, and took a lease of the theatre in June 1850, coupling it with a renewal of management at the Sheffield Theatre Royal. February 1851 saw the production, first in Sheffield and three days later in Manchester, of the drama with which his name was ever after primarily associated: the adaptation by Charles Webb of Dennery and Fournier's *Paillasse* under the title of *Belphegor the Mountebank*. The *Manchester Examiner*, which normally ignored the lowly Queen's, sent a representative, who to his surprise found that 'with situations affording scope for rant and exaggeration, he [i.e. Dillon] never stepped beyond the limits of nature and good taste' (22 Feb. 1851).

But Clara Dillon's health was proving precarious; Dillon himself collapsed in the summer of 1850, and by the end of 1851 these factors, combined with a notorious carelessness in business matters, moved the Manchester correspondent of the *Era* to adjudge that Dillon 'is not exactly fit for management; that he would find it more lucrative to be a leading actor than a manager'. But as an actor,

In domestic tragedy – call it melo-drama if you list – few men can approach Dillon. He touches the heart, moves the sensibilities, seizes opportune moments to hit off some every day action, which at once strikes the spectator as natural and truthful, and makes the auditor deeply sympathise with the character so vividly presented before him. Dillon is truly the actor for the people.   (*Era*, 14 Dec. 1851)

That final sentence might well be the proud epitaph for the whole hardworking race of provincial tragedians: truly actors for the people.

In July 1852 Dillon leased the Queen's Theatre, Dublin, managing it, with various absences to star in England, till November of the following year. Like the Queen's in Manchester, it was the city's secondary theatre, in competition with a Theatre Royal, but for the first year Dillon's management was successful, if not particularly innovative. Its greatest historical interest lies in the engagement as principal low comedian of J. L. Toole, whom Dillon had seen in amateur theatricals at the Walworth Institute.

Again, however, Dillon seems to have over-extended himself in his first season; for much of the second, he was away 'starring', and eventually, on 6 November 1854, he had to apply under the Insolvent Debtors Protection Act. Under that protection, he returned to engagements in his old stamping grounds – Sheffield, Wolverhampton, Hull, the Queen's in Manchester – with one atypical foray to Bath and Bristol in 1855. This was where the young Marie Wilton played Henri to his Belphegor so appealingly that Dillon promised her: 'If ever I have a London theatre I shall give you an engagement' (Bancroft, 1904, vol. 1 pp. 32–3).

By this time, despite bankruptcy (which few actor–managers seem to have escaped), Dillon was gaining confidence in himself as a classical actor, this being reflected in the almost complete dropping of the lesser melodramas from his repertoire. Everywhere, however, *Belphegor* continued the greatest attraction: by the end of February 1855 he had played it nearly 550 times. The Sheffield *Iris* (28 Feb. 1855) declared:

The provinces have no such other actor as Mr Dillon, and we shall be very much out in our calculations if he does not ere long occupy a position in the metropolis second to no member of the theatrical profession.

It was to be another year before this prophecy was tested – a year mainly spent in Dillon's favourite Sheffield, but this time without his usual success. He had to meet an increased rent; the supporting company which Arthur Dillon had engaged on his stepson's behalf was of deplorable standard, and the additional tenancy of the minor theatre in Sheffield, the Adelphi, was a further drain on his resources. Well might the *Sheffield Daily Telegraph* (8 Apr. 1856) echo Manchester in assigning his failure to the fact that 'he is not adapted for the drudging detail necessary in so peculiar a speculation as a theatre'.

Playing almost nightly, Dillon had again to enlarge his stock of characters, alternating Bulwer Lytton, Shakespeare and *Louis XI* with *The Wrecker's Daughter*, *The Black Doctor*, and, of course, *Belphegor*. This led to a dilemma faced by almost every leading actor of the period, including Macready and Charles Kean: that success in melodrama led to prejudice against acceptance as a 'legitimate' actor. 'Veritas', writing in the *Sheffield Free Press* (17 Nov. 1855), thought this unjust:

To be a successful melo-dramatic delineator, the actor must possess good mental power, force of action, and spirit; be a good reader, and also gifted by nature with a well-formed face and figure. Now, if such are the requisites for effectively displaying melo-drama, what more, we will ask, is required for *Macbeth*, a Shakespearian character?

Of this prejudice Dillon was well aware. When eventually he appeared in London, at Sadler's Wells in May 1856, it was in *Belphegor*. He is said later to have expressed regret that he had not opened in *Othello*, for his success in *Belphegor* 'was so great it overshadowed him in other characters'.[1] But there is little doubt that the choice was right; in Shakespeare he would have had to face current competition from Charles Kean and Phelps.

The success of *Belphegor* was tremendous, with splendid notices from critics as influential as those of *The Times* and the *Athenaeum*. A fortnight's engagement was prolonged for two weeks more, enabling Dillon to show his abilities in a greater variety of parts, though still not in

Shakespeare. Before the month was over, it was announced that Dillon was to lease the Lyceum Theatre, with the backing of his stepfather-in-law Ben Conquest.

Charles Dillon opened the Lyceum on 15 September 1856 with *Belphegor*, followed by a new extravaganza by William Brough, *Perdita; or, The Royal Milkmaid*, which burlesqued Charles Kean's production of *A Winter's Tale*. In the company were Marie Wilton (in fulfilment of Dillon's earlier promise) and J. L. Toole, who established their reputations during this season.

For the first two months almost all Dillon's vehicles were essentially melodramatic, except for a new five-act play by Westland Marston, *A Life's Ransom*; then at the end of November came *Othello*. The *Athenaeum* (6 Dec. 1856), in a detailed analysis of the 'temptation scene', makes it clear that Dillon was capable of very careful, indeed meticulous, building up of character, and provides evidence of those alternations of mood within a scene which were so often to be remarked on as a feature of his acting. *Hamlet* was staged in mid-March, though it has to be said that the ghost effects attracted more attention than Dillon's performance; in Hamlet's scene with Gertrude 'the spirit of his father occupies one of the pictures in the tapestry, which is transparent, and passes along the back of the whole scene until he reaches the portal' (*Athenaeum*, 28 Mar. 1857), which must have provided quite a *frisson*.

Unfortunately, at the end of an apparently triumphant season everything began to go amiss. Dillon was under contract to George Webster to return to Sadler's Wells but was persuaded to take the company to Drury Lane for a week instead; Webster promptly took him to court. When Dillon did play at the Wells, at the end of May, because of ill health and for other causes the engagement turned into a shambles.[2] What should have been a triumphant reappearance in Sheffield at the Surrey Music Hall (both regular theatres being closed) was blocked by the magistrates. Worst of all, the summer opera season at the Lyceum was so long extended that Dillon was unable to regain possession till Christmas, when he was immediately faced with major expenditure on a new Christmas extravaganza.

Two more new plays – *Lovers' Amazements*, by the veteran Leigh Hunt, and another shorter piece by Westland Marston, *A Hard Struggle* – were quickly introduced. The latter brought an enthusiastic tribute to Dillon's acting from Charles Dickens, which the actor was often to quote proudly in his advertisements (Marston, 1888, vol. 2, p. 185; Pascoe, 1880, pp. 119–25). To put more substance into the programme, and quite certainly to capitalise on her drawing power, Dillon engaged Helen Faucit in mid-

February, primarily to play Lady Macbeth to his Macbeth. By now in desperate straits, Dillon took on a parallel engagement at the Standard, sometimes playing both theatres the same night. Nevertheless the season collapsed on 22 March, Dillon forfeiting his deposit of over £1000 for surrendering the lease before the expiry date, and the first hearing of his bankruptcy was on 23 April, an ironic date for a Shakespearean actor. The *Era* (28 Mar. 1858) summed up, fairly enough: 'Mr Dillon has had all the elements of success, but they have lacked judicious combination.'

This sad ending was, it has to be said, the pattern for most provincial tragedians attempting theatrical management in London. It was to happen to Barry Sullivan at the Holborn, and James Anderson and John Coleman at Drury Lane. It is questionable whether even Henry Irving would have succeeded had not the Batemans established the enterprise first.

So now it was back to touring, usually with members of the London company, including Barrett as acting manager, Calhaem in supporting roles and Eliza Webb, Charles Webb's daughter, who replaced Marie Wilton in the second Lyceum season, and on tour often substituted for an ailing Clara Dillon – eventually both on stage and off. By the autumn of 1859 Dillon's marriage had broken down.

As early as July 1858 Dillon had advertised his intention of touring abroad, but any such plans were dropped when E. T. Smith offered him an engagement at Drury Lane in February 1860, which unfortunately turned out totally unproductive. Dillon was at an impasse in his career, and he may have felt an overseas tour now to be the only way forward.

However, when eventually Charles Dillon followed the example of so many provincial stars in setting off for America, it seems to have been totally on impulse, with no pre-planning, and could hardly have been worse timed. Surely no one but he would have taken ship for New York in the middle of winter, without a single advance contact, and with a Civil War in imminent prospect at his destination. To add, undeservedly, to all this, he broke his ankle during a terrible storm on the passage out, and was still limping when he arrived in New York early in January 1861.

Had Dillon not been befriended by Sam Cowell and his wife, he would have had to return with his tail between his legs – indeed, he was twice on the verge of doing so; but Cowell got him a one-night stand at the Winter Gardens, where Edwin Booth was just making his name, and, despite a blizzard on the evening of performance, enough spectators and critics arrived to make *Belphegor* an artistic, if not a financial, success (Disher, 1934, pp. 243–5).

After a few months on the eastern seaboard, where his 'naturalism' was well received, he moved over the border to Canada. Here he encountered again Eliza Webb, who had taken an engagement at the Theatre Royal in Montreal; soon they were touring as 'Mr and Mrs Charles Dillon'.

During the next five and a half years Charles and Eliza worked their passage halfway round the world and back again. It was a gruelling experience, in which elements both human and natural seemed often to be in league against the provincial tragedian abroad. In California, where they spent eight months, Dillon was literally washed out of his theatres several times by flash floods; in Tasmania and New Zealand numerous performances were 'rained off'; takings were affected by trade depression, especially in New Zealand; and an engagement at Valparaiso was cancelled when the Spanish fleet arrived to blockade the port. Managements were unreliable, sometimes non-existent.

Prolonged stays in towns of limited population meant the introduction of an exceptionally wide range of plays. Some of these, especially in San Francisco, Melbourne and Sydney, were melodramatic vehicles of twenty-five years back, but they also included Marston's *Strathmore*, Byron's *Manfred* and *Sardanapalus* and several new Shakespearean parts. *A Midsummer Night's Dream* was given in May 1864 at the Prince of Wales's, Sydney, allegedly its 'First night in the Colonies', Dillon playing Bottom, in which he was described by the *Morning Herald* (7 May 1864) as 'inimitably good'. In July he produced a condensed version of *Timon of Athens*, which he repeated in Dunedin, New Zealand, with some success, though his rendering of Timon was criticised by the *Otago Daily Times* (8 June 1865) as being 'one sustained rage throughout'. One of Dillon's last parts in New Zealand was Falstaff in *1 Henry IV*, in which he was excellently reviewed. It was in the course of this tour, too, that Dillon revived and extensively worked on the role of King Lear.

Eventually, at the beginning of December 1865 Charles and Eliza reached New York, where Eliza died of typhoid fever on 12th. Dillon himself was seriously ill, probably from the same cause, but early in January began another American and Canadian tour.

This time he did secure New York engagements: first at Niblo's for two and a half weeks in May, playing safe with *Belphegor*, and later at the Broadway Theatre in November 1866. Here he made his major bid in *King Lear*, receiving an excellent notice from the *New York Herald* (6 Nov. 1866):

Through all the transitions of the unhappy King, from credulous trust and rash aversion to rage, madness, partial sanity and death, the identity of the king was never sacrificed to the actor; it was Lear who spoke and moved in every scene, not Dillon.

It has to be said that not all critics were so favourable; 'Bayard' in *Wilkes'*

Spirit of the Times (17 Nov. 1866) claimed to find the mannerisms of Belphegor intruding unsuitably into Lear.

When finally Dillon returned to England in March 1867, he still had fourteen years' acting before him. From the point of view of public prestige they provided him with little advance in his profession: he had been too long away, though he was still enthusiastically received in the provinces.

What most distinguished Dillon in this period, and made him remarkable among provincial tragedians, was his continuous search for new characters. Shortly after his return to England he revived *Timon of Athens* in his cut version, though this met with little success and was soon dropped; a more successful Shakespearean 'novelty' was a revival in 1872 of *Coriolanus* of which the prompt-book is in the Birmingham Shakespeare Library. W. C. Day adapted *The Bridal* for him; Joseph Fox and W. G. Wills provided new plays.

Dillon did have a number of London opportunities after his return, the first of which was an engagement at Sadler's Wells in February 1868. He had played Belphegor at the Theatre Royal Glasgow on the evening of Saturday, 15 February, and on Monday he opened in Islington, with an almost entirely strange company, as King Lear. This behaviour, which would be unimaginable today, can, however, be paralleled many times: John Coleman relates how he played Macbeth to Isabella Glyn's Lady in Newcastle without rehearsal on one occasion (Coleman, 1904, vol. 2, p. 567); George Melville stepped from the Edinburgh coach into the Theatre Royal Bristol ready to go on stage as Hamlet. All of which is eloquent testimony to the efficiency of the stylisation accepted in the production of Shakespeare, if not to the artistry achieved.

A year later Dillon appeared at Drury Lane, alternating leading parts with Samuel Phelps in *Macbeth*, *The School for Scandal*, *Othello* and *1 Henry IV*, the last of which enabled him to play Falstaff again. The *Illustrated London News* (6 Mar. 1869) flatteringly saw the two actors as 'now at the head of their profession' – Phelps outstanding for his careful characterisation but now somewhat monotonous of speech, Dillon at the other extreme:

Not a speech, not a sentimer.r, not a line, but shows an immense amount of study; and the meaning is brought out by all the resources of the histrionic art – the emphasis, the pause, the intonation in all its varieties of modulation and falsetto, whatever can convey the significance of the poet's words to the audience, are all put into requisition, and his interpretation, both of the poetry and the passion, is managed with exquisite skill and consummate power.

It is easy to imagine how this could also be seen as merely stagey and artificial.

Dillon's last two London appearances were somewhat unexpected: two months playing Manfred in Byron's piece of *diablerie* at the Princess's in the late summer of 1873, and an engagement in *A Winter's Tale* at Drury Lane in the autumn of 1878. Despite the fact that he had never acted Leontes before, Dillon played in Wolverhampton up to Wednesday, 25 September and on the following Saturday opened at the Lane. It is tempting to speculate how well Dillon might have played the part had the opportunity come earlier. Tackling it at the age of sixty, with minimal rehearsal, it is hardly surprising that he gave an uneven performance: *The Times* (30 Sept. 1878) tactfully put it that 'his prolonged absence from the more fastidious audiences has apparently told on his style'. Other reviewers were kinder, but the *Illustrated Sporting & Dramatic News* fairly summed up the reasons why it was now too late for Dillon to re-establish himself as a major star; that changes in dramatic fashion had made his method of Shakespearean interpretation seem 'somewhat antiquated' to the new generation (23 Nov. 1878).

The last years were sad. Between and after the London engagements there was continual and exhausting touring in the provinces, where those same changes in dramatic fashion, and in internal organisation, were increasingly tending to isolate provincial tragedians like Dillon. In the larger cities, the best managers were still able to mount their own Shakespearean productions in the Charles Kean manner, as Saker did in Liverpool; but in the smaller towns, so far as the remaining stock companies were concerned, Shakespeare and the 'Macready plays' were often restricted to one-off benefit performances.

Thus it became more and more necessary for Dillon, if he was to secure an adequate number and sequence of dates, to tour his own company – a business responsibility of which he became less and less capable. More and more, too, the notices betray how specialised, not to say unfashionable, the repertoire of the remaining provincial tragedians was becoming, despite Dillon's genuine attempts to revive unusual classics and sponsor new dramas. Repeatedly the line taken by the press is to stress the rare opportunity of seeing legitimate plays represented by one of the grand old elocutionary school: 'Superfluous lags the veteran on the stage.'

Dillon simply could not afford to retire, and went on doing the round with his third and last partner, Bella Mortimer, a provincial actress with whom he had played at George Stanley's Tyne Theatre in Newcastle. His itinerary shows him acting in smaller and smaller towns, in areas where he had never before played (such as Wiltshire), or had not visited for many years (such as East Anglia and Tyneside). It was at Hawick on the Borders that he collapsed and died in the street on 24 June 1881, his last performance, fittingly, having been Othello the previous evening.

Why did Dillon, like so many other provincial tragedians, fail to establish himself at the top of his profession? In his particular case, so many people comment on his cheerful negligence over business detail, both as manager and star, that it is impossible to ignore this as a major factor. The quality of his acting is less easy to evaluate. It is rather too simplistic to say, as Westland Marston does, that 'Mr Charles Dillon was an actor of great emotional gifts, but very deficient in intellectual ones' (1888, vol. 2, p. 190). It is true that he seems to have been an intuitive rather than a ratiocinative actor throughout his career; and he was probably conditioned to seeing the human emotions expressed in even the greatest plays through the medium of gaslight rather than of natural light. But he was far from unintelligent; he worked steadily at his major roles, as notices repeatedly testify, while his little pamphlet published in the 1870s, *A Slight Analysis of the Character of Hamlet*,[3] is clearly the work of a thinking man tempered by the experience of a practical actor.

Like the great majority of provincial tragedians, Dillon was not a 'pictorial' actor – naturally enough, given the conditions of his career. It was not yet possible to tour quantities of scenery, or large numbers of 'auxiliaries' – it was the latter difficulty which restricted the success of his Coriolanus. W. C. Day's vignette, 'Coriolanus at the Sea-Side', in *Behind the Footlights* (1885, pp. 31–47), mischievously illustrates the potential for disaster in this area. The provincial tragedian had to rely on personal charisma, above all on his voice, on 'elocution'.

The grand manner of a Kemble was not natural to Dillon, though there are enough approving comments on his curse in *King Lear* and on his Coriolanus to suggest that he could rise to a very near approximation; but pathos he had in abundance, and appreciation of the lights and shades of character. He may sometimes have been wrongheaded in his interpretations, but he was never dull. Moreover, in no single notice of all the hundreds I have read, is he ever accused, even in his last days, of 'walking through' a performance – which cannot be said of all his contemporaries.

Simply because, by definition, the provincial tragedians failed to make a permanent name in London, they should not be written off as unimportant. They played a vital part in the resurgence of the regional theatre in the 1850s and early 1860s; and when the Indian summer faded, and the stock companies gave way to the ever-increasing flood of touring attractions, the 'legitimate' would have had a poor showing indeed in the provinces had it not been for actresses like Alice Marriott, Isabella Glyn and Mary Scott-Siddons, and actors like James Bennett, Sullivan, Henry Loraine, George Melville, Walter Montgomery and Charles Dillon.

By 1880 provincial tragedians were an almost extinct breed. Of Barry Sullivan's death in 1888 W. J. Lawrence writes: 'the people were no longer able to raise the old cry "The King is dead; long live the King," – for, sooth to say, the dynasty had gone its way for ever with the potentate' (1893, p. 9).

But that was not quite true: the spirit of Sullivan, of Dillon, and of a dozen more, lived on in such companies as those led by Frank Benson, Edward Compton and the Tearle cousins. They were actors the British theatre should be proud to have on its roll.

NOTES

1 Letter from Algernon Cooper to *Era*, 30 July 1881.
2 See particularly *Era*, 26 and 31 May 1857.
3 This little pamphlet is undated, but it includes a reprint of a talk by George Dawson published in the *Birmingham Morning News*, which dates it between 1871 and 1876.

Select Bibliography

References to printed books are on the author-date system. References to newspapers, magazines, learned journals, unpublished theses and manuscript sources are given in the text or the footnotes accompanying each chapter.

Ackermann, R. *Microcosm of London*, London, 1808–11.

Agate, James. *Brief Chronicles*, London, 1943.

Albery, James. *The Dramatic Works of James Albery*, ed. Wyndham Albery, London, 1939.

Allaway, A. J. *Vaughan College, Leicester*, Leicester, 1962.

Allen, Shirley. *Samuel Phelps and Sadler's Wells Theatre*, Middleton, Ct. 1971.

Archer, Frank. *An Actor's Notebook*, London, 1912.

Archer, William. *Masks or Faces*, London, 1888; repr. New York, 1957.

   The Old Drama and the New, London, 1923.

Art Treasures Examiner, The, Manchester, 1857.

Ashton, Geoffrey. *Shakespeare's Heroines in the Nineteenth Century*, Buxton, 1980.

Badawi, M. M. *Coleridge: Critic of Shakespeare*, Cambridge, 1973.

Baker, Michael. *The Rise of the Victorian Actor*, London, 1978.

Baldensperger, F. *Études d'histoire littéraire*, II, Paris, 1910.

Baldick, Robert. *The Life and Times of Frederick Lemaître*, London, 1959.

Ball, Robert Hamilton. *Shakespeare and the Silent Film*, London, 1968.

Bancroft, Marie and Squire. *Mr and Mrs Bancroft on and off the Stage*, London, 1904.

Barclay, Tom. *Memoirs and Medleys: The Autobiography of a Bottle Washer*, Leicester, 1934.

Baring, Maurice. *Sarah Bernhardt*, London, 1933.

Barker, Kathleen M. D. *Theatre Royal Bristol 1766–1966*, London, 1974.

Barzum, Charles. *Berlioz and his Century*, 3rd edn, Chicago, Ill., 1982.

Bassan, Fernande, and Chevalley, Sylvie. *Alexandre Dumas père à la Comédie-Française*, Paris, 1972.

Beerbohm, Max. *More*, London, 1899.

   Around Theatres, London, 1924.

Benzie, William. *Dr F. J. Furnivall: Victorian Scholar-Adventurer*, Norman, Okla., 1983.

Bernhardt, Sarah. *My Double Life*, London, 1907.

   L'Art du théâtre, Paris, 1923.

Besterman, Theodore, ed. *Voltaire on Shakespeare*, Geneva, 1967.

Biancolli, Louis, ed. *The Opera Reader*, New York, 1953.

Billson, Charles. *Leicester Memories*, Leicester, 1924.

Bingham, Madeleine. *The Great Lover: The Life and Art of Herbert Beerbohm Tree*, London, 1978.

Blanchard, E. L. *The Life and Reminiscences of E. L. Blanchard with Notes from the Diary of Wm. Blanchard*, ed. Clement Scott and Cecil Howard, London, 1891.

Booth, Michael. *English Melodrama*, London, 1965.

  ed. *English Plays of the Nineteenth Century*, London, 1969–76.

  ed. *The Revels History of Drama in English, Volume VII: 1750–1880*, London, 1975.

  Victorian Spectacular Theatre, London, 1981.

Borgerhoff, J.–L. *Le Théâtre anglais à Paris sous la Restauration*, Paris, 1912.

Bouchor, Maurice. *La Tempête*, Paris, 1888.

  Les Chansons de Shakespeare, Paris, 1896.

Bradby, David, James, L., and Sharratt, B., eds. *Performance and Politics in Popular Drama*, Cambridge, 1980.

Bradley, A. C. *Shakespearean Tragedy*, London, 1904; repr. 1961.

Bragaglia, Leonardo. *Shakespeare in Italia*, Rome, 1973.

Brereton, Austin. *'H. B.' and Laurence Irving*, London, 1922.

Briggs, Asa. *Victorian People*, rev. edn, Chicago, Ill. 1955.

  Victorian Cities, London, 1963; repr. 1968.

Briggs, K. M. *The Anatomy of Puck*, London, 1959.

Busi, Anna. *Otello in Italia (1777–1972)*, Bari, 1973.

Calvert, Charles, ed. *The Merchant of Venice*, Manchester, 1871.

Caretti, L., ed. *Il teatro del personaggio*, Rome, 1979.

Carr, Alice Comyns. *Reminiscences*, ed. Eve Adams, London, 1923.

Catalogue of Pictures and Sculptures, Royal Shakespeare Theatre Picture Gallery, 5th edn, Stratford-upon-Avon, 1964.

Catalogue of Pictures, Sketches and Designs, Exhibiting at 29, Castle Street, Edinburgh, being the Majority of the Works of the Late David Scott, RSA, Edinburgh, 1849.

Churchill, Randolph. *Winston S. Churchill*, London, 1967.

Cibber, Theophilus. *The Lives and Characters of the most Eminent Actors and Actresses of Great Britain and Northern Ireland*, London, 1753.

Clark, Kenneth. *The Gothic Revival*, London, 1928.

Cole, J. W. (J. W. Calcraft). *The Life and Theatrical Times of Charles Kean*, London, 1859.

Coleman, John. *Plays and Playwrights I Have Known*, Philadelphia, Pa, 1880.

  Fifty Years of an Actor's Life, London and New York, 1904.

Collier, Constance. *Harlequinade*, London, 1929.

Collier, J. Payne. *The History of English Dramatic Poetry to the Time of Shakespeare; and Annals of the Stage to the Restoration*, London, 1831.

Collison-Morley, L. *Shakespeare in Italy*, London, 1916.

Cook, Dutton. *Nights at the Play*, London, 1883.

Cooke, W. *The Elements of Dramatic Criticism*, London, 1775.

Cooper, Thomas. *The Life of Thomas Cooper*, London, 1872; repr. Leicester, 1971.

Cowell, J. *Thirty Years Passed among the Players in England and America*, New York, 1845.

Craig, Edward Gordon. *Henry Irving*, London, 1930.

Cressonois, Lucien, and Samson, Charles. *Hamlet*, Paris, 1886.

Crinò, A. M. *Le traduzione de Shakespeare in Italia nel settecento*, Rome, 1950.

Crosse, Gordon. *Shakespeare Playgoing 1890–1952*, London, 1953.

Cunnington, C., Willett and Phillis. *Handbook of English Costume in the Sixteenth Century*, 2nd rev. edn, London, 1970.
    Handbook of English Medieval Costume, 2nd rev. edn, London, 1969.
Cuvelier. *Le More de Venise ou Othello, pantomime entremêlée de dialogues*, Paris, 1818.

David, Richard. *Shakespeare in the Theatre*, Cambridge, 1978.
Day, W. C. *Behind the Footlights*, London, 1885.
de La Place, Pierre-Antoine. *Le Théâtre anglois*, London, 1746–9.
de Marly, Diana. *Costume on the Stage 1600–1940*, London, 1982.
de Musset, Alfred. *Lorenzaccio*, ed. Armond d'Artois, Paris, 1898.
de Neuville, Lemercier. *Histoire anecdotique des marionettes modernes*, Paris, 1892.
de Sainte-Beuve, Charles-Augustin. *Causeries de lundi*, 6, Paris, 1853.
de Vigny, Alfred. *Œuvres complètes*, ed. F. Baldensperger, Paris, 1955–8.
Dibdin, James C. *The Annals of the Edinburgh Stage*, Edinburgh, 1888.
Dickins, R. *Forty Years of Shakespeare on the English Stage*, London, 1907.
Dillon, Charles J. *A Slight Analysis of the Character of Hamlet*, n.d.
Disher, M. Willson. *The Last Romantic: Sir John Martin-Harvey*, London, n.d.
    ed. *The Cowells in America*, London, 1934.
Douce, Francis. *Illustrations of Shakespeare, and of Ancient Manners*, London, 1807–8.
Downer, Alan S. *The Eminent Tragedian: William Charles Macready*, Cambridge, Mass., 1966.
Ducis, Jean-François. *Œuvres*, Paris, 1826.
Durian, Hans. *Jocza Savits und die Münchener Shakespearebuhne*, Emsdetten, 1937.

East, Rev. J. *The Pulpit Justified and the Theatre Condemned*, London, 1844a.
    The Theatre – a Discourse on Theatrical Amusement and Dramatic Literature, London, 1844b.
Eliot, T. S. *Murder in the Cathedral*, ed. Nevill Coghill, London, 1965.
Elliston, Robert. Advertisement in *Shakespeare's Tragedy of King Lear, Printed Chiefly from Nahum Tate's Edition, with some Restorations from the Original Text*, London, 1820.
Esher, Viscount, ed. *The Girlhood of Queen Victoria*, London, 1912.

Faucit, Helena Lady Martin. *On Some of Shakespeare's Female Characters*, 4th edn, Edinburgh, 1891.
Fellner, Richard. *Geschichte einer deutschen Musterbuhne*, Stuttgart, 1888.
Field, Kate. *Adelaide Ristori: A Biography*, New York, 1867.
Fitzgerald, Percy. *Henry Irving*, London, 1893.
Fleetwood, Frances. *Conquest*, London, 1953.
Fletcher, George. *Studies of Shakespeare*, London, 1847.
Forbes-Robertson, Johnston. *A Player under Three Reigns*, London, 1925.
Forster, John, and Lewes, George Henry. *Dramatic Essays for the 'Examiner' and 'The Leader'*, London, 1896.
Foulkes, Richard. *The Shakespeare Tercentenary of 1864*, London, 1984.
France, Anatole. *Œuvres complètes*, Paris, 1926.
Friedman, Winifred H. *Boydell's Shakespeare Gallery*, New York, 1976.

G[reen]-A[rmytage], R.N., ed. *The Book of Martin Harvey*, London, 1932.
Ganzel, Dewey. *Fortune and Men's Eyes: The Career of John Payne Collier*, London, 1982.
Gatti, H. *Shakespeare nei teatri Milanese dell'ottocento*, Bari, 1968.

Gaunt, William. *The Pre-Raphaelite Tragedy*, London, 1942.

Geller, G. G. *Sarah Bernhardt*, trans. E. S. G. Potter, London, 1933.

Genée, Rudolf. *Die Entwicklung der scenischen Theaters und die Buhnenreform in Munchen*, Stuttgart, 1889.

Genest, J. *Some Account of the English Stage*, Bath, 1832.

Gielgud, Kate. *A Victorian Playgoer*, ed. Muriel St. Clare Byrne, London, 1980.

Gilbert, W. S. *Original Plays*, Second Series, London, 1881; Third Series, London, repr. 1922.

Gilman, Margaret. *Othello in France*, Paris, 1925.

Glasstone, Victor. *Victorian and Edwardian Theatres*, London, 1975.

Goethe, J. W. *Werke*, Hamburg, n.d.

Goode, John, ed. *The Air of Reality: New Essays on Henry James*, London, 1972.

Gould, F. J. *History of the Leicester Secular Society*, Leicester, 1900.

Granger, J. *A Bibliographical History of England from Egbert the Great to the Revolution*, 4th edn, London, 1804.

Granville-Barker, Harley. *Prefaces to Shakespeare*, London, 1930.

Graves, Algernon, comp. *The Royal Academy of Arts: A Complete Dictionary of Contributors and their Work from its Foundation in 1769 to 1904*, London, 1905–6; repr. 1970.

Gray, John M. *David Scott, R. S. A. and his Works with a Catalogue of his Paintings, Engravings and Designs*, Edinburgh, 1884.

Green, Frederick. *Literary Ideas in 18th-Century France (olim Minuet)*, 1935; repr. New York, 1966.

Grove, George. *Dictionary of Music and Musicians*, London, 1879–89.

Hare, A. *Theatre Royal Bath: The Orchard Street Calendar*, Bath, 1977.
  George Frederick Cooke: The Actor and the Man, London, 1980.

Hartnoll, Phyllis ed. *Shakespeare in Music*, London, 1964.

Hazlitt, William. *Complete Works of Hazlitt*, ed. P. P. Howe, London, 1930.

Hedgcock, Frank A. *Garrick and his French Friends*, 1912; repr. New York, 1969.

Herbert, D., ed. *The Operas of Benjamin Britten*, London, 1979.

Hertz, Henrik. *King René's Daughter: A Danish Lyrical Drama*, trans. Theodore Martin, London, 1850.

Hiatt, Charles. *Ellen Terry and her Impersonations*, London, 1898.

Hill, John. *The Actor*, London, 1750; 2nd edn, 1755.

Hillebrand, H. *Edmund Kean*, New York, 1933.

Hingston, E. P. *Adelaide Ristori*, London, 1856.

Hodges, C. Walter. *The Globe Restored*, 2nd edn, London, 1968.

Hogan, Charles Beecher. *Shakespeare in the Theatre 1701–1800*, Oxford, 1952–7.

Holbrook, Catherine. *Memoirs of an Actress*, London, 1807.

Holmes, M. R. *Stage Costumes and Accessories in the London Museum*, London, 1968.

Hood, Thomas. *The Poetical Works of Thomas Hood*, Chandos Edition, London, n.d.

Horn-Monval, M. *Répertoire bibliographique des traductions et adaptations françaises du théâtre étranger du XVe siècle à nos jours*, V, Paris, 1963.

Horne, R. H. *A New Spirit of the Age*, London, 1844.

Houghton, Walter E. *The Victorian Frame of Mind 1830–1870*, New Haven and London, 1957.

Houseman, John. *Run-Through*, New York, 1972.

Hughes, Alan. *Henry Irving, Shakespearean*, Cambridge, 1981.

Hunt, W. Holman. *Pre-Raphaelitism and the Pre-Raphaelite Brotherhood*, London, 1905; 2nd edn, 1913.

Hunter, James. *The Story of Hamlet Condensed and Interspersed with the Text of Shakespeare's Tragedy in Three Parts*, Leicester, 1866.

Immermann, Karl. *Werke*, ed. Benno von Wiese, Frankfurt, 1971.

Irving, Henry. *The Drama: Addresses*, London, 1893.

    ed. with F. A. Marshall *The Henry Irving Shakespeare*, London, 1892.

Irving, H. B. *The Life of Judge Jeffreys*, New York, 1899.

    Studies of French Criminals of the Nineteenth Century, London, 1901.

    Occasional Papers, Dramatic and Historical, London, 1906.

    ed. *Hamlet As Arranged for the Stage*, London, 1909.

    Some Thoughts on 'Hamlet', Sydney, 1911a.

    The Trial of Franz Muller, Toronto, 1911b.

    The Trial of Mrs. Maybrick, Philadelphia, Pa, 1912.

    A Book of Remarkable Criminals, New York, 1918.

    The Trial of the Wainwrights, Toronto, 1920.

    Last Studies in Criminology, London, 1921.

Irving, Laurence. *Henry Irving*, London, 1951.

    The Successors, London, 1967.

    The Precarious Crust, London, 1971.

Irwin, David and Francina. *Scottish Painters At Home and Abroad 1700–1900*, London, 1975.

Jacobs, Arthur. *Arthur Sullivan, A Victorian Musician*, London, 1984.

James, Henry. *The Scenic Art*, ed. A. Wade, London, 1949.

Jameson, Mrs (Anna Brownell). *Characteristics of Women, Moral, Poetical and Historical*, 2nd edn, London, 1833.

    Shakspeares Women, London, 1879.

Jarro. *Vita Aneddotica di Tommaso Salvini*, Florence, 1908.

Joannidès, A. *La Comédie-Française de 1680 à 1900*, 1901; repr. Geneva, 1970.

    Relevé des representations de Mounet-Sully à la Comédie-Française, Paris, 1917.

Jones, Henry Arthur. *The Shadow of Henry Irving*, London, 1931.

Jusserand, J. J. *Shakespeare en France sous l'Ancien Régime*, Paris, 1898.

Kean, Charles, ed. *King Lear by William Shakespeare Arranged for Representation . . . by Charles Kean*, London, 1855; ed. G. K. Hunter, 1970.

    Shakespeare's Play of King Richard II Arranged for Representation by Charles Kean, London, 1857; ed. D. Rittenhouse, 1970.

Kelly, F. M. *Shakespearian Costume for Stage and Screen*, London, 1938; rev. edn, 1970.

Kerslake, J. F. *Catalogue of Theatrical Portraits in London Public Collections*, London, 1961.

Kindermann, Heinz. *Theatergeschichte Europas*, Salzburg, 1964.

Knepler, Henry. *The Gilded Stage*, London, 1968.

Knight, Charles. *Old England*, London, 1845–6.

Knight G. Wilson. *Shakespearian Production*, London, 1964.

Knight, Joseph. *Theatrical Notes*, London, 1893.

Knowles, James Sheridan. *The Elocutionist, A Collection of Pieces in Prose and Verse*, 9th edn, Belfast, 1832.

    The Dramatic Works of James Sheridan Knowles, Calcutta, 1838.

    The Dramatic Works of James Sheridan Knowles, London, 1856.

    The Dramatic Works of James Sheridan Knowles, ed. Emma Knowles, London, 1873–4.

Knowles, James Sheridan. *Lectures on Dramatic Literature*, London, 1873.
Knowles, Richard Brinsley. *The Life of James Sheridan Knowles*, London, 1872.
Koller, Ann Marie. *The Theatre Duke: George II of Saxe-Meiningen and the German Stage*, Stamford, Ill., 1984.
Kott, Jan. *Shakespeare Our Contemporary*, London, 1964.

Lacroix, Jules. *Le Roi Lear*, Paris, 1868.
Lamb, Charles. *The Works of Charles and Mary Lamb*, ed. E. V. Lucas, London, 1903–5.
Lamb, Margaret. *'Antony and Cleopatra' on the English Stage*, London, 1980.
Langhans, Edward A. *Restoration Promptbooks*, Urbana, Ill., 1981.
Laroche, Benjamin. *Œuvres complètes*, Paris, 1844.
Lawrence, W. J. *Life of Gustavus Vaughan Brooke*, Belfast, 1892.
    Barry Sullivan, London 1934.
    Old Theatre Days and Ways, London, 1935.
Leacroft, Richard and Helen. *Theatre and Playhouse: An Illustrated Survey of Theatre Building from Ancient Greece to the Present Day*, London, 1984.
Leathes, Victor. *British Entertainers in France*, Toronto, 1959.
Leech, Clifford, and Craik, T. W., eds. *The Revels of History of Drama in English, Volume VI: 1750–1880*, London, 1975.
Leicester Domestic Mission Annual Reports, Leicester, 1846–73.
Lemaître, Jules. *Impressions du théâtre*, 4, Paris, 1890.
Lewes, G. H. *On Actors and the Art of Acting*, London, 1875; repr. New York, 1952.
LeWinter, Oswald, ed. *Shakespeare in Europe*, London, 1970.
Lodge, Edmund. *Portraits of Illustrious Personages of Great Britain*, London, 1825–34.
Lombroso and Ferri. *The Descent of Man*, 2nd edn, London, 1881.

Maas, Jeremy. *Victorian Painters*, London, 1969.
Macready, William Charles. *Reminiscences, Diary and Letters*, ed. Sir Frederick Pollock, London, 1875 (2 vols.), London, 1876 (1 vol.): ed. William Toynbee, London, 1912, repr. 1969; ed. J. C. Trewin, London, 1967.
Macqueen-Pope, W. *Gaiety, Theatre of Enchantment*, London, 1949.
Malone, Edmond. *Historical Account of the Rise and Progress of the English Stage*, 1790; repr. as vol. 3 in *The Plays and Poems of William Shakespeare, with the Corrections and Illustrations of Various Commentators: Comprehending a Life of the Poet, and an Enlarged History of the Stage by the late Edmond Malone*, ed. J. Boswell, London, 1821.
Mander, Raymond, and Mitchenson, Joe. *Hamlet through the Ages: A Pictorial Record from 1709*, London, 1952.
Manvell, Roger. *Shakespeare and the Film*, London, 1971.
Marcus, Steven. *The Other Victorians*, London, 1966.
Margueritte, Paul. *Le Petit Théâtre*, Paris, 1888.
Marqusee, Michele, ed. *Hamlet*, with 16 lithographs by Eugène Delacroix, New York, 1976.
Marshall, Dorothy. *Fanny Kemble*, London, 1977.
Marston, J. Westland. *Our Recent Actors*, London 1888; repr. 1890.
Martin, Lady (Helena Faucit). *On Some of Shakespeare's Female Characters*, Edinburgh, 1885; 4th edn, 1891.
Martin, Theodore. *Helena Faucit*, London, 1900.
Martineau, Harriet. *Autobiography*, London, 1877.

Select Bibliography

Mason, Edward Tuckerman. *The Othello of Tommaso Salvini*, New York and London, 1890.

Mathews, Brander, ed. *Papers on Acting*, repr. New York, 1958.

Mayer, David, and Scott, Matthew. *Four Bars of 'Agit': Music for Victorian and Edwardian Melodrama*, London, 1983.

Mayhew, Henry. *London Labour and the London Poor*, London, 1861.

Mazer, Cary. *Shakespeare Refashioned: Elizabethan Plays on Edwardian Stages*, Ann Arbor, Mich., 1981.

Meeks, Leslie Howard. *Sheridan Knowles and the Theatre of his Time*, Bloomington, Ind., 1933.

Meisel, Martin. *Realizations*, Princeton, NJ, 1983.

Merchant, W. Moelwyn. *Shakespeare and the Artist*, London, 1959.

Mesmer, Friedrich Anton. *Mesmerism*, intro. Gilbert Frankau, London, 1948.

Minto, W., ed. *Autobiographical Notes of the Life of William Bell Scott H.R.S.A., LL.D.*, London, 1892.

Moncrieff, W. T. *The Lear of Private Life*, 2nd edn, London, 1828.

Moore, G. E. *Principia Ethica*, Cambridge, 1903.

Morley, Henry. *The Journal of a London Playgoer*, London, 1891; ed. M. Booth, Leicester, 1974.

Morgan, A. A. *The Mind of Shakespeare*, London, 1860.

Mounet-Sully. *Souvenirs d'un tragédien*, Paris, 1917.

Murray, Christopher. *Robert William Elliston Manager*, London, 1975.

Nagler, A. M. *A Source Book in Theatrical History*, New York, 1952; repr. 1959.

National Gallery of Scotland Catalogue of Paintings and Sculpture, 51st edn, Edinburgh, 1957.

Nicoll, Allardyce. *A History of Early Nineteenth Century Drama, 1800–50*, Cambridge, 1937.

A History of Late Nineteenth Century Drama 1850–1900, Cambridge, 1946.

Nussell, Heide. *Rekonstruktionen der Shakespeare-Buhne auf dem deutschen Theater*, Cologne, 1967.

Odell, George C. D. *Shakespeare from Betterton to Irving*, New York, 1920; repr. 1966.

O'Donoghue, Freeman. *Catalogue of Engraved British Portraits Preserved in the Department of Prints and Drawings in the British Museum*, London, 1908–25.

Opie, Amelia. *Father and Daughter*, London, 1807.

Oxenford, John, trans. *Conversations of Goethe with Eckermann and Soret*, London, 1850.

Palmer, David, ed. *Writers and Their Background: Tennyson*, London, 1973.

Palmer, John. *Political Characters in Shakespeare's Plays*, London, 1945.

Park, Roy. *Hazlitt and the Spirit of the Age*, Oxford, 1971.

Parris, Leslie, ed. *Pre-Raphaelite Papers*, London, 1984.

Pascoe, C. E. *The Dramatic List*, London, 1880.

Pastore, A., ed. *Shakespeare degli italiano*, Turin, 1950.

Patterson, Alfred Temple. *Radical Leicester*, Leicester, 1954.

Pearson, Hesketh. *Beerbohm Tree: His Life and Laughter*, London, 1956.

Pemberton, J. Edgar. *Ellen Terry and her Sisters*, London, 1902.

Penley, B. S. *The Bath Stage*, London, 1892.

Pevsner, Nikolaus. *Some Architectural Writers of the Nineteenth Century*, Oxford, 1972.

Phelps, W. May, and Forbes-Robertson, J. *The Life and Life-Work of Samuel Phelps*, London, 1886.

Pick, John. *The West End Mismanagement and Snobbery*, Eastbourne, 1983.

Pickering, R. *Reflections upon Theatrical Expressions in Tragedy*, London, 1755.

Pinches, J. H. and R. V. *The Royal Heraldry of England*, London, 1974.

Planché, James Robinson. *History of British Costume*, London, 1834; 3rd edn, 1881.
Oberon, London, [1865?].
Recollections and Reflections, London, 1872; rev. edn. 1901.
A Cyclopaedia of Costume or Dictionary of Dress, London, 1876–9.

Poel, William. *Monthly Letters*, London, 1929.

Reece, Robert. *Perfect Love: A Spectacular Fairy Play*, London, 1871.

Rees, Terence. *Theatre Lighting in the Age of Gas*, London 1978.

Reynold, Ernest. *Early Victorian Drama 1830–1870*, Cambridge, 1936.

Richards, Kenneth, and Thomson, Peter, eds. *Nineteenth Century British Theatre*, London, 1971.

Richardson, Joanna. *Sarah Bernhardt*, London, 1959.

Rinder, Frank, and McKay W. D. *The Royal Scottish Academy, 1826–1916: A Complete List of the Exhibited Works*, Glasgow, 1917.

Ripley, John. *'Julius Caesar' on Stage in England and America 1599–1973*, Cambridge, 1980.

Ristori, Adelaide. *Ricordi e studi artistica*, Turin, 1887.

Robertson, W. Graham. *Time Was*, London, 1931; repr. 1981.

Robinson, Henry Crabb. *The London Theatre 1811–1866: Selections from the Diary of Henry Crabb Robinson*, ed. Eluned Brown, London, 1966.

Ross, Michael. *Alexandre Dumas*, Newton Abbot, 1981.

Rossi, Ernesto. *Quarant 'anni di vita artistica*, Florence, 1887.

Rowell, George. *The Victorian Theatre*, London, 1956; repr. 1978.
ed. *Victorian Dramatic Criticism*, London, 1971.
Queen Victoria Goes to the Theatre, London, 1978.
Theatre in the Age of Irving, Oxford, 1981.

Ruskin, John. *Modern Painters*, London, 1843–60; 3rd edn, 1900.
Complete Works, ed. E. T. Cook and Alexander Wedderburn, London, 1903–4.

Russell, Willy. *Educating Rita*, London, 1981.

Ryan, Richard. *Dramatic Table Talk*, London, 1825–30.

St. John, Christopher. *Ellen Terry*, London, 1907.
ed. *Ellen Terry and Bernard Shaw: A Correspondence*, New York, 1931.

Salvini, Celso. *Tommaso Salvini nella storia del teatro italiano e nella vita del suo tempo*, Bologna, 1955.

Salvini, Tommaso. *Leaves from the Autobiography of Tommaso Salvini*, London, 1893.
Ricordi, aneddoti ed impressioni, Milan, 1895.

Sand, George. *Théâtre complet*, 4e série, Paris, 1867.

Sands, Molly. *Robson of the Olympic*, London, 1979.

Santaniello, A. E., intro. *The Boydell Shakespeare Prints*, New York, 1979.

Scarff, W. *Leicestershire and Rutland at the Opening of the 20th Century*, Brighton, 1902.

Scharf, George, jun. *Recollections of the Scenic Effects of the Covent Garden Theatre . . .* , London, 1838.
Observations on the Westminster Abbey Portrait of Richard II, London, 1867.

Select Bibliography

Schoenbaum, Samuel. *Shakespeare's Lives*, London, 1970.
 William Shakespeare: A Documentary Life, London, 1975.
Schwob, Marcel. *Œuvres complètes*, Paris, 1928.
Scott, Clement. *From 'The Bells' to 'King Arthur'*, London, 1896.
 The Drama of Yesterday and Today, London, 1899.
 Ellen Terry, London, 1900.
 Some Notable Hamlets of the Present Time, London, 1900; ed. L. Arthur Greening, New York, 1969.
Scott, David. *British, French and German Painting: Being a Reference to the Grounds which Render the Proposed Painting of the New Houses of Parliament Important as a Public Measure*, Edinburgh, 1841.
Scott, William B. *Memoir of David Scott R.S.A.*, Edinburgh, 1850.
 Selections from the Works of the late David Scott, R.S.A., Glasgow, 1866–7.
Sessely, Annie. *L'Influence de Shakespeare sur Alfred de Vigny*, Bern, 1928.
Shattuck, Charles, ed. *Bulwer and Macready: A Chronicle of the Early Victorian Theatre*, Urbana, Ill., 1958.
 The Shakespeare Promptbooks: A Descriptive Catalogue, Urbana, Ill., 1965.
 ed. *The John Philip Kemble Promptbooks*, Charlottesville, Va, 1974.
Shaw, G. B. *Our Theatre in the Nineties*, London, 1932.
Sheridan, Paul. *Penny Theatres of Victorian London*, London, 1981.
Sheridan Knowles's Conception and Mr. Irving's Performance of Macbeth, London, 1876.
Simonsuuri, Kirsti. *Homer's Original Genius: Eighteenth-Century Notions of the Early Greek Epic*, Cambridge, 1979.
Sims, George R. *My Life: Sixty Years' Recollections of Bohemian London*, London, 1917.
Skinner, Basil. *Shakespeare in Scottish Art*, Edinburgh, 1964.
Smith, Goldwin. *Guesses at the Riddles of Existence*, London, 1898.
Smythe, Arthur J. *The Life of William Terriss, Actor*, London, 1898.
Somerset, Charles A. *Shakespeare's Early Days*, London, n.d.
Soulie, Frédéric. *Roméo et Juliette*, Paris, 1828.
Southern, Richard. *Changeable Scenery: Its Origins and Development*, London, 1952.
 The Victorian Theatre: A Pictorial Survey, Newton Abbot, 1970.
Speaight, Robert. *Shakespeare on the Stage*, London, 1973.
Sprague, A. C. *Shakespeare and the Actors*, Cambridge, Mass., 1948.
 Shakespeare's Histories, London, 1964.
Stahl, Ernst Leopold. *Shakespeare und das deutsche Theater*, Stuttgart, 1947.
Stanislavsky, C. *My Life in Art*, London, 1924.
Stavisky, Aron Y. *Shakespeare and the Victorians*, Norman, Okla., 1969.
Stevenson, George. *The Legitimate Drama*, Leicester, 1864.
Stoker, Bram. *Personal Reminiscences of Henry Irving*, London, 1906.
Strong, Roy. *Tudor and Jacobean Portraits*, London, 1969a.
 The English Icon: Elizabethan and Jacobean Portraiture, London, 1969b.
 And When Did You Last See Your Father? The Victorian Painter and British History, London, 1978.
Styan, J. L. *The Shakespeare Revolution*, Cambridge, 1977.
Summerson, John, ed. *Concerning Architecture Essays on Architectural Writers and Writing presented to Nikolaus Pevsner*, London, 1968.

Tallis's History and Description of the Crystal Palace, London, 1851.
Taranow, Gerda. *Sarah Bernhardt: The Art within the Legend*, Princeton, NJ, 1972.

Select Bibliography

Tate, Nahum. *The History of King Lear*, London, 1681.
Terry, Ellen. *The Story of My Life*, 2nd edn, London, 1908.
    Ellen Terry's Memoirs, ed. Edith Craig and Christopher St. John, London, 1933.
Tieck, Ludwig. *Kritische Schriften*, Leipzig, 1848.
    Romane, ed. Marianne Thalmann, Munich, n.d.
Trewin, J. C. *Mr. Macready*, London, 1955.
    Benson and the Bensonians, London, 1960.
Trewin, Wendy. *All on Stage: Charles Wyndham and the Alberys*, London, 1980.
Tyson, Nancy Jane. *Eugene Aram: Literary History and Typology of the Scholar Criminal*, Hamden, Conn., 1983.

Vacquerie, Auguste, and Meurice, Paul. *Falstaff, scène de la taverne*, Paris, 1895.
van Abbe, Derek Maurice. *Christoph Martin Wieland 1733–1813: A Literary Biography*, London, 1961.
van der Merwe, Pieter. *Clarkson Stanfield 1793–1867*, Tyne and Wear, 1979.
van Tieghem, Philippe. *Les Influences étrangères sur la littérature française (1550–1880)*, Paris, 1961.
Vicinus, Martha. *The Industrial Muse*, London, 1974.
Vincent, David. *Bread, Knowledge and Freedom*, London, 1981.
von Weber, Baron Max. *Carl Marie von Weber: The Life of an Artist*, trans. J. Palgrave Simpson, London, 1865.

Warrack, John. *Tchaikovsky*, New York, 1973.
Watson, E. B. *Sheridan to Robertson*, Cambridge, 1926.
Webb, Charles. *Belphegor the Mountebank*, London, [1860?].
Weinstock, Herbert. *Rossini*, London, 1968.
    Vincenzo Bellini, London, 1972.
Wells, Stanley, ed. *Nineteenth Century Shakespeare Burlesques*, London, 1977.
Wicks, Charles Beaumont. *The Parisian Stage: Alphabetical Indexes of Plays and Authors, 1800–1900*, Alabama, 1950–79.
Wieland, Christoph Martin. *Oberon*, trans. William Sotheby, London, 1844.
Willement, Thomas. *Regal Heraldry*, London, 1821.
Williams, Robert Folkstone. *Shakespeare and his Friends*, London, 1838.
Wood, Christopher. *The Pre-Raphaelites*, London, 1981.

Young, G. M. *Portrait of an Age*, Oxford, 1936.

Zanco, A. *Shakespeare in Russia e altri saggi*, Turin, 1945.

Index

Index

307

309

Index

Index